Measuring Advertising Effectiveness

ADVERTISING AND CONSUMER PSYCHOLOGY

A series sponsored by the Society for
Consumer Psychology

Measuring Advertising Effectiveness

Edited by

William D. Wells

University of Minnesota

LEA LAWRENCE ERLBAUM ASSOCIATES, PUBLISHERS
1997 Mahwah, New Jersey   London

Lawrence Erlbaum Associates, Inc., Publishers
10 Industrial Avenue
Mahwah, New Jersey 07430

Cover design by Kevin Kall

Library of Congress Cataloging-in-Publication-Data

Measuring advertising effectiveness / edited by William D. Wells.
        p. cm.
    "Includes edited versions of papers presented at the 1994
Advertising and Consumer Psychology Conference"—Pref.
Includes bibliographic references and index.
ISBN 0-8058-1901-0 (cloth : alk. paper) ISBN 0-8058-2812-5
(paper : alk. paper
        1. Advertising—Research—United States—Congresses.
I. Wells, William D.
HF5815.U5M38 1996
659.1—dc20   96-8021
                                              CIP

Books published by Lawrence Erlbaum Associates are printed on
acid-free paper, and their bindings are chosen for strength and durability.

Printed in the United States of America

10 9 8 7 6 5 4 3 2 1

Contents

Preface

From the earliest days of applied psychology and scientific marketing, researchers have sought reliable and valid measures of the effects of advertising. Darrell Blaine Lucas and Steuart Henderson Britt's (1963), *Measuring Advertising Effectiveness*, was an influential early summary of psychology's contributions. Roy H. Campbell's (1969), *Measuring the Profit and Sales Results of Advertising*, was an equally influential summary of the aggregate, market-oriented approach.

This volume continues that search. It includes edited versions of papers presented at the 1994 Advertising and Consumer Psychology Conference, co-sponsored by the Society for Consumer Psychology, the Marketing Science Institute, the University of Minnesota, and the Minneapolis advertising agency Campbell-Mithun-Esty. The conference was co-chaired by William D. Wells of the University of Minnesota and Thomas Jonas, then of Campbell-Mithun-Esty. The volume also includes commentary by both academic and industry-based participants in that event. Like Lucas and Britt's *Measuring Advertising Effectiveness*, this volume seeks to unravel and measure the complex details of individual response. Like Campbell's *Measuring the Profit and Sales Results of Advertising*, it examines market-oriented outcomes from a more applied stance.

All of the chapters and commentaries show healthy tension between the more theoretical interests and dispositions of the academic community and the more applied, results-oriented interests and dispositions of real-world research. The bottom line, as the real-world participants would say, is that measuring advertising effectiveness is so complicated that, although it is both a valid, important academic topic and a consequential applied problem, neither academic researchers nor industry researchers are likely to make decisive progress without help. Instead, reliable and valid measures of advertising effectiveness are most likely to emerge from constructive criticism and mutually supportive interaction between the two camps. On that conclusion, the long history of the topic and the exchanges at this conference fully concur.

In combining the academic and applied approaches, this volume contributes up-to-date theoretical formulations, methodological advances, and optimistic views of future research.   It offers partial added answers to some important problems and insightful forecasts of next steps.

The co-chairs of the conference wish to thank the co-sponsors for their essential support.   We especially acknowledge the key contributions of Mary Achartz and Linda Wilson of the University of Minnesota, who managed hundreds of organizational details, and of Lara Carls-Lissick, also of the University of Minnesota, who checked and double-checked the final draft.

I

Effects and Effectiveness

In 1963, Lucas and Britt published *Measuring Advertising Effectiveness*, a summary of the state of the art. The first half of their review—about 200 pages—covered "measurement of advertising messages." Its main topics were techniques of measurement, recognition tests, recall and association tests, opinion and attitude ratings, projective methods, laboratory testing and analyses of content, and inquires and sales measure. The second half covered media analysis.

Lucas and Britt's summary was a blend of academic psychology, marketing theory, survey methodology, and practical experience. Real-world applications, and real-world problems and limitations, were stressed throughout.

In 1994, the annual Advertising and Consumer Psychology Conference of the Society for Consumer Psychology covered some of the same territory. Like the Lucas and Britt volume, it was a blend of academic psychology, marketing theory, survey methodology, and practical experience. And, like Lucas and Britt's summary, it stressed problems and limitations.

There were, however, some important differences. In the original *Measuring Advertising Effectiveness*, the authors devoted entire chapters to recognition and recall. In this volume, recognition is scarcely mentioned, and recall comes in for heavy criticism. This is a sign of progress. We no longer believe that memorability, however measured, is necessary or sufficient. Instead, we know that advertisements are subtle, diverse, complex phenomena that require detailed individual investigation. We also know that *advertising effects* are different from *advertising effectiveness*, and that neither effects nor effectiveness can be evaluated in isolation.

The three chapters in this section open the discussion stressing the multidimensional nature of advertising's diverse effects. In chapter 1, Christine Wright-Isak of Young & Rubicam, Advertising and Ronald J. Faber and Lewis R. Horner of the University of Minnesota distinguish between academic, theory-oriented studies of effects and practical, in-context evaluations of effectiveness. They delineate the differences between those two domains, and propose separate strategies for solving evaluation problems.

In chapter 2, William A. Cook of the Advertising Research Foundation and Arthur J. Kover of Fordham University distinguish among the duties and perspectives of advertising researchers who work for advertisers, advertising agencies, advertising research suppliers, and universities. They outline conflicts among those points of view and search for common interests.

The discussion, by Esther Thorson of the University of Missouri, echoes and adds to both chapters. It acknowledges the complexity of a psychology and sociology of mediated persuasion, and it stresses that, despite all differences, more and better communication among the communities is the quickest route to solving common problems.

1

Comprehensive Measurement of Advertising Effectiveness: Notes From the Marketplace

Christine Wright-Isak
Young & Rubicam, Advertising

Ronald J. Faber
Lewis R. Horner
University of Minnesota

When the economic environment becomes difficult, marketers demand proof of advertising's effectiveness, preferably in numerical terms. Unfortunately, few marketers can agree on what standards advertising is expected to meet, or even what constitutes definitive proof. We are in such a period now. In a time of recurring recession and in an environment of advancing globalization of companies, products, and brands, many brands are experiencing low growth in unit volume and increasing competition from private brands and generics (Eechambadi, 1993). In this business climate, advertisers want to know what they are getting for their advertising dollars. Industry researchers are often asked whether academic research will provide answers.

The proof called for is usually short term. Brand managers must account for yearly budgets to their division heads. The question asked about the advertising is whether its performance justified its proportion of last year's marketing budget. Agencies scramble to produce facts that indicate a positive evaluation of the advertising contribution. Everyone is on the defensive. Effects are hard to isolate because advertising merges with other elements of the marketing mix and with nonmarketing aspects of the message environment.

To further complicate the problem, stress on short-term evidence ignores some of the most important contributions advertising can make. In a speech to the Association of National Advertisers, Richard Costello (1991), Corporate Communications Manager for General Electric, declared that the value of corporate advertising was long-term creation and maintenance of goodwill that enhanced his company's ability to do business. He went on to state that effectiveness can be calculated by taking the difference between the market

3

price of GE's stock and the book value of the tangible assets of the company. However, Costello was concerned with corporate advertising. The more common situation—selling a specific product to a target market—does not lend itself to similar calculations. Nevertheless, Costello made an important point by noting that the true value of advertising is its long-term contribution to the brand. The goodwill created through advertising can reduce the cost of doing business and prepare markets for positive responses to subsequent selling efforts.

ACADEMIC RESEARCH: MEASURING ADVERTISING EFFECTS

Although long-term contribution is of vital interest to advertising practitioners and their clients, it is not frequently discussed in academic journals. Academic research tends to focus on specific elements within ads and how these elements influence viewer responses. Which dependent measure is examined is typically determined by the theory used to frame the research. This type of research might best be termed the study of advertising *effects*.

Academic research typically focuses on manipulating a few variables to isolate their respective impact. Although several effects may be tested in one study, each is usually considered separately, and no summary statement across measures is expected. Although a few academic studies have looked at interrelationships among effects (e.g., Okechuku & Wang, 1988; Stewart & Furse, 1984–1985; Stewart & Koslow, 1989), they have been the exception rather than the rule.

Are advertising effects the same as advertising effectiveness? Although the two are certainly related, distinctions between them must be clearly understood. Advertising effectiveness is concerned with making a tangible contribution to a company or brand. This benefit must exceed its cost if it is to be considered worthwhile. Effectiveness is cumulative over time and affects feelings, attitudes, and behaviors.

Assessments of effectiveness are typically made over longer time spans than measures of effects. They involve multiple exposures to ads and multiple executions within campaigns. In contrast, most effects research involves limited numbers of executions and exposures. Effects are as likely to be evaluated in an experimental setting as in a natural field setting. Effectiveness must be determined within a complex environment where other marketing activities and competitive actions greatly add to the difficulty of assessing advertising's value. For a full understanding of effectiveness we need to know which effects contribute to effectiveness, and we need to know whether effective campaigns show similar patterns.

Korgaonkar, Moschis, and Bellinger (1984) asked a large sample of advertising agency executives to describe the most and least successful campaigns in their experience. They concluded that successful campaigns "are based on market research findings; they are backed with adequate financial and managerial resources, they are based on careful media planning; and, they are likely to use messages that are perceived to be creative and unique" (p. 49). A year later, Korgaonkar and Bellinger (1985) followed up with an identically designed study with similar results. Both sets of findings focused on organizational and situational correlates of successful campaigns, with success defined as a composite score that includes sales, attitude, and awareness. Although Korgaonkar and Bellinger (1985) did not directly address the issue of how success is demonstrated, respondents in both agency and client samples agreed that a good client–agency relationship is one of the correlates. A "good" relationship was defined as consistent key personnel on both sides during the campaign's development and a lack of client–agency personality conflicts.

INDUSTRY MEASUREMENTS: JUSTIFYING AD BUDGETS IN TERMS OF SALES RESULTS

Because "effectiveness" has tended to refer to whether the cost of advertising is returned to the advertiser in the form of current or potential sales revenue, several authors have proposed using sales as the primary criterion. However, because additional variables act as channels or barriers (we often do not know which) between message and purchase, many other authors have argued for measures of consumer knowledge and beliefs (Aaker, Batra, & Myers, 1992; Colley, 1961; Schultz, 1990). However, as Schreiber and Appel (1990–1991) argued, the exact nature of the relationship between these surrogate measures and actual sales is not known; thus what constitutes the appropriate measure of effectiveness remains highly debatable (Abraham & Lodish, 1990; McDonald, 1993; Schroer, 1990; Steiner, 1987).

To understand effectiveness in a real-world context we need to have some systematic collection of facts that tell us the probability that the intended audience saw the campaign, what intervening phenomena affected the campaign's impact, and the net impact of those phenomena and the campaign on purchase behavior. Combining this collection of facts with data about specific ad effects may help us understand the performance of the campaigns, as well as contribute to theory development.

To further complicate the issue, we also have to consider the role of competitors' budgets, or what the industry calls *share of voice* (SOV). It has been argued that the most appropriate measure of effectiveness is market share to market voice ratio (Jones, 1990). An additional, virtually unaddressed area is the content of the media in which the advertising message appears (Bogart, 1976).

Little in the academic literature has helped to resolve these issues. Instead, advertising effects are typically studied in controlled experiments that employ one-shot exposures to single messages over relatively short periods of time. They fail to capture the effects of multiple related messages in natural environments, each designed to achieve different changes in consumers.

An exception to this general rule was recently presented by Eechambadi (1993). He addressed:

1. The issue of long-term versus short-term time frames for assessing expected impact.
2. The fact that advertising often involves multiple objectives.
3. The problem that the link between advertising and sales is usually indirect.

His econometric approach to these problems in car sales creates a chain of evidence that estimates (on the basis of previous performance) the likely number of inquiries or showroom visits to be generated out of an expected number of recipients of the advertising message. He then anticipated the likely proportion of actual prospects included in this estimate of inquiries, and the likely proportion of actual sales of this number of prospects. By estimating each link in this chain and multiplying the number of anticipated sales times the value of each sale, he arrived at a number that estimates the value of the advertising.

This approach relies heavily on accurate information about the relationships among key variables, and it focuses on relatively short-term results. Nonetheless, it provides valuable insights into what effectiveness entails.

FOUR CRITERIA FOR DEMONSTRATING EFFECTIVENESS

Effects are clearly individual-level phenomena. Effectiveness is not simply an aggregation of effects across consumers. We might better conceive of effectiveness as a societal-level concept, observable through consensus of a community of professionals. Examination of debate within the industry indicates convergence on four main criteria for demonstrating advertising effectiveness. To be comprehensive and compelling in demonstrating value advertising professionals must do the following.

1. *Make the role of each advertising effort explicit in the context of multiple marketing goals and program alternatives.* Advertising is only one component of a broader marketing mix designed to build sales. To evaluate advertising's contribution to the larger effort, it is necessary to specify in advance what particular goals the advertising is intended to achieve. For example, advertising may be used to build a particular brand identity, to change existing perceptions, or to create trial purchase. Specifying objectives in advance allows for the establishment of specific performance criteria.

2. *Establish a chain of evidence to demonstrate the indirect linkages between the advertising, its expected impact, and the ultimate expected business outcome.* The more indirect the outcome for which advertising is held accountable, the more necessary it is for a chain of evidence to be established. This is the evaluative counterpart of defining the particular

role advertising is expected to play in the marketing mix. Not only must advertising and marketing goals be shown to have been achieved, but evidence indicating that advertising contributed to the larger marketing objectives must also be provided. Additionally, the ability to rule out non-advertising-related situational factors may also help to strengthen the desired linkages.

3. *Identify and account for the contribution of creative. The main focus of a large portion of effects research is on the impact of specific elements of the creative message.* Measures of effectiveness must also consider the contribution of creative work, but this should take the entire creative message into account and not be restricted just to specific parts of it.

4. *Recognize that advertising has long-term as well as short-term value.* Specification of the long- and short-term contribution of the advertising investment is crucial to a fair evaluation of its performance. When we set short-term performance standards we should also consider their role in long-term strategies. It has long been recognized in work on media and budget models that advertising has carryover effects (Leckenby & Wedding, 1982; Palda, 1964). Carryover effects have sometimes been subdivided into two types—delayed response and customer holdover effects (Kotler, 1971; Leckenby & Wedding, 1982). Delayed response effects occur when there is a delay between the time advertising dollars are spent and a consumer response (purchase) is made. Customer holdover effects refer to the fact that an ad can have an effect on subsequent repurchases. Thus an ad might continue to influence a consumer's buying choice not only in the next purchase situation, but in later ones as well.

A LONG-TERM VIEW OF ADVERTISING EFFECTIVENESS

Because brand knowledge and image are cumulative effects of many campaigns, it may take years to assess the full impact of advertising. Ironically, the group that stresses long-term effects the most is the critics of advertising. Critics tend to make assertions such as:

- Advertised products lead children to develop poor nutritional habits.
- Commercial messages promote materialistic values.
- Models shown in ads lead to an overemphasis on beauty and thinness for women.
- Adolescents start to smoke because cigarette ads show attractive, adventurous, and popular people smoking.
- Stress on superficial attributes (both for products and political candidates) leads people to develop poor decision-making strategies.

Although these issues involve a range of target audiences and outcomes, the common underlying theme is that consistent messages over long periods of time have important impacts on beliefs, and these beliefs influence behavior. Applied more generally to our understanding of advertising effectiveness, this theme suggests that consistent messages over time create beliefs about brands and brand users that ultimately influence choice processes and create tangible benefits for the advertiser.

Ivory Soap provides a positive example. In 1882, Ivory ran a newspaper ad that showed a drawing of a pair of hands and a large bar of Ivory soap, followed by five dense paragraphs of copy. The first paragraph stressed that Ivory had "the fine qualities of a choice Toilet Soap" and (in bold) that it was 99 and 44/100% pure. One hundred and twelve years later, Ivory ran ads in which photographs of people dominated the page. In one case the photo showed a close-up of a 14-year-old girl; another pictured a young father and son. The only copy appeared in a strip down the right-hand side of the page. In large print, one word at a time, the copy said, "You're never too old to baby your skin." In between each word in smaller print the copy said, "no greasy creams," "no heavy perfumes," "no deodorants," "just the basics." The bottom of the column included a color picture of a wrapped bar of Ivory and the statement "99 44/100% pure," which is now a registered trademark of Ivory.

The look of the Ivory ad has certainly changed to fit the times, but even with these changes, for more than 100 years Ivory has continued to say that it is 99 and 44/100% pure. In 1882 this point needed to be placed in bold in the first paragraph. By 1994, all that was needed was a simple reminder in small print below the bar. By consistently stressing this one claim, Ivory has captured the attribute of purity (and perhaps associated attributes such as mildness and gentleness). The value for Ivory of having used this consistent advertising message is that it would now be extremely difficult, if not impossible, for any other brand to challenge Ivory on this dimension. This equity that advertising has created needs to be recognized in any discussion of advertising effectiveness.

We can easily find several other examples. When one thinks of a dependable washing machine, the first brand that comes to mind is Maytag. With years of consistent advertising, Maytag has dominated the claim of dependability and generated widespread brand awareness, even though Maytag's advertising budget is typically well below that of its major competitors. This example suggests that long-term consistent advertising messages can create an image that keeps the brand in the consumer's mind. If a company strongly associates itself with a particular attribute or image, it can afford to reduce its advertising budget or even stop advertising for brief periods of time without significantly hurting its sales. This tangible economic benefit must be considered in assessing advertising effectiveness.

Originally, Maytag stressed dependability to overcome the perceived financial risk inherent in buying a washing machine instead of a washboard. Today, in a more hectic and complex world, families are concerned about the potential loss of time and convenience that can be caused by an undependable appliance. Maytag has understood this and reexpressed its equity through the lonely Maytag repairman who is never called because Maytag appliances never break. Thus, Maytag capitalized on its initial efforts by updating its imagery to fit the times, while continuing to stand for the same value: dependability.

LONG-TERM VERSUS SHORT-TERM VIEWS
OF EFFECTIVENESS

Not surprisingly, long-term effectiveness and short-term effectiveness must be assessed in different ways. Differences include type of effect examined, time period considered, measurement method, and target audience.

Type of Effects

Short-term effectiveness is best assessed by demonstrating a chain of effects that includes sales, brand perceptions, and advertising awareness or attitudes. Failure to show any of these effects would raise questions about either effectiveness or causality. The more clearly and convincingly the ties between each of these effects can be made and the greater the degree to which alternative causes can be ruled out, the more compelling the case that advertising created an impact.

A long-term perspective of advertising effectiveness would focus more on cumulative perceptions. Here too, it would be important to show that outcomes match the prime focus of a brand's campaigns over the years. Because other elements of the marketing mix will normally be consistent with the long-term advertising image or benefit when a campaign is successful, it will be more difficult here to identify advertising's unique contribution.

Time Period

In the short term, effectiveness can be assessed in time periods ranging from a few minutes to a year. To directly establish that advertising made an impact, copy test results that examine attitude change immediately after exposure may be an appropriate measure. To show that the campaign affected sales, the appropriate time period may range from monthly or quarterly changes to 1 year. The time required to measure changes in brand perceptions is typically shorter.

In measuring long-term changes in brand beliefs, 10 years or longer would not be unusual. Although studies of this sort do not fit the time frames brand managers generally have to demonstrate their ability, they provide vital evidence about the importance of advertising and they increase marketers' ability to use advertising effectively.

Appropriate Outcome Measure

In assessments of short-term advertising effectiveness, the most common measurement is the change in awareness, brand knowledge, attitudes, or sales. Because it is also important to show that changes are due to advertising and not some other cause, the test brand's change scores should be compared with those of its major competitors. This comparison can help allay concerns that the change was due to a change in economic or market conditions or some other confounding factor.

Although change is the predominant way of assessing short-term advertising effectiveness, change is not always appropriate when examining long-term effectiveness. Here, the goal is to associate a brand with a clear and recognizable attribute or image. Thus, the objective should be consistency over time rather than change. The most appropriate way to assess long-term effectiveness is to examine the strength of association between the desired image or attribute and the brand. As with short-term effectiveness, it may be worthwhile to compare the performance of the target brand with its major competitors. When a campaign has been effective, the brand will have a stronger linkage to its advertised image or attribute than any rival.

Target Audience

The final difference between the long-term and short-term views of advertising effectiveness is the target audience. Some authors have recently written about the importance of focusing just on current prospects in assessing short-term measures of advertising effectiveness (Swenson, 1994; Wells & Swenson, 1994). They argue that including nonprospects in a sample creates error in estimating effectiveness because nonprospects are unlikely to respond to advertising in the same way as prospects do.

However, when we talk about long-term effectiveness, people who are not currently prospects but who might one day become buyers may be the most important group to consider. These people do not wake up one day and become prospects for a product without prior ideas or information. Rather, they have images and conceptions about brands and brand users prior to reaching a consideration phase in buying.

If a brand can project a clear and consistent image or a strong association with an attribute, it is more likely that future prospects will remember the brand and know something about it when they reach the product consideration stage. This effect is analogous to McGraw-Hill's campaign to promote use of ads in business publications to support personal selling. In the McGraw-Hill ads, a stern looking man is seated in a chair. The copy quotes him as saying:

> I don't know who you are.
> I don't know your company.
> I don't know your company's product.
> I don't know what your company stands for.
> I don't know your company's customers.
> I don't know your company's record.
> I don't know your company's reputation.
> Now—what was it you wanted to sell me?

Below the picture, the moral of this tale is spelled out for the reader, "Sales start **before** your salesman calls—with business publication advertising."

What was true for the role of business ads in personal selling may also be true of the long-term role of advertising for consumer products and services. By creating a clear and recognizable image or attribute association through long-term consistent advertising, advertisers can assure that future prospects will come to the buying situation with a feeling that they know the advertiser's brand, its customers, its reputation, and what it stands for. This is another important long-term benefit of advertising.

CONCLUSION

Advertising is under increasing pressure to demonstrate that it makes a difference and is worth its cost. However, given advertising's salience, there is a surprising lack of consensus regarding its effectiveness. We have tried to resolve some of the problems by differentiating advertising effectiveness from advertising effects. Effectiveness involves assessments of actual campaigns in natural settings, whereas effects involve responses to individual ads.

We proposed that effectiveness may best be thought of as a societal-level concept whose meaning is established by the consensus of a community of professionals. As such, a first step in future research might be to determine what information professionals use in judging effectiveness. One potential source of useful data is the Advertising Effectiveness Awards, commonly known as Effies. Entrants for this award provide descriptions of campaign objectives and background situation, creative and media strategy, and most importantly, evidence of the results of the campaign. A pool of more than 300 judges representing clients, agencies, marketing research companies, and a few academics, assess the effectiveness of each entry. The research question would be what criteria these professionals use to judge effectiveness in this context.

As useful as it might be, this information is limited to short-term effectiveness. A more complete conceptualization of effectiveness must take into account a campaign's ability to contribute to long-term brand equity. Greater consideration of ways to measure this contribution is clearly needed.

REFERENCES

Aaker, D. A., Batra, R., & Myers, J. G. (1992). *Advertising management* (4th ed.). Englewood Cliffs, NJ: Prentice-Hall.

Abraham, M. M., & Lodish, L. M. (1990). Getting the most out of advertising and promotion. *Harvard Business Review, 68,* 50–60.

Bogart, L. (1976). Mass advertising: The message, not the measure. *Harvard Business Review, 54,* 107–116.

Colley, R. H. (1961). *Defining advertising goals for measured advertising results.* New York: Association of National Advertisers.

Costello, R. (1991, April). *The B-to-B opportunity: Focus on the brand.* Presentation to the Association of National Advertisers Business to Business Marketing Communication Conference, Atlanta, GA.

Eechambadi, N. (1993, October). *Valuing the contribution of advertising in the nineties.* Presentation to the Advertising Accountability Research Workshop, New York.

Jones, J. P. (1990). Ad spending: Maintaining market share. *Harvard Business Review, 68,* 38–42.

Korgaonkar, P. K., & Bellinger, D. (1985). Correlates of successful advertising campaigns: The manager's perspective. *Journal of Advertising Research, 25,* 34–39.

Korgaonkar, P. K., Moschis, G. P., & Bellinger, D. (1984). Correlates of successful advertising campaigns. *Journal of Advertising Research, 24,* 47–53.

Kotler, P. (1971). *Marketing decision making: A model building approach.* New York: Holt, Rinehart & Winston.

Leckenby, J. D., & Wedding, N. (1982). *Advertising management: Criteria, analysis and decision making.* Columbus, OH: Grid.

McDonald, C. (1993). Point of view: The key is to understand consumer response. *Journal of Advertising Research, 33,* 63–69.

Okechuku, J., & Wang, G. (1988). The effectiveness of Chinese print advertisements in North America. *Journal of Advertising Research, 28,* 25–34.

Palda, K. (1964). *The measurement of cumulative advertising effects.* Englewood Cliffs, NJ: Prentice-Hall.

Schreiber, R. J., & Appel, V. (1990–1991). Advertising evaluation using surrogate measures for sales. *Journal of Advertising Research, 30,* 27–31.

Schroer, J. C. (1990). Ad spending: Growing market share. *Harvard Business Review, 68,* 44–48.

Schultz, D. E. (1990). *Strategic advertising campaigns* (3rd ed.). Lincolnwood, IL: NTC Business Books.

Steiner, R. L. (1987). Point of view: The paradox of increasing returns in advertising. *Journal of Advertising Research, 27,* 45–53.

Stewart, D. W., & Furse, D. H. (1984–1985). Analysis of the impact of executional factors on advertising performance. *Journal of Advertising Research, 24,* 23–26.

Stewart, D. W., & Koslow, S. (1989). Executional factors and advertising effectiveness: A republication. *Journal of Advertising, 18,* 21–32.

Swenson, M. R. (1994, April). Attention to advertisements by prospects and non-prospects. In K. Whitehill King (Ed.), *Proceedings of the 1994 Conference of the American Academy of Advertising Conference* (pp. 207–212). Athens, GA: American Academy of Advertising.

Wells, W. D., & Swenson, M. R. (1994). *Consequences of contamination.* Unpublished manuscript, University of Minnesota.

2

Research and the Meaning of Advertising Effectiveness: Mutual Misunderstandings

William A. Cook
Advertising Research Foundation

Arthur J. Kover
Fordham University

Any discussion of advertising research and measurement of advertising effectiveness needs to consider advertising research as a marketing problem. If marketing is defined as the art of meeting consumers' needs, advertising effectiveness must be defined in relation to the needs of advertisers. We contend that these needs are quite diverse; we believe that these differing needs reflect important differences in definition among academic and practitioner researchers.

Such a relativistic approach may worry some readers. They may say, "What about scientific objectivity?" We say that we are examining a language phenomenon. Scientific objectivity is but an example of one language and does not represent the single standard of excellence. From our relativistic position, we attempt to articulate how this state of confusion about advertising effectiveness has evolved. We also propose some means to move beyond the present deadlock in which we talk amongst ourselves but the words have different meanings.

Four groups of people have different needs for something called advertising effectiveness: (a) advertising agency researchers, (b) syndicated advertising research services, (c) marketing managers (who nominally use the research), and (d) academicians.

Each has different sets of needs and activities, different reward systems, and different definitions of advertising effectiveness and the means to measure effectiveness. These differences do not grow smaller; they are enduring and even growing.

INDUSTRY DEFINITIONS OF EFFECTIVENESS

The role of the advertising agency researcher has changed radically in the past 10 years (Zaltman & Moorman, 1988–1989). Removed from a central position in the marketing process (O'Donoghue, 1994), the advertising researcher has three central preoccupations. The first preoccupation is ensuring that the agency's advertising looks good to the client. Two major means are open to accomplish this: qualitative research (Achenbaum, 1993) and the use of a syndicated service to pretest finished advertising. Other advertising research functions, such as market definition, tracking, or even selection of the syndicated service, are now generally reserved by clients. Second, increasing competition among agencies for scarcer business (O'Donoghue, 1994) saddles agency researchers with frequent new business pitches. The meaning of "effectiveness" here often becomes showmanship: subtly integrating (usually qualitative) research with presentations of speculative creative work. Finally, advertising researchers have another role, providing consumer depictions to the creatives. These (qualitative) depictions are often the researchers' most important contribution to advertising and ultimately to advertising effectiveness.

Many syndicated advertising research providers emphasize in-market measurement and models that translate the traditional copy research measures to sales effects (see chaps. 18 and 19, this volume). At the same time, syndicated research providers attempt to link copy quality, media weight, and scheduling to sales effectiveness. These sales-anchored validations are in response to clients' expressed needs to justify advertising expenditures (as contrasted to, say, promotion expenditures) in the most direct way possible. Although some of these syndicated services are constructed around attitude and belief change, most recent efforts have concentrated on bridging the gap between their key normative measurements and sales.

Marketing managers are spending less time addressing copy-related issues and when they do, they are treating them in the context of other elements of the marketing mix. Just as advertising is viewed by marketers today as part of a larger, more complex array of consumer communications tools, marketing itself has broadened in scope. Matters of finance, distribution, and trade relations are taking up larger amounts of the marketers' long days. Common denominators in those dialogues are sales and profits. Consequently, when advertising issues are addressed by marketing management, it is increasingly in those terms. Because advertising effectiveness is viewed in this context, it too is seen by marketing managers in terms of dollars and cents. Thus, marketing managers and providers of syndicated services are adopting similar definitions of advertising effectiveness. This is not surprising because syndicated services must market their products; they must tailor their offerings to their clients' expressed needs (Adams & Blair, 1992; Kuse, chap. 7, this volume).

ACADEMIC DEFINITIONS OF EFFECTIVENESS

What do academicians define as effectiveness? Perhaps the best way to charac-terize academic research practice is to contrast it with that of practitioners.

Table 2.1 presents our evaluation of that contrast. The subjects of the 1993 Advertising Research Foundation Workshops agendas provided the key practi-tioner issues. This agenda is contrasted with academicians' articles in the 1993 issues of the *Journal of Advertising, Journal of Consumer Research, Journal of Consumer Marketing, Journal of Marketing,* and *Journal of Advertising Research.* Generally, the topics explored by practitioners centered on measurement and strategies; academicians, by contrast, were more concerned with theory.

Table 2.2 attempts to reach one higher level of abstraction, contrasting the more general research orientations of practitioners and academicians. Not surprisingly, these general orientations suggest that academicians are most concerned with understanding as an end rather than as a means to action. Even though many of the academic articles had sections labeled "Implications for Marketing Managers," the implications seemed to be self-evident or difficult to execute. Therefore, by extension, for the academic audience, effectiveness was defined in the language of theory, not practice.

TABLE 2.1
Practitioner Versus Academic Research Orientations

	Practitioners[a]	Academicians[b]
What's new/changes	X	
Advertising measurement[c]	X	
Advertising strategy	X	
Viewer data/ media measurement	X	
Branding/brand equity	X	
Specific measurement tools/sales effects	X	
General theory		X
Advertising response/affect/attitudes		X
Consumer decision-making models		X
Integrated communications		X
New products/line extension		X
Organization of marketing/marketing research		X

[a]ARF Workshops in 1993. [b]Articles on advertising research (1993) in *Journal of Advertising, Journal of Consumer Research, Journal of Consumer Marketing, Journal of Marketing, Journal of Advertising Research.* [c]Defined as specific copy research techniques and issues about specific meas-urements and their relationship to some payoff measurement.

TABLE 2.2
Practitioner Versus Academic General Orientations

	Practitioners[a]	Academicians[b]
Application	Now; generally only to immediate practice	Not necessarily now. Perhaps application only to theory, not practice
Model	S→R	S→Affect→R
Focus on	Measurement	Theory
	"Results"	Consumer
	What affects my work	What affects larger structures
	Inputs (brands, advertising)	Structures/affects
	Action based on results	Understanding to understand

[a]ARF Workshops in 1993. [b]Articles on advertising research (1993) in *Journal of Advertising, Journal of Consumer Research, Journal of Consumer Marketing, Journal of Marketing, and Journal of Advertising Research.*

WHY DIFFERENT DEFINITIONS OF ADVERTISING EFFECTIVENESS?

The term *effectiveness* involves demonstrating that some effect has occurred. It shifts emphasis from descriptive approaches to causal ones (whatever "causal" means). Despite these common threads, it should be apparent from our brief descriptions that advertising effectiveness means different things to those four audiences. Why is this? Does our answer to the "why" provide some clues as to a rapprochement among the different groups of researchers?

We believe that the crux of the problem was laid out by Wittgenstein in his idiosyncratic version of language theory. Wittgenstein (1953) stated that language comes from what people do, their actions and behaviors. Therefore, the different nature of the academic and practitioner occupations means that words (even the same words, such as *research*) have different meanings.

Wittgenstein wrote about "language games" to describe the languages associated with different activities. See Table 2.3 for a simplified description of language games. The marketing managers' highly pragmatic, financial-results-oriented activities and the academics' highly conceptual activities have very different "rules" of how to win and who is winning and even of what winning is (Kover, 1976). Consequently, even when academicians and practitioners use the same words, effective performance means vastly different things.

In the starkly different contexts of the faster changing business world and the slower changing academic world, the meanings of familiar words are diverging even more than in the past. Although academicians and practitioners may use the same words, they are not necessarily talking about the same things. Because practitioners are behaving differently today, the terms they use have different shadings from what they have had in the recent past. *Effectiveness* has come to mean either sales results or some kind of accepted surrogate for sales results. Previously accepted measures, such as attitude change, are slowly being left behind (or relegated to qualitative research, particularly focus groups) as pressure increases for advertising to justify itself against alternative forms of promotional spending.

No matter how good or bad business has been recently, managers of publicly owned companies must convey to present and would-be stockholders that things are going to get better next quarter or sooner. The resulting short-term focus has altered the behavior of these firms and of those who work there in several significant ways. The meaning of such terms as *sample, brands* and *brand equity, loyalty, advertising impact,* and, of course, *effectiveness* has radically changed even though the terms are the same. As the activities change, the words remain but the meanings gradually transform.

For practitioners, profitability is not the only financial construct gaining marketing management attention. Accountability is also a focus. Emphasis on "absolutes" is being replaced by emphasis on "relatives." The frequently heard question from marketers today, "How much should we be spending on advertising?" is a surface manifestation of the accountability issue sometimes expressed as "What is my advertising spending doing for my bottom line?" This is a shorthand version of the real question for which management is seeking an answer: "What is my advertising spending doing for my bottom line relative to other elements of the marketing mix?" This latter question forces comparisons among advertising, consumer promotion, trade promotion, customer service, and other ways in which marketers can seek to improve profitability. When measuring advertising effectiveness, academicians seldom consider such issues.

Following the lead of marketing practitioners, the major syndicated services have begun to concentrate heavily on relating results studies to sales. An example is the joint advertising effectiveness modeling by NPD and McCollum/Spielman Worldwide. In a recent presentation of their model, Poling (1994) indicated that although attitudes are a critical part of this model, attitudes are inside the black box (see also Mehta & Purvis, chap. 18, this volume). It is sales that are visible and, for now, sales are the core trend in evaluation.

TABLE 2.3
Language, Word Games, Meaning
(An Oversimplified Précis of Some of Wittgenstein's Later Theory)

Basic idea: "meaning as use"

No "logic of language" but a vast collection of practices, each with its own meaning.

The grammar of each language is a kind of logic based on the different activities for which each language is used. "Language games" are any and all of the language-using activities in which we engage. Wittgenstein sees a multiplicity of language games; they differ according to the activities of which they are a part.

The meaning of a word is its use in the language. That use is tied to the activity with which it is used.

"To understand a sentence means to understand a language. To understand a language means to be master of a technique" (Wittgenstein, *Philosophical Investigations*, 1953, Par. 199)

LOSS OF OBJECTIVITY

As a result of their emphasis on single (if essential) measures of effectiveness, marketers apparently are willing to sacrifice researcher objectivity to gain researcher expertise in business contexts and languages. Researchers can be used to "sound like science" even as they lose objectivity. Perhaps this is one reason (beside that of perceived costs) for the growth of qualitative research. The format of qualitative research allows for greater "latitude" in interpreting findings, particularly those that can be shown to sound like sales influence (Achenbaum, 1993). Decentralization has reduced the behavioral distance between the researcher and the marketer and probably has reduced the language gap as well. The narrowing of that distance may be a danger for applied researchers as they become more similar to marketers. The greater the similarity between research practitioner and marketer, the greater the gap between the research practitioner and academician.

THE ACADEMIC PERSPECTIVE

The need system for academicians is focused on creating theory (Kover, 1976). Advertising effectiveness can be (and often is) defined by criteria other than sales: greater insight into the structure of consumers' decisions, more understanding of attitude and attitude change, ever more abstract models. It is not necessary within that language to come up with sales changes (or their surrogates).

For the outsider, the academic enterprise seems to be a disjointed series of individual efforts, a set of loosely connected clusters of people and orientations. Each cluster has its own particular orientation—cognitive, semiotic, cultural, and so on—and each orientation selects a definition of effectiveness that best fits its own measurements.

These differences, these language differences between practitioners and academicians and within the academic world, mean that communication, in the sense of shared understanding, is very difficult (Brinberg & Hirchman, 1986). Practitioners deride academicians as distant, fragmented, not applied, not concerned with the real world, and not caring. Like creatures of the Galapagos Islands, they are cut off from the academic foundations that gave them origin. Academicians deride practitioners as atheoretical, using sloppy research, not building, and not caring. Like poor cousins, they press their noses against the window to view what seem to be huge research funds used to repeat the same dull projects. Both are right. And wrong.

How can applied researchers act as translators between these different activity structures? An appeal to empathy will not do. The reward structures, themselves a part of the activity structure (Ayer, 1985), are quite different between the two spheres and offer little promise of motivating incremental changes in the differing activity streams. Still, there are some possibilities.

1. Can the reward structures be changed? Is it possible that practitioners can be rewarded for expanding knowledge? In the early 1980s, Irv Gross recommended that DuPont institute sabbaticals for marketing researchers as they had for chemists and physicists.
2. Can new structures be created? Can companies and agencies form small theory units? Can academic institutions form applied units?
3. Can crossover people be treated and rewarded differently? Can they be used to find and recruit others who can benefit both business and the academy?
4. If different languages are results of different activities, can activities be found that can draw both kinds of people into joint effort? The question of effectiveness is one such effort.

A SHARED TASK

In our view, working in a task-oriented environment in which shared activity is the key, in which the rewards (both internal and external) come from successful completion of meaningful goals, in which the two groups must work together is the most promising way to overcome the language barrier.

We believe that the emergence of the new infotainment options that have taken off in recent years have created a sense of urgency that could generate this kind of effort. As the home computer muscles its way into the living rooms and family rooms of the United States, it is creating new communications imperatives. As the virtual community flashes into existence, the traditional ad agencies are virtually out of the picture.

Leading advertisers are telling their agencies that dramatic changes are necessary. At the annual conference of the American Association of Advertising Agencies in May 1994, Edwin Artzt, then CEO of Procter and Gamble, proclaimed, "From where we stand, we can't be sure that ad-supported TV programming will have a future in the world being created—a world of video-on-demand, pay-per-view and subscription television" (Yahn, 1994). He called for an industry summit and focused ad agencies on the new media issues.

We believe and propose that this call, and the complex series of developments that precipitated it, represent the single best hope for overcoming the language barrier between academicians and practitioners. We also believe that the importance and the magnitude of the problem offer substantial rewards to cooperative efforts that call forth skillful applications of the unique abilities and perspectives of both parties.

REFERENCES

Achenbaum, A. A. (1993). The future challenge to market research. *Marketing Research, 5*(2), 12–18.

Adams, A. J., & Blair, M. H. (1992). Persuasive advertising and sales accountability: Past experience and forward validation. *Journal of Advertising Research, 32*(2), 20–25.

Ayer, A. J. (1985). *Wittgenstein*. London: Weidenfeld & Nicholson.

Brinberg, D., & Hirschman, E. C. (1986). Multiple orientations for the conduct of marketing research: An analysis of the academic/practitioner distinction. *Journal of Marketing, 50*(4), 161–173.

Kover, A. J. (1976, November). Careers and non-communication: The case of academic and applied marketing research. *Journal of Marketing Research, 13*, 339–344.

O'Donoghue, D. (1994). Account planning: The state of the art. *Admap, 29*, 1.

Poling, F. (1994, April 18). *Measuring advertising's influence on your brand's vital signs*. Speech presented at the Advertising Research Foundation's 40th Annual Conference, New York.

Wittgenstein, L. (1953). *Philosophical investigations* (G. E. M. Anscombe, trans.), Oxford, UK: Blackwell.

Yahn, S. (1994, May 16). Advertising's grave new world. *Advertising Age, 1*.

Zaltman, G., & Moorman, C. (1988–1989). The management and use of advertising research. *Journal of Advertising Research, 28*(6), 11–18.

Comments on Chapters 1 and 2

Esther Thorson
University of Missouri—Columbia

Chapters 1 and 2 demonstrate why advertising effectiveness is sufficiently difficult and intriguing to warrant the focus of an entire volume. Interestingly, these important chapters approach advertising effectiveness in quite different ways. Chapter 1 by Wright-Isak, Faber, and Horner suggests that what ad effectiveness really means is debatable, and that there are some consistent rules concerning how it should be approached. Chapter 2 by Cook and Kover agrees that ad effectiveness has a number of different definitions, and asserts that all have value. What is needed in view of these differing definitions is a system of cross-talk among those holding the different definitions, so that the whole enterprise can move ahead more quickly and effectively. In spite of their differing orientations, however, these chapters offer insights into the issue. I showcase these insights, and then offer some further thoughts about how the two approaches can be reconciled and about how both chapters provide significant insight into advertising's rapidly changing world of new media and new technologies.

Both chapters distinguish between what academicians and practitioners in advertising research are actually doing. Academicians are looking mainly for generalizable statements about how features of ads determine their impact. They are almost never interested in how well a particular brand performs in the marketplace. Practitioners, on the other hand, are interested solely in just that impact. Only when a campaign is in the development stage are practitioners even vaguely interested in generalizations about the influence of ad features—features such as ad length, the psycholinguistic structure of the language used in the copy, how illustrations relate to copy points, the category of emotion that is elicited by the ad, or the number of nouns in the headline. Even at the time of ad creation, it is likely that creatives believe that the uniqueness of the ad and how it captures meaning are more important than any set of rules about what features work best (see similar comments by Crimmins, chap. 7, this volume).

So is the academic study of advertising effects completely useless? No. It is just that the purpose of academic advertising research is not to aid practitioners, but to develop a psychology and sociology of mediated persuasion. In such a social science, the structure of messages is linked to internal and external behaviors via a set of generalized rules or laws. Eventually, this body of knowledge may become sufficiently well developed to be used by anyone interested in figuring out how to persuade via the media. Presently, however, this knowledge is ignored by most advertising practitioners.

As the authors of both chapters observe, practitioners are mostly interested in knowing whether ads create enough impact to warrant their cost. This means that the focus is on individual ads for individual brands. There is virtually no interest in generalizations across brands. The practitioner is not selling all brands, just one. What makes the practitioner's question difficult is, first, the complicated and variable linkage between exposure to ads and persuaded behavior (e.g., purchase). Second, getting a fix on all the relevant occurrences in the linkage is expensive. Both of these facts have led to a situation in which, although a lot of claims are made about measuring advertising effectiveness, most of those claims are only that. There is not much in the way of scientifically valid data to support them.

So what do we do when academicians provide little or nothing of relevance to advertising effectiveness issues, and practitioners who know what they want do little to provide valid demonstrations? Chapter 1 suggests that when the term *ad effectiveness* is used, everyone must accept four criteria for investigating effectiveness. First, it needs to be clear to everyone involved what the goals of the advertising are in the first place. If the goal is to improve the percentage of people who recognize the brand as representing a particular category of product, then that effect is what must be tested. If the goal of the advertising is to increase the number of inquiries received, then that effect is what must be tested.

Second, the authors suggest that how advertising fits into the chain of events in the marketing effort must be identified. This criterion appears to be closely related to identification of the goal(s) of the advertising. Creating greater brand recognition is an event very early in the chain from ad to purchase, but one might argue that it is critically important. If consumers do not know that Compaq sells computers, they will not know to ask about them, and may be more hesitant to try one when it is recommended by their local computer dealer. To determine whether advertising is effective under these conditions, it would be necessary to first establish that indeed more people were coming to know that Compaq made computers, and that dealerships where advertising was heavier had salespeople who reported greater receptiveness in the showroom. In other words, when advertising is not designed to drive a sale directly, its stated purpose must be demonstrated, and how that accomplishment is eventually related to a sale must also be examined. Only then can ad effectiveness truly be demonstrated. Reynolds, Olson, and Rochon (chap. 19, this volume) make similar comments.

Third, Wright-Isak, Faber, and Horner point out that an ad is more than the sum of its individual parts. It may create emotion, be easy to understand in terms of its linguistic structure, and have an optimal number of words in its headline, but it is more than these features. It is a whole message, the impact of which must be measured.

The last requirement that Wright-Isak, Faber, and Horner suggest is that advertising effectiveness is likely to have meaning both in the short term and the long term. Short-term effects occur as a result of one or two viewings. Long-term effects occur as a result of many viewings—the effects of which are presumably cumulative. It is clear that one of the reasons that advertising has been losing out to promotion is that short-term effects of advertising are often much less than those of promotion. Promotions, on the other hand, are likely to have little or no positive long-term value.

These four criteria for evaluating advertising effectiveness are unarguably important. They are probably most important for practitioners because they are based on the goal of the practitioner—that is, to index the impact that advertising has on marketing objectives and compare that impact to its cost. They are also important for academicians with the goal of developing a social science of advertising because they help explain why the knowledge the academicians are producing is unlikely to prove particularly interesting to practitioners. I hasten to say, however, that sometimes a finding that crops up first in academic research on advertising (i.e., the predictive value of attitude toward the ad) can prove quite useful to practitioners.

A comment made by Wright-Isak, Faber, and Horner provides a good segue into the chpter by Cook and Kover. Wright-Isak et al. say that "advertising effectiveness is a societal level concept whose meaning lies within a community of professionals" (p. 4). Cook and Kover point out that different research communities have different meanings for ad effectiveness, and that the communities do not communicate very well because although the meanings are different, the words used are not. Cook and Kover articulate four such communities. The first are ad agency researchers, the second are researchers at syndicated research companies, the third are marketing managers in companies marketing brands, and the fourth are academicians.

Quite rightly, Cook and Kover note that these four communities have different goals. Ad agency researchers want to make their agency's work look good to the client, have material to use in new business pitches, and be able to paint a detailed picture of the potential customer for creatives who have to communicate to that customer. Syndicated researchers want to help clients compare an ad's impact to its cost. Marketing managers are generally interested in the same thing. Academicians are interested in what the authors call "theory," generalized social science laws that link general characteristics of ads to responses to ads.

Whereas Wright-Isak et al. suggest that the practitioner definition of ad effectiveness is the one that should be adopted, Cook and Kover suggest that if the four ad research communities are forced to interact with each other, a new definition of ad effectiveness may emerge—one that combines the best of the several communities. Cook and Kover even go so far as to suggest how the communities might be formed; for example, having practitioners visit as professors and having universities form applied research units. Most importantly, they suggest that new media technologies have created a situation of enough uncertainty that agencies and advertisers might be willing to invest in think tanks of the type Cook and Kover recommend.

The bottom line is that advertising effectiveness, a phrase used by both academicians and practitioners, is not understood at all in the same way by the two groups. The Wright-Isak et al. chapter suggests how the phrase should be understood, and what research should therefore look like. The Cook and Kover chapter concludes that the various parties using the term should get together in a serious, long-term enterprise to understand what advertising effectiveness really means.

In the chapters that follow, the reader will clearly see these distinctions. Interestingly, however, not all the distinctions are predictable based on whether the authors are academicians or practitioners. In some cases (e.g., Percy & Rossiter, chap. 15), the academicians are much in agreement with the criteria set up by Wright-Isak et al. If Cook and Kover are right, what we really need is more and better communication among the communities, and this volume will likely prove an excellent starting point for that to occur.

Finally, it should be noted that advertising effectiveness is not going to become less important with the coming of the information superhighway. No matter whether the advertising occurs in an electronic newspaper or magazine or in interactive television, the question of its effectiveness will be critical. If we can build toward a science of mediated persuasion that can identify generalizations about the components of a campaign and how they operate, then this knowledge will serve us well, no matter what the technology.

II

Subtle Processing

Chapters 1 and 2, and the comments that follow them, stress differences between the academician's theoretical orientation and the practitioner's profit-based concerns. At times it seems as though the needs and values of academicians who are interested in developing a psychology and sociology of mediated persuasion and the needs and values of practitioners who are interested in measuring real-world effects are so far apart that the two groups (if they are groups) have little, if anything, in common.

The chapters and discussions in Part II present strong evidence to the contrary. Even though the three chapters in this part all describe classically "academic" experiments, they offer new ways of thinking about important profit-oriented questions. Chapter 3 asks if advertisements are effective even when the audience is inattentive. Chapter 4 asks if an advertisement's context affects its effectiveness. Chapter 5 asks if repetition enhances persuasion. To all three questions, the answer is "yes."

These chapters and the comments on them demonstrate the productivity of academician–practitioner interaction. They note potential applications and they go beyond the obvious to propose extensions. They raise important issues for both academic and applied research.

Chapter 3 is authored by Stewart Shapiro of the University of Baltimore, Susan E. Heckler of the University of Arizona, and Deborah J. MacInnis of the University of Southern California. Chapter 4 is authored by Youjae Yi of Seoul National University, Korea. Chapter 5 is authored by Sharmistha Law and Scott A. Hawkins of the University of Toronto. The comments are by Larry Percy, a former advertising agency research director who is also a textbook coauthor and an independent consultant, and by James C. Crimmins, Director of Strategic Planning and Research at DDB Needham Worldwide, a multinational advertising agency. Both Percy and Crimmins are authors of other chapters in this volume.

3

Measuring and Assessing the Impact of Preattentive Processing on Ad and Brand Attitudes

Stewart Shapiro
University of Baltimore

Susan E. Heckler
University of Arizona

Deborah J. MacInnis
University of Southern California

A typical yet frustrating situation for advertisers is that consumers pay little or no attention to advertisements. For example, they are likely to be engaged in conversation or driving when exposed to broadcast ads or reading an article when a print ad is present. Conventional wisdom holds that the resulting low levels of ad processing under such conditions reduce the ad's effectiveness, because conscious processing of ads is thought to be necessary for ads to impact consumers' preferences. Indeed, a number of measures of advertising effectiveness (i.e., recall, recognition, comprehension) assume consumers are aware of and can remember an ad.

Recent research in psychology suggests that information that is present but "ignored" can, in fact, be processed, albeit at a nonconscious, preattentive level. Furthermore, recent theory suggests that this type of processing can lead to changes in judgments about the preattentively processed information (i.e., increased liking for the ad and brand), even though consumers cannot recall having seen the preattentively processed stimulus before. Even more interesting is that some empirical work in an advertising context has shown that preattentively processed stimuli can affect consumer judgments about an ad or brand (Janiszewski, 1988, 1993; Shapiro & MacInnis, 1992).

Unfortunately, past research is limited in demonstrating that observed effects are due to the preattentive processing of ads as opposed to alternative explanations. Moreover, there currently exists no stringent methodology for stimulating or measuring preattentive processing. Of particular concern is whether the methodology ensures that no conscious processing of the ads occurs during the exposure and measurement activities. If, however, these methodological issues were resolved, and if preattentively processed ads were shown to impact consumer judgments, we would have evidence that exposure itself is, in some situations, likely to affect consumers' brand judgments. Thus, substantially new theory about advertising exposure and consumer information processing would be evidenced. Moreover, we would have novel insights into alternative measures of advertising effectiveness. For example, if advertisements that are ignored still affect brand attitudes, care must be taken in interpreting measures of advertising effectiveness based solely on recognition, recall, or comprehension.

The purpose of this research is threefold. First, a new, more stringent method designed to investigate preattentive processing of print ads is tested. Second, using this new method and novel indicators of preattentive processing, more convincing evidence will be given regarding the relationship between preattentive processing and consumer attitudes than has been offered in the past. Third, a direct comparison is made between the impact of consciously processed and preattentively processed ads on consumers' attitudes toward the ad and brand.

LITERATURE REVIEW

As indicated in greater detail later, emergent literature in advertising and psychology suggests that individuals can process information that is just outside the focus of attention, even though they are not consciously aware of it. The processing of this information has been shown to influence individuals' judgments about (i.e., affect their attitude toward) the stimulus processed preattentively. Before discussing this literature in more detail and describing the issues examined in this research, we first describe preattentive processing, and distinguish it from related research streams. Table 3.1 guides the discussion.

A majority of research on advertising effects focuses on consumers' conscious processing of an advertisement (Stream I in Table 3.1). In this research, respondents' primary task is to direct their attention to the information in the ad, and they are fully conscious of what the information is (i.e., they have the ability to acknowledge that they are being presented with the information; Kihlstrom, 1990). Research in this area typically focuses on the effects of

TABLE 3.1
Distinguishing Streams of Research in Information Processing

Streams of Research	Attentional Focus on the Ad vs. Surrounding Context	Who Determines Whether the Ad Achieves Awareness	Is Awareness of the Ad Achieved?
I. Conscious processing	Ad	Consumer	Yes
II. Preconscious processing	Ad	Advertiser	No
III. Preattentive processing	Surrounding context	Consumer	No

processing different types of ads on consumers' memory (e.g., Childers, Heckler, & Houston, 1986; Costley & Brucks, 1992; Heckler & Childers, 1992; Keller, 1987), beliefs (e.g., Lutz, 1975, 1977; Mitchell & Olson, 1981), and attitudes (e.g., Edell & Staelin, 1983; MacKenzie, Lutz, & Belch, 1986; Mittal, 1990).

A second, less heavily researched stream labeled preconscious processing (Stream II in Table 3.1) focuses on respondents' processing of information typically presented at such a fast rate or in such a degraded form that it cannot be consciously perceived, even though they focus their attention directly on the spot where information is being delivered. Respondents are unaware of the existence of this information because it is presented subliminally (i.e., just below the perceptual threshold; Marcel, 1983a, 1983b; Moore, 1988; Reber, 1985; Synodinos, 1988). A main characteristic of this phenomenon is that the denied access to consciousness of information is controlled by the advertiser (i.e., information is deliberately presented below the perceptual threshold). Although there is evidence in both marketing and psychology for the existence of subliminal perception, evidence for its effects on consumers' attitudes and behaviors is unclear. The research remains controversial and the practice is generally regarded as unethical.

A third and distinct research stream labeled preattentive processing (Stream III in Table 3.1) focuses on respondents' "processing" of information that is just outside their focus of attention. Such would be the case, for example, when consumers flip through a magazine looking for or reading a particular article (thus focusing their attention on the article), and in the process "overlook" the many ads to which they are exposed. Like research on preconscious processing, this research stream deals with situations in which consumers are unaware of the nonattended information. Unlike research on preconscious processing, however, consumers, not advertisers, are responsible for denied access of information to consciousness (i.e., they are not conscious of it because they are paying attention to something else, not because advertisers control the nature of the exposure).

Given the enormity of advertising clutter (Britt, Adams, & Miller, 1972; Webb & Ray, 1979), and given that consumers are often involved in tasks that occupy their attention and thus limit their opportunity to attend to and process ads (MacInnis, Moorman, & Jaworski, 1991), understanding the potential impact of ads processed at a preattentive level is important.

Some research on preattentive processing has appeared in the marketing literature. In the studies conducted to date, consumers were exposed to a mock newspaper containing several articles and target ads. Ads, either pictorial or verbal in nature, were placed to either the right- or left-hand side of an article in the newspaper. Subjects were told to read the articles, and were later tested for their liking for and recognition of the target ads. This research examined situations that facilitate preattentive processing (Janiszewski, 1988, 1993) and provided evidence that preattentively processed ads and brands are evaluated more favorably despite the fact that consumers cannot remember having previously seen the ads (Janiszewski, 1988, 1993; Shapiro & MacInnis, 1992).

Unresolved Issues

Despite these intriguing results, several issues need to be resolved before one can feel confident about the effects of preattentively processed information on ad and brand attitudes. These include issues regarding (a) the control of attention during the exposure activity, (b) the identification of valid measures of attention, (c) the identification of valid measures of preattentive processing, and (d) the measurement of any differential impact of attentive versus preattentive processing of ads on ad and brand attitudes.

Controlling Attention. Studying preattentive processing requires a method that controls the focus of attention so that attention is focused on the surrounding context and not on the ad. Unfortunately, prior methods have had consumers simply read a mock newspaper—a procedure that allows consumers considerable freedom to glance at the surrounding ad content. For example, 20% of the consumers in Experiment 3 of Janiszewski's (1993) study claimed to recognize the target ad, suggesting that these consumers used conscious versus preattentive processing to process the target ads. Although some conscious processing may be a natural part of the typical consumer viewing context, it is not desirable for the careful study of preattentive processing.

Measuring Attention. In addition to providing a method that provides greater control over attentional focus, it is necessary to have some independent measure of attention so as to determine that processing is indeed operating at a preattentive level. Previous studies by Janiszewski (1988) and Shapiro and MacInnis (1992) did not provide this evidence. Janiszewski (1993) did provide eye tracking data in one experiment to provide "online" evidence of attentional focus. However, individuals can devote attentional resources to information not in focal view (Posner, 1980; Sperling & Melchner, 1978). Thus although eye tracking data may accurately reflect where consumers are focusing their attention, it does not accurately reflect where subjects are devoting attentional resources. Moreover, eye tracking equipment is cumbersome and certainly does not reproduce normal viewing behavior. Ideally then, measures of attention that do not interfere with normal viewing behavior, and that provide better insight into the allocation of attentional resources are needed.

Measuring Preattentive Processing. In addition to measuring the allocation of attentional resources, independent measures are needed to demonstrate that preattentive processing has occurred. All information, whether processed consciously or at a preattentive level, activates a memory representation of the material. This activation, known as priming, increases the likelihood that the activated stimulus will be retrieved from memory. If consumers process a brand name at a preattentive level, there is a greater likelihood that they will mention that name when asked to name brands in the product category than if they had not been exposed to the brand name at all. Therefore, evidence of this priming effect is necessary to support that preattentive processing has occurred. Priming is often assessed using an implicit memory task (Graf & Schacter, 1985; Schacter, 1987) in which individuals' memory performance is shown to be facilitated even though they report no awareness of having been exposed to the object before. Janiszewski provided no independent measures of priming. Shapiro and MacInnis (1992) did use an implicit memory task to assess priming, however due to the small sample size (all Ns less than 9) further investigation is needed before any conclusions can be reached.

Measuring the Differential Impact of Attentive Versus Preattentive Processing

Finally, it seems important to examine the impact of preattentively processed ads on ad and brand attitudes compared to ads that have been processed at an attentive (conscious) level. From the standpoint of measuring advertising effectiveness it would be interesting to determine whether ads processed preattentively create ad and brand attitudes that are as favorable or perhaps even more favorable than ads processed at a fully attentive, conscious level.

The objectives of this research are thus (a) to develop and test a method that will control attentional focus and measure the allocation of attentional resources, (b) to show a direct link between preattentive processing, and ad and brand attitudes, and (c) to investigate the differential impact of preattentively versus attentively processed ads on ad and brand attitude.

With respect to the last two objectives we expect that:

- Processing an ad in a preattentive manner will prime the brand depicted within the ad and thus create an implicit memory trace for the brand even though recognition of the ad will be at levels no greater than that expected by chance.
- Processing an ad in a preattentive manner will lead to an increased evaluation of the ad and brand even though recognition of the ad will be at levels no greater than that expected by chance.
- Ads processed preattentively will create ad and brand attitudes that are as favorable or more favorable than ads processed attentively.

RESEARCH METHOD

Controlling and Measuring Attentional Resources

One of the primary contributions of this research is the development of a new methodological tool that allows the researcher to retain a high level of control in the exposure process while presenting subjects with realistic information. Specifically, to gain better control over subjects' use of attentional resources, this study uses a computer-based magazine rather than a paper-based magazine. A picture of the computer screen can be seen in Fig. 3.1. The computer screen is divided into three columns by two thin lines running vertically down the computer screen. The article to be attended is displayed in the middle column. The information in all three columns scrolls up the computer screen line by line at a predetermined rate. Subjects' task is twofold. One task is to comprehend as much of the article displayed in the middle column as they can as the article is scrolling line by line up the computer screen. At the same time, subjects are asked to perform a cursor-moving task.

As shown in Fig. 3.1, the computer screen contains a happy face cursor fixated vertically on the second to the top line of the middle column (hereafter called the attended line). The cursor can move to the left and right on the attended line within the boundaries of the middle column. Subjects' task is to move the cursor in such a way that it is positioned between two words when the next line of text scrolls up. In other words, the goal is to avoid having the cursor hit a word. If the cursor does hit a word, an error is detected and an audible beep is sounded. Although this cursor-moving task is not completely representative of an actual viewing situation, it does simulate the attentional requirements of driving a car, having a conversation, or quickly reading a magazine article, when also being exposed to advertisements.

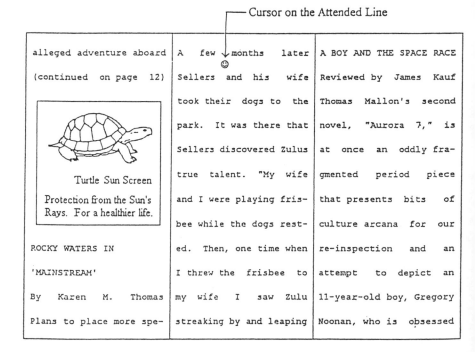

FIG. 3.1. Processing instrument.

The brand depicted in the target ad was in direct line with the attended line, but in subjects' peripheral vision, for approximately 2.5 seconds as it scrolled up the computer screen and out of sight. Based on previous research (Janiszewski, 1988), pictorial ads were placed to the left of the middle column. Additional articles displayed above and below the target ads were present simply to make the computer-based magazine more similar to an actual magazine (or newspaper).

This method not only allows greater control over attentional focus, it also provides a manipulation check measure of attentional focus. Specifically, if subjects do shift their attention away from the middle column and toward the left- or right-hand column of the computerized magazine when something as different as an ad passes by the attended line in the subjects' periphery (i.e., in the left- or right-hand column), we would find more errors than when only text material is in their periphery. The number of errors when the target ad is passing relative to the number of errors made immediately before and after exposure to the target ad therefore provides independent evidence of attentional focus. Equal numbers of errors indicate that subjects did not shift their attention during ad exposure. To enhance subjects' skills in using the cursor, and thus rule out lack of experience in using the cursor as an explanation for the number of errors, subjects were given practice sessions in using the cursor. Furthermore, the cursor task begins well before exposure to the target ads and continues well after exposure to the target ads.

Measures of Preattentive Processing

In addition to using the manipulation check measure given earlier to determine attentional focus, several measures were taken to assess whether information was preattentively processed. The existence of preattentive processing is indicated by two measures: (a) implicit memory for the target brand name, and (b) no evidence for recognition of the target ad.

Measures of Implicit Memory.   Evidence for priming of verbal information is typically conducted by using word fragments. Specifically, if a word such as *hope* had been primed in memory, subjects presented with the word fragment h _ _ _ should be more likely than subjects who were not primed with this word to fill in the blanks to make the word *hope* versus different words (like *hill, hole,* or *help*). In this study, pictorial implicit memory measures are needed to provide evidence that the ads and brands depicted in the target ads are preattentively processed and thus primed in memory.

Although similar measures have rarely been used to assess implicit memory for pictorial stimuli, considerable effort at developing these measures has been undertaken by the authors. Through several rounds of pretesting, picture fragments were developed for the target brands. As illustrated in Fig. 3.2, each brand picture was fragmented so that there were a total of nine fragment levels with Level 9 being the completed picture and Level 1 being the most fragmented

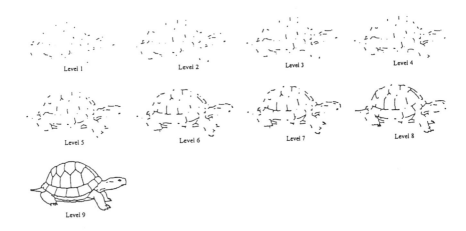

FIG. 3.2. Implicit memory picture fragment measure for Turtle Sun Screen.

picture (Snodgrass & Corwin, 1988). To assess implicit memory, subjects are shown each fragment one level at a time starting with Level 1. The task is to try to identify the object (i.e., brand depiction) at each level correctly. The measure of interest is the level at which subjects can correctly identify the object. Implicit memory would be demonstrated if subjects who had been exposed to the ad (presumably at a preattentive level) recognize the object at a lower level of completion (i.e., more fragmented) than a control group who had been exposed only to the computer magazine, but not the target ads.

Recognition Memory.   Priming by itself does not, however, indicate preattentive (vs. conscious) processing. In addition to showing priming effects, preattentive processing requires that subjects do not report recognition of the ad. To measure recognition memory, subjects were shown six ads—the two target ads and four distractor ads. They were instructed to think back to the computer task and indicate whether they recognized having seen any of the ads at any point during their exposure to the magazine articles. Lack of conscious awareness of the ads would be indicated if subjects who had been exposed to the target ads show no greater awareness of the target ads than a control group of subjects who had been through the same experimental procedure without having been exposed to the ads.

To test our first hypothesis, we expect to find greater levels of implicit memory for subjects exposed to ads in the processing task versus subjects in the control group who performed the same processing task devoid of any ads. We also expect to find equal levels of recognition of ads for subjects in the preattentive processing experimental group and control group.

Measuring the Differential Impact of Attentive Versus Preattentive Processing

The brand names and ads used in this research were based on several rounds of pretesting designed to allow the measurement of any differential impact of preattentive versus conscious processing. To assess this differential impact, it is important to select brands and ads for which prior attitudes have not been established. Thus, novel and fictitious brands and ads are used in the study. Additionally, ads and brands evaluated as neutral in pretests have been identified to provide the opportunity for affect change. Finally, in order to create pictorial ads, concrete brand names were selected that could be communicated through a single object.

Brands were evaluated on three 9-point bipolar scales: unappealing/appealing, unlikable/likable, and unpleasant/pleasant ($\alpha > .95$). A set of related ads were evaluated on four 9-point bipolar scales: unappealing/appealing, likable/unlikable, unpleasant/pleasant, and unattractive/attractive ($\alpha > .93$). The ads and brands selected for the study elicited statistically equivalent neutral ratings. The ads and mean rating responses can be seen in Fig. 3.3.

To test the other two hypotheses, we expect to find that participants in the preattentive processing experimental group will show more favorable brand and ad attitude versus those in the control group, and will show as favorable (or perhaps more favorable) brand attitudes as participants in the attentive processing group.

Subjects

Subjects were 48 undergraduate students who participated in the experiment for course credit. Experimental sessions were conducted over a 3-week period and ranged in sizes from 3 to 12 subjects per session.

Design and Procedures

A mixed factorial design was used with three groups (control, preattentive, and attentive) as the between-subjects factor and two experimental ads (Rabbit Car Battery and Turtle Sun Screen) as the within-subject factor. The control group of subjects ($N = 16$) were exposed to the computer magazine and completed

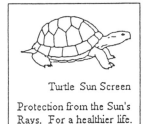

Turtle Sun Screen

Protection from the Sun's Rays. For a healthier life.

Rabbit Car Battery

The battery which never needs a jump.

| Mean Ad Attitude Rating | = 5.51 |
| Mean Brand Attitude Rating | = 5.53 |

| Mean Ad Attitude Rating | = 5.28 |
| Mean Brand Attitude Rating | = 4.97 |

FIG. 3.3. Experimental ads and mean rating responses given in pretest.

the task in exactly the same manner as the other subjects, except they were not exposed to the target ads. The experimental subjects ($N = 32$) followed the same procedure as the control subjects with respect to exposure to the computer magazine, except they were exposed to the two target ads. Half the subjects in the experimental group were told that they would also be asked questions regarding the ads that pass by in the left-hand column of the processing task (the attentive processing group) and half were not told anything about the presence or absence of ads in the processing task (the preattentive processing group). Within each of these two conditions, all subjects were exposed to both ads, allowing for a sample size of 32 for each processing condition. Order of ad exposure was counterbalanced between subjects.

All subjects were told that the purpose of the study was to determine how distraction affects their ability to recall and comprehend magazine articles. Subjects were given the processing task instructions and were allowed to practice with the cursor-moving portion of the processing task before completing the experimental portion. Following the processing task, subjects completed a distraction task, the implicit memory fragment completion measure, ad and brand attitude measures, and the ad recognition task. Subjects in all groups also completed several covariate measures. All subjects were then debriefed.

RESULTS

Assessing the Validity of the Method

An examination of the total number of errors made while performing the processing task can provide some indication of how involving the processing task was, and therefore the extent to which it occupied attentive resources. Error rates close to zero would provide evidence that subjects did not need to devote all their attentive resources to the assigned processing task. If this were the case, it could be argued that subjects had the ability to complete the processing task and consciously process the target ads simultaneously. Additionally, error rates near 100% might suggest that the processing task was too difficult, causing subjects to give up and thus freeing up attentive resources to process the target ads consciously. The mean number of errors made out of a possible 54 in the processing task was 15.69 (29.1%), 16.56 (30.1%), and 17.56 (32.5%) in the control group, preattentive processing group, and attentive processing group respectively. T test comparisons indicate that these differences between experimental groups are not significant (all $ps > .5$). This result indicates that the processing task was equally challenging across experimental groups, and yet not so difficult that subjects would give up.

To assess the validity of the computerized magazine method further, its ability to detect shifts in attention was examined. Because subjects in the attentive processing group were also instructed to pay attention to the ads passing by in the left-hand column of the computer magazine, they should have at some point shifted their attention away from the middle column and toward the left-hand column when performing the processing task. If this method is valid, it should be sensitive enough to detect this shift in attention. An increase in the number of errors in the cursor-moving task would be evidence of a shift in attention away from the middle column of the processing task. Hence, an increase in the number of errors in the attentive processing group versus the preattentive processing group and control group during ad exposure would be evidence that those in the preattentive processing group did not shift their attention to the ads and thus did not consciously process the ads.

To ascertain when subjects in the attentive processing group shifted their attention toward the ads, several questions were asked of these subjects after the experiment was completed. Subjects reported having looked at each ad only once ($X = 1.4$, mode $= 1$) as the ads scrolled up the computer screen, and further, that they looked at each ad when the ads were approximately 5 lines ($X = 4.7$, mode $= 5$) below the attended line. Therefore, four sections of the processing task were investigated: 8 to 10 lines before the target ads, 4 to 6 lines before the target ads (where subjects in the attentive processing group indicated they shifted their attention to the target ads), the three lines as the brand depiction was passing the attended line, and the three lines just after the ads passed the attended line. Hereafter, these sections are referred to as the Before-Before section, Before section, During section, and After section respectively (see Fig. 3.4).

An analysis of variance (ANOVA) was run to test for the main effect of group (attentive vs. preattentive vs. control) on the error rate for each section of the processing task. Results support the ability of the method to detect shifts in attention and suggest that subjects in the preattentive processing group did not shift their attention to the target ads when completing the processing task. The average number of errors made in Lines 4 through 6 (i.e., in the Before section) was significantly greater in the attentive ($X = .97$) versus preattentive processing group ($X = .50$) and control group ($X = .56$, $F = 4.37$, $p < .02$).[1] This result is consistent with earlier findings from those subjects in the attentive processing group who claimed to have looked at the ads approximately five lines before the target ads were in line with the attended line. Additionally, the error rate between the preattentive processing group and control group was not significantly different in the Before section, indicating that those in the preattentive processing group did not shift their attention to the target ads at this point in the processing task. Further, the number of errors made in the Before-Before section, During section, and After section were not significantly different across the three groups (all $Fs < .2$, ps all $> .8$; see Fig. 3.4), indicating that subjects in the attentive and preattentive processing groups did not shift

---

[1]Because the text in the processing task was double spaced, a maximum of 2 errors could be made in Lines 4 through 6, for errors can only be made on the even numbered lines. Odd numbered lines represent the spaces between two lines of text.

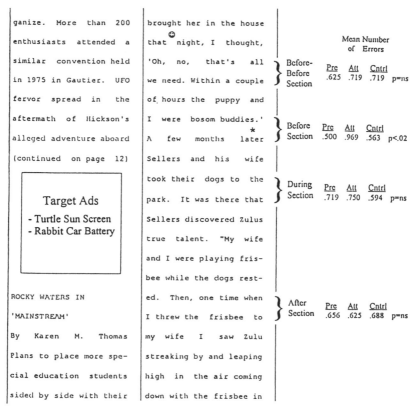

ganize. More than 200 enthusiasts attended a similar convention held in 1975 in Gautier. UFO fervor spread in the aftermath of Hickson's alleged adventure aboard (continued on page 12)

Target Ads
- Turtle Sun Screen
- Rabbit Car Battery

ROCKY WATERS IN
'MAINSTREAM'

By Karen M. Thomas

Plans to place more spe-
cial education students
sided by side with their

brought her in the house
that night, I thought,
'Oh, no, that's all
we need. Within a couple
of hours the puppy and
I were bosom buddies.'
A few months later
Sellers and his wife
took their dogs to the
park. It was there that
Sellers discovered Zulus
true talent. "My wife
and I were playing fris-
bee while the dogs rest-
ed. Then, one time when
I threw the frisbee to
my wife I saw Zulu
streaking by and leaping
high in the air coming
down with the frisbee in

Mean Number
of Errors

	Pre	Att	Cntrl	
Before-Before Section	.625	.719	.719	p=ns
Before Section	.500	.969	.563	p<.02
During Section	.719	.750	.594	p=ns
After Section	.656	.625	.688	p=ns

Pre = Preattentive Processing Group
Att = Attentive Processing Group
Cntrl = Control Group

* Line where those in the Attentive Processing Group claimed to have shifted their attention to the Target ads.

FIG. 3.4. Errors made with the cursor-moving task: An indication of shifts of attention.

their attention to the target ads in any of these portions of the processing task. Combined, these results suggest that those subjects in the attentive processing group shifted their attention to each target ad once while completing the processing task, whereas those in the preattentive group did not shift their attention to the targets ads at all.

The recognition results further support these findings. Chi-square tests indicate that a greater percentage of subjects in the attentive processing group (100%) claimed to recognize the target ads versus those in the preattentive processing group (25%) and control group (28.1%, χ^2 both > 22, ps < .001). Thus, consistent with the error rate data, these results suggest that only those subjects in the attentive processing group shifted their attention to the target ads while completing the processing task.

Testing the Hypotheses

Our first hypothesis states that processing an ad in a preattentive manner would create an implicit memory trace for the brand. ANOVAs were run for each of the two picture fragment measures with group (attentive, preattentive, and control) as the independent variable. Results indicate that group had no effect on the picture fragment completion measures, $F = 1.89, p > .16$ for Rabbit and $F = .03, p > .90$ for Turtle). Thus, the first hypothesis was not supported.

It is thought that a lack of support for this hypothesis might be due to the implicit memory measure itself, and not the theory. Specifically, if this measure was valid, one would expect to find a priming effect with the attentive processing group. For this reason, the other two hypotheses were examined despite the lack of support for the first one.

The second hypothesis examines the effect of preattentive processing on ad and brand attitude. Differences were found in ad attitude between the Rabbit ad ($X = 5.97$) and Turtle ad ($X = 5.20$), $t = 3.16, p < .003$, and thus the two ads were analyzed separately. ANOVAs indicate that group had no effect on subjects' attitude toward the Rabbit Car Battery ad, $F = .807, p > .40$, but did for the Turtle Sun Screen ad, $F = 3.54, p < .04$. A contrast indicates that those in the preattentive processing group ($X = 5.72$) evaluated this ad more positively than those in the control group ($X = 4.28$), $t = 2.39, p < .02$. Thus, the first part of our second hypothesis was partially supported. An ANOVA on brand attitude indicates that group has no effect on brand attitudes, $F = 1.12$, $p > .30$. Thus the second part of this hypothesis was not supported.

The final hypothesis examines ad and brand attitude under conditions of preattentive versus attentive processing and suggests that ads processed in a preattentive manner may be evaluated equally or more favorably than ads processed in an attentive manner. Because no effect was found for group in conjunction with the Rabbit Car Battery ad, analysis of ad attitude focuses on the ad for Turtle Sun Screen. Contrasts indicate that those in the preattentive processing group ($X = 5.72$) evaluated the ad as highly as those in the attentive processing group ($X = 5.59$), $t = .826, p > .80$, and that both of these groups evaluated the ad more highly than those in the control group ($X = 4.28$; both $ps < .05$). Thus, support was found for the first part of this hypothesis. Because no effect was found for group on brand attitude, brand attitude was not analyzed to test the second part of the final hypothesis.

Matching Activation

Because only minimal support was found for many of the hypotheses, further examination of previous theories investigating the effects of preattentive processing on ad attitude was undertaken in an attempt to find mediating or moderating variables that can affect the preattentive processing—affect relationship. Previous research investigating this relationship suggests that matching activation may affect the likelihood of forming a mental representation of the preattentively processed material (see Janiszewski, 1993). Matching activation states that the availability of processing resources of one hemisphere of the brain can be increased with an increased use of processing resources of the opposing hemisphere. Thus, if a subject were completing a task primarily requiring use of the left hemisphere (e.g., reading an article), the availability of processing resources in the right hemisphere would increase in anticipation of an increased processing load. The increased availability of resources in the right hemisphere would then increase the likelihood that information (e.g., a picture) initially sent to the right hemisphere would be processed.

When completing the processing task in this study, subjects could have used primarily right or left hemispheric resources depending on whether they concentrated more of their efforts on maneuvering the cursor (a right hemisphere task) or reading the article (a left hemisphere task). According to matching activation theory, subjects who devoted a greater amount of their efforts to reading the article would have a larger amount of right hemispheric resources available for processing, and given that the processing of pictorial information is thought to be primarily compatible with the right hemisphere versus the left hemisphere, these subjects would then have an increased likelihood of preattentively processing the pictorial ads.

Responses to the distraction task performed after completing the processing task allow us to divide subjects into those who used relatively more versus less left hemispheric resources when completing the processing task. One part of the distraction task involved having subjects write down what they could remember about the article they read in the computerized magazine. A greater number of facts recalled is one indication that a subject used relatively more left hemispheric resources when completing the processing task, and thus had a relatively greater amount of right hemispheric resources available to process the pictorial ads preattentively.

One of the researchers and an assistant, both blind to the experimental conditions, coded subjects' responses to this question as to the number of correct facts mentioned from the article (intercoder reliability = 94%). Discrepancies were discussed among the two coders until a resolution was reached. The mean number of correct facts recalled was 3.07, with the mode also equaling 3.[2] This variable was then made into a dichotomous variable with zero to three correct facts recalled given a code of 1, and four or more facts recalled given a code of 2. A code of 1 (2) indicates a relatively low (high) amount of left hemispheric resources being used when completing the processing task and

---

[2]The specific question asked in the distraction task was to briefly describe the article by writing down the central idea of the article, what events occurred, and the names of the central characters. Because of the way the question was worded, and because the article was mostly descriptive, there were not a large number of facts that could be recalled.

thus a relatively low (high) level of right hemispheric resources available for processing the pictorial ads.[3]

Analyses were rerun on the attitude measures with group and hemisphere as the independent variables. Matching activation would predict a two-way interaction between group and hemisphere, with a greater effect on the ad and brand attitude measures from high versus low left hemisphere subjects in the preattentive processing group.

The results are consistent with the theory of matching activation. The results of the ANOVAs for ad and brand attitude are depicted graphically in Fig. 3.5. Ad attitude is higher for those in the preattentive processing group classified as using a relatively high versus low amount of left hemispheric resources when completing the processing task (X = 7.62 vs. 5.07 for the Rabbit Car Battery ad, and 7.04 vs. 4.93 for the Turtle Sun Screen ad, both ps < .05). Similar results were found for brand attitude (X = 7.39 in the high and 4.57 in the low left hemispheric resource condition, p < .05).

This analysis also provides support for our last two hypotheses. Those in the preattentive processing group who used a relatively high amount of left hemispheric resources when completing the processing task evaluated the ads and brands more favorably compared to those in the control group (for Rabbit Car Battery X = 7.62 vs. 5.53, for Turtle Sun Screen X = 7.04 vs. 4.28, for brand attitude X = 7.39 vs. 4.70, all ps < .05). This result supports our second hypothesis.

Additionally, those in the preattentive processing group who used a relatively high amount of left hemispheric resources when completing the processing task also evaluated the ads more favorably compared to those in the attentive processing group (for Rabbit Car Battery X = 7.62 vs. 6.32 and for Turtle Sun Screen X = 7.04 vs. 5.59, all ps < .05). These results provide support for the stronger version of our final hypothesis (that ads processed preattentively will be evaluated more highly than ads processed attentively).

Results for brand attitude support the weaker version of the last hypothesis (that attitudes are equivalent for preattentively vs. attentively processed brands). Because of differences between the high and low left hemisphere conditions in the attentive processing group with brand attitude (see Fig. 3.5), the conservative comparison of interest is the difference in brand attitude between the preattentive and attentive processing groups in the high left hemisphere condition. Results indicate no differences between these two groups (X = 7.39 in the preattentive processing group and X = 6.57 in the attentive

---

[3]Further analyses were conducted on the low and high left hemispheric resource conditions in order to rule out any individual differences for accounting for any effects that might be found with the hemisphere variable. Subjects in the low and high left hemispheric resource conditions did not differ in handedness (χ^2 = 1.34, p > .50), gender (χ^2 = .751, p > .3), visual (t = 1.60, p > .10), or verbal (t = 1.0, p > .92) style of processing, video game experience (t = .63, p > .535), ad recognition (χ^2 = .045, p > .80) or error rate in any of the four sections analyzed (all ps > .10). Thus, any differences found between the two hemisphere conditions cannot be attributed to any of these other factors.

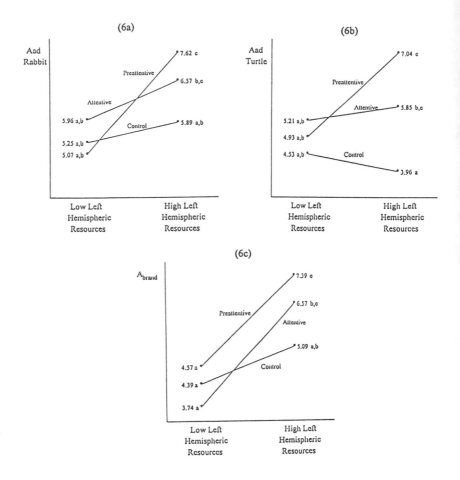

Means with different letters are significantly different from one another at p < .05

FIG. 3.5. Attitude toward the ad and brand by the extent of left hemispheric resources utilized while performing the processing task.

processing group, $p > .05$). Hence, those brands that were attentively processed were evaluated as highly as those that were preattentively processed.

DISCUSSION

The validation of the method used in this study is important in that it contributes significantly to our future study of preattentive processing. This method has been found to foster preattentive processing of advertisements while simultaneously providing an online measure of where subjects are devoting their attentional resources. Without a method such as the one used in this study, which provides clear evidence that the target ads are unattended, it is difficult to attribute any findings to preattentive versus attentive processing.

Additionally, support of the preattentive processing–affect relationship using this more rigorous method lends more credence to the importance of studying preattentive processing. This is particularly so because it was found that under certain conditions, preattentive processing leads to more favorable ad evaluations than attentive processing.

Additional research, however, is warranted to ascertain the strength, duration, and effects of preattentive processing before any managerially useful recommendations can be made about whether and how to develop advertising effectiveness measures that capture the effects of preattentively processed advertisements. To this end, research is presently being conducted that examines whether preattentively processed ads can affect subjects' purchase processes. Specifically, the authors are using the same computerized method as they used in this study, but are examining the effect of preattentively processed ads on consideration set formation rather than attitude change. It is thought that similar research should be conducted in the future manipulating ad content, time between exposure and test, number of ad exposures, and the extent of competitive ad interference in order to better understand the boundaries of the preattentive processing effect.

ACKNOWLEDGMENT

The second and third authors are listed in alphabetical order. The authors would like to thank Ann Perez for her time and efforts involved in developing the computer program used in this study.

REFERENCES

Britt, S. H., Adams, S. C., & Miller, A. S. (1972, December). How many advertising exposures per day? *Journal of Advertising Research, 12,* 3–9.

Childers, T. L., Heckler, S. E., & Houston, M. J. (1986). Memory for the visual and verbal components of print advertisements. *Psychology and Marketing, 3,* 137–150.

Costley, C. L., & Brucks, M. (1992). Selective recall and information use in consumer preferences. *Journal of Consumer Research, 18,* 464–474.

Edell, J. A., & Staelin, R. (1983, June). The information processing of pictures in print advertisements. *Journal of Consumer Research, 10,* 45–61.

Graf, P., & Schacter, D. L. (1985). Implicit and explicit memory for new associations in normal and amnesiac subjects. *Journal of Experimental Psychology: Learning, Memory, and Cognition, 11,* 501–518.

Heckler, S. E., & Childers, T. (1992). The role of expectancy and relevancy in memory for verbal and visual information: What is incongruency. *Journal of Consumer Research, 18,* 475–492.

Janiszewski, C. (1988). Preconscious processing effects: The independence of attitude formation and conscious thought. *Journal of Consumer Research, 15,* 199–209.

Janiszewski, C. (1993, December). Preattentive mere exposure effects. *Journal of Consumer Research, 20,* 376–392.

Keller, K. L. (1987). Memory factors in advertising: The effect of advertising retrieval cues on brand evaluations. *Journal of Consumer Research, 14,* 316–333.

Kihlstrom, J. F. (1990). The psychological unconscious. In L. Pervin (Ed.), *Handbook of personality theory and research* (pp. 445–464). New York: Guilford.

Lutz, R. J. (1975). Changing brand attitudes through modification of cognitive structure. *Journal of Consumer Research, 1,* 49–59.

Lutz, R. J. (1977). An experimental investigation of causal relations among cognitions, affect, and behavioral intention. *Journal of Consumer Research, 3,* 197–208.

MacInnis, D. J., Moorman, C., & Jaworski, B. J. (1991). Enhancing and measuring consumers' motivation, opportunity, and ability to process brand information from ads. *Journal of Marketing, 55,* 32–53.

MacKenzie, S. B., Lutz, R. J., & Belch, G. E. (1986). The role of attitude toward the ad as a mediator of advertising effectiveness: A test of competing explanations. *Journal of Marketing Research, 23,* 130–143.

Marcel, A. J. (1983a). Conscious and unconscious perception: An approach to the relations between phenomenal experience and perceptual processes. *Cognitive Psychology, 15,* 238–300.

Marcel, A. J. (1983b). Conscious and unconscious perception: Experiments on visual masking and word recognition. *Cognitive Psychology, 15,* 197–237.

Mitchell, A. A., & Olson, J. C. (1981). Are product attribute beliefs the only mediator of advertising effects on brand attitude? *Journal of Marketing Research, 28,* 318–332.

Mittal, B. (1990). The relative roles of brand beliefs and attitude toward the ad as mediators of brand attitude: A second look. *Journal of Marketing Research, 28,* 209–219.

Moore, T. E. (1988). The case against subliminal manipulation. *Psychology & Marketing, 5,* 297–316.

Posner, M. I. (1980). Orienting of attention. *Quarterly Journal of Experimental Psychology, 32,* 3–25.

Reber, A. S. (1985). *The Penguin dictionary of psychology.* Middlesex, UK: Penguin.

Schacter, D. L. (1987). Implicit memory: History and current status. *Journal of Experimental Psychology: Learning, Memory and Cognition, 13,* 501–518.

Shapiro, S., & MacInnis, D. J. (1992). Mapping the relationship between preattentive processing and attitude. In J. F. Sherry, Jr., & B. Sternthal (Eds.), *Advances in consumer research* (Vol. 19, pp. 505–513). Chicago: Association for Consumer Research.

Snodgrass, J. G., & Corwin, J. (1988). Perceptual identification thresholds for 150 fragmented pictures from the Snodgrass and Vanderwart picture set. *Perceptual and Motor Skills, 67,* 3–36.

Sperling, G., & Melchner, M. J. (1978). The attention operating characteristic: Examples from visual search. *Science, 202,* 315–318.

Synodinos, N. E. (1988). Review and appraisal of subliminal perception within the context of signal detection theory. *Psychology & Marketing, 5,* 317–336.

Webb, P., & Ray, M. (1979). Effects of TV clutter. *Journal of Advertising Research, 19,* 7–12.

Comments on Chapter 3

Larry Percy
Marketing Communications Consultant

The ideas explored in chapter 3 have enormous potential for advertisers. A demonstration that advertising may not need to be consciously or "attentively" processed to elicit a positive response to the brand means that advertising is probably more effective than most people think, not less. Although a number of practical problems get in the way of measuring such effects for real-world advertising, this should not obviate the importance of the issue being studied.

Unfortunately, the chapter is loaded with just the sort of thing that leads managers to conclude that "pure research" is of no practical use. For example, the extremely small sample size is likely to attract a manager's attention. This point is aggravated by the authors saying early in the chapter that "more work is needed before conclusions can be reached" (p. 29) from earlier research that used samples of "only 9," when some of the analysis in this study is based on a sample of only 16. We can also hear managers objecting that the contrived presentation of the stimulus ads is not "real," or pointing out that many of the hypotheses remained partially supported at best.

The problem is that most practitioners are so conditioned to asking questions and expecting simple answers that they have little or no interest in looking beyond to understand what may be causing the answer. Although managers do not need to conduct this type of research themselves, it is critical that they be encouraged to look beyond their criticism of academic research, and begin to appreciate the issues being explored.

In this case, the issue being explored is important to anyone making decisions about advertising. The implication of the research is that advertising (at least most print advertising) is going to register and communicate something as long as a person is exposed to the visual field that contains the advertising (e.g., the page of a newspaper or magazine), even if that person's attention is held by other material in that visual field. Although that "something" may not be that the brand has a special feature, it could very well be a simple positive response to the brand. Wouldn't it be great if we actually generate significant positive feelings toward our brands among their target market even if they do not consciously attend to and process our message? This would mean that current measures of advertising effectiveness are underestimating advertising's utility.

Interestingly, a great deal of related work (Kroeber-Riel, 1988, 1993; Percy, 1993; Ruge, 1988) suggests that one need not actually fully attend to advertising for that advertising to have a positive effect. Kroeber-Riel especially felt that visual images, when appropriately and uniquely matched to a brand and its

45

primary attribute, can elicit positive associated responses without cognitive processing of the advertising. The eye must merely cross the page.

The authors discuss a very similar phenomenon early in chapter 3. People may be unaware of an ad simply because they are paying attention to the editorial copy on the page, something else in their environment, or a limited, subcognitive impression that identifies the material as advertising, and move on. However, if the advertising falls within their peripheral field of vision, something is (or could be) communicated.

So, although the thrust of the chapter itself may seem to be more on the validation of the method than on the potential strength of preattentive processing, managers should not be discouraged by the seeming irrelevance of the technique to real-world applications. The procedure is only a means, and a good one, of demonstrating that the phenomenon of preattentive processing does indeed occur.

Although many of the findings were not statistically significant, and some of the hypotheses were not sustained, preattentive processing was in evidence. This alone is encouraging enough. That is not to say it is better when people are inattentive to advertising (after all, the stimuli were hardly finished ads designed to encourage strong affect), but that even if one is not paying strict attention, advertising may nonetheless stimulate a positive response for the brand.

More research here should certainly be encouraged—first, as the authors suggest, to refine measures to deal with more realistic advertising stimuli, but also to learn what it might be about an execution that can enhance positive preattentive processing when one is not paying active attention. As we all know, that will be most of the people, most of the time.

REFERENCES

Kroeber-Riel, W. (1988). *Advertising in saturated markets.* Saarbrücken, Germany: Institut für Konsumund und Verhallensforschung, International Series.

Kroeber-Riel, W. (1993). *Bild Kommunikation* [Pictoral Communication]. Munich: Verlag Franz Vahlen.

Percy, L. (1993). Brand equity, images and culture: Lessons from art history. In W. F. vanRaaij & G. J. Bamossy (Eds.), *Advancing consumer research* (Vol. 1, pp. 569–573). Provo, UT: Association for Consumer Research.

Ruge, H.-D. (1988). *The imagery-differential.* Saarbrücken, Germany: Institut für Konsumund und Verhallensforschung, International Series.

4

Advertising Effectiveness and Indirect Effects of Advertisements

Youjae Yi
Seoul National University

Advertisements frequently emphasize salient attributes of products so that people's beliefs about these attributes will change. It is commonly accepted that changes in beliefs lead to changes in attitude. Much research has therefore focused on changes in attacked beliefs and related these changes to attitude change.

Substantial evidence suggests that advertising can affect unattacked elements as well. An audience may infer beliefs about aspects of a product not mentioned in the ad. Thus, communication messages about one attribute can influence beliefs about other attributes. That is, advertisements can have indirect effects on attitudinal elements (e.g., Yi, 1990d, 1993). As a consequence, for a full understanding of advertising effectiveness we need to understand when and how these indirect effects take place.

Then, two questions arise:

1. Which beliefs will be indirectly affected?
2. Under what conditions will the indirect effects be likely to be strong?

Two general factors have been found to provide answers to these questions: attribute interdependence and attribute accessibility. The purpose of this chapter is to provide an integrative review of the relevant research findings (e.g., Yi, 1990a, 1990b, 1990c, 1990d, 1991, 1993).

ATTRIBUTE INTERDEPENDENCE

Yi (1990d) examined the indirect effects an ad designed to change a belief has on other attitudinal elements. Attribute interdependence is posited to moderate the indirect effects on unmentioned beliefs. In this section, Yi's (1990b) study is briefly reviewed.

Conceptual Framework

Interdependent attributes refer to attributes perceived to be associated or related. One type of interdependent attribute is causally related attributes. For example, if consumers believe that the reliability of a car will reduce maintenance costs, the two attributes may be negatively associated in a causal sense. Attributes can also be interdependent as a result of measuring the same concept or by sharing a common antecedent. Several findings suggest interrelationships or interdependence among attributes (Yi, 1989).

What are the implications of such interdependence for predicting indirect effects of ads? For an indirect effect to occur for an attribute, the attribute should be accessible to the ad recipient. When an attribute is activated by the ad exposure, the activation is likely to spread to other attributes connected with the attribute, and these attributes may become accessible to ad recipients (Collins & Loftus, 1975). That is, product attribute beliefs are retrieved and accessed according to the manner in which attributes are organized in memory. As a result, people are likely to make inferences about the attributes that are interdependent with the mentioned attribute, and change beliefs about these attributes accordingly. Thus, it is hypothesized that an ad designed to change a belief will affect other unmentioned beliefs that are interdependent with the belief.

A distinct characteristic of this study should be noted, compared with previous studies of indirect effects. This study investigates indirect effects of advertisements on individual attitudinal elements, and thus differs from some studies that examined global indirect effects. Lutz (1975), for example, found indirect effects of advertisements. The anticipated changes for the attacked attributes ($\Delta\Sigma_i \, B_i a_i$) were labeled first-order cognitive effects, whereas the changes in unattacked elements ($\Delta\Sigma_k \, B_k a_k$) were second-order cognitive effects. Second-order cognitive effects, however, do not reveal what the effects are for individual attributes, and do not distinguish effects on beliefs (B_i) from effects on attribute evaluations (a_i). This study questions which attributes are indirectly affected, and distinguishes indirect effects on beliefs from indirect effects on attribute evaluations.

Method

The subjects for this study were 120 MBA students and business school staff at a major west coast university in the United States. An automobile was selected as the test product. A focus group was interviewed to identify salient attributes of the product. Eight attributes mentioned by at least 30% of the individuals were selected as modally salient attributes. They were durability, dependability, ease of maintenance, repair costs, roominess, style, riding comfort, and sportiness.

This study used a 2 × 2 between-subject design with directness of belief change attempts (direct or indirect) and visual cue (present or absent) as the factors. Because a pilot study revealed that repair costs were considered as a weak attribute of the test brand, repair costs were selected as an intended attribute, an attribute to be changed by the ad. Dependability and repair costs were found to be highly associated in the focus group interview, and these attributes were the foci of the ad stimuli.

Directness of belief change attempts was manipulated by varying verbal claims in the ads. In the direct attempt, the ads made verbal claims about low repair costs. In the indirect attempt, the ads made verbal claims about high dependability. Visual cue was manipulated by either including or not including a picture that suggested the intended attribute, repair costs.

Results

The interdependence among product attributes was investigated using a structural equation modeling framework with LISREL (Jöreskog & Sörbom, 1988). There were four dimensions, EV1 through EV4; these reflect (a) reliability (durability and dependability), (b) maintenance costs (ease of maintenance and repair costs), (c) comfort (riding comfort and roominess), and (d) appearance (style and sportiness). Also, EV2 (maintenance costs) was hypothesized to be causally dependent on EV1 (reliability) according to the pilot study. Figure 4.1 provides the proposed representation of expectancy-value (EV) attitude. The fit of the model was assessed with maximum likelihood ratio chi-square test; it was satisfactory in terms of the usual .05 cut-off level. Other measures of the overall fit also suggested that the model was satisfactory. See Bagozzi and Yi (1988) for a discussion on the evaluation of structural equation models.

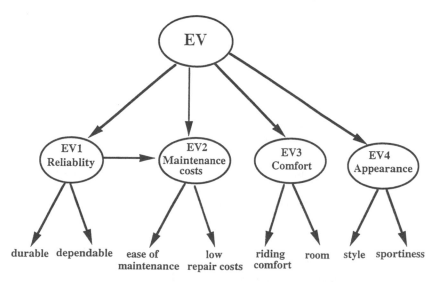

FIG. 4.1. Representation of expectancy-value attitude.

The path from EV1 (reliability) to EV2 (maintenance costs) was tested for significance with the chi-square difference test. Specifically, we compared the model having the path from EV1 to EV2 free to one with the path fixed to zero. The difference in fit of the two models was significant. The standardized value for this path is 0.54 ($t = 4.73$), suggesting that reliability is causally associated with low maintenance costs. The four attributes (i.e., durability, dependability, ease of maintenance, and low repair costs) measuring these two dimensions were thus found to be interdependent.

The hypothesis concerning indirect belief changes was tested by examining belief changes in the indirect attempt conditions. Specifically, it was tested by examining whether the ad changed the unmentioned beliefs that are interdependent with the mentioned belief. It can be noted that dependability was mentioned in the ads under the indirect attempt. Recall that three attributes were found to be interdependent with the mentioned attribute (dependability); that is, durability, ease of maintenance, and repair costs.

Belief change, measured as post-minus preexposure belief scores, was tested for statistical significance both for the ads with the visual cues and for those without the visual cues. The indirect belief change was significant for the three interdependent attributes. In contrast, the belief change was not significant for any of the noninterdependent attributes. Overall, there is strong support for the hypothesis.

Discussion

An ad had indirect effects on beliefs not mentioned in the ad. Advertisers might use an understanding of the interdependence in designing ad messages. In general, some beliefs are more difficult to change through external attempts than others. In such cases, it may be useful to attack beliefs that are more vulnerable yet are related to the intended beliefs. Even when beliefs are equally difficult to change, ads can merely suggest related beliefs and/or their interdependence with the intended beliefs. This might be especially fruitful when the direct attribute achieves wearout.

The findings fit with the structural representation of EV. Because EV is a cognitive network of interdependent beliefs, an ad effect on one belief is expected to bring about changes in other related beliefs. This is consistent with the spreading activation theory (Collins & Loftus, 1975). That is, when one is exposed to an ad, clusters of interdependent beliefs (not just a mentioned belief) change together. Recent studies of EV attitude have focused on the existence of substructures (Bagozzi, 1982, 1985; Burnkrant & Page, 1988; Shimp & Kavas, 1984), but its implications have not been fully investigated. This study has shown that an understanding of attitude structure can be useful for predicting advertising effects.

The results are also consistent with the wisdom of marketers for copy testing. It is not sufficient to examine a postexposure change in the target belief, because there might be second-order effects on other beliefs that could have consistent or inconsistent effects on overall attitudes. The fact that what is communicated goes beyond the literal verbal content also suggests that we need to be concerned about misleading or socially irresponsible advertising.

ATTRIBUTE ACCESSIBILITY

A second questions was: Under what conditions will the indirect belief change be facilitated? For an inference to be made about an attribute so that the belief is changed, the attribute should be accessible to a person. But what factors determine accessibility of attributes? I examine several factors that are likely to enhance the accessibility of attributes to ad recipients.

Priming Within the Ad: Visual Cues

Yi (1990d) posited that visual stimuli in the ad can prime certain attributes and make them accessible. Lynch and Srull (1982) noted that self-generated or externally generated cues can facilitate information accessibility. In the advertising context, visual cues suggesting an unmentioned attribute may work as retrieval cues that directly enhance awareness of the attribute by directing one's attention toward that attribute. Based on these arguments, Yi (1990d) hypothesized that an indirect effect of an ad on an unmentioned belief will increase with the existence of visual cues that suggest that belief.

In Yi's (1990d) study, the visual cues were about repair costs. Thus, the effect of visual cues was tested by comparing the indirect belief change scores for this attribute between the ads with visual cues and those without visual cues. Table 4.1 summarizes the results of this study. The results show that the visual cues had the predicted effects: Inclusion of visual cues increased the indirect belief change. That is, an indirect effect on an unmentioned belief increased with the visual cues suggesting that belief. This finding suggests that visual cues in the ad can enhance the indirect effects.

Priming by Ad Context: Contextual Priming

Yi (1990b) proposed that contextual factors can affect the indirect effects of product information in the ad by priming certain attributes of the product category. Specifically, contextual materials may activate particular product attributes and guide consumers' interpretations of product information. These interpretations may result in the formation or change of beliefs about the advertised brand, thereby affecting consumers' evaluations of the advertised brand.

TABLE 4.1
Belief Change Scores (ΔB_i) After Ad Exposure

Beliefs	Belief Change Scores ($\Delta B_i s$)		Difference Score[a]
	Ads Without Visual Cues (n = 30)	Ads With Visual Cues (n = 30)	Effects of Visual Cues
Highly dependable[b]	1.07**	1.43**	0.36
Highly durable	1.23**	1.33**	0.10
Easy to maintain	0.83*	0.53	−0.30
Requires low repair costs[c]	1.00**	1.70**	0.70*
Provides riding comfort	0.13	0.20	0.07
Provides enough room	0.67	0.30	−0.37
Has an appealing style	−0.50	−0.40	0.10
Has a sporty appearance	0.03	−0.27	0.30

Note. Visual cues have suggested the intended belief (i.e., repair costs).

[a]The difference in belief change score between the ads with visual cues and those without visual cues.   [b]This is a belief explicitly mentioned in the ad messages.   [c]This is an intended belief to be changed ultimately by the ad.

*$p < .05$. **$p < .01$.

Conceptual Framework

In many instances, an ad may contain product information that can be interpreted in several different ways. For example, when one hears that a car is large, one might infer either that the car will be comfortable or that the car will need a large amount of gasoline; that is, a certain product characteristic (e.g., the size of a car) can imply several benefits or consequences (e.g., comfort or gas consumption). In such a case, interpretations of size as high comfort would enhance brand evaluation, whereas interpretations of size as low gas mileage would lower brand evaluation. What then determines the particular interpretation given to the presented information?

Many studies show that people's interpretation of information often depends on the particular knowledge structures (e.g., concepts and schemas) that are currently active (Higgins & King, 1981; Wyer & Srull, 1981). For example, information that someone gave a friend an answer during an exam could be interpreted as either dishonest or kind. Which interpretation is actually given seems to depend on which of the related concepts (dishonest or kind) is most easily accessible at the time information is received (Srull & Wyer, 1980). Active or accessible concepts serve to direct attention to selective aspects of information and are likely to be used to interpret information. These findings suggest that highly accessible attributes are likely to be used in interpreting product information in a given ad.

Given that attribute accessibility guides interpretations of product information, it becomes important to identify what determines attribute accessibility. Although a variety of factors can make certain attributes accessible to ad recipients, of particular interest to this study is the immediate environment for the ad. When the ad context provides people with exposure to a certain attribute (e.g., when they read a magazine article mentioning the attribute), this attribute is likely to become accessible. Subsequently, that attribute is likely to be used in processing ad information and evaluating the advertised brand. Research in social cognition has shown that the accessibility of certain concepts is enhanced by prior exposure to the concepts (Higgins & King, 1981; Wyer & Srull, 1981).

The impact of the ad context on brand evaluation would therefore depend on the attribute primed or activated by the ad context (e.g., magazine article) prior to ad exposure. When the ad context primes an attribute (e.g., comfort) that has positive implications for the evaluation of the advertised brand, overall product evaluations will be enhanced. In contrast, when the context primes an attribute (e.g., gas consumption) whose evaluative implication is negative, overall product evaluations will be lowered. This suggests that the same ad can have different effects, depending on the context in which the ad appears. Thus, it is hypothesized that an ad context priming specific product attributes can have either a positive or negative effect on the evaluation of the advertised brand by altering the way ambiguous product information in an ad is interpreted.

Method

Forty subjects participated in the experiment. Personal computers were selected as a focal product. A pretest revealed that the variety of product features could be perceived either negatively or positively. Specifically, numerous features of a personal computer can imply either that the computer is not user friendly or that the computer is versatile. Therefore, the availability of various features was chosen as the key message in the target ad.

The target ad focused on numerous features of a new personal computer (PC-3000). The ad featured a headline in boldface, "Get the PC-3000, satisfy your lust for power and performance." The ad contained three paragraphs of text emphasizing that the PC-3000 personal computer has numerous features. The ad also contained a picture of one person standing by the computer.

After the general instructions, participants were given three booklets and told to complete the booklets in the order presented. In the first booklet, subjects were asked for general background information. The second booklet contained two advertisements: an ad designed to prime certain product attributes, and an ad for the target brand (PC-3000). The first ad in this booklet represented the priming manipulation. Consequently, two different ads were created that emphasized one of the two attributes (i.e., versatility or ease of use). Each of the prime ads featured a personal computer (which is different from the target brand) that can activate one of the attributes that might be relevant to evaluating the target brand.

Half of the subjects saw a prime ad for the personal computer with a brand name in boldface, "Versa-Com." Centered at the top of this prime ad was the headline, "I didn't know it could do that," emphasizing the fact that the Versa-Com computer can perform many functions. The other half saw a prime ad emphasizing ease of use for the computer with its brand name in boldface, "EZ-Com." This prime ad had the headline, "Our frills require no skills," at the top and contained a picture of a child working at the computer terminal. After completion of the priming manipulation, subjects saw the target ad for PC-3000.

In the third booklet, subjects were asked to generate salient attributes of a personal computer that would come to mind if they considered purchasing one. They listed in an open-ended format the characteristics of a personal computer that they would consider. Subjects were then asked to turn to the next page, where they were asked for brand evaluations such as brand attitudes and purchase intentions.

Results

A one-way analysis of variance (ANOVA) was run on attitude toward the advertised brand. Table 4.2 summarizes the results of this study. Results indicated that contextual priming had significant effects on brand attitude. As expected, brand attitude was higher when the versatility attribute was primed, compared with the case when ease of use was primed (4.98 vs. 3.97).

TABLE 4.2
Cell Means for Key Variables

Variables in the study	Attribute Primed by the Ad Context	
	Versatility	Ease of Use
Brand evaluations		
A_b	4.98	3.97
PI	4.57	3.33
Accessibility of attribute		
Frequency of mention		
Versatility	55%	25%
Ease of use	30%	55%
Order of mention		
Versatility	6.2	7.1
Ease of use	7.7	6.0

Note. A_b = attitude toward the brand; PI = purchase intention.

By examining brand evaluations, we have implicitly assumed that if priming effects on overall judgments were observed, the attribute must have been activated. However, because priming effects depend ultimately on the enhanced accessibility of primed attributes, it is important to assess whether different attributes were indeed accessible to consumers across the two priming conditions. In this regard, the data from the attribute elicitation task were analyzed to gain insights into the processes underlying the priming effects.

Two measures were constructed from the free elicitation data in order to operationalize the accessibility of attributes: frequency of mention and order of mention. The frequency of mention measure was examined first. For the attribute of versatility, the priming manipulation had significant effects on the frequency of mention: 55% of the subjects mentioned versatility in the versatility condition, whereas 25% mentioned versatility in the ease-of-use condition ($p < .03$). On the other hand, ease of use was more frequently mentioned in the ease-of-use condition than in the versatility condition (55% vs. 30%; $p < .06$). The order of mention measure was also compared across groups. For the attribute of versatility, the mean order of mention was 6.2 in the versatility condition, compared with 7.1 for the ease-of-use condition ($p < .05$). Similarly, ease of use was elicited earlier in the ease-of-use condition than in the versatility condition (6.0 vs. 7.7; $p < .05$). The results indicated that the priming manipulation did indeed affect the relative accessibility of product attributes.

In summary, the results supported the hypothesis. Evaluations of the target brand were affected by the ad context priming different product attributes. Furthermore, an examination of the attribute-level data indicated that contextually primed attributes were indeed more accessible to consumers than unprimed attributes, consistent with the hypothesis. Yi (1991) also showed a similar result by employing the structural equation analysis of experimental data (Bagozzi & Yi, 1989; Bagozzi, Yi, & Singh, 1991).

Discussion

Yi's (1990b) study extended existing studies in several aspects. First, this study incorporated research on priming in investigating the effects of contextual materials preceding the ad (Herr, 1989). This study has found that contextual factors may influence judgments of the advertised brand by priming different product attributes. The same product features in an ad can be evaluated in different ways, depending on the adjacent materials.

Second, this research linked information accessibility and ad context effects within a single framework. On the one hand, researchers have found that information accessibility affects brand choice and attitudinal judgments (e.g., Biehal & Chakravarti, 1983). On the other hand, many studies have shown that ad contexts affect advertising effectiveness (e.g., Soldow & Principe, 1981). The research reported here suggests that the two streams of research can be integrated fruitfully. The results show that consumers render evaluatively different judgments of the same product, depending on which attribute is made accessible by contextual factors.

This research is also relevant to practitioners of advertising. First, it suggests that an ad context can alter the impact of a particular ad on brand evaluations. By showing that an ad context is not merely a benign background but that it can influence the effectiveness of an ad, this study expands the scope of both strategic and tactical approaches to persuasion. Second, this study provides a new perspective into the effects of competitive advertising. The study suggests the possibility that ads for competing brands might be beneficial if competing brands can prime certain product attributes that would lead to positive interpretations of the information about the target brand.

Limitations of this study should be mentioned. First, this study used somewhat strong priming manipulations in a lab experiment. One might argue that such priming is unlikely to occur in the natural advertising context. However, advertisements for brands that employ product features or benefits as a basis for positioning (e.g., Crest toothpaste and Budget Rent-A-Car) may prime certain attributes (e.g., cavity prevention and economy) to consumers. One should assess the extent to which the general ad context primes product attributes and examine whether the findings are generalizable. In fact, Yi (1990a) found similar contextual priming effects with magazine articles preceding the ad.

MODERATOR OF CONTEXTUAL PRIMING: PRIOR KNOWLEDGE

Yi's (1990a, 1990b) research provides evidence for contextual priming effects on the evaluation of the product in print ads. However, contextual priming does not guarantee influence. The impact of contextual priming may be strong or negligible depending on the characteristics of the audience. We need to understand the individual difference variables that are likely to mitigate or enhance contextual priming effects. In this regard, Yi (1993) examined one variable to address this issue: prior knowledge. This section provides an overview of this study.

Conceptual Framework

Ambiguous product information is potentially associated with several attributes. Contextual priming effects will occur when one of these related attributes is primed by the ad context and the relationship of ambiguous information with this attribute is activated. Contextual priming effects thus assume the existence of perceived relationships among product attributes in memory.

Experienced consumers may develop knowledge about the possible relationships among elements of a product class (Rao & Monroe, 1988). For example, consumers who use automobiles may come to learn certain relationships among engine size, fuel efficiency, and safety. This knowledge should allow consumers to encode the ambiguous information in terms of related attributes. However, inexperienced or low-knowledge consumers would lack such knowledge structures representing relationships among product attributes (Herr, 1989). As a consequence, they would not be able to encode ambiguous information in terms of other related product attributes. Thus, contextual priming effects are less likely for consumers with little knowledge.

On the other hand, too much knowledge may also decrease contextual priming effects. As consumers develop a great deal of expertise within a product category, they might acquire knowledge of criteria useful for judging alternatives in that category. Because experts possess well-established decision criteria (Bettman & Sujan, 1987; Wright & Rip, 1980), product attributes are likely to be highly accessible to them, regardless of contextual priming. Highly knowledgeable individuals are thus likely to consider a product in terms of all the relevant attribute dimensions that are chronically accessible to them. As a result, contextual priming effects would also be reduced for highly knowledgeable consumers.

Moderately knowledgeable individuals may have some idea as to what attributes are important in evaluating a product. However, because these attributes are not readily accessible from memory, they may not evaluate the product along all the relevant attribute dimensions. Thus, moderately knowledgeable individuals may be more susceptible to contextual priming effects in that they are likely to consider only those attributes that are made temporarily accessible by the context.

Based on these arguments, it is proposed that prior knowledge would moderate the impact of contextual priming on product evaluations. Specifically, it is hypothesized that contextual priming effects on brand attitudes and purchase intentions will be pronounced among consumers with moderate product class knowledge and sharply diminish among consumers with low or high knowledge.

Method

A pretest was conducted to identify a product attribute that has different implications for other attributes. The results indicated that the size of a car was negatively related to fuel economy, but positively related to safety. That is, the large size of a car tended to imply that the car is not fuel efficient or that the car is safe. Therefore, the size of a car was chosen as a focal attribute in the ad. Accordingly, fuel economy was chosen as the attribute to be primed by the ad context in the negative priming condition, whereas safety was chosen as the salient attribute in the positive priming condition.

A print ad was created that focused on the size of the advertised car. The ad introduced a fictitious brand as a new car in order to reduce any confounding due to subjects' familiarity with the test brand. Presenting product information in four short paragraphs, the ad emphasized the fact that the car was large. A picture of the car was also included.

This study used a 2 × 3 factorial between-subjects design with two factors: product attributes (safety or fuel economy) primed by the ad context and prior knowledge about the product class (low, moderate, or high). These two factors will be hereafter called contextual priming and prior knowledge, respectively. Magazine articles were used as the ad context by placing the appropriate article before the ad.

Contextual priming was manipulated by varying the theme of the article so that it would activate different attributes. In the safety condition, the article dealt with the safety of air travel with a headline in boldface, "How safe is air travel?" In the fuel economy condition, the article contained a story of an oil entrepreneur with a headline in boldface, "Oil's new mavericks."

The subjects were 120 students at the business school of a major university. Subjects were randomly assigned to one of the two priming conditions that differed in terms of magazine articles preceding the ad. After the general instructions, each subject read a magazine article that primed one of the two attributes (oil or safety). After reading the article, they completed a one-page questionnaire on their reactions to the magazine article, including their current feelings.

Next, subjects were told that a preproduction version of an advertisement for a new car had been obtained for the study. Each subject was given a photocopy of the ad and was told to examine it as if they had seen it in a magazine. All subjects saw the same ad, although they had read a different article. They were then asked for attitude toward the ad, attitude toward the advertised brand, and purchase intentions.

After responding to these measures, subjects completed a test to measure individual subject's actual product knowledge held in memory. The knowledge scale consisted of 16 multiple-choice questions that assessed subjects' knowledge of automobiles. The subjects were divided into low-, moderate-, and high-knowledge groups using their scores on the knowledge scale.

Results

A 2 × 3 multivariable analysis of variance (MANOVA) was run on the set of dependent variables (i.e., A_b, for attitude toward the brand, and PI, for purchase intention) with contextual priming and prior knowledge as the independent variables. MANOVA results showed that contextual priming and prior knowledge had a significant interaction effect on these measures of brand evaluations. The main effects were nonsignificant.

For an understanding of priming effects on individual variables, separate 2 × 3 ANOVAs were subsequently run on each dependent variable: A_b and PI, respectively. The interaction effects of contextual priming and prior knowledge were significant for both A_b and PI. Contextual priming had significant main effects on A_b, but its effects on PI were not significant. The main effects of prior knowledge on A_b and PI were nonsignificant.

The cell means for the dependent variables show that contextual priming effects were significant for subjects with moderate knowledge. Specifically, A_b was higher in the positive priming condition than in the negative priming condition (4.50 vs. 3.18, $p < .01$). The same pattern was observed for PI (2.47 vs. 1.48, $p < .01$). However, little contextual priming effects occurred for the subjects with low or high knowledge. In the low-knowledge group, neither A^b nor PI was different between the positive and negative priming conditions. The same patterns of A_b and PI were observed for the high-knowledge subjects.

Discussion

The fact that contextual priming effects are an inverted U-shape function of prior knowledge suggests that the relationships between priming and expertise might be subtler than found in earlier studies. For example, Bettman and Sujan (1987) demonstrated that prior knowledge decreased the effects of priming different decision criteria on product evaluations, whereas Herr (1989) found that prior knowledge increased priming effects. Note that both findings can be explained under the nonlinear relationship. Depending on which levels of prior knowledge are employed, each of the two seemingly conflicting results can be observed in a particular study.

Although contextual priming effects diminished among those with both low and high knowledge, different mechanisms seem to underlie such diminished effects. First, consumers with little product knowledge may not perceive the relevance of the accessible attribute to the evaluation at hand. Thus, although a product attribute is made accessible by the ad context, the consumers may not be able to draw the implication of ambiguous product information in terms of that attribute.

On the other hand, high-knowledge consumers are relatively immune to accessibility manipulations by contextual priming, perhaps because their evaluative standards are well established and already highly accessible (e.g., Bettman & Sujan, 1987; Wright & Rip, 1980). Contextual priming of a pertinent attribute may only remind highly knowledgeable consumers of what they already know. That is, situational manipulations of attribute accessibility are redundant for them, because most attributes are chronically accessible to them.

This research has several theoretical implications. First, this study extends the research on consumer inference making by considering situations where several benefits or consequences can be inferred from the same set of product features. Previous research tended to examine whether or not or when inferences are made, assuming that the inferences made in a given situation are similar (e.g., Ford & Smith, 1987). This study allows for the existence of several inferences that may differ in evaluative implications, examines which inferences are made out of several possible ones, and investigates contextual priming as a determinant of inferences. By investigating the moderator variable of contextual priming effects, this research also provides insights into the situations when contextual effects may be pronounced. That is, the results of this study should be informative of when ad context influences consumers' product evaluations.

CONCLUSION

A review of indirect effects suggests that understanding indirect effects can extend research on advertising effects in several ways. First, this study incorporates research on priming in investigating the influences of ad environment. This study models psychological processes that occur as a result of print ads being embedded in certain environments and examines the way in which the ad context influences particular measures of advertising effectiveness.

Second, this research links ad context and information accessibility within a single framework in explaining cognitive priming effects. On the one hand, many studies have shown that ad contexts affect advertising effectiveness (e.g., Singh & Churchill, 1987). On the other hand, studies of information accessibility suggest that once a concept is primed or activated, its relative salience is enhanced, and the likelihood of its use in encoding subsequent information increases (e.g., Wyer & Srull, 1981). This research suggests that an integration of the two streams of research can be fruitful.

Third, this study extends the research on inferential beliefs by considering situations where several different, potentially opposing, inferences are possible. That is, cognitive priming effects in this study might be seen as special types of inferential beliefs. Studies of human inference suggest that people may go beyond the given information by forming inferential beliefs about unmentioned aspects of a stimulus (e.g., Ford & Smith, 1987; Huber & McCann, 1982). As a consequence, an ad designed to change a belief may indirectly affect other beliefs that are not mentioned in the ad. However, previous research tended to examine whether or not inferences are made, with relatively little attention given to the possibility of multiple inferences. In this regard, this study can be seen as an extension of the research on inference; it allows for the existence of several inferences that may differ in their evaluative implications, examines which inferences are made out of several possible ones, and investigates attribute salience as a determinant of inferences.

This research is also relevant to practitioners of advertising. First, the ad context is not merely a benign background for ads, but it can also become an effective communication itself. By providing an understanding of context effects, this study expands the scope of both strategic and tactical approaches to persuasion. The findings suggest an indirect persuasive attempt in which one provides seemingly neutral information (e.g., weight of a bag) and primes consumers to encode the information in terms of the target benefit (e.g., ease of handling). Table 4.3 illustrates the direct and indirect approaches to persuasion. Such indirect approaches to persuasion are likely to offer several advantages over traditional techniques claiming the target benefit directly. Yi (1990c) showed that indirect approaches can offer certain advantages over direct approaches. For example, indirect approaches tend to yield persuasion that is more stable over time and reduce unfavorable cognitive responses generated among the audience.

Second, this study helps advertisers understand potentially dysfunctional second-order effects of the ad context. The findings can help advertisers to understand and predict the unintended effects of the ad context. If the ad context primes negative interpretations of the product, perceptions of the advertised product will be negatively affected. One should avoid placing the ad in such an unfavorable environment. Alternatively, one might proactively create a favorable context that can enhance the effect of an ad. For example, advertisements emphasizing a certain product feature (e.g., air bags) may benefit by having an adjacent article (e.g., crime story) that can prime the target benefit (e.g., safety). This suggests that advertisers might wish to have more control over not only media outlets, but also specific editorial content.

Third, the results of this study can be useful for understanding the positive or negative context effects of commercial clutter. Finally, ad context effects may be important for copy testing. Because ad effectiveness varies across contexts, ads must be tested in a setting that closely resembles the actual ad environment.

Kirmani and Yi (1991) argued that the influence of advertising context may be either cognitive or affective. Cognitive influence occurs when the context influences consumers' processing of product information in ads. Affective influence, on the other hand, occurs when the context generates affective responses such as mood states or feelings (see Goldberg & Gorn, 1987). Contextual priming effects reviewed in this chapter are cognitive in nature. However, it is also possible that contextual priming manipulations might have induced unintended affective influences. See Yi (1990a) for an investigation of affective influence.

Magazine articles and competitive advertisements were found to affect the interpretation of product attributes. Future research can focus on the identification of other factors (e.g., point-of-purchase stimuli) that enhance the likelihood that certain attributes are accessible to consumers in processing product information.

TABLE 4.3
Direct and Indirect Approaches to Persuasion

Persuasive Approach	Intended Attribute[a]	Mentioned Attribute[b]
Direct	A	A
Indirect	A	B

[a]An ad intends to change beliefs about this attribute.   [b]An ad contains verbal messages about this attribute.

REFERENCES

Bagozzi, R. P. (1982). A field investigation of causal relationships among cognitions, affect, intentions, and behavior. *Journal of Marketing Research, 19*, 562-584.

Bagozzi, R. P. (1985). Expectancy-value attitude models: An analysis of critical theoretical issues. *International Journal of Research in Marketing, 2*, 43-60.

Bagozzi, R. P., & Yi, Y. (1988). On the evaluation of structural equation models. *Journal of the Academy of Marketing Science, 16*, 74-94.

Bagozzi, R. P., & Yi, Y. (1989). On the use of structural equation models in experimental designs. *Journal of Marketing Research, 26*, 271-284.

Bagozzi, R. P., Yi, Y., & Singh, S. (1991). On the use of structural equation models in experimental designs: Two extensions. *International Journal of Research in Marketing, 8*, 125-140.

Bettman, J. R., & Sujan, M. (1987). Effects of framing on evaluation of comparable and noncomparable alternatives by expert and novice consumers. *Journal of Consumer Research, 14*, 141-154.

Biehal, G., & Chakravarti, D. (1983). Information accessibility as a moderator of consumer choice. *Journal of Consumer Research, 10*, 1-14.

Burnkrant, R. E., & Page, T. J. (1988). The structure and antecedents of the normative and attitudinal components of Fishbein's theory of reasoned action. *Journal of Experimental Social Psychology, 24*, 66-87.

Collins, A. A., & Loftus, E. F. (1975). A spreading activation theory of semantic processing. *Psychological Review, 82*, 407-428.

Ford, G., & Smith, R. A. (1987). Inferential beliefs in consumer evaluations: An assessment of alternative processing strategies. *Journal of Consumer Research, 14*, 363-371.

Goldberg, M. E., & Gorn, G. J. (1987). Happy and sad TV programs: How they affect reactions to commercials. *Journal of Consumer Research, 14*, 387-403.

Herr, P. M. (1989). Priming price: Prior knowledge and context effects. *Journal of Consumer Research, 16*, 67-75.

Higgins, E. T., & King, G. A. (1981). Accessibility of social constructs: Information processing consequences of individual and contextual variability. In N. Cantor & J. Kihlstrom (Eds.), *Personality, cognition, and social interaction* (pp. 69-122). Hillsdale, NJ: Lawrence Erlbaum Associates.

Huber, J., & McCann, J. (1982). The impact of inferential beliefs on product evaluations. *Journal of Marketing Research, 19*, 324-333.

Jöreskog, K. G., & Sörbom, D. (1988). *LISREL 7: A guide to the program and applications.* Chicago: SPSSX.

Kirmani, A., & Yi, Y. (1991). The effects of advertising context on consumer responses. In R. Holman (Ed.) *Advances in consumer research* (Vol. 18, pp. 414-416). Provo, UT: Association for Consumer Research.

Lutz, R. J. (1975). First-order and second-order cognitive effects in attitude change. *Communication Research, 2*, 288-299.

Lynch, J. G., & Srull, T. (1982). Memory and attentional factors in consumer choice: Concepts and research methods. *Journal of Consumer Research, 9*, 18-37.

Rao, A. R., & Monroe, K. B. (1988). The moderating effect of prior knowledge on cue utilization in product evaluations. *Journal of Consumer Research, 15*, 253-264.

Shimp, T. A., & Kavas, A. (1984). The theory of reasoned action applied to coupon usage. *Journal of Consumer Research, 11*, 795-809.

Singh, S. N., & Churchill, G. A. (1987). Arousal and advertising effectiveness. *Journal of Advertising, 16*(11), 4-10.

Soldow, G. F., & Principe, V. (1981). Response to commercials as a function of program context. *Journal of Advertising Research, 21,* 59-65.

Srull, T. K., & Wyer, R. S. (1980). Category accessibility and social perception: Some implications for the study of person memory and interpersonal judgments. *Journal of Personality and Social Psychology, 38*(June), 841-856.

Wright, P., & Rip, P. (1980). Product class advertising effects on first time buyers' decision criteria. *Journal of Consumer Research, 7,* 176-188.

Wyer, R. S., & Srull, T. K. (1981). Category accessibility: Some theorical and empirical issues concerning the processing of social stimulus information. In E. T. Higgins, C. P. Herman, & M. P. Zanna (Eds.), *Social cognition: The Ontario Symposium* (pp. 161-197). Hillsdale, NJ: Lawrence Erlbaum Associates.

Yi, Y. (1989). An investigation of the structure of expectancy-value attitude and its implications. *International Journal of Research in Marketing, 6,* 71-83.

Yi, Y. (1990a). Cognitive and affective priming effects of the context for print advertisements. *Journal of Advertising, 19,* 40-48.

Yi, Y. (1990b). Contextual priming effects in print advertisements. *Journal of Consumer Research, 17,* 215-222.

Yi, Y. (1990c). Direct and indirect approaches to advertising persuasion: Which is more effective? *Journal of Business Research, 20,* 279-291.

Yi, Y. (1990d). The indirect effects of advertisements designed to change product attribute beliefs. *Psychology and Marketing, 7,* 47-63.

Yi, Y. (1991). The influence of contextual priming on advertising effects. *Advances in Consumer Research, 18,* 417-425.

Yi, Y. (1993). Contextual priming effects in print advertisements: The role of prior knowledge. *Journal of Advertising, 22,* 1-10.

Comments on Chapter 4

James C. Crimmins
DDB Needham Chicago

Yi's chapter begins from the idea that advertising changes the way we think about a brand in two ways, directly and indirectly. Advertising can directly and explicitly attack our current beliefs in frontal assault, and advertising can indirectly and implicitly attack our beliefs in a flanking maneuver that causes us to draw inferences about the brand. When indirect advertising works well, we tell ourselves in inference what we might hesitate to believe under frontal assault.

Advertising practitioners are certainly familiar with advertising's ability to work directly and indirectly. In their Pepsi Challenge spots, Pepsi told us directly that a lot of people prefer Pepsi to Coke in a blind sip test. Tylenol tells us directly about the quality of Tylenol, reminding us that Children's Tylenol is the one most pediatricians give their own children. At the same time, Nike has said volumes about the kind of company they are, the kind of shoe they make, and what it feels like to wear their shoes all indirectly by dramatically exhorting us to "Just Do It." People might believe that compared to other salty snacks, pretzels are boring. Frito-Lay confronted that belief not by saying directly that Fat Free Rold Gold pretzels are fun, but indirectly by demonstrating the fun of Fat Free Rold Gold pretzels with their "It Must Be the Pretzels" campaign, which wildly exaggerated what can happen when you eat Fat Free Rold Gold pretzels.

When advertising practitioners design advertising that leads us to conclusions rather than confronts us with conclusions, they work not from a disciplined analysis of how this process works but intuitively as artists have always worked, using music, movement, color, and symbol to evoke emotions and thoughts in the audience.

Although the process of creating indirect advertising cannot be formularized, Yi's chapter helps us begin to think about the process in a clearer, more disciplined way.

Yi's biggest contribution to the practice of advertising is in challenging us to address three fundamental questions about advertising that works indirectly.

When is indirect advertising most useful? Yi suggests that indirect advertising may be most useful when the belief we are trying to change is resistant to change through the direct approach. This is a straightforward suggestion but a provocative one. It means that indirect advertising may be most useful under the following conditions.

- The belief is firmly held.
- The belief is emotionally charged.
- The belief change suggested is large.
- The audience is skeptical of the advertiser's truthfulness.
- The suggested belief change invites counterarguing.
- The belief is a subjective opinion, not an objectively verifiable fact (e.g., style, product personality, product image).
- The belief has to do with perceptions of the product users rather than product qualities.
- The belief has to do with the way others will perceive you if you use the product.
- The belief has to do with the emotional rewards of using the product.
- A direct statement of a product attribute will have the completely opposite effect on the belief (e.g., explicitly stating that the product is cool, in the social sense, will strongly suggest that the product is the opposite).

Many common circumstances seem appropriate for indirect advertising communication. This list of possibilities is long and, I am sure, incomplete. Each possibility serves as an interesting hypothesis for future research.

Which beliefs will be indirectly affected by what we say? This question assumes a fixed message and explores the range of possible results. However, practitioners are interested in a fixed result (the desired belief), and explore the range of messages that will possibly lead to it. Therefore, practitioners might rephrase the question by reversing it: What can we say to indirectly influence the targeted belief?

Yi looks for the answer in attribute independence. Yi defines interdependent attributes as "attributes perceived to be associated or related" (p. 46).

Suppose we wanted to communicate to children that fruit is fun, but children believe that fruit is not fun. If the foods that children believe are fun are generally sweet and cold, we might communicate that fruit is sweet and cold in an effort to infer that fruit is fun. This approach might work if sweet, cold, and fun are interdependent attributes. Attribute interdependence is often used by practitioners in persuasion.

In order to communicate indirectly that fruit is fun, we might communicate that some obviously fun people like Robin Williams or the Power Rangers are crazy about fruit. Children may accept, in a very undeliberate and unself-conscious way with little counter-arguing, that fruit must be more fun than they originally thought.

When are indirect effects likely to be strong? Yi demonstrates that a message saying a car is large will be interpreted more positively in an environment that raises the salience of safety than in an environment that raises the salience of fuel economy. The inferences people draw from a message depend in part on the issues salient in that communication environment.

As Yi suggests, his results seem to have direct implications for media buying. Putting ads in environments that raise the salience of the point we are trying to make should increase our effectiveness. The impact of environment on inference, however, may be less dramatic than Yi found in his experiments. Yi demonstrated the impact of environment on a relatively ambiguous message; for example, saying a car is big without specifying the advantages of bigness. When advertising is done well, it contains few if any ambiguous messages. It would be interesting to examine the influence of an environment in which safety is salient on reactions to an ad that already relates a car's size to its added safety.

In addition to investigating the impact of media environment on inference, we may also want to spend time investigating the impact of social environment on inference. DDB Needham once tested a commercial for a loan service in the United States, English-speaking Canada, and French-speaking Canada. The visuals were identical in all three tests. The audio was modified for French-speaking Canada by professional translators and announcers. In the United States and English-speaking Canada, respondents drew a number of very positive inferences about the lending institution from the commercial. In French-speaking Canada, respondents drew a number of negative inferences about the lending institution from the commercial. We checked to make sure the problem was not in the translation; it was not. Two different audiences were drawing very different inferences from essentially the same stimulus.

It seemed that people in French-speaking Canada were much more conservative financially than English-speaking Canadians or people in the United States. The illustrations of how one could use the borrowed money struck English-speaking Canadians and people in the United States as reasonable and struck French-speaking Canadians as frivolous. English-speaking Canadians and people in the United States concluded that the lending institution was offering a welcome service. French-speaking Canadians concluded that the lending institution was trying to get people further in debt by encouraging them to borrow for insignificant, trivial reasons. Environment, in this case social environment, influences our interpretation of advertising.

Academic studies of advertising such as Yi's stimulate the practitioner by addressing fundamental issues, issues that practitioners are often too wrapped up in day-to-day crises to address. Progress demands that we learn from our experience. Practitioners spend too much time immersed in experience and too little time learning from it.

5

Advertising Repetition and Consumer Beliefs: The Role of Source Memory

Sharmistha Law
Scott A. Hawkins
University of Toronto

Convincing consumers of a product's benefits is crucial to the success of an advertising campaign. To achieve this goal, a strategy commonly adopted by marketers is to repeat simple product claims—we have heard on numerous occasions that, "Campbells soup is good food." Therefore, an enduring question in the study of advertising effectiveness concerns the effect of repetition on the consumer (for reviews, see Calder & Sternthal, 1980; Pechmann & Stewart, 1989). Repeating an ad has been found to enhance memory for the advertised brand (Belch, 1982; Cacioppo & Petty, 1979). Multiple exposures of the same ad have also been found to first increase and then decrease positive attitude toward the advertised products (Cacioppo & Petty, 1979; Sawyer & Ward, 1979). Although the effect of repetition on consumers is clearly an important concern for marketers, very little research has been done on the impact of repetition on consumer *beliefs*. The objectives of this research are to (a) confirm prior findings that repetition increases belief in marketing claims, and (b) further our understanding of the memory mechanisms underlying the effect of repetition on beliefs.

Repetition-induced belief was first reported by Hasher, Goldstein, and Toppino (1977), who found that subjects rated repeated statements as being more truthful than new statements. This phenomenon has since been called the "truth effect." Two causal mechanisms have been proposed for this effect.

First, it is argued that subjects' sense of having seen the item before (i.e., sense of familiarity) leads to heightened validity ratings: A statement will seem true if it expresses facts that feel familiar (e.g., Bacon, 1979; Hawkins & Hoch, 1992). The only study in the marketing literature that has examined the truth effect is reported by Hawkins and Hoch (1992), who observed that repetition-induced familiarity leads to increases in belief of simple product claims. In an initial session, subjects were shown consumption-related trivia statements selected to be plausible but of uncertain truth value. During a later session, half of the original statements were re-presented along with a set of new statements.

Subjects were asked to first rate each statement for validity and then determine which statements had been presented in the previous experimental session. Analysis of individual subjects' responses indicated that (a) repetition increased belief, (b) repetition increased familiarity, and (c) when both repetition and familiarity were included in a multiple regression, only familiarity significantly increased belief.

A second explanation of the truth effect is that it occurs because of *source misattribution*, or a decline in memory for the context in which a fact is learned. According to this hypothesis, a statement will seem truer if it is believed to have been heard from multiple sources. In other words, it is suggested that source misattribution results in the convergent validity for a statement and thus heightens its truth ratings (e.g., Arkes, Hackett, & Boehm, 1989; Arkes, Boehm, & Xu, 1991; Schwartz, 1982).

Arkes et al. (1991) found some support for the source misattribution hypothesis. They had subjects assess statements for perceived validity, familiarity, and the source of prior occurrence on two separate occasions. Analysis of their results in a structural equation model revealed an across-session, but not a within-session effect of source misattribution on truth ratings: items attributed to sources outside the experiment in Session 1 were rated more true in Session 2. However, no significant relationship between misattributed statements in Session 2 and their truth ratings in the same session (that is, Session 2) were found. In addition, they reported that source dissociation has an indirect effect on belief through its effect on familiarity: subjects who misattributed a statement to a source outside the experiment rated the statement as more familiar, and more familiar items received higher truth ratings.

Source misattribution has not been investigated in the marketing context. However, there is reason to believe that source misattribution plays an important role in the manifestation of the truth effect within this context. People may be naturally skeptical about marketing claims (Wright, 1986), but their failure to recall the source of a claim may reduce their initial skepticism toward it. In everyday situations, one often remembers a fact (e.g., that Japanese cars are very reliable) but forgets where or when the fact was encountered. Hence, a message gained from a questionable source may be recollected, and because of its familiarity and a failure to recall its source, judged to be credible. The central question in this study is: Does a decline in source memory lead to increased belief?

The preceding discussion suggests the following hypotheses:

H1: Statements shown during study and repeated at test will be rated more valid compared to statements shown only at test (the classic truth effect).

H2: Statements perceived to be repeated—that is, correctly or incorrectly recognized as having been seen before—will be rated more valid compared to statements perceived to be new (the effects of familiarity).

H3: Statements presented during the experiment but misattributed to a source outside of the experiment will be rated the highest in validity (the effects of source misattribution).

METHOD

Design

The study involved a completely within-subject design with item type (Old vs. New) being the repeated factor.

Stimuli Construction

The experimental stimuli consisted of marketing statements about brands and product claims. Two stages of pretesting were done to ensure that the brand names were familiar and that the claims were plausible to Canadian consumers.

Pretest 1. Previous research suggests that the truth effect is most apparent for statements relating to concepts already familiar to subjects (Arkes et al., 1991). This pretest, which had a sample of 14 subjects, was conducted to identify highly familiar brand names. Subjects were given a list of 112 brand names spanning 50 product categories (e.g., shampoos, airlines, car rental companies) and were required to rate their familiarity with each on a scale ranging from 1 (*very unfamiliar*) to 5 (*very familiar*). Brand names with an average familiarity of 2.5 or higher were then paired with fictitious facts to form plausible product related statements. Examples of the claims used are: "MacLeans is the most popular magazine amongst middle-class Canadians today; Six of CIBC Mutual funds have been awarded AAA rating by Canadian Bond Rating service; The price of reusable canvas grocery bags has almost doubled since 1981." Some of the statements were taken from lists used in the Hawkins and Hoch (1992) studies.

Pretest 2. One hundred and fifty-nine sentences created in Pretest 1 were then pretested for plausibility using another 11 subjects. Subjects rated the validity of each statement on a scale ranging from 1 (*definitely false*) to 5 (*definitely true*). From this group of statements, those with a mean truth rating of approximately 3.0, standard deviation of less than 1, and with a unimodal distribution were included in the experimental stimuli list. One hundred twenty-six statements meeting the selection criteria were randomly divided into two lists of 30 statements each: one list represented the "old" claims (i.e., presented at both study and test), whereas the second set was used as "new" claims (i.e., shown only at test). The mean plausibility rating of 3.07 and standard deviation of 0.82 were included in the main experiment.

Two versions of the study booklet—Booklet A and Booklet B—consisting of 30 target items were created and rotated across groups of subjects such that "old" items shown to half of the subjects would be the "new" items shown to the other half and vice versa. In addition, to minimize further potential confounds that could result from primacy or recency effects, the first and last five items presented to subjects at study were filler items and were not repeated during test. Subsequent analysis of the results showed no significant effect of study booklet, $F(1,90) = 0.55, p > .5$, confirming that the process of stimulus randomization had its desired effect.

The study list consisted of 45 product-related statements, 30 of which were repeated during test. The test booklet contained 75 product-related statements (30 "old" items repeated from the study list; 30 "new" items; and 15 filler items that were included to reduce primacy and recency effects and to increase list length).

Subjects and Procedure

Twenty-four undergraduate commerce students volunteered for the study in exchange for extra course credit. They were told that the purpose of the study was to assess the effectiveness of product claims. Subjects were run in small groups of 2 to 6, with each group being randomly assigned to one of the two booklet conditions. One subject was unable to follow the instructions and was thus dropped from the analysis.

The study consisted of three parts: study, filler, and test. During the study session, subjects were shown 45 statements for 10 seconds each. They were instructed to first form a mental image of the claim and then rate how easy or hard the imagery task was. The purpose of this task was to increase memory, but not evaluation of the claims (Hawkins & Hoch, 1992). Following the initial presentation and rating of the statements, personal data (such as their age, years of education, etc.), and a vocabulary test score were collected from each subject for use in another experiment. This part of the study lasted for about 25 minutes and served as a filler task to minimize the effects of short-term memory. At testing, subjects were told that they would see another set of marketing statements and were informed that some of the 75 statements were repeated from Session 1. For each statement displayed, subjects were given 12 seconds in which to fill out the three dependent measures (to be discussed shortly). They were also instructed not to leave any questions blank.

Dependent Measures

The order of the dependent measures was as follows. First, subjects were required to rate the truth of each statement. Following this, they indicated if they recognized the statement. Finally, they were asked to indicate the source of their prior experience with the statement, if any.

Truth Ratings. Subjects' belief about facts was measured on a continuous 16 cm Likert scale anchored at "definitely false" and "definitely true." Belief was measured as the distance from the left side of the scale.

Recognition. Subjects circled "Y" if they remembered seeing the item before and "N" if they did not. Subjects were informed that they did not have to recall the source of the claim.

Source Attribution.   For statements reported as having been seen before, subjects had to indicate where they had first encountered the statement: outside of the experiment (newspaper, friend, personal experience, etc.), or during the study phase of the experiment. Because all statements were made-up facts, an item seen during study but attributed to an outside source constitutes a source misattribution.

RESULTS

Role of Actual Repetition

Figure 5.1 provides a graphical summary of the truth ratings. To test Hypothesis 1, we calculated a mean response to old items and a mean response to new items for each subject during the test sessions. This comparison showed a robust truth effect; old items were judged to be more true than new items, $M_{old} = 10.13$; $M_{new} = 9.38$; $t(23) = 3.35, p < .01$.

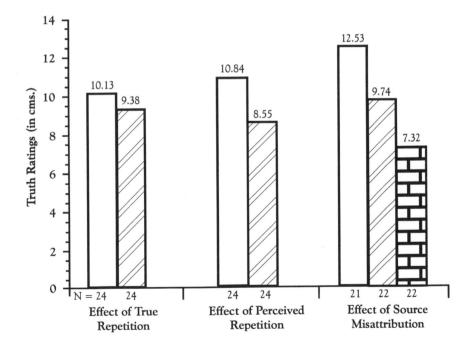

FIG. 5.1 The figure shows the effect of *true repetition* (left); the effect of *perceived repetition* or familiarity (middle); and the effect *of source misattribution* (right) on truth ratings. True repetition effect is the truth ratings for old (black bar) and new (light grey bar) items. Perceived repetition effect is the truth ratings for items thought to be repeated (black bar) and items thought to be new (light grey bar). Source misattribution effect is the truth ratings for items actually repeated and attributed to an outside source (black bar), attributed to the experiment (light grey bar) and items thought to be new (dark grey bar). All the comparisons are significantly different at $p < 0.01$; please see text for details.

Role of Perceived Recognition

As shown in the middle section of Fig. 5.1, statements recognized and hence thought to be repeated (correctly or incorrectly) were rated as being more true than statements perceived to be not repeated, $M_{Perceived Old} = 10.84$; $M_{Perceived New} = 8.55$; $t(23) = 7.38, p < .001$. Hypothesis 2 was thus confirmed. In addition, we compared the mean difference between the truth ratings of actual old and new items with the mean difference between the truth ratings of items perceived to be old and those perceived to be new. Results indicated that the effect of perceived repetition on the truth effect was significantly higher compared to the effect of true repetition, $t(23) = 5.32, p < .001$.

Role of Source Misattribution

The most interesting result concerning the relationship between rated truth and memory judgements occurred when we analyzed the role of source misattribution (Hypothesis 3). A within-subject ANOVA revealed a significant main effect of source misattribution, $F(2,88) = 80.90, p < .001$. Among statements actually repeated in the study, those statements thought to have been seen before outside of the experiment were given higher truth ratings (12.53) than those thought to have been seen in the experiment (9.74), which in turn, were given higher ratings than those thought not to have been seen before (7.32). A Scheffe post hoc test indicated that all means were significantly different at $p < .01$.

These results indicate that one basis for belief is memory for source; people generally believe statements that confirm remembered information and are even more likely to believe those statements that they think they have heard before in a different context. Hence, the key finding of this study is that repetition has the greatest impact on belief when consumers remember the message but forget where they heard it.

DISCUSSION

Repetition of ads is a common occurrence in today's advertising campaigns. This study replicates previous research by showing that repetition increases the perceived validity of a statement. Therefore, these results demonstrate that the truth effect is a quite general and robust phenomenon. Hawkins and Hoch (1992) concluded that familiarity is a primary determinant of the truth effect. Our results support such a contention: subjects rate those statements that they think they have seen before as more true.

Furthermore, this experiment demonstrates that the truth effect is influenced not only by subjects' feelings of perceived repetition or familiarity, but also by whether or not the feeling is accompanied by recall of the source of the prior experience. Our results, which correspond to findings reported in Arkes et al. (1989), show that subjects are more likely to believe statements that they misattribute to an outside source, regardless of whether or not they were truly repeated. One explanation of this may be that subjects consider extraexperimental sources, such as friends, personal experience, and so on as being more credible than the experimental material. Alternatively, as Arkes et al. (1991) suggested, source misattribution may indirectly increase belief by enhancing the perceived familiarity of the statements. Finally, it could be that when people forget the source of a statement that feels familiar, they think it is a part of their general (or semantic) knowledge, and thus are less likely to subject it to careful scrutiny.

As is the case for most laboratory studies, the experiment described here represents an abstraction of how repetition of advertising affects consumer beliefs in more real-life settings. Specifically, the conditions for message processing were atypical in that subjects were instructed to form mental images of the experimental stimuli. In order to increase the generalizability of these findings, the relationship between source memory and the truth effect should be studied in a variety of exposure contexts.

A question for future research is: What impact does the rate of forgetting have on consumer belief over a longer time interval? A general finding is that the rate of forgetting occurs rapidly at first and then slows down (Wickelgren, 1972). It is important to note that from a truth effect perspective, an increase in time delay would be expected to: (a) increase source misattributions, which would lead to inflated truth ratings, and (b) decrease familiarity, which in turn would reduce truth ratings (Arkes et al., 1991). However, with respect to a decline in source memory over time, there is some conflicting evidence about whether there is any forgetting at all. Arkes et al. (1991) found no increase in source misattributions when the time interval between the first and the second exposure increased from 1 to 5 weeks. On the other hand, Gardiner and Java (1991), conducting a recognition-memory experiment, found that memory for source declined at a different rate than memory for words over short retention intervals. They report that memory for source declined more sharply than memory for words over a 24-hour time interval, after which both forms of memory declined gradually and at a similar rate. Hence, one explanation for why Arkes et al. (1991) did not find a decline in source memory over time could be the relatively long delay (1–5 week intervals) they had chosen. A pertinent question for future research then, is to explore the relationship between the forgetting rates of the two types of information (content and source) and the impact of different time intervals of repetition-induced beliefs.

Another area of future research suggested by these findings is to examine the effects of integrative communications on consumer beliefs.[1] Given that source attributions are an important determinant of consumer beliefs, it will be interesting to see if multimedia advertising campaigns (that is, campaigns run simultaneously on TV, radio, and in print) are more persuasive compared to

---

[1]We are grateful to Esther Thorson for formulating this idea.

campaigns run in a single medium. A related research question would be to investigate media effects: Are different media differentially responsive to repe-tition-induced beliefs? Also, are different media perceived to be differentially credible?

Finally, how familiarity and source misattribution contribute causally in increasing belief has not been addressed in this chapter. This study was limited to correlational evidence, so the direction of causal influence is not clear. It is possible that the feeling of familiarity is used as a cue to the source of an item; the greater the feelings of familiarity, the higher the chance of attributing that familiarity to an external source. Alternatively, it may be that feelings of familiarity are a product of unconscious source attributional processes. Our future research agenda is aimed at clarifying the respective roles of familiarity and source misattribution in determining consumer beliefs.

ACKNOWLEDGMENT

Sharmistha Law is a doctoral candidate and Scott A. Hawkins is an Assistant Professor of Marketing in the Faculty of Management at the University of Toronto. This research was supported in part by a grant to Scott A. Hawkins from the Social Sciences and Humanities Research Council of Canada.

REFERENCES

Arkes, H. R., Hackett, C., & Boehm, L. (1989). The generality of the relation between repetition and judged validity. *Journal of Behavioral Decision Making, 2,* 81–94.

Arkes, H. R., Boehm, L., & Xu, G. (1991). Determinants of judged validity. *Journal of Experimental Social Psychology, 27,* 576–605.

Bacon, F. T. (1979). Credibility of repeated statements: Memory for trivia. *Journal of Experimental Psychology: Human Learning and Memory, 5*(3), 241–252.

Belch, G. E. (1982). The effects of television commercial repetition on cognitive response and message acceptance. *Journal of Consumer Research, 9,* 56–66.

Cacioppo, J., & Petty, R. (1979). Effects of message repetition and position on cognitive response, recall and persuasion. *Journal of Personality and Social Psychology, 37,* 97–109.

Calder, B. J., & Sternthal, B. (1980). Television commercial wearout: An information processing view. *Journal of Marketing Research, 17,* 173–186.

Gardiner, J. M., & Java, R. I. (1991). Forgetting in recognition memory with and without recollective experience. *Memory and Cognition, 19*(6), 617–623.

Hasher, L., Goldstein, D., & Toppino, T. (1977). Frequency and the conference of referential validity. *Journal of Verbal Learning and Verbal Behavior, 16*(1), 107–112.

Hawkins, S. A., & Hoch, S. J. (1992). Low-involvement learning: Memory without evaluation. *Journal of Consumer Research, 19,* 212–225.

Pechmann, C., & Stewart, D. W. (1989). Advertising repetition: A critical review of wearin and wearout. *Current Issues and Research in Advertising, 11*(1–2), 285–330.

Sawyer, A. G., & Ward, S. (1979). Carry-over effects in advertising communication. In J. N. Sheth (Ed.), *Research in Marketing, 2* (pp. 259–314). Greenwich, CT: JAI.

Schwartz, M. (1982). Repetition and rated truth value of statements. *American Journal of Psychology, 95,* 393–407.

Wickelgren, W. A. (1972). Trace resistance and the decay of longterm memory. *Journal of Mathematical Psychology, 9,* 418–455.

Wright, P. (1986). Schemer schema: Consumers' intuitive theories about marketers' influence tactics. In R. J. Lutz (Ed.), *Advances in Consumer Research, 13* (pp. 1–3). Provo, UT: Association for Consumer Research.

III

The ELM Model

In the three decades since Lucas and Britt's (1963) *Measuring Advertising Effectiveness*, one of the most influential developments was Petty and Cacioppo's (1986) *Elaboration Likelihood Model* (ELM) of persuasion. In particular, their distinction between central and peripheral processing has influenced academic and applied analysis of advertising ever since.

In chapter 6, the first of two chapters devoted to the ELM model, Curtis P. Haugtvedt of Ohio State University and Joseph R. Priester of the University of Michigan emphasize the importance of *strong attitudes*—attitudes that are "relatively persistent over time, resistant to change in the face of attack, and more predictive of behavior" (p. 79). They assert that strong attitudes are most likely to emerge from central processing of issue-relevant arguments, and present some surprising evidence to that effect.

In chapter 7, James C. Crimmins of DDB Needham Worldwide looks at the ELM model from a practitioner's point of view. He notes that the distinction between central and peripheral processing is difficult to apply in practice because real-world relationships among stimuli, involvement, and respondent are often circular, and because practitioners cannot duplicate the involvement manipulations on which much of the ELM model is based. As later discussions show, Crimmins' comments have important practical consequences. They also have significant implications for ELM-based academic advertising research.

6

Conceptual and Methodological Issues in Advertising Effectiveness: An Attitude Strength Perspective

Curtis P. Haugtvedt
Ohio State University

Joseph R. Priester
University of Michigan

Consider a typical scenario in the development and pretesting of marketing communications. First, objectives are identified for a particular audience. Effort then focuses on creative executions that convey important arguments in favor of a product.[1] To assess the effectiveness of an advertisement or persuasive message, attempts are made to measure influences on the memories, attitudes, and beliefs of audience members. The success of a communication is typically determined by its ability to produce changes in memory, attitudes, or beliefs of individuals exposed to it. That is, observations of changes in a positive (or desired) direction are seen as indicative of effectiveness.

In this chapter, we argue that advertisers and marketers might benefit by considering additional measures and methods to obtain a more complete picture of the effectiveness of their communications. In brief, we suggest that the creation, maintenance, or enhancement of strong attitudes constitutes an important component of what should be meant by the term *advertising effectiveness*. By strong attitudes, we mean attitudes that are relatively persistent over time, resistant to change in the face of attack, and more predictive of behavior. We first provide a brief overview of the theoretical foundations of our work and then focus on methodological issues relevant to basic researchers, advertising practitioners, and marketing managers interested in assessing the strength of attitudes formed or changed as a result of exposure to persuasive communications.

---

[1] These arguments can certainly be more than the typical cognitive or verbal arguments used in most academic research to date. For example, under the appropriate circumstances, anticipated or experienced affect can serve as an argument in support of a person, issue, or product. A brief discussion of this issue is presented at the end of this chapter.

Consistent with the majority of work in the domain of persuasion, we use the term *attitude* to refer to a general favorable, unfavorable, or neutral evaluation of a person, object, or issue. In addition, our focus on attitude as an indication of marketing effectiveness is based on the important roles attitudes have been shown to have in influencing perceptions, organizing information, and guiding behavior in a variety of domains (for recent reviews see Eagly & Chaiken, 1993; Perloff, 1994; Petty, Priester, & Wegener, 1994).

CONCEPTUAL BACKGROUND

One of the first systematic attempts to study persuasion was initiated by Yale psychologist Carl Hovland and his colleagues in the late 1940s (Hovland, Janis, & Kelley, 1953; Hovland, Lumsdaine, & Sheffield, 1949) and continued by McGuire (1969, 1978) and others. The Yale perspectives on persuasion relied heavily on learning theory. That is, learning of message content was emphasized as the process by which persuasion was achieved and maintained (see Eagly, 1974; Hovland, Janis, & Kelley, 1953). A contrasting position was taken by later researchers who viewed the thoughts and ideas evoked by exposure to a communication as the basis for immediate attitude change as well as its long-term maintenance (see Cacioppo & Petty, 1981; Perloff & Brock, 1980; Petty, Ostrom, & Brock, 1981).

Noting that persuasion can also take place without extensive issue-relevant thought and in an attempt to account for differential persistence of experimentally induced attitude change, Petty (1977) outlined the Elaboration Likelihood Model of persuasion (ELM). In brief, the ELM holds that although people want to hold correct attitudes, the amount of effortful cognitive activity in which they are motivated and able to engage varies with individual and situational factors. Thus, the ELM focuses on the extent to which people's attitudes are determined by their careful examination, consideration, and elaboration of all of the available information in the persuasion environment along the dimensions perceived central to the merits of the advocacy (*central route* to attitude change), versus their reliance on relatively simple "cues" in the persuasion setting that determine attitudes via simpler association (*peripheral route*; see Petty & Cacioppo, 1981, 1986). As shown later, the extent and nature of message-relevant elaboration play important roles in the development of strong attitudes.

Inducing Message Elaboration

The ELM differs from many previous theories of attitude change processes by explicitly recognizing the moderating role of numerous factors associated with the likelihood of extensive message-relevant elaboration. That is, rather than suggesting an invariant process of attitude change, the ELM notes that certain kinds of processes are likely to be more or less responsible for attitude changes under specifiable conditions. For example, research has shown that attitude changes are more likely to be mediated by cognitive responses under conditions of relatively high motivation. Under low motivation conditions, attitude changes are more likely to be mediated by factors such as perceived source expertise or attractiveness rather than thoughts about product attributes. Numerous consumer and advertising-relevant variables have been shown to influence the extent of message-relevant elaboration (for a review see Petty, Unnava, & Strathman, 1991), although changes in the nature of advertising (in form and context), as well as the nature of a particular application, make the continued assessment of the likelihood of elaboration an important task for both basic researchers and practitioners.

The ELM explicitly notes that attitudes changed via central route processes are likely to be more persistent over time, more resistant to change in the face of attack, and more predictive of behavior than attitudes changed by peripheral route processes. Because central route change processes occur under conditions fostering high levels of elaboration, it is important for researchers to be able to discern the extent to which a particular combination of factors influences elaboration. Thus, in the following section we briefly review some methodological techniques that have been successfully employed to assess levels of message-relevant elaboration in previous research.

Assessing the Extent of Message-Relevant Elaboration

Assessing the extent to which consumers engage in extensive message-relevant elaboration of a persuasive message has always been an important goal for advertisers. However, perhaps because of the strong influence of the message learning perspective as well as the ease of data collection and coding, until recently much research has focused on measures of the extent to which consumers can recall aspects of a message as an indication of effectiveness. That is, ads for which consumers are able to recall more information were assumed to have been processed more extensively than ads associated with less recall. Unfortunately, and consistent with the basic research in social psychology, recall has not proven to be a reliable indicator of persuasive success (see reviews by Arnold & Bird, 1982; Gibson, 1983; Greenwald, 1968; Stewart, Pechmann, Ratneshwar, Stroud, & Bryant, 1984).

As suggested earlier, the cognitive response approach was developed in response to the failure of message learning to account for attitude change as well as its long-term maintenance. From the cognitive response perspective, an individual's idiosyncratic reactions to the persuasive appeal were seen as better predictors of attitude and the thought-listing technique (designed to capture these reactions) employed by cognitive response researchers offers one way to assess the extent of message-relevant elaboration. This technique typically involves having people write down the thoughts they recall having at the time they were exposed to an advertisement or persuasive message. The extent and nature of these thoughts about different advertisements or in different contexts can offer insights about the extent to which (and how) a particular variable influences message relevant elaboration (see reviews by Cacioppo, Harkins, & Petty, 1981; Stephens & Russo, chap. 10, this volume; Wright, 1973).

An alternative (or complement) to inferring the extent of elaboration from thought-listing protocols is to vary the quality of product attributes or message arguments contained in a communication. That is, argument quality manipulations can be used as a methodological tool for indexing the extent of argument-based processing (see Petty & Cacioppo, 1986). In brief, weak arguments in support of a position are those that are easily counterargued when processed under high elaboration conditions. That is, persons thinking about the material would experience more unfavorable thoughts than favorable thoughts about the promoted product. On the other hand, strong arguments are those that are difficult to counterargue when processed under high elaboration conditions. Persons thinking extensively about strong arguments in support of a position would experience relatively more favorable than unfavorable thoughts. Consumers exposed to strong versus weak versions of advertising copy, therefore, should express very different attitudes if they were engaged in extensive elaboration. Lower levels of elaboration would be characterized by less extreme differences—perhaps to a point where no difference in final attitude is observed (although it is the pattern of data showing significant enhancement or reduction of differences that is most important).

In sum, an argument quality manipulation allows researchers and practitioners "to determine under what conditions individuals are thinking about and elaborating upon the arguments provided" (Cacioppo, Petty, & Stoltenberg, 1985, p. 224). As can be seen in the following discussions, insights regarding the extent of message-relevant elaboration during advertising pretesting are likely to be useful in understanding and predicting the relative strength of attitudes formed or changed.

Attitude Persistence

According to the ELM, and consistent with perspectives from cognitive psychology, greater degrees of message-relevant elaboration (occurring at the time of message exposure or continuing after message exposure) are hypothesized to increase persistence, resistance, and attitude–behavior consistency. In brief, greater elaboration is hypothesized to create more extensive associative networks, increasing the likelihood that more elements will be available to maintain the attitude over time as well as to fend off attacks. Likewise, the greater number and salience of certain thoughts increases the likelihood that the attitude will be available to guide behavior (see Haugtvedt & Petty, 1992; Petty, Haugtvedt, & Smith, 1995, for a more complete description). Thus, for example, research has shown that newly changed attitudes of individuals who intrinsically enjoy thinking (and therefore engage in greater degrees of elaboration) tend to decay less over time than the attitudes of individuals who do not enjoy thinking to the same degree (and therefore tend to engage in less elaboration). Importantly, and related to the purpose of this chapter, attitudes expressed by the two groups of individuals are equally positive (i.e., equally extreme) when assessed soon after exposure to an advertisement or persuasive message. It is only by examining changes over time that the difference in strength is revealed (Haugtvedt & Petty, 1992).

The personality variable of need for cognition (Cacioppo & Petty, 1982; Haugtvedt, Petty, & Cacioppo, 1992) is but one way to operationalize differential motivation to elaborate. Similar findings of differential attitude persistence have also been observed in studies employing situational manipulations of personal relevance (e.g., Haugtvedt, 1989; Haugtvedt & Strathman, 1990). The important point for this discussion is that equally extreme positive attitudes can be formed by very different processes, and these processes have important implications for the ability of the attitude to persist over time.[2]

In sum, as the empirical studies described earlier clearly show, attitudes that are equally extreme in a positive direction can vary with regard to strength. One way to assess the strength of the attitudes formed would be to assess the extent of decay over time. In the following section, we discuss an alternative methodology designed to examine another indicator of attitude strength: the extent to which an attitude remains relatively unchanged in the face of attack.

Attitude Resistance

As noted earlier, stronger attitudes are those that change relatively less in the direction of the contrary information or that require a stronger attack in order to change.[3] This research approach does not require that attitudes be measured over time, but rather that one examine the reactions of individuals to counter-persuasive material after they have viewed a pro-product advertisement. Attitudes that change less in the face of attack would be considered stronger than those that change to a greater degree.[4]

---

[2]The academic research has examined relative influences of different factors (such as the arguments and cues contained in the same advertisement) in conjunction with individual differences or manipulations of processing motivation for theory-testing purposes, and the same methods might be employed in applied contexts to compare the effectiveness of two different versions of an advertisement or advertising campaign. That is, the extent to which the advertisements can stimulate or support extensive elaboration can be examined by employing cognitive response measures and/or argument quality manipulations. In addition, one could and should also compare the relative persistence of attitudes formed or changed by the communications.

[3]For similarities and differences regarding the ELM perspective on resistance and that of McGuire (1964), see Haugtvedt and Petty (1992) and Petty, Haugtvedt, and Smith (1995).

[4]In addition, by varying aspects of the countermaterial, one can begin to assess the extent to which different aspects are more or less critical in the maintenance or demise of a consumer's attitude.

In a study that provides an example of this approach, Haugtvedt and Petty (1992) provided subjects who were high or low in need for cognition with an initial message about the safety of a well-known food additive. This initial message contained strong arguments from an expert source and was followed by an opposing message containing weak arguments from a different expert source. Haugtvedt and Petty (1992) hypothesized that because the attitudes of individuals with high need for cognition (HNC) would be based more on their reactions to the strong arguments in the initial message, they would be less susceptible to the relatively weak arguments in the attack message. However, because individuals with low need for cognition (LNC) should have based their positive product attitudes more on reactions to the expert source than from a careful analysis of what was said, they should have been more susceptible to an expert source arguing just the opposite.

Results of the study were as predicted. That is, although both HNC and LNC individuals were persuaded equally by the initial message, the attitudes of the HNC participants were more resistant to the attacking message. Analysis of process data suggested that the source of the attacking message was a more important determinant of the attitude changes for LNC participants.

A study by Haugtvedt, Wegener, and Warren (1994) provided a direct test of the notion that the resistance of low-elaboration participants is dependent on source expertise. Using the senior comprehensive exam topic and a manipulation of personal relevance, equally positive attitudes were created in two groups of participants. Like the previous study, the attack message was designed to contain relatively weak arguments against the exam. However, in this study, two versions of the attack were employed. The introduction to one version contained the photograph of an individual characterized as a distinguished professor from Harvard (a high expert source). The introduction to the alternate message contained a slightly different version of the same photograph in which the individual appeared unshaven and less distinguished and was characterized as an administrative associate at a 2-year college (a low expert source).[5]

Individuals whose initial positive attitudes were formed under the high or low relevance (elaboration) conditions were randomly assigned to read the attack message from the Harvard professor or the administrative associate. Replicating the earlier research in which the second message was presented by an expert source, attitudes formed under high-relevance conditions were more resistant to the influence of the attack message than attitudes formed under low-relevance conditions. Importantly, however, when the source of the attacking message was a low-status individual, low-elaboration subjects resisted the attacking message to the same extent as high-elaboration subjects. Stated differently, high-elaboration subjects resisted the second message regardless of

---

[5]Of course, just as it is critical to pretest product attribute information for argument quality, it is also important to pretest source information to verify the intended perceptions by the intended target audiences.

the status of the second source, but the resistance of the low-elaboration subjects was dependent on whether the attack came from a Harvard professor or a lower status administrative associate.

The results of this study clearly show that initial attitudes based on peripheral route processes are more susceptible to source factors in attack messages. The results also suggest that just as initial attitude change can be based on different processes, so too can resistance. If this study had used only a low-status person as the source of the attacking message, it would have appeared as if high- and low-elaboration subjects were equally resistant to counterpropaganda. The inclusion of attacking messages from both high- and low-status sources demonstrated that the resistance of the low-elaboration group is tied to the source cues contained in the attacking message, whereas the resistance of the high-elaboration group is more dependent on the strength of their initial attitudes.

Independence of Persistence and Resistance

Thus far, we have suggested that attitudes based on greater degrees of elaboration should be relatively more persistent and resistant than attitudes based on less elaboration. In the following section, we discuss situations in which persistence and resistance may be distinct. In a demonstration of the potential independence of attitude persistence and resistance, Haugtvedt, Schumann, Schneier, and Warren (1994) presented one group of participants with an advertising campaign for a consumer product in which the substantive message arguments for the campaign were varied across multiple exposures of the ads. Another group of participants was presented with a campaign in which the ads were varied cosmetically, but not in substance.

The cosmetic variation strategy involved keeping the arguments the same across ad exposures but varying the positive cues contained in the advertisements. Variation strategies are often used by advertisers to forestall the onset of tedium effects—situations in which continued exposure to an advertisement actually results in the development of negative product attitudes (see Schumann, Petty, & Clemons, 1990). Substantive variation strategies encourage attitude formation via the central route, whereas cosmetic variations encourage attitude formation via the peripheral route. Such exposures, therefore, could serve as tests of the elaboration predictions regarding attitude persistence and resistance. Previous research comparing central and peripheral routes to persuasion had typically involved a single exposure to multiple arguments but relatively few cues. Thus, such research may have provided central route participants with memorial advantages over peripheral route participants.

Consistent with the idea that a complex associative network underlying central route attitudes could provide memorial advantages over single-cue peripheral route attitudes, Haugtvedt et al. (1994) hypothesized that providing more cues (or at least a repetition of the cues) might result in equal persistence for substantively varied ads and cosmetically varied ads. However, they also hypothesized that attitudes based on more elaboration should be relatively more resistant to an attack than attitudes based on cues. Results of their experiment supported these hypotheses. Although attitudes created by substantive and cosmetically varied ads were equally positive and equally persistent over 1 week, attitudes based on exposure to substantively varied ads were more resistant in the face of an attack that occurred 1 week after exposure. The results of this study thus suggest that it remains important to consider the measure of attitude strength. If resistance measures had not been employed, it would have been easy to conclude that any type of repetition would be successful in producing strong attitudes.

Attitude–Behavior Consistency

As the earlier examples show, understanding the extent of elaboration is likely to have important implications for the persistence of attitudes over time as well as their resistance to attack. The ELM also suggests that attitudes created or changed via the relative operation of central route processes should be more predictive of behavior than attitudes changed via peripheral route processes. Most studies examining the issue of attitude–behavior consistency have focused on preexisting attitudes. Few studies have examined the ability of newly changed attitudes to guide behavior. Many studies demonstrating high levels of attitude–behavior consistency, however, can be interpreted as supportive of the idea that attitudes based on greater elaboration should be better guides to behavior than those based on less elaboration. For example, the attitudes of HNC individuals, which tend to be based on a careful consideration of issue-relevant arguments, have been shown to be more predictive of their behavior than the attitudes of LNC individuals (Cacioppo, Petty, Kao, & Rodriguez, 1986).

Studies in which attempts have been made to vary initial information processing have also shown that attitudes created or changed under conditions of relatively high elaboration are more strongly linked to behavior or behavioral intention (e.g., Leippe & Elkin, 1987; Petty, Cacioppo, & Schumann, 1983; Sivacek & Crano, 1982). Thus, the existing data support the idea that attitudes based on greater degrees of elaboration are more predictive of behavior.

EXAMINING THE IMPACT OF AN
ADVERTISING RELEVANT VARIABLE:
THE CASE OF SOURCE TRUSTWORTHINESS

In this section, we briefly review recent research showing that the source of a persuasive message might influence the extent to which persons engage in message-relevant elaboration. This example also serves to illustrate methodological techniques that can help us understand how a new advertisement might influence consumers' judgments.

Some practitioners believe that a highly trustworthy endorser is likely to be more persuasive than a moderate or low trustworthy endorser. Indeed, the fact that Nancy Kerrigan (an Olympic skater widely perceived as highly trustworthy) received several endorsement contracts following the 1994 Winter Olympics whereas Tonya Harding (an Olympic skater widely perceived as highly untrustworthy) received no endorsement offers would seem to support the existence of such beliefs.

The general idea that consumers are likely to be more influenced by endorsers believed to be honest and sincere is indeed reasonable. The specific components most often hypothesized to constitute credibility are expertise and trustworthiness (Hovland, Janis, & Kelley, 1953). *Expertise* refers to a communicator's ability to confer accurate information (i.e., an expert source possesses the knowledge necessary to provide accurate information). *Trustworthiness* refers to a communicator's intent to transmit accurate information (i.e., a trustworthy source is believed to be honest rather than deceptive; see Hovland et al., 1953, chap. 2 for further discussion).

Recent research by Priester and Petty (1994) sought to examine the implications of endorser trustworthiness on message processing and persuasion, holding endorser expertise constant.[6] Their research drew on the ELM to study the mechanisms through which endorser trustworthiness might influence persuasion. Reviewing previous literature and empirical findings, they suggested that if message recipients can be confident that a source will provide accurate information, they will forgo the effortful task of scrutiny and unthinkingly accept the message as valid. In contrast, if message recipients are unsure of the accuracy of the information, they are likely to expend the energy necessary to scrutinize the arguments.

Specifically, although popular canon supports the use of trustworthy endorsers such as skating star Nancy Kerrigan, theoretical perspectives suggest that the use of the less trustworthy Tonya Harding might lead to greater scrutiny of the issue-relevant information and more thoughtful attitude change. To test these ideas, an experiment was conducted immediately prior to and after the women's figure skating finals at the 1994 Winter Olympics. During this time Kerrigan was widely perceived to be a highly trustworthy person, whereas Harding was widely perceived to be a person of, at best, questionable trustworthiness. Advertisements for a fictitious brand of inline roller skates were created. This product was chosen because both Kerrigan and Harding could be expected to have relatively high and comparable expertise.

---

[6]One reason the literature on the effects of source credibility has produced complicated—and sometimes apparently conflicting—results is that researchers typically have not separated expertise and trustworthiness in their research, and these components of credibility might have different effects on the processes of attitude change (Priester & Petty, 1995; for a review of the effects of source credibility, see Sternthal, Phillips, & Dholakia, 1978).

To test the idea that source trustworthiness might serve to influence the extent of elaboration, the quality of the arguments contained in the advertisement was manipulated (between subjects) to allow inferences regarding the influence of source trustworthiness on message scrutiny. Some participants viewed an advertisement containing strong arguments with Nancy Kerrigan as the endorser for the skates, and others viewed an advertisement containing weak arguments with Kerrigan as the endorser. Other participants were randomly assigned to view the same ads with Tonya Harding as the endorser.

When individuals are exposed to a message under conditions that foster message scrutiny (such as an untrustworthy source), those who read strong arguments should be more persuaded than those who read weak arguments. On the other hand, as message scrutiny decreases, argument strength should have less impact on product attitudes. Participants in the study were 60 undergraduate students. The critical skate advertisement was presented with other advertisements and text materials in the context of a proposed college student magazine. After reading the material, participants were asked to provide their evaluations of the magazine and the products contained in the advertisements, the product endorsers, and other aspects of the ads. Finally, participants were asked to write down all of the thoughts they recalled going through their minds at the time they read the advertisement for the inline skates.

Analyses revealed that although Nancy Kerrigan and Tonya Harding were perceived as equally expert, Kerrigan was perceived as significantly more trustworthy. An analysis of product attitude data revealed the predicted interaction. Persons exposed to the Kerrigan advertisements liked the product equally well regardless of the strength of the arguments contained in the advertisement. Persons exposed to the Harding advertisements, however, liked the product to the same high degree as the persons exposed to the Kerrigan ads only when it contained strong arguments. They expressed significantly less positive attitudes when the Harding advertisement contained weak arguments. The pattern of the attitude data, then, support the idea that an untrustworthy source would lead to greater message-relevant processing. The effects of the strong and weak versions differed more when Harding was the endorser than when Kerrigan was the endorser. Additional analysis provided further support for the hypothesized processes. Perceptions of source trustworthiness were significantly and positively correlated with attitudes expressed by persons exposed to the Kerrigan versions of the advertisement, but not with attitudes expressed by persons exposed to the Harding versions. Further, product-related cognitive responses were significantly correlated with product attitudes only for persons exposed to the Harding versions.

These results suggest that if an advertiser's goal is to increase information processing, the use of a relatively untrustworthy source may be one method by which to accomplish this. Interestingly, the attitudinal results of this study contrast with participants' evaluations of the advertisements. That is, the Kerrigan versions of the ads were rated higher than the Harding versions with regard to perceived effectiveness.

METHODOLOGICAL INTRICACIES

The research described in this chapter was conducted to test basic theoretical propositions. However, we firmly believe that the general principles underlying this research have important implications for the practice of advertising. We also believe that methods used here can be employed in applied settings. In the following section, we identify some important methodological considerations.

What Are Cues and What Are Arguments?

As noted earlier in the chapter, attitudes based on simple inferences or peripheral cues are weaker than attitudes based on elaboration of issue-relevant arguments. It is therefore reasonable to ask what aspects of a persuasive appeal are likely to serve as the basis for simple inferences (and hence peripheral route attitudes), and what aspects of a persuasive appeal serve as the basis for product-relevant elaborative thoughts (central route attitudes). A first important consideration is that from the ELM perspective, numerous variables, processes, and effects fall along various continua (cf. Petty, Wegener, Fabrigar, Priester, & Cacioppo, 1993). Thus, for example, the ELM considers the attitude construct as falling along a nonattitude–attitude continuum (e.g., Fazio, 1989) rather than making a qualitative distinction between attitude formation and change. In addition, central versus peripheral routes are conceptualized as a continuum rather than as absolutes (see Petty & Cacioppo, 1986; Petty, Kasmer, Haugtvedt, & Cacioppo, 1987). Relative predictions are made regarding attitude strength as outcomes of the relative operation of central versus peripheral processes (see Haugtvedt & Petty, 1992; Haugtvedt & Wegener, 1994; Petty et al., 1995).

The ELM has explicitly avoided the placement of variables (e.g., source attractiveness, number of message arguments) as central or peripheral factors in a list of "cues" versus "arguments." The most important theoretical and practical reason for this perspective relates to the interactive nature of variables under particular conditions. That is, depending on the meaning of a variable in a specific context and the likelihood of elaboration, variables can sometimes serve as cues, sometimes act as arguments, and sometimes affect the extent or direction of elaboration (Petty & Cacioppo, 1986). For example, in some situations, a variable like beautiful background scenery can serve as a peripheral cue in an advertisement for a new car but is likely to serve as an argument in an advertisement for a vacation destination (see Petty, Unnava, & Strathman, 1991).

Importantly, the ELM does not suggest that any variable will serve any role at any time. Indeed, the model offers predictions as to when a particular variable is likely to assume a particular role. As a general rule, variables are most likely to operate as peripheral cues when elaboration is low. When elaboration likelihood is high, variables are likely to affect persuasion either by serving as arguments or by biasing the ongoing elaboration. When elaboration likelihood is moderate, variables can affect persuasion by influencing the decision of audience members to engage or not engage in extensive elaboration. In our earlier example, source trustworthiness played this role. For more examples of perspectives on the multiple roles of variables see Petty, Gliecher, and Baker (1991); Petty, Cacioppo, and Haugtvedt (1992); and Petty, Schumman, Richman, and Strathman (1993).

In the research described in this chapter, materials were pretested to assure that attitudes formed via elaboration were equal in extremity to attitudes formed via peripheral route processes. Likewise, because of the theory-testing nature of the research, interest was in capturing differences in attitude decay and not the rate of decay. From an applied standpoint, however, researchers may be very interested in the rate of decay in order to most efficiently schedule repeats or variations of the advertisement in order to maintain attitude and awareness above some threshold level (see discussion of rate of decay by Kuse, chap. 17, this volume).

An additional methodological consideration in persistence research is the fact that process data (e.g., cognitive responses, argument recall, etc.) should not be obtained from the same people because the process of listing one's thoughts is likely to artificially increase the extent of elaboration.

What Kind of Message Does One Use to Study Resistance?

In the preceeding discussions, we suggested that one way to assess advertising effectiveness may be to challenge the attitudes of people exposed to an advertisement or campaign. From a practical perspective, consideration needs to be given to the nature of attacks a consumer might encounter. In general, the academic research has used relatively weak arguments in attack messages (but see Haugtvedt & Wegener, 1994). From an applied standpoint, it would be important to examine different aspects of attacks so messages can be tailored to aid in the creation of attitudes strong enough to withstand the likely attacks of competitors (see Haugtvedt, Leavitt, & Schneier, 1993).

SUMMARY

Our goal in this chapter was to introduce attitude strength as an important component of advertising effectiveness. To illustrate our points, we reviewed research showing that very different attitude change processes can lead to equally positive attitudes, and that the ways attitudes are formed have important implications for their ability to persist over time, resist attack, and predict behavior.

A critical factor in creation of strong attitudes is the extent to which people engage in extensive message-relevant elaboration. We described how such elaboration might be assessed using argument quality manipulations as well as thought-listing data. A recent study on the issue of source trustworthiness provided an example of how these techniques could be employed to understand how an advertising-relevant variable can influence the extent of elaboration. We ended the chapter with a discussion of the multiple roles variables can play and some important methodological considerations. In sum, we are hopeful that the attitude strength perspective will prompt new ways of thinking about and assessing the impact of advertising and other persuasive techniques.

REFERENCES

Arnold, S. J., & Bird, J. R. (1982). The day after recall test of advertising effectiveness: A discussion of the issues. *Current Issues and Research in Advertising, 1,* 59–68.

Cacioppo, J. T., Harkins, S. G., & Petty, R. E. (1981). The nature of attitudes and cognitive responses and their relationships to behavior. In R. E. Petty, T. M. Ostrom, & T. C. Brock (Eds.), *Cognitive responses in persuasion* (pp. 31–54). Hillsdale, NJ: Lawrence Erlbaum Associates.

Cacioppo, J. T., & Petty, R. E. (1981). Social psychological procedures for cognitive response assessment: The thought listing technique. In T. Merluzzi, C. Glass, & M. Genest (Eds.), *Cognitive Assessment* (pp. 309–342). New York: Guilford.

Cacioppo, J. T., & Petty, R. E. (1982). The need for cognition. *Journal of Personality and Social Psychology, 42,* 116–131.

Cacioppo, J. T., Petty, R. E., Kao, C. F., & Rodriguez, R. (1986). Central and peripheral routes to persuasion: An individual difference perspective. *Journal of Personality and Social Psychology, 51*(5), 1032–1043.

Cacioppo, J. T., Petty, R. E., & Stoltenberg, C. (1985). Processes of social influence: The elaboration likelihood model of persuasion. In P. Kendall (ed.), *Advances in cognitive behavioral research and therapy* (Vol. 4, pp. 215–274). New York: Academic Press.

Eagly, A. H. (1974). Comprehensibility of persuasive arguments as a determinant of opinion change. *Journal of Personality and Social Psychology, 29,* 758–773.

Eagly, A. H., & Chaiken, S. (1993). *Psychology of attitudes.* Fort Worth, TX: Harcourt, Brace, Jovanovich.

Fazio, R. H. (1989). On the power and functionality of attitudes: The role of attitude accessibility. In A. R. Pratkanis, S. J. Breckler, & A. G. Greenwald (Eds.), *Attitude structure and function* (pp. 153–180). Hillsdale, NJ: Lawrence Erlbaum Associates.

Gibson, L. D. (1983). If the question is copy testing, the answer is . . . not recall. *Journal of Advertising Research, 23*(1), 39–45.

Greenwald, A. G. (1968). Cognitive learning, cognitive response to persuasion, and attitude change. In A. G. Greenwald, T. C. Brock, & T. M. Ostrom (Eds.), *Psychological foundations of attitudes* (pp. 147–170). New York: Academic Press.

Haugtvedt, C. P. (1989). *Persistence and resistance of attitude change: Individual and situational approaches.* Unpublished doctoral dissertation, University of Missouri, Columbia.

Haugtvedt, C. P., & Petty, R. E. (1992). Personality and persuasion: Need for cognition moderates the persistence and resistance of attitude changes. *Journal of Personality and Social Psychology, 63,* 308–319.

Haugtvedt, C. P., Leavitt, C., & Schneier, W. L. (1993). Cognitive strength of established brands: Memory, attitudinal, and structural approaches. In D. A. Aaker & A. L. Biel (Eds.), *Brand equity and advertising: Advertising's role in building strong brands* (pp. 247–261). Hillsdale, NJ: Lawrence Erlbaum Associates.

Haugtvedt, C. P., Petty, R. E., & Cacioppo, J. T. (1992). Need for cognition and advertising: Understanding the role of personality variables in consumer behavior. *Journal of Consumer Psychology, 1,* 239–260.

Haugtvedt, C. P., Schumann, D. W., Schneier, W. L., & Warren, W. L. (1994). Advertising repetition and variation strategies: Implications for understanding attitude strength. *Journal of Consumer Research, 21,* 176–189.

Haugtvedt, C. P., & Strathman, A. (1990). Situational personal relevance and attitude persistence. *Advances in Consumer Research, 17,* 766–769.

Haugtvedt, C. P., & Wegener, D. T. (1994). Message order effects in persuasion: An attitude strength perspective. *Journal of Consumer Research, 21,* 205–218.

Haugtvedt, C. P., Wegener, D. T., & Warren, W. (1994, May). *Personal relevance, attack source expertise, and resistance of newly changed attitudes.* Paper presented at the annual meeting of the Midwestern Psychological Association, Chicago.

Hovland, C. I., Janis, I. L., & Kelley, H. H. (1953). *Communication and persuasion.* New Haven, CT: Yale University Press.

Hovland, C. I., Lumsdaine, A., & Sheffield, F. (1949). *Experiments on mass communication.* Princeton, NJ: Princeton University Press.

Leippe, M. R., & Elkin, R. A. (1987). When motives clash: Issue involvement and response involvement as determinants of persuasion. *Journal of Personality and Social Psychology, 52*(2), 269–278.

McGuire, W. J. (1964). Inducing resistance to persuasion: Some contemporary approaches. In L. Berkowitz (Ed.), *Advances in experimental social psychology* (Vol. 1, pp. 191–229). New York: Academic Press.

McGuire, W. J. (1969). The nature of attitudes and attitude change. In G. Lidzey & E. Aronson (Eds.), *The handbook of social psychology* (2nd ed., Vol. 3, pp. 136–314). Reading, MA: Addison-Wesley.

McGuire, W. J. (1978). An information-processing model of advertising effectiveness. In H. L. Davis & A. J. Silk (Eds.), *Behavioral and management sciences in marketing* (pp. 156–180). New York: Wiley.

Perloff, R. M. (1993). *The dynamics of persuasion.* Hillsdale, NJ: Lawrence Erlbaum Associates.

Perloff, R. M., & Brock, T. C. (1980). And thinking makes it so: Cognitive responses to persuasion. In M. Roloff & G. Miller (Eds.), *Persuasion: New directions in theory and research* (pp. 67–100). Beverly Hills, CA: Sage.

Petty, R. E. (1977). *A cognitive response analysis of the temporal persistence of attitude changes induced by persuasive communications.* Unpublished doctoral dissertation, Ohio State University, Columbus.

Petty, R. E., & Cacioppo, J. T. (1981). *Attitudes and persuasion: Classic and contemporary approaches.* Dubuque, IA: William C. Brown.

Petty, R. E., & Cacioppo, J. T. (1986). *Communication and persuasion: Central and peripheral routes to attitude change.* New York: Springer-Verlag.

Petty, R. E., Cacioppo, J. T., & Haugtvedt, C. P. (1992). Involvement and persuasion: An appreciative look at the Sherifs' contribution to the study of self-relevance and attitude change. In D. Granberg & G. Sarup (Eds.), *Social judgment and intergroup relations: Essays in honor of Muzifer Sherif* (pp. 147–175). New York: Springer-Verlag.

Petty, R. E., Cacioppo, J. T., & Schumann, D. W. (1983). Central and peripheral routes to advertising effectiveness: The moderating role of involvement. *Journal of Consumer Research, 10*, 135–146.

Petty, R. E., Gleicher, F., & Baker, S. M. (1991). Multiple roles for affect in persuasion. In J. Forgas (Ed.), *Emotion and social judgments* (pp. 181–200). Oxford, UK: Pergamon.

Petty, R. E., Haugtvedt, C. P., & Smith S. M. (1995). Elaboration as a determinant of attitude strength: Creating attitudes that are persistent, resistant, and predictive of behavior. In R. Petty & and J. Krosnick (Eds.), *Attitude strength: Antecedents and consequences* (pp. 93–130). Mahwah, NJ: Lawrence Erlbaum Associates.

Petty, R. E., Kasmer, J. A., Haugtvedt, C. P., & Cacioopo, J. T. (1987). Source and message factors in persuasion: A reply to Stiff's critique of the Elaboration Likelihood Model. *Communication Monographs, 54*(3), 233–249.

Petty, R. E., Ostrom, T. M., & Brock, T. C. (1981). Historical foundations of the cognitive response approach to attitudes and persuasion. In R. E. Petty, T. M. Ostrom, & T. C. Brock (Eds.), *Cognitive responses in persuasion* (pp. 5–29). Hillsdale, NJ: Lawrence Erlbaum Associates.

Petty, R. E., Priester, J. R., & Wegener, D. T. (1994). Cognitive processes in attitude change. In R. S. Wyer & T. K. Srull (Eds.), *Handbook of social cognition* (Vol. 2, pp. 69–142). Hillsdale, NJ: Lawrence Erlbaum Associates.

Petty, R. E., Schumann, D. W., Richman, S. A., & Strathman, A. J. (1993). Positive mood and persuasion: Different roles for affect under high and low elaboration conditions. *Journal of Personality and Social Psychology, 64*, 5–20.

Petty, R. E., Unnava, H. R., & Strathman, A. J. (1991). Theories of attitude change. In T. S. Robertson & H. H. Kassarjian (Eds.), *Handbook of consumer behavior* (pp. 241–280). Englewood Cliffs, NJ: Prentice-Hall.

Petty, R. E., Wegener, D. T., Fabrigar, L. R., Priester, J. R., & Cacioppo, J. T. (1993). Conceptual and methodological issues in the Elaboration Likelihood Model of persuasion: A reply to the Michigan State critics. *Communication Theory, 3*, 336–362.

Priester, J. R., & Petty, R. E. (1994). *Endorser trustworthiness and message scrutiny: Comparing perceived versus actual advertising effectiveness.* Unpublished manuscript, Department of Psychology, Ohio State University, Columbus.

Priester, J. R., & Petty, R. E. (1995). Source attributions and persuasion: Perceived honesty as a determinant of message scrutiny. *Personality and Social Psychology Bulletin, 21*, 637–654.

Schumann, D. W., Petty, R. E., & Clemons, D. S. (1990). Predicting the effectiveness of different strategies of advertising variation: A test of the repetition-variation hypotheses. *Journal of Consumer Research, 17*, 192–202.

Sivacek, J., & Crano, W. D. (1982). Vested interest as a moderator of attitude-behavior consistency. *Journal of Personality and Social Psychology, 43*(2), 210–221.

Sternthal, B., Phillips, L. W., & Dholakia, R. (1978). The persuasive effect of source credibility: A situational analysis. *Public Opinion Quarterly, 42*(3), 285–314.

Stewart, D. W., Pechmann, C., Ratneshwar, S., Stroud, J., & Bryant, B. (1984). Methodological and theoretical foundations of advertising copy testing: A review. *Current Issues and Research in Advertising, 2*, 1–74.

Wright, P. L. (1973). The cognitive processes mediating acceptance of advertising. *Journal of Marketing Research, 4*, 53–62.

7

Inference and Impact

James C. Crimmins
DDB Needham Chicago

Inference is audience participation. In inference the audience members go beyond the message presented in advertising and draws their own conclusions about the brand.

Although inference is critical to persuasion, inference is the one step in the communication process that has received the least attention in commercial analyses of advertising effectiveness. The Advertising Research Foundation (ARF) copy research validity project investigated 36 measures commonly used to evaluate advertising in commercial copy testing systems (Haley, 1990). None were measures of inference. None were measures of the conclusions the audience drew about the brand as a result of being exposed to the advertising.

Inference has received more attention in academic research. The cognitive processing school of advertising research specifically explores the thoughts simulated by an advertisement.

The most common way of collecting cognitive processing data is by thought-listing techniques. In thought listing, respondents are asked a series of open-ended questions such as: "As you were looking at the commercial, what thoughts or ideas went through your mind and what feelings did you have?" and "Besides trying to sell the product, what was the main idea?"

Thought listing captures those inferences arrived at through deliberate, explicit, and self-conscious processing; but it misses those inferences that are arrived at through implicit, nondeliberate, and subconscious processing.

To illustrate inferences captured and inferences missed in thought listing, let us look at the reactions of beer drinkers to a Coors Light television commercial. The commercial featured young adults enjoying various ski resort activities and drinking Coors Light, as well as a voice-over that tells us "you know looking good isn't just for summer," Coors Light "won't slow you down," and Coors Light is "the right beer now."

Two hundred respondents were recruited. All were drinkers of light beer. Half the respondents were assigned to the control group and half were assigned to the test group. The number of Coors Light drinkers was balanced between groups.

The test group was shown the Coors Light commercial. After seeing the commercial they were asked the following questions:

- As you were looking at the commercial, what thoughts or ideas went through your mind and what feelings did you have?
- Did anything else come to your mind while looking at the commercial that you would like to mention?
- Besides trying to sell the product, what was the main point of the commercial?

Their open-ended responses were coded and the most common responses are listed in Table 7.1. The explicit, self-conscious messages people played back were about qualities of the beer and occasions for drinking it. After a few more open-ended questions, the test group was asked how well each of a set of individual adjectives describe Coors Light beer and, lastly, how well each of a set of individual adjectives describe the Coors Light beer drinker.

The control group, recruited in exactly the same fashion, was not shown the commercial nor asked the open-ended question, but just asked how well the individual adjectives describe Coors Light beer and the Coors Light drinker. To understand the inferences that people drew from the advertising, we compared the descriptions of Coors Light and Coors Light drinkers from those who had just seen the ad (the test group) and those who had not (the control group).

Table 7.2 lists the percentage point differences in responses from the test group and the control group. The inferences people drew about the Coors Light product from the advertising are similar to the explicit playback uncovered in the thought-listing technique. However, the inferences drawn about the Coors Light *drinker* never showed up in the thought-listing technique. Those inferences were implicit, nondeliberate, and subconscious.

Thought-listing techniques and cognitive processing research in general underestimate the actual mental processing that occurs. They capture self-conscious, deliberate inferences but miss subconscious, nondeliberate inferences.

A major evolutionary step occurred in the school of cognitive processing with Petty and Cacioppo's Elaboration Likelihood Model (ELM; 1986). The

TABLE 7.1
Most Common Thought Listing Responses to Coors Light Advertisement

Response	Percentage
A beer for good times	28%
Stay slim, low cal	24%
Good tasting	22%
The right beer now	20%
It is light	19%
Less filling	18%
Won't slow you down	18%
A beer for anytime	18%

TABLE 7.2
Brand Rating Differences Between Test and Control Groups

Change in Product Description (Test-Control)		Change in User Description (Test-Control)	
Less filling	+18%	Up-to-date	+19%
Clean tasting	+14	Adventurous	+17
Pleasant	+13	Fun loving	+14
Refreshing	+9	Self-assured	+13
Mellow	+1	Sophisticated	+10
Full-bodied	0	A serious beer drinker	+1
		Hard working	0
		Dependable	−1

ELM acknowledges that inference can occur in both self-conscious, central processing and also in subconscious, peripheral processing. In central processing, the receiver actively and consciously considers the merits of the central arguments of the persuasive message. In peripheral processing, the receiver is either unmotivated or unable to engage in deliberate analysis of the central arguments and instead reacts to peripheral cues with simple affect or simple inference. According to the model, if the receiver is able to process the message actively, the receiver's involvement is the principal determinant of which form of processing takes place. The more involved the receiver, the more likely that the processing focuses on the merits of the central arguments. The more uninvolved the receiver, the more likely processing focuses on peripheral cues.

The ELM is of interest to advertising practitioners because it deals with both self-conscious and subconscious inference. However, the ELM has proven difficult to apply to advertising in practice. What follows are a practitioner's problems in applying the ELM and some suggestions for making the ELM more useful in the day-to-day practice of advertising.

Confusion Between Central Arguments and Peripheral Cues

The ELM makes a fundamental distinction between central arguments and peripheral cues, but distinguishing one from the other in practice is difficult. The concepts of central argument and peripheral cue lack workable definition.

Petty and Cacioppo (1983) distinguished central arguments from peripheral cues in a somewhat circular fashion. If an element has an effect on attitude change that they expect a central argument to have, then it is a central argument. For example, they expected that a picture of an attractive model would serve as a peripheral cue in a shampoo ad. According to the ELM, involved viewers should pay attention only to the central arguments and not be influenced by peripheral cues. Their experiment, however, showed that the picture had a positive influence on the attitudes of involved viewers. Because the picture of the attractive model acted like a central argument, Petty and Cacioppo concluded that the picture must be a central argument.

In another paper, Cacioppo and Petty (1989) said a central argument is whatever the audience member believes is a central argument. Unfortunately, consumers usually are not explicitly aware of how they make decisions. Marketers have long known that the consumer's own importance rating is among the least valid measures of an attribute's true importance in making brand choices. When consumers are mistaken about the real perceptual basis of their choice, what might appear to be central processing may in fact just be rumination about product qualities that will have little real impact on brand choice. If by central argument, we mean an element of an ad that is central to persuasion, the consumer is a poor judge of what does and does not qualify.

What is central and what is peripheral seems largely a matter of perspective. What the audience believes is central will be different from what is in fact central to their choice. Both will be different from what is objectively central to brand performance. All three may be different from what the advertiser believes is central to the sale.

The concepts of central argument and peripheral cue are difficult to work with in practice not only because of their definitions, but also because of their connotations. Argument suggests a rational, logical proposition but advertising often has no more to do with rational logic than does friendship or romance. Peripheral suggests unimportant or unintended. However, for the practitioner, a well-crafted ad should have no unimportant or unintended elements. In a well-crafted ad, every element should contribute to the desired inference.

Here is how Jack Mariucci (1992), a well-known and gifted art director, talked about the details in an ad:

> From the birth of an idea until its final execution there can be hundreds of details that can mean the difference between success and failure. While great art directors may differ in their approach to details, they all agree on one thing—there is one detail that every other detail must bow down before and that is the idea, the concept. If each and every one of your details don't support the idea, they are bogus, bankrupt and fraudulent.

For Mariucci, there are no peripheral elements, at least not by design. Every detail, no matter how small, must serve the central advertising idea. Whether the ad is for an expensive, luxury, image product or a mundane, household, nonimage product, the principle is the same.

What could be more nonimage than drain openers? In the early 1980s, Liquid Drano held the lion's share of the market (well above a 50% share of market) and was unassailable. As long as the consumer's decision frame was a choice among drain openers, Liquid Drano had the advantage because their name defined the category. Liquid Plum'r was a distant number two brand.

During the mid and late 1980s, Liquid Plum'r ran a new campaign. In the typical commercial of this new campaign, silly cartoonlike plumbers are frustrated by phone calls that they hoped would be for them but were instead for Liquid Plum'r. The idea and the line was "Liquid Plum'r is the plumber to call first."

That campaign turned the drain opener category on its head. After 5 years, market shares were reversed with Liquid Plum'r holding over half the market and Drano a distant second. During this period the prices of the brands were comparable and there was little or no real difference in the products. By changing the consumer's decision frame from a choice among drain openers to a choice among plumbing alternatives, these ads took the advantage away from Drano and gave it to Liquid Plum'r.

What was central and what was peripheral in those ads? The ads did not put forth a new logical, factual argument for the superiority of Liquid Plum'r; such an argument could not have been made. The ads did successfully lead people to adopt a new decision frame for brand choice. The creators of those ads would maintain that there were no peripheral elements. Every element contributed to the central idea that "Liquid Plum'r is the plumber to call first." Judging from the results in the marketplace they are probably right.

From a practitioner's point of view, rather than classifying elements of an ad into central arguments and peripheral cues, we would classify elements into those that lead to the desired inference and those that do not, and we would do our best to eliminate the latter.

Central and Peripheral Processing Versus Self-Conscious and Subconscious Processing

Although the difference between central arguments and peripheral cues seems arbitrary and largely a matter of perspective, the difference between central processing and peripheral processing is critical. Central processing is self-conscious, deliberate, and explicit, whereas peripheral processing is subconscious, intuitive, and implicit.

I recommend relabeling central processing as self-conscious processing and peripheral processing as subconscious processing. Self-conscious and subconscious are far more descriptive of the activities they reference and less value laden than central and peripheral.

Little Attention Paid to Subconscious Processing

Petty and Cacioppo postulated that attitude change that results from self-conscious (central) processing is far more enduring than attitude change that results from subconscious (peripheral) processing. As a result, the main emphasis in ELM research has been on self-conscious processing. Subconscious processing has gotten little attention and has been simply relegated to the unimportant "peripheral" category.

In reality, self-conscious, deliberate, explicit processing may apply to only a small portion of the attitudes we form and the decisions we make. How many of us, for example, have sat back and explicitly considered the pros and cons of spending time with all the people we know to arrive at a decision on who we would make our friends or even our spouse. What decisions could be more important? Yet our mental processing in selecting people to spend time with is quite informal and spontaneous. We develop expectations of what it would be like to share their company without explicit, deliberate, self-conscious processing.

The friendships we make with brands are made in much the same way; not through explicit, self-conscious, rational evaluation of the benefits of a brand but by gradually forming an expectation of what using a brand would be like. In many categories, factual differences between brands are so minimal that there is little to weigh in a deliberate and self-conscious manner. However, the emotional associations that surround the brands and the decision frames that brands call to mind can be quite different.

The Liquid Plum'r ad was wonderfully effective not by stimulating explicit consideration of the pros and cons of the product, but by simply encouraging people through subconscious, implicit, nondeliberate processing to think of Liquid Plum'r as an alternative to a plumber rather than as an alternative to other drain openers.

The body of work surrounding the ELM would be more useful to practitioners if more emphasis was placed on the way in which inferences are drawn from subconscious processing. Most processing of advertising massages is subconscious, implicit, and intuitive.

Beyond Laboratory Involvement

The ELM has justly highlighted the impact of involvement on the way a message will be processed. According to the ELM, high involvement will lead to self-conscious, deliberate processing. Low involvement will lead to nondeliberate, subconscious processing. Advertising practitioners would agree that involvement determines the extent of mental processing that will occur. However, practitioners would maintain that high involvement leads to both more self-conscious processing and more subconscious processing.

In ELM experiments, subjects are generally divided into a high-involvement group and a low-involvement group. High involvement is typically generated by leading that group to believe that the ad is immediately relevant (e.g., they will very shortly have to make a decision about the product advertised). Low involvement is generated by leading the other group to believe that the ad is irrelevant to them (e.g., the ad is for a product that they cannot and will not ever be able to purchase).

Advertisers do not have the ability to manipulate the relevance of the choice as typically occurs in ELM experiments. However, advertisers do use three other approaches to make sure they are speaking to an involved audience.

- First, advertisers select to speak with only those who would logically be interested or historically have shown interest in products of the type being sold (e.g., sending a foot remedy message to people with foot problems).
- Second, advertisers seek to reach their target at a time or place in which they will be open to suggestion. For example, the time to sell products for the relief of foot problems is when the audience's feet hurt, such as on their way home from work in the evening.
- Third, advertisers use the message itself to involve the audience. They design the message to arrest the attention of the distracted and get a reaction.

This last point is little understood but basic to the practice of advertising. It deserves repeating. Advertisers use the message itself to involve the audience. They design the message to arrest the attention of the distracted and get a reaction. The typical consumer is exposed to over 700 commercial messages in the course of a normal day. The messages come from television, radio, outdoor ads, magazines, newspapers, direct mail, telephone, and other sources. The consumer obviously cannot take the time and effort for extensive mental processing of each message. They pick and choose those they will pay attention to. The message itself must capture their attention. The message itself must involve the audience if it is to be noticed and effective. Therefore, to speak to an involved audience, the practitioner attempts to direct the message to those who will find it relevant when they will find it relevant, and attempts to use the message itself to engage their interest. The practitioner will find it much easier to apply the learning from academic experiments that generate involvement with tools the practitioner can use.

SUMMARY

In inference, audience members go beyond the message and draw their own conclusions about the brand. In our experience, understanding the inferences the audience draws from the advertising is the best way to learn why an ad is working or not working.

Although inference is a critical step in the process of persuasion, it is largely neglected by commercial copy testing systems. Academic research has more actively investigated inference. The cognitive processing approach has focused on inferences drawn in self-conscious, explicit, deliberative mental processing but misses inferences drawn in subconscious, less deliberative processing.

The ELM was a significant evolution of the cognitive processing approach. It considers inferences drawn from deliberate or central processing and also inferences drawn from nondeliberate or peripheral processing.

The ELM has proven useful in guiding academic experimentation; however, the ELM has been less useful in the practice of advertising. I offer here a practitioner's perspective on four aspects of the ELM that limit its usefulness.

1. The distinction between central arguments and peripheral cues is arbitrary. What is central and what is peripheral changes depending on one's perspective. What is central to brand performance in some objective sense is different from what the audience believes is central, and both will be different from what advertising practitioners believe is central to their case. From the practitioner's point of view, a more useful distinction is between elements that lead to the desired inference and elements that do not. In good advertising there are no peripheral elements. Every element in the ad should contribute to the desired inference. Elements that do not lead to the desired inference should be eliminated.

2. Having dropped the arbitrary distinction between central arguments and peripheral cues, it is helpful to relabel the routes to persuasion from central and peripheral routes as self-conscious and subconscious routes. Self-conscious processing is deliberate and explicit. Subconscious processing is implicit and intuitive. Both lead to inference. Both lead to changed expectations for the brand. Both lead ultimately to changed behavior.

3. Most decisions we make about brands—in fact, most decisions we make in our lives—are made on the basis of inferences drawn from subconscious processing. Yet most of the attention in research using the ELM has focused on self-conscious processing. Subconscious processing seems dismissed as merely peripheral. The study of how inferences are drawn from subconscious processing of advertising messages is a wide open and exciting area for future research.

4. The ELM has rightly highlighted the role of involvement in determining the level of processing that a message receives. However, the manipulation of involvement in academic experiments is unlike situations practitioners normally confront. Practitioners can increase involvement by:

- Aiming at an audience for whom the message is relevant.
- Attempting to reach that audience when they are open to our suggestion.
- Crafting the message to arrest the attention of the distracted. In the competition for the attention of our audience, a message that is not involving will be ignored.

Experiments that work with the tools the practitioner can use to generate involvement will lead much more directly to application of the results in the practice of advertising.

I predict that when involvement is generated using tools available to the advertiser (targeting, timing, and arresting attention), involvement will lead to both more self-conscious and subconscious inferences.

REFERENCES

Cacioppo, J. T., & Petty, R. E. (1989). The elaboration likelihood model: The role of affect and affect-laden information processing in persuasion. In P. Cafferata & A. Tybout (Eds.), *Cognitive and affective responses to advertising* (Vol. 5, pp. 69–88). Lexington, MA: Lexington Books.

Haley, R. I. (1990). *The ARF copy research validity project, final report*. New York: The Advertising Research Foundation.

Mariucci, J. (1992). *God is in the details*. Presentation to DDB Needham Creative Directors Conference.

Petty, R. E., & Cacioppo, J. T. (1983). Central and peripheral routes to persuasion: Application to advertising. In L. Percy & A. Woodside (Eds.), *Advertising and consumer psychology* (pp. 3–23). Lexington, MA: Lexington Books.

Petty, R. E., & Cacioppo, J. T. (1986). The elaboration likelihood model of persuasion. In L. Berkowitz (Ed.), *Advances in experimental social psychology* (Vol. 19, pp. 123–205). New York: Academic Press.

Comments on Chapters 6 and 7

William D. Wells
University of Minnesota

Whereas chapters 1 and 2 of this volume advocated increased contact between academic and applied researchers, and chapters 3, 4, and 5 highlighted potential academic contributions to that partnership, chapters 6 and 7 show that academic and applied researchers become more sophisticated when they interact.

Chapter 6 shows that the ELM model—and in particular the ELM model's core distinction between central and peripheral processing—disentangles logical, rational, obvious influences from less logical, less rational, and less obvious influences. Even more tellingly, it shows how to elicit what practitioners want most—positive responses that influence behavior and resist attack.

Chapter 7 applies some of the constructs reviewed in chapter 6 to real-world advertising problems. In the course of that application, it reveals some critical ambiguities in the original formulations. In attempting to resolve those ambiguities, it proposes a shift from central versus peripheral processing to self-conscious versus unself-conscious processing.

Chapter 7 offers two concrete examples of the benefits of academician–practitioner interaction. It shows how academic constructs and academic methods provided core ideas that influenced the way practitioners went about their work. It also shows how confrontation between laboratory-based theories and real-world outcomes generate potentially important feedback. If academic researchers take this feedback seriously, new theory-building insights are likely to result.

IV

Cognitive Elaboration

The research reviewed by Haugtvedt and Priester in chapter 6 and the applications described by Crimmins in chapter 7 converge on the proposition that inferences produced by self-relevant elaboration influence the strength and durability of the effects of persuasive messages. One way to examine those inferences is to ask respondents to list their thoughts during or after exposure to an ad. Chapters 8, 9, and 10 focus on findings from, and refinements of, the thought-listing technique.

Chapter 8, by Peggy Lebenson and Max Blackston of Research International, reviews a large and diverse collection of copy tests in which real-world consumers verbalized their cognitive and emotional responses to a wide range of ads. It demonstrates that responses to advertisements for frequently purchased grocery and drug store items are likely to differ from responses to advertisements for less frequently purchased durable goods and services in essential ways. It also demonstrates that advertisements for different kinds of products, employed for different purposes under different circumstances, have three very different kinds of effects.

Sharon Shavitt and Michelle Nelson's comments on chapter 8 provide more evidence of the value of real-world–academic interaction. Shavitt and Nelson discuss the impact of Lebenson and Blackston's chapter on their thinking, and go on to offer useful new ideas of their own.

Chapter 9—by Michelle Nelson, Sharon Shavitt, Angela Schennum and Jacqueline Barkmeier, all of the University of Illinois, Urbana–Champaign—documents another major difference among products. It demonstrates that cognitive and emotional responses to advertisements for "instrumental" products are likely to be quite different from cognitive and emotional responses to "social identity" products. It also shows that these differences are likely to interact with differences in proclivity to monitor the self. Like the differences documented by Lebenson and Blackston, these differences can change outcomes of all thought-listing research.

Chapter 10, by Debra J. Stephens and J. Edward Russo, is useful methodological shop talk. It shows that thought-list investigations become more sensitive and more reliable when investigators replay stimuli before respondents report their reactions, when respondents self-code valences, and when valence ratings include intensity. These procedures improve the sensitivity (and thereby the usefulness) of both academic and applied thought-list research. Stephens and Russo are university-based researchers, the former at Villanova, the latter at Cornell.

8

Pretesting Advertising Using Cognitive Response Analysis: Some Conclusions and Hypotheses Based on Practical Experience

Peggy Lebenson
Max Blackston
Research International, USA

Research International (RI) is a very large custom research firm with offices in 44 countries. RI has extensive copy testing involvement, and over the years has evolved an approach to methodology based on "best current practice." In practical terms, that means using custom samples with forced exposure of the advertising, and asking a series of evaluative and diagnostic questions. Although action standards are sometimes set using a comparison to an unexposed control sample, for the most part we use our database of test results as a normative guide. In the early 1990s, RI incorporated cognitive response measures into our standard copy testing method-ology. Since then, we have conducted over 200 copy tests in the United States, Europe, and the Pacific Rim using Cognitive Response Analysis[SM], and have accumulated a database of test results that is now sufficiently broad for analysis.

The subject of this chapter is the analysis of this database. We have looked at the relationships between the different measures commonly used as criteria of advertising effectiveness as well as measures based on Cognitive Response Analysis[SM]. This analysis has led us to hypothesize a four-way classification system for evaluating and predicting advertising effects.

THE ORIGINS OF COGNITIVE RESPONSE ANALYSIS (CRA[SM])

Cognitive Response Analysis[SM] is based on the theory of cognitive processing. Although this theory is by no means new, its application to the evaluation of advertising most certainly is. It was first proposed and experimented with by Shavitt and Brock (1985).

The Importance of Self in Advertising

Brock and Shavitt's basic premise was that consumers are not passive, objective receivers of advertising messages. Rather, they interact with the message: They interpret it for themselves, they associate it with other information, they compare it to their own experience, and they argue with it. Thus, the greater the degree of cognitive processing of an advertising message, the more likely that message is to change attitudes.

Shavitt and Brock's original hierarchy for the analysis of CRA[SM] responses classified thoughts, ideas, and reactions into three primary types:

- Self-relevant thoughts—thoughts indicating a high degree of cognitive processing (whether positive or negative).
- Product-related thoughts—thoughts that simply and unambiguously relate to the product, brand, or service being advertised.
- Execution thoughts—thoughts that relate directly to executional elements or aspects of production.

Research International

In 1987, Brock and Shavitt's work was taken up by the Ogilvy Center for Research and Development under its then director, Alexander Biel. Together, this team brought Cognitive Response Analysis[SM] to the point where it was an applicable research technique. In 1989, RI realized the potential of the technique as a means of advertising pretesting and incorporated CRA[SM] measures into our standard methodology.

CRA[SM] is therefore the application of the cognitive processing model to the evaluation of advertising effectiveness. It is a method for systematically exploring consumers' "inner dialogue" with advertising and, through that, predicting the likely effectiveness of that advertising in changing attitudes and behavior.

THE CRA[SM] METHODOLOGY

The way in which CRA[SM] is administered and applied by RI is simple and direct. After viewing the advertising, respondents are asked to write down all the thoughts, reactions, and ideas that went through their minds as they were seeing the advertising for the first time. Respondents are then asked to classify each thought as positive, negative, or neutral.

Responses are coded using a hierarchical structure designed to identify "personal reaction" to the advertising. The respondent's own response valence (positive or negative) is incorporated into this structure.

Early experience using the Brock–Shavitt hierarchy in pretesting led us to discover that self-relevance actually operates at different levels and could equally well apply to the product or the execution. In addition, we added a third content category we called *communicator*, which includes comments that link product and execution. This resulted in a modification of the hierarchy, which allowed self-relevance (or its absence) to permeate across all content categories.

By incorporating the valence assigned by respondents to their responses (positive or negative) we come to a set of 12 possible response categories (Fig. 8.1).

International Data Bank

The international data bank records—by test—all of these 12 categories of CRA[SM] response, together with means and distributions of responses to other more conventional measures, such as likability, overall opinion of the brand, purchase intent, and many diagnostic measures (Fig. 8.2).

POSITIVE RESPONSES	NEGATIVE RESPONSES

◆ SELF-RELEVANT
  ► PRODUCT
  ► COMMUNICATOR
  ► EXECUTION
 	
◆ NON SELF-RELEVANT
  ► PRODUCT
  ► COMMUNICATOR
  ► EXECUTION
	◆ SELF-RELEVANT
	  ► PRODUCT
	  ► COMMUNICATOR
	  ► EXECUTION
	
	◆ NON SELF-RELEVANT
	  ► PRODUCT
	  ► COMMUNICATOR
	  ► EXECUTION

FIG. 8.1 CRA response categories.

CRA[SM] RESPONSE CATEGORIES	COPY TESTING MEASURES
AVERAGE NUMBER OF RESPONSES (THOUGHTS/IDEAS) PER RESPONDENT	OVERALL OPINION
	PURCHASE INTEREST
PERCENTAGE OF SELF-RELEVANT RESPONSES	LIKABILITY
	BELIEVABILITY
PERCENTAGE OF POSITIVE RESPONSES	DIAGNOSTICS
PERCENTAGE OF PRODUCT VS. EXECUTIONAL RESPONSES	

FIG. 8.2 International data bank.

Analysis of the Database

Our analysis is based on two groups of advertising tests:

- A database of tests on packaged goods brands. This is the larger database consisting of some 139 tests conducted over the last 5 years.
- A database consisting of about 30 tests on durable goods and service brands.

All of the tests followed a similar format:

- Exposure of the test advertisement twice—first in a clutter reel of eight ads, and subsequently by itself.
- Following the second exposure, the CRA^{SM} thought and idea listing is administered, followed by open-ended message comprehension and a series of evaluative scales.
- The evaluative scales consist of likability of the advertising, overall opinion of the brand advertised, and a purchase intent question. These latter two scales vary in format and wording between the two databases, reflecting the different nature of packaged goods and nonpackaged goods purchasing.

Our analysis consists of a comparison of pairs of variables on each of the two databases. First of all, we compare three conventional "persuasion" measures—likability, overall opinion, and purchase intent. Then we compare each of these to two measures derived from the CRA^{SM}—the valence of respondents' thoughts (the percentage of thoughts rated as positive by respondents), and the percentage of thoughts classified as self-relevant and having a positive valence.

ANALYSIS OF PACKAGED GOODS ADVERTISING TESTS—"PERSUASION" MEASURES

Liking Versus Overall Opinion

Figure 8.3 shows a scatter plot of the packaged goods tests with likability (% top two box) on the horizontal axis, and overall opinion (% top three boxes of a 7-point scale) on the vertical. This shows a very strong positive relationship between liking the ad and rating the brand highly. The simple correlation between these two variables is 0.74.

Liking Versus Purchase Intent

Liking the advertising also shows a strong relationship with purchase intent. The correlation of 0.63 is only slightly lower than that of liking and overall opinion (Fig. 8.4).

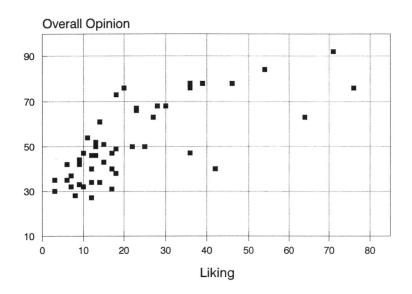

FIG. 8.3 Packaged goods advertising: Correlation between liking and overall opinion.

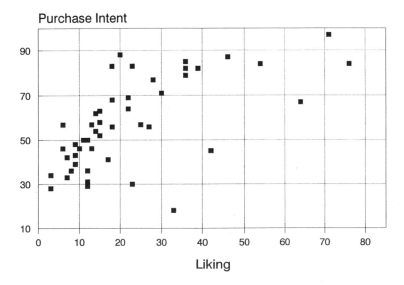

FIG. 8.4 Packaged goods advertising: Correlation between liking and purchase intent.

Overall Opinion Versus Purchase Intent

The relationship between overall opinion and purchase intent is also very consistent, with a correlation of 0.74 (Fig. 8.5).

Summary: Packaged Goods "Persuasion" Measures

Our conclusion is that, for packaged goods, liking the advertising and liking the brand go hand in hand. This confirms the commonsense view that for a frequently purchased (and low ticket) item, the advertising itself is as much a product attribute or consumer benefit as any other.

Furthermore, as both liking the advertising and overall opinion are associated with high purchase intent, any of these three measures may be regarded as a measure of the persuasiveness of the advertising (Fig. 8.6).

ANALYSIS OF NONPACKAGED GOODS ADVERTISING TESTS—"PERSUASION" MEASURES

Liking Versus Overall Opinion

This chart shows the same pair of variables for the nonpackaged goods tests. The data are somewhat equivocal, as it is possible to see a general relationship between the two, but there are clearly a number of exceptions that fall well off

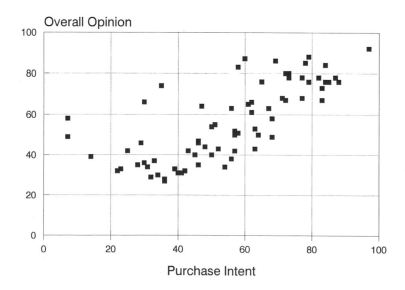

FIG. 8.5 Packaged goods advertising: Correlation between overall opinion and purchase intent.

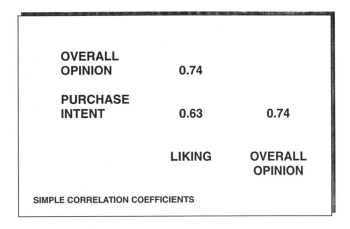

FIG. 8.6 Packaged goods advertising: Correlations between evaluative scales.

the line. The simple correlation between the two variables (0.57) is lower than its equivalent for packaged goods advertising (Fig. 8.7).

Liking Versus Purchase Intent

For nonpackaged goods, there is clearly no consistent relationship between liking the advertising and purchase intent (Fig. 8.8).

Overall Opinion Versus Purchase Intent

For nonpackaged goods, again, there is no one-for-one relationship between product evaluation and purchase intent (Fig. 8.9).

Summary: Nonpackaged Goods "Persuasion" Measures

For less frequently purchased, higher ticket goods it seems that likable advertising and high product approval are not so closely linked as they are for packaged goods. Furthermore, if we believe that purchase intent is our main "bottom line" measure of advertising effectiveness, then both liking the advertising and overall opinion would be very poor indicators of effectiveness (Fig. 8.10).

ANALYSIS OF PACKAGED GOODS ADVERTISING TESTS—COGNITIVE RESPONSES MEASURES

Valence

Before addressing the issue of self-relevance, the degree of cognitive processing of the advertising, we take a look at valence—the self-assessment of each

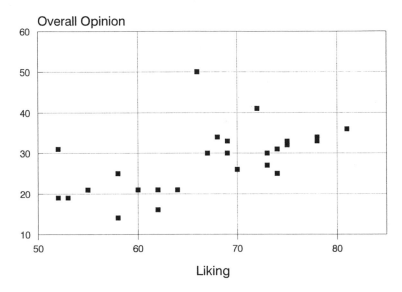

FIG. 8.7 Nonpackaged goods advertising: Correlation between liking and overall opinion.

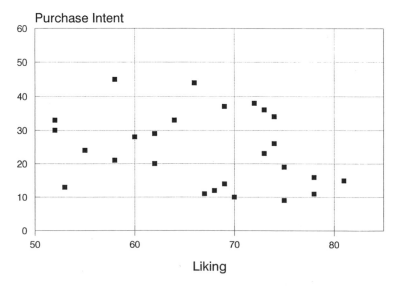

FIG. 8.8 Nonpackaged goods advertising: Correlation between liking and purchase intent.

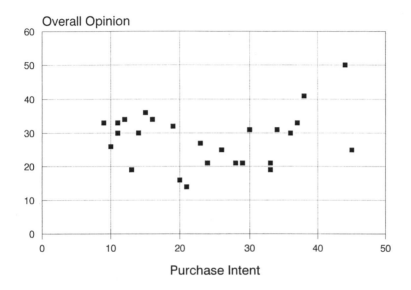

FIG. 8.9 Nonpackaged goods advertising: Correlation between overall opinion and purchase intent.

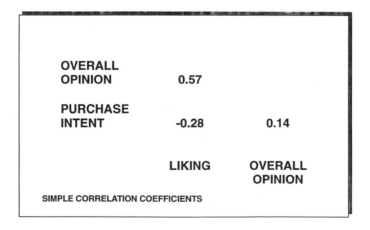

FIG. 8.10 Nonpackaged goods advertising: Correlations between evaluative scales.

thought as positive, negative, or neutral. It is important to note that this an assessment of the thought itself—not whether it resulted in positive or negative feelings about the brand. A number of studies, most recently Stephens and Russo (chap. 10, this volume), suggest that this type of positive valence is a very strong predictor of A_{Brand}.

Positive Valence Versus Liking

The relationship between positive valence and likability is a fairly strong one, although there are a significant number of outliers (Fig. 8.11).

Positive Valence Versus Overall Opinion

The relationship between positive valence and overall product opinion is again generally positive, but with significant deviation (Fig. 8.12).

Positive Valence Versus Purchase Intent

The relationship between positive valence and purchase intent is in fact the strongest of the three. This suggests that—at least for packaged goods—valence is a good predictor of A_{Brand}. Furthermore, from the relative strengths of these relationships, it would appear that the relationship of positive valence to purchase intent is not mediated by either advertising likability or overall product evaluation (Fig. 8.13).

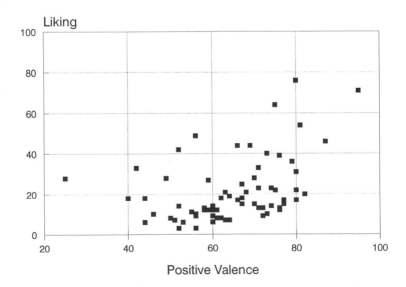

FIG. 8.11 Packaged goods advertising: Correlation between positive valence and liking.

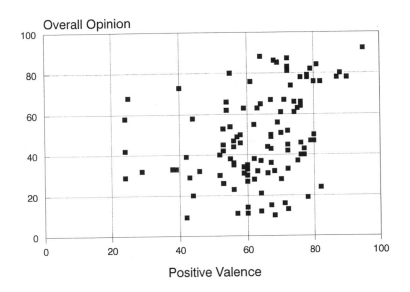

FIG. 8.12 Packaged goods advertising: Correlation between positive valence and overall opinion.

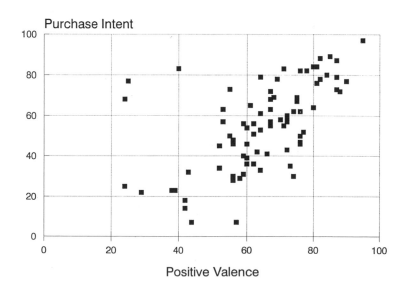

FIG. 8.13 Packaged goods advertising: Correlation between positive valence and purchase intent.

ANALYSIS OF NONPACKAGED GOODS ADVERTISING TESTS—COGNITIVE RESPONSE MEASURES

Positive Valence Versus Liking

For our nonpackaged goods tests, the relationship between positive valence and liking is also a strong one, stronger in fact than its equivalent for packaged goods (Fig. 8.14).

Positive Valence Versus Overall Opinion

The relationship between positive valence and overall opinion is also significant but slightly less strong than with likability (Fig. 8.15).

Positive Valence Versus Purchase Intent

In the case of nonpackaged goods, there is no relationship at all between positive valence and purchase intent (Fig. 8.16).

Our conclusions are that, for packaged goods advertising, positive valence appears to converge with the other measures of advertising effectiveness. For nonpackaged goods, positive valence is most directly related to A_{Ad}, and secondarily to A_{Brand} (Fig. 8.17).

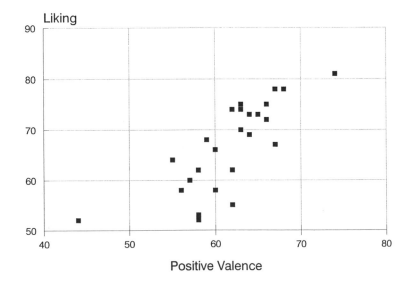

FIG. 8.14 Nonpackaged goods advertising: Correlation between positive valence and liking.

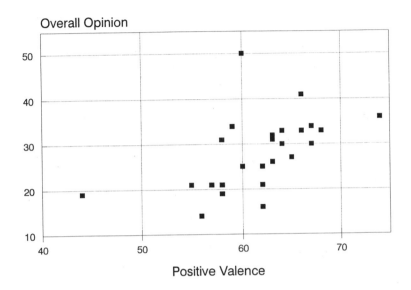

FIG. 8.15 Nonpackaged goods advertising: Correlation between positive valence and overall opinion.

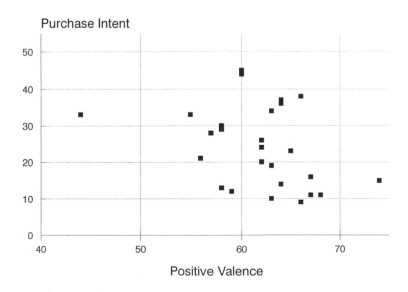

FIG. 8.16 Nonpackaged goods advertising: Correlation between positive valence and purchase intent.

	PACKAGED GOODS	NONPACKAGED GOODS
LIKING	0.40	0.77
OVERALL OPINION	0.47	0.52
PURCHASE INTENT	0.57	-0.36
SIMPLE CORRELATION COEFFICIENTS		

FIG. 8.17 Correlations between evaluative scales and positive valence.

Self-Relevance

Finally, we can see from this summary of correlation coefficients that self-relevance is weakly related to all of the other measures in packaged goods advertising, and not at all for nonpackaged goods tests (Fig. 8.18).

SUMMARY

Our findings can thus be summarized as follows:

- For packaged goods advertising tests, all measures of advertising effectiveness except self-relevance appear to converge strongly.
- For non-packaged goods, only A_{Ad} (liking) and A_{Brand} (overall opinion) have a consistent relationship—but not sufficiently strong for one to be a predictor of the other—and both purchase intent and self-relevance measures are independent.

What do we make of all this? Our ingoing assumption about CRA^{SM} and self-relevance specifically was that it was a "better mousetrap"—a better measure of advertising effectiveness than scale measures—because it did not require an introspective evaluation by the respondents of the effect of the advertising on their own attitudes and likely behavior. We expected to get some convergence between self-relevance and other measures, but not that they would all point in the identical direction under all circumstances. Our objective was that the various measures should each serve as both evaluative and diagnostic criteria for coming to a point of view on an ad.

The fact that in one case—packaged goods—we do get convergence, and in the other we get a great deal of divergence has forced us to make a more explicit set of hypotheses about the different effects we are in fact measuring. We make these hypotheses for the general case, and argue that packaged goods advertising falls within this general structure, but with certain special characteristics that bring about convergence between the different effects.

Effects 1 and 2: Two "Persuasion" Effects

- Effect 1 is what we call the *brand effect*, measured by overall opinion and other such measures that evaluate consumers' feelings about a product or service without reference to purchase consideration.
- Effect 2 is the *call to action effect*, which is measured by purchase interest and other measures that directly address likelihood of purchase, or change in behavior.

These effects are shown in Fig. 8.19. As we have seen, for packaged goods the brand effect is closely associated with purchase intent, and we can use either of these as a measure of the persuasiveness of the advertising. However, for nonpackaged goods, there is virtually no association between these two effects.

The high correlation between the two effects for packaged goods as opposed to the low correlation for nonpackaged goods makes intuitive sense. For

	PACKAGED GOODS	NONPACKAGED GOODS
LIKING	0.54	0.19
OVERALL OPINION	0.52	0.33
PURCHASE INTENT	0.40	-0.03
SIMPLE CORRELATION COEFFICIENTS		

FIG. 8.18 Correlations between evaluative scales and self-relevance.

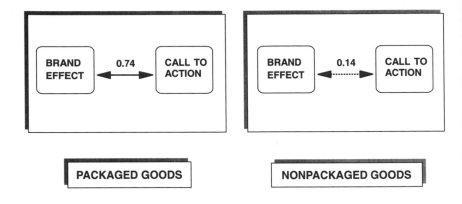

FIG. 8.19 Two persuasion effects.

packaged goods, which are generally frequently purchased low ticket items, a favorable opinion of the product or brand is usually a sufficient reason to buy. For higher risk, higher ticket items such as durables, a favorable opinion of the brand or product may be necessary but not sufficient to close the sale.

In our practical experience with nonpackaged goods clients, it proves quite helpful to separate the different persuasion effects, because the objective of the advertising may include one but not the other. For example, some manufacturers may use advertising to create a favorable opinion and a sales force to close the sale. Or they may use two different types of advertising—for example, in the automobile industry where a main product or brand campaign is used to shape product opinion and dealer advertising is used to provide a call to action.

Effect 3: "Feel Good" Advertising Effect

We have hypothesized a third effect that can operate independently of the two persuasion effects. We call this the *feel good* advertising effect (Fig. 8.20).

For packaged goods, we have seen how the feel good effect and the brand effect go hand in hand. Furthermore, because the feel good effect and the brand effect are both associated with call to action, any of these three effects may be regarded as a good predictor of the bottom-line effectiveness of the advertising.

For nonpackaged goods, the picture is very different. We have seen that the association of the feel good effect and the brand effect is weak and there is virtually no association with call to action. We would hypothesize that the feel good effect is not a good predictor of A_{Brand} outside of the realm of packaged goods advertising. This has important practical implications for advertisers in their evaluation of prospective ads. Although it may be helpful for a nonpackaged goods advertisement to be likable, advertising that simply makes consumers feel good may not be very effective. Similarly, we can all think of examples of negative advertising that have effectively sold the product.

This finding is consistent with other considerations from outside of the data itself. Whereas we can hypothesize that much advertising for packaged goods serves the purpose of reinforcing existing users and encouraging brand loyalty, for larger ticket items, advertising plays a different role in the purchase process; it is more likely to be used by nonusers of the product as a source of information, rather than confirmation. The evaluation of product information gleaned from the advertising is therefore likely to be more independent of the evaluation of the advertising itself.

Effect 4: Self-Relevance Effect

For packaged goods, we have seen that the overall level of positive self-relevance has a relatively weak relationship with the other evaluative measures we have looked at, and for nonpackaged goods there is virtually no relationship at all. Thus we have postulated a fourth effect that we call *self-relevance* (Fig. 8.21).

We have formulated a hypothesis about the meaning of self-relevance based on the theory of cognitive processing. We believe that self-relevance is a measure of the viewer's active involvement with the advertising. Self-relevant advertising is more likely to produce durable changes in attitudes. Furthermore, self-relevant advertising is more likely to engage the viewer at a second and subsequent exposure, and so take longer to wear out.

Testing the Hypothesis

Simply stated, our hypothesis is that attitude changes induced by exposure to self-relevant (i.e., cognitively processed) advertising will decay more slowly over

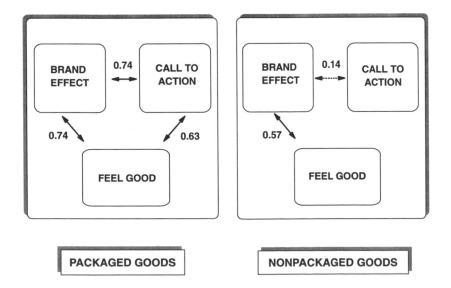

FIG. 8.20 "Feel good" advertising effect.

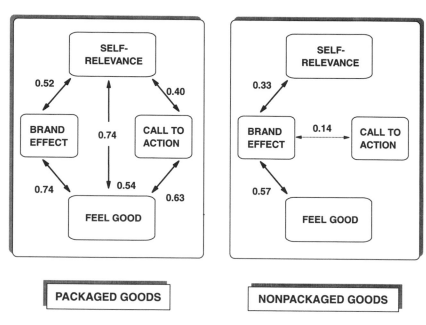

FIG. 8.21 Self-relevance effect.

time. In this sense, self-relevance—combined with other desirable attitude changes—becomes the key criterion for judging how effectively an ad will meet its objectives in the market.

Aside from the academic work and various bits of anecdotal evidence, there is a piece of experimental work on advertising that supports this hypothesis. This was carried out by Brock and sponsored by the Ogilvy Center for Research & Development. In this experiment, heightened processing of a piece of advertising (for a Canadian brand of margarine) was artificially created for one sample of consumers by a procedure known as *buttressing*—essentially telling them that, after seeing the ad, they would be asked to pass on the information about the product to someone else. A second sample saw the same advertising without any buttressing. Both samples rated the advertising and the product.

Eight weeks later these two samples were recontacted by telephone under the auspices of a quite separate and unconnected survey. Buried among the questions were the same scales they had been administered right after exposure to the advertising. At this point in time, the scores from the unbuttressed sample had declined virtually to the level of the unexposed control sample's. In contrast, those consumers who had had the boosted processing still rated the product significantly higher than the control sample (Fig. 8.22).

This study was carried out among real consumers and used real advertisements as stimuli. However, it used buttressing as a way of artificially stimulating processing, rather than measuring the "natural" processing that takes place when people are exposed to advertising. At RI, we decided to take it one step further into the "real" world by repeating this type of experimental study on a much broader scale. We conducted a study in the United States and two European countries to test our hypothesis that self-relevance in advertising makes other changes produced by the advertising more long-lived.

The design for this experiment was very straightforward:

- Eighteen standardized copy tests of television ads were conducted, six each in the United States, the United Kingdom, and Germany. The ads were a mix of packaged and nonpackaged goods, including durables (autos, computers) and services (insurance, telecom).
- In each test, measures included standard likability rating, overall opinion plus a number of specific attributes, and a purchase intent question. In addition, CRA[SM] was administered in the standard format.
- Three weeks later, follow-up telephone interviews were conducted with the same respondents. In these interviews, detailed recall of the ads seen in the prior copy test was elicited, and the brand rating scales were repeated.

This research design has allowed us to test our hypothesis about self-relevance in a variety of ways, involving analyses both at the aggregate sample level as well as analyses of shifts. For the present purpose, we stick to the aggregate sample analyses.

A very straightforward measure of the longevity of advertising effects on the brand is the difference in overall brand ratings between the copy test and the follow-up interview. We have calculated an index of "longevity" for each ad as the ratio of the top three box percentages (on a 7-point scale). In each case the copy test score is the denominator. The scatter plot shows the longevity index plotted against the level of positive self-relevance (Fig. 8.23).

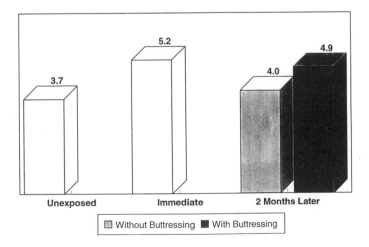

FIG. 8.22 Attitude change over time: Product advertisement.

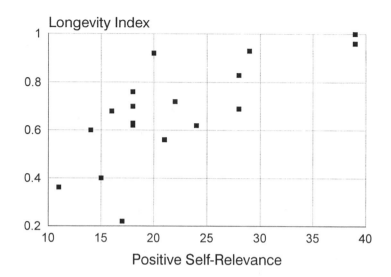

FIG. 8.23 Longevity of brand effect: Correlation between longevity index and positive self-relevance.

The scatter plot shows a very clear pattern of increased longevity with higher levels of positive self-relevance. It seems likely that the longevity of advertising effects is a complex phenomenon, and is not just the result of a single variable. For example, there is a negative relationship between longevity and negative self-relevance (Fig. 8.24).

A multiple regression using both positive and negative self-relevance as independent variables gives a very good fit (adjusted R^2 of 0.62) with significant coefficients for both variables. The coefficient measuring the influence of positive self-relevance on the longevity of brand effects is roughly twice the magnitude of the coefficient for negative self-relevance.

CONCLUSIONS

In conclusion, this preliminary analysis of our database has caused us to question some of our ingoing assumptions about applying CRA[SM] to the practical task of copy testing. We originally thought that CRA[SM] would be a better measure of ad effectiveness than more conventional measures and add some diagnostic insight to our pretesting methodology. However, we have found that cognitive processing, as measured by CRA[SM], seems to work quite independently of other advertising effects that are measured by more conventional copy testing techniques.

We have hypothesized that cognitive processing, rather than being a predictor of persuasiveness or likability, serves to imprint these effects, as well as other

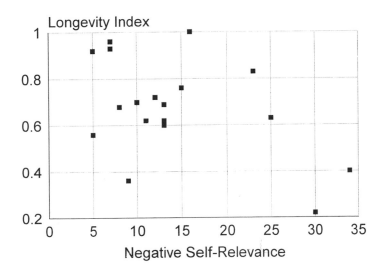

FIG. 8.24 Longevity of brand effect: Correlation between longevity index and negative self-relevance.

attitudinal changes, more firmly in the minds of consumers. If this hypothesis is proven true, then cognitive processing takes on a more important role than a diagnostic one. It becomes a key criterion for evaluating how effectively an ad will meet its objectives in the market.

We hypothesize that cognitive processing is necessary but not sufficient in and of itself, to produce effective advertising. Self-relevance in advertising must be combined with other elements that produce the two desired persuasion effects (brand effect and call to action) and feel good effect. We would suggest that an effective ad should have a balance of these four effects. Depending on the objectives of the advertising, some ads may be stronger on one of the effects than the others, but each of the four effects should be achieved at least at a minimum level.

The four effects we have postulated have proved to be quite helpful, thus far, as a practical tool for interpreting the results of individual copy tests. With further testing and analysis, we hope that this schema will provide even deeper insight into how advertising works and help our clients to create more effective advertising.

REFERENCES

Shavitt, S., & Brock, T. (1985). Improving cognitive response prediction of persuasion: Towards a semantic hierarchy. In D. Stewart (Ed.), Proceedings of the Division of Consumer Psychology (pp. 13–14). San Antonio, TX: American Psychological Association.
The Ogilvy Center For Research and Development. (1989). Attitude change: Making it stick.

Comments on Chapter 8

Sharon Shavitt
Michelle R. Nelson
University of Illinois at Urbana–Champaign

The studies conducted by Research International and reported here by Lebenson and Blackston are an excellent example of the interrelationship between academic and industrial research efforts. The initial work on the types of cognitive response measures described in chapter 8 was conducted by Shavitt and Brock (1986; see also Shavitt & Brock, 1985) at Ohio State University. Research International (RI) modified and successfully applied these measures to large-scale industrial testing needs. Lebenson and Blackston's chapter reports the results of their extensive and intriguing studies. We are delighted to offer comments on this work from an academic perspective.

First, it must be said that any academician would covet the sort of database described by Lebenson and Blackston. The painstaking coding of the thoughts (into 12 theory-relevant categories), the large sample sizes, the different product types represented, the variety of criterion measures collected (including purchase intention ratings), and the breadth of countries represented make these data ideal for testing a vast array of hypotheses about cognitive processing and ad effectiveness. With access to such a database, an academic researcher could happily retire from data collection altogether!

Data generated in the laboratory are, unfortunately, impoverished by comparison. Small and homogeneous samples responding to limited sets of stimuli in often artificial circumstances constrain the generalizability of our findings. Moreover, these limitations can also constrain the breadth of our theories to the extent that our studies cannot encompass enough of the key variables that face advertising decision makers.

Thus, it is gratifying when the concepts and methods developed in our laboratories can find a useful purpose in the real world of advertising. The knowledge gained in the course of applying that work can feed back into the refinement of laboratory-based concepts and methods. The result is a better theoretical understanding of advertising effects.

SELF-RELEVANT COGNITIVE RESPONSES

One of the notable aspects of the RI database described by Lebenson and Blackston is the detailed and informative coding of cognitive responses into content categories. In particular, the distinction drawn between self-relevant and nonself-relevant thoughts provides a powerful basis for identifying those thoughts that are likely to play a long-term role in persuasion.

Thoughts that involve the self can be conceptualized in terms of two separate dimensions: origin and target. The origin dimension refers to how much of the thought originates in the self versus in the commercial. According to this conceptualization, self-relevant thoughts are any thoughts that indicate significant processing or elaboration on the ad. The target dimension reflects what the thought is about—that is, the respondent's focus of attention. According to this conceptualization, self-relevant thoughts are any thoughts that are about the self, including references to past experiences and personal needs. There is research precedent for analyzing self-relevance in message processing along either of these dimensions (see Greenwald, 1968; Krugman, 1965, 1967; Leavitt, Waddell, & Wells, 1970).

In our work (Shavitt & Brock, 1986), we placed the role of the self in cognitive responding in the context of a cross-cutting framework of origin and target. In terms of the target dimension, thoughts could be about the self, the product, or the execution. In terms of origin, thoughts could be message originated, recipient modified, or recipient originated. These dimensions cross-cut each other completely with the exception that self thoughts are not considered message originated; thoughts about oneself (one's own experiences, beliefs, and goals) are by definition more than mere playbacks of the ad.

Lebenson and Blackston define self-relevance in terms of the origin dimension (i.e., how much of the thought originates in the self vs. in the advertisement). Self-relevant thoughts in the RI database are those thoughts that reflect elaborated processing "from the literal use of the personal pronoun ('I like that product'; 'I don't believe that') to the use of emotionally charged language ('That's garbage')" (Blackston, Bunten, & Chadwick, 1994, p. 49).

Whereas the extent of elaboration is certainly important in evaluating message processing, it is also useful to consider what the thoughts are about (i.e., the target of the thoughts). In our experience, many elaborated thoughts are actually about the endorser or the ad's executional elements (e.g., "That actor plays in a soap opera" or "I hated the music"). Although these responses can reflect substantial elaboration, they nevertheless may not have the same significance in terms of a call to action as would thoughts that are literally about the self (e.g., "I'm not the sort of person who would cook something like that").

PACKAGED VERSUS NONPACKAGED GOODS

We call attention to the target of the thoughts in order to address Lebenson and Blackston's finding that self-relevant thoughts for packaged goods were more predictive of ad effectiveness criteria than self-relevant thoughts for nonpackaged goods. We suggest that self-relevant thoughts for the different product types may have had different targets.

Ads for nonpackaged goods such as computers and cars, which were probably less relevant to respondents' future purchase plans, may have elicited self-relevant thoughts that focused primarily on the communicators and the executional elements of the ads. However, ads for frequently purchased packaged goods, such as foods or grooming products, may have elicited self-relevant thoughts that were more focused on the products and their suitability for purchase. Thus, whereas both sets of self-relevant thoughts may have been equally elaborated (recipient originated), one might expect that the content of the latter type of self-relevant thoughts would be more predictive of brand attitudes and call to action criteria.

Future study of the RI database could address this possibility. The detailed coding of thoughts in the database includes content categories for three types of targets—product, execution, and communicator—and these are cross-cut with the self-relevant and nonself-relevant categories. Thus, one could determine whether self-relevant thoughts toward ads for packaged goods were more likely to be about the product (and less likely to be about the executional elements) than were self-relevant thoughts toward ads for nonpackaged goods. If one could separate buyers from nonbuyers in the nonpackaged goods category, one could also examine whether buyers' self-relevant thoughts were more likely to be about the product than those of nonbuyers.

Perhaps most importantly, future research could determine whether the favorability of self-relevant thoughts targeted toward the product was more predictive of ad effectiveness criteria than the favorability of other types of self-relevant thoughts, and whether these relationships vary with type of product and other factors (see Shavitt & Brock, 1986, 1990).

Based on a comparison of their results for nonpackaged versus packaged goods, Lebenson and Blackston distinguish the advertising persuasion processes likely to be associated with these different product types. They draw critical distinctions between *brand effects, call to action effects,* and *feel good effects*—distinctions that have general theoretical importance.

Indeed, Lebenson and Blackston's arguments in this regard are quite consistent with Fishbein and Ajzen's (1975) theorizing about the prediction of behavioral intentions. As Fishbein and Ajzen argued, one's attitude toward a product is often much less useful in predicting purchase intention than one's attitude toward the act of purchasing the product. This seems particularly likely to be true for expensive, durable goods. As Lebenson and Blackston suggest, for such higher risk items, liking of the product or brand may not be sufficient to motivate purchase. The call to action effect for nonpackaged goods might instead be better predicted by measures assessing consumers' evaluations of purchase or usage behaviors (see Fishbein & Ajzen, 1975).

Lebenson and Blackston's hypotheses regarding the role of feel good effects in predicting A_{Brand} also mesh well with theorizing about A_{Ad} (Mitchell & Olson, 1981; Shimp, 1981) and the conditions under which it mediates A_{Brand} and purchase intention (e.g., Lutz, 1985; MacKenzie & Lutz, 1989). The consistency between processes tested in the laboratory and those emerging from the present industrial data lends further support to Lebenson and Blackston's arguments.

LONG-TERM EFFECTS

Lebenson and Blackston conclude that self-relevant processing serves to imprint attitudinal changes more firmly or durably in the minds of consumers. Their report of findings demonstrating the role of self-relevant thoughts in the longevity of advertising effects is particularly intriguing. In the laboratory, we have also found that when self-focused, elaborated thinking is elicited in response to an ad, the consistency between brand attitudes and subsequent brand choice behavior is increased (Shavitt & Brock, 1986). More recent data suggest that recall may play a role in the long-term effects of self-relevant thinking; thoughts about the self seem more likely to be remembered at a delay than thoughts about other targets (Shavitt & Brock, 1990).

In the next chapter (chap. 9), we present our own current work on the role of cognitive responses in predicting long-term advertising persuasion. This research focuses on the role of goal-relevant thoughts—thoughts that are relevant to the consumer's enduring motives or to the goals served by the product—in predicting brand attitudes at a delay. In line with Lebenson and Blackston's findings, our data suggest that product type can influence the predictiveness of listed thoughts. Our results also point to the importance of the consumer's personality in identifying which types of thoughts will be most predictive.

Although we have not yet examined the self-relevance of thoughts in this data set, goal-relevant and self-relevant thought categories likely overlap. Not surprisingly, thoughts that are relevant to desired or undesired outcomes often have the self as referent. It remains for future research to investigate the relationship between these important categories of cognitive response, and the implications for predicting long-term advertising effects.

REFERENCES

Blackston, M., Bunten, N., & Chadwick, S. (1994). Cognitive response analysis after circumnavigating the world. In K. Finlay, A. A. Mitchell, & F. C. Cummins (Eds.), Proceedings of the Society for Consumer Psychology (pp. 48–54). Clemson, SC: CtC Press.

Fishbein, M., & Ajzen, I. (1975). Belief, attitude, intention, and behavior: An introduction to theory and research. Reading, MA: Addison-Wesley.

Greenwald, A. G. (1968). Cognitive learning, cognitive response to persuasion and attitude change. In A. G. Greenwald, T. C. Brock, & T. M. Ostrom (Eds.), Psychological foundations of attitudes (pp. 147–170). New York: Academic Press.

Krugman, H. E. (1965). The impact of television advertising: Learning without involvement. Public Opinion Quarterly, 29, 349–356.

Krugman, H. E. (1967). The measurement of advertisement involvement. Public Opinion Quarterly, 30, 583–596.

Leavitt, C., Waddell, C., & Wells, W. D. (1970). Improving day-after recall techniques. Journal of Advertising Research, 10, 13–17.

Lutz, R. J. (1985). Affective and cognitive antecedents of attitude toward the ad: A conceptual framework. In L. F. Alwitt & A. A. Mitchell (Eds.), *Psychological processes and advertising effects* (pp. 45–63). Hillsdale, NJ: Lawrence Erlbaum Associates.

MacKenzie, S. B., & Lutz, R. J. (1989). An empirical examination of the structural antecedents of attitude toward the ad in an advertising pretesting context. *Journal of Marketing, 53,* 48–65.

Mitchell, A. A., & Olson, J. C. (1981). Are product attribute beliefs the only mediator of advertising effects on brand attitude? *Journal of Marketing Research, 18,* 318–332.

Shavitt, S., & Brock, T. C. (1985). Improving cognitive response prediction of persuasion: Towards a semantic hierarchy. In D. Stewart (Ed.), *Proceedings of the Division of Consumer Psychology* (pp. 13–14). San Antonio, TX: American Psychological Association.

Shavitt, S., & Brock, T. C. (1986). Self-relevant responses in commercial persuasion: Field and experimental tests. In K. Sentis & J. Olson (Eds.), *Advertising and consumer psychology* (Vol. 3, pp. 149–171). New York: Praeger.

Shavitt, S., & Brock, T. C. (1990). Delayed recall of copytest responses: The temporal stability of listed thoughts. *Journal of Advertising, 19*(4), 6–17.

Shimp, T. A. (1981). Attitude toward the ad as a mediator of consumer brand choice. *Journal of Advertising, 10,* 9–15.

9

Prediction of Long-Term Advertising Effectiveness: New Cognitive Response Approaches

Michelle R. Nelson
Sharon Shavitt
Angela Schennum
Jacqueline Barkmeier
University of Illinois at Urbana–Champaign

In industry, interest appears to be growing in measures of advertising effectiveness that focus on consumer response at the individual level (e.g., Lebenson & Blackston, chap. 8, this volume; McDonald, 1993). However, responses to measures that offer rich and diagnostic insights into consumer reactions can be difficult to obtain, particularly in samples large enough to provide reliable assessments of ad effectiveness. One approach that has shown promise in this regard focuses on consumers' cognitive responses. As yet, however, very few studies have examined the predictiveness of cognitive responses after a delay (but see Chattopadhyay & Alba, 1988), so not much is known about the stability of cognitive responses and the degree to which they predict long-term advertising effectiveness. Indeed, as Sawyer and Ward (1979) lamented, "little is known about the delayed effects of advertising at the individual level" (Chattopadhyay & Alba, 1988, p. 1).

In this chapter, we present research on listed-thought cognitive response measures and their relation to long-term advertising effectiveness. The first part of the chapter focuses on new, goal-relevant dimensions of listed thoughts, their role in the persuasion process, and their prediction of delayed persuasion outcomes. We also examine consumer personality differences and product characteristics as variables that affect the predictiveness of listed thoughts. These findings emerge from a program of research on the antecedents and consequences of consumer motivations. The second part of the chapter reports research exploring a new cognitive response methodology. This research gauges consumers' insight into the thoughts underlying their attitudes.

GOAL-RELEVANT DIMENSIONS
OF COGNITIVE RESPONSE

Listed-thought measures of cognitive response reflect the by-products of information-processing activity—the reactions that one generates in the course of receiving an ad or other persuasive message, relating it to prior knowledge, and evaluating it (Petty, Ostrom, & Brock, 1981). The content of these thoughts typically provides a rich source of information about idiosyncratic responses to messages. Hence, listed-thought measures have become a commonly used method for determining individuals' reactions to advertising messages (e.g., Batra & Ray, 1986; Chattopadhyay & Alba, 1988; Leavitt, Waddell, & Wells, 1970; Lutz & MacKenzie, 1982). Cognitive response researchers (e.g., Petty et al., 1981; Shavitt & Brock, 1986, 1990) have suggested that the cognitive responses elicited by a persuasive message contribute strongly to message effectiveness because such responses reflect enduring and personally relevant thought processes.

Which types of listed thoughts should be particularly personally relevant? Theory and research on attitude functions (e.g., Katz, 1960; Kelman, 1958, 1961; Smith, Bruner, & White, 1956), the motives or goals that attitudes serve for individuals, suggest that thoughts reflecting goal-relevant content should be particularly important.

Consumers may have different goals in mind when evaluating a product.[1] For example, consumers' goals may involve conveying a particular social image or identity through consumption of a product, expressing one's values, or gaining social approval. Such *social identity attitudes* toward a product are generally based on perceptions of others' product attitudes, and what they imply about the image and characteristics of the product and user. On the other hand, consumers may have the goal of maximizing utilitarian rewards or minimizing the punishments obtained from a product. *Utilitarian attitudes* are generally based on those product attributes that provide intrinsically satisfying or unsatisfying outcomes (Shavitt 1989, 1990).

The goals that are served by evaluating a product can determine the conditions under which the evaluation will change (Shavitt, 1990; Snyder & DeBono, 1985). Thus, thoughts that reflect one's personally relevant goals provide a basis for determining which types of advertising messages are likely to change product attitudes. More importantly for evaluating ad effectiveness, listed thoughts toward an ad that reflect the goals associated with one's product attitude provide a basis for predicting the effects of the ad on an individual.

In addition to examining goal-relevant cognitive processes involved in attitude formation, our work has attempted to develop new methods for

---

[1]To be sure, consumers may differ in the extent to which they have any goals in mind when exposed to an advertisement. However, to the extent that their cognitive responses reflect goal-relevant thinking, those responses should be particularly useful in the long-term prediction of persuasion.

eliciting thoughts in key categories. The research presented here offers an initial evaluation of these methodologies, as well as insight into the long-term relationships between listed thoughts and attitudes.

Classifying the Content of Listed Thoughts

In earlier research (Shavitt, 1990; Shavitt, Lowrey, & Han, 1992), a coding method was developed and validated for classifying the motives or functions reflected in listed thoughts to advertisements. The coding focuses primarily on two major categories of motivational themes. The utilitarian category includes references to product quality, thoughts about features or attributes of the product, and references to rewards or punishments associated with the product. The social identity category includes thoughts about the product's image, as well as references to others' attitudes toward the product, what the product symbolizes, and what the product communicates to others. Across a variety of products and situations, this coding method has proven effective in distinguishing attitudes that serve different functions (e.g., Shavitt, 1990; Shavitt & Fazio, 1991; Shavitt et al., 1992). Moreover, studies employing this coding method have pointed to a number of variables that can influence consumers' product evaluation goals. One of these studies is outlined here.

The Interactive Role of Products and Personality

Shavitt et al. (1992) examined the roles of products and personality to determine how each may affect consumers' product evaluation goals. Would the functions a product serves differ with the type of product or the personality of the consumer? Would the types of advertising appeals consumers find persuasive depend on these factors as well?

Attitude objects (such as products) have been shown to play an important role in attitude functions. A product's perceived value for attaining specific goals may be defined by its intrinsic characteristics and by societal or cultural definitions of the product. Therefore, the purposes a product can serve vary from product to product, with some products fulfilling multiple functions (e.g., sunglasses, which provide utilitarian benefits and express a certain social image). Others are generally limited to serving a single function, for example, a utilitarian function (aspirin) or a social identity function (high school class ring; Johar & Sirgy, 1991; Shavitt, 1989, 1990).

These limitations on the functions products serve suggest that products may interact with personality or other variables in influencing attitude functions and the persuasiveness of appeals. That is, individual differences in consumer goals may emerge for some product categories but not for others. For instance, when the product serves multiple functions, it presents an opportunity to focus on different functional goals. The functional goals that will be salient may then vary with a number of factors, including the personality of the consumer.

Personality has already been shown to influence product evaluation goals. For example, research by Snyder and DeBono (1985) has suggested that high and low self-monitors differ in the functions that their product attitudes tend to serve. High self-monitors (identified by their relatively high scores on the Self-Monitoring Scale; Snyder, 1974) are typically concerned with projecting social images that allow them to meet the requirements of different social situations. For example, a high self-monitor would be more likely to endorse a statement such as, "When I am uncertain how to act in a social situation, I look to the behavior of others for cues" (Snyder, 1974). Low self-monitors, on the other hand, are less concerned with social appropriateness and more concerned with being consistent with their internal feelings and preferences. A low self-monitor would agree with a statement such as, "I would not change my opinions (or the way I do things) in order to please someone else or win their favor." Indeed, self-monitoring level has been shown to predict a variety of judgments and social behaviors, including friendship patterns, romantic attractions, policy evaluations, and attitude–behavior relationships (Snyder, 1987).

In the product domain, Snyder and DeBono (1985) suggested that low self-monitors tend to be concerned with dimensions related to product quality, such as the taste of coffee or the cleaning performance of shampoo (but see Brannon & Brock, 1994). In contrast, high self-monitors tend to be concerned with the self-presentational significance of products, such as the image associated with using or serving a particular type of coffee. These differences between high and low self-monitoring consumers are associated with differences in the types of advertising appeals they find persuasive (Snyder & DeBono, 1985). For example, high self-monitors are typically more persuaded by appeals about the social image or status associated with the product, whereas low self-monitors are more persuaded by claims about the product's quality or attributes. In the functional categorization employed here, then, low self-monitors' responses appear to reflect utilitarian goals, whereas high self-monitors' responses reflect social identity goals.

The studies described next (Shavitt et al., 1992) examined the interactive roles of product and personality to investigate whether differences in the functions of high and low self-monitors' product attitudes would be more likely to emerge for some types of products than for others.

Method and Rationale

In two studies, subjects wrote their own advertisements for different types of products: (a) utilitarian function products: air conditioner, aspirin; (b) multiple-function products: watch, sunglasses; and (c) social identity function products: class ring, school flag. These products were selected based on functional criteria identified in previous research (Shavitt, 1990). After writing the ads and completing some other measures, subjects completed the 25-item Self-Monitoring Scale (Snyder, 1974).

It was expected that product type would exert a strong influence on subjects' responses. For example, it was predicted that subjects would use primarily quality-based arguments when writing an ad for a utilitarian product and would use mostly image-based claims when advertising a social identity product. Further, it was expected that differences between high and low self-monitors in the types of appeals they write would emerge mainly in the multiple-function product category.

The advertising headlines and copy that subjects wrote were coded by independent judges to assess the functions they reflected using the coding scheme for goal-relevant categories described earlier (see Shavitt, 1990). Utilitarian arguments included claims about the product's quality, features, or rewards. Social identity arguments included claims about the product's image, what it symbolizes or communicates to others, and how others feel about the product.

Results and Discussion

Consistent with previous research (Shavitt, 1990), product type did strongly influence the content of the ads that subjects wrote. Subjects tended to use utilitarian arguments for utilitarian products (aspirin or air conditioner) and image-based claims for social identity products (class ring or school flag). As predicted, self-monitoring differences played the greatest role for the multiple-function products (watch or sunglasses). That is, when writing ads for sunglasses or watches, high self-monitors tended to use more image-based arguments and headlines, whereas low self-monitors tended to use more quality-based arguments and headlines.

This research confirmed that variables such as personality and product type both can influence consumers' product evaluation goals as well as what types of appeals they find convincing. In cases where the product serves primarily a single function, the product itself may be a very important variable in predicting the functions of the consumer's attitude. However, when the product serves multiple functions (e.g., sunglasses), differences in the types of functions that individuals focus on may emerge depending on their personalities. Consequently, when there is opportunity to focus on multiple dimensions of a product, personality may be an important factor in predicting the persuasiveness of appeals.

This initial research also demonstrated that the coding scheme originally developed to classify the functional relevance of subjects' listed thoughts could be extended to a new context, to code the advertisements that subjects write. Thus, the coding scheme appears flexible enough to be used in coding the functions reflected in a variety of open-ended responses.

Investigating the Long-Term Predictiveness of Listed Thoughts

In our most recent study, we investigated further the roles of product and personality in determining attitude functions and the persuasiveness of appeals, focusing on functions as revealed in subjects' listed thoughts. What types of thoughts would be most relevant in attitude formation, and would these same thoughts continue to be important after a week's delay? We were interested both in how well subjects' listed thoughts correlated with their attitudes at a delay, and how consistent their recalled thoughts were with their attitudes. Also, would social identity thoughts be more predictive of long-term attitudes than utilitarian thoughts for high self-monitors, and vice versa for low self-monitors? Would the type of product being advertised matter? This study was designed to address these questions.

To measure the predictiveness of listed thoughts for long-term attitudes, we used two listed-thought measures: (a) subjects' initial listed thoughts and (b) subjects' recalled thoughts at a delay. In each case, we wanted to evaluate the degree to which subjects' thoughts predicted or were consistent with their attitudes. We included an examination of the thoughts that subjects recalled at a delay because this may more closely resemble the role of cognitive responses in a purchasing situation, when consumers must try to remember their thoughts about the ad or the product. Those thoughts that consumers are able to recall may also be those that are most important to their attitudes.

Method

Fifty-seven students from an introductory advertising class participated in this two-session study of advertising effects. The study consisted of a 3 (product type: utilitarian, social identity, and multiple-function) × 2 (self-monitoring level: high vs. low) between-subjects design. Within subjects, thoughts were coded to reflect an additional two-level thought type factor (utilitarian vs. social identity).

In the first session, participants were shown print advertisements for a variety of products and listed their thoughts about these ads according to instructions designed to elicit their utilitarian and social identity thoughts. A week later, subjects reported their attitudes toward the advertised brands, then attempted to recall the thoughts that they had listed during the first session. Finally, subjects completed several other measures, including the 25-item Self-Monitoring Scale (Snyder, 1974).

Product Characteristics.   Consistent with earlier research, we expected that the functional relevance of the product being advertised may make a difference in the predictiveness of listed thoughts. Thus, products featured in the ads were selected for their relevance to particular functional goals (utilitarian, social identity, or multiple-function) based on criteria identified in previous research (Shavitt, 1990; Shavitt et al., 1992). All products were pretested to confirm their a priori categorization by asking another student sample (a) to rate their attitude toward each product and then (b) to indicate (on a 5-point scale) the degree to which utilitarian considerations (past experience and satisfaction with product's performance) and social identity considerations (own identity and friends' reactions) contributed to their attitude. The chosen utilitarian products had significantly greater "utilitarian" contribution scores than "social identity" contribution scores, and social identity products showed greater social identity contribution scores than utilitarian scores. Multiple-function products revealed approximately equal contribution means.

Based on these data, the utilitarian products selected were toothbrush, laundry detergent, and paper towels. The social identity products were flowers, greeting cards, and school banners. The multiple-function products were mineral water, school sweatshirts, and gourmet coffee. Pretest data also indicated that all of these items are frequently purchased by students, validating the use of a student sample for our selection of products. In addition, the products are all typically available in full-service supermarkets (at a modest cost). Thus, although the products we selected vary greatly in terms of their functional relevance, they are similar in terms of their retail purchase context and their relevance to the student subject population.

Advertising Stimuli. The ads employed were for fictitious brands of these products (so as to avoid any effects of prior attitude), but were modeled after real ads for actual brands and appeared very realistic. Ads contained a headline, a visual, and between 35 and 150 words of copy. The ads in this study differed from those of stimulus ads in previous studies of attitude functions (Shavitt, 1990; Snyder & DeBono, 1985) in that we attempted to balance utilitarian and social identity claims within each ad. This allowed us to maintain consistency in the type of advertising content used across products in different function categories. For example, for laundry detergent the utilitarian claim was, "Nouvelle Detergent is formulated to protect colors better than any other liquid detergent," and the social identity argument was, "So you can always look your best in your favorite clothes." For flowers, the utilitarian claim was, "We have fresh flowers brought in daily and prices to suit any budget," and the social identity argument was, "No matter what it is you want to express, do it with flowers."

Procedure. Subjects were told that a local ad agency was copy testing a series of ads that were going to be placed in student publications, and that the agency wanted the students' responses to the ads. At the first session, subjects examined three randomly assigned product ads (out of a possible nine), viewing one ad in each function category: utilitarian, multiple-function, and social identity. The order in which they responded to the three function categories was counterbalanced in a Latin-square design.

After viewing each ad, subjects read standard thought-listing instructions (Cacioppo & Petty, 1981) and then were given approximately 3 minutes to list their thoughts on forms on which six boxes were printed. Next, subjects were asked to rate each of those thoughts according to whether the thought was favorable to the product, unfavorable to the product, or neutral, on a scale from −2 (*very unfavorable*) to +2 (*very favorable*).

Following the rating task, subjects responded to a new set of thought-listing tasks for each of the three products. Because the goal of this study was to explore the role of function-relevant cognitive responses in predicting subsequent attitudes, it was important to access any relevant thoughts subjects had in each function category. Thus, in order to encourage subjects to report thoughts relevant to the utilitarian or social identity aspects of the product, new "directive" instructions had been developed and pretested in a separate study. The social identity version of the directive instructions read as follows:

> In addition to the thoughts you have already listed, if any (other) thoughts or feelings occurred to you as you were reading the (brand name) ad that were related to the [image of the product or its user (for example, what the product symbolizes or what it communicates to others)] please list them below.

In the utilitarian version of the directive instructions, the bracketed portion read, "quality of the product (for example, features or attributes of the product)." Three boxes were included on each directive instruction form. All subjects responded to both directive instructions in counterbalanced order. Then, subjects proceeded to rate each of those thoughts on the +2 to –2 favorability scale used to rate their initial thought list. Results of a pretest indicated that these directive instructions did not seem to affect how subjects thought about the product.[2]

Subjects returned to the lab a week later. At that time, their attitudes toward each of the advertised products they had seen were assessed using semantic differential scales anchored by –4 to +4 (good–bad, desirable–undesirable, and favorable–unfavorable), and other measures were taken. Next, subjects were asked to recall any of the thoughts that they had listed the previous week (including thoughts from directive instructions). For each product, subjects

---

[2]In the pretest, subjects examined a packet of print ads and then listed their thoughts using standard thought-listing instructions toward the target ad for a fictitious campus restaurant. Subjects then rated their thoughts for favorability (on the +2 to –2 scale), and indicated their attitudes on a series of 9-point semantic differential scales. Next, subjects responded to one of the two versions of the directive instructions, randomly assigned, and then (after completing several other measures) indicated their attitudes again, this time on a 7-point self-rating scale. Attitudes measured at Time 1 and Time 2 were converted to standardized scores and compared. No significant differences were found between attitudes at Time 1 and Time 2. In addition, no significant differences were found between directive instruction groups in their attitudes at Time 2. This is particularly important as the target ad was designed to elicit any potential effects of the directive instructions by providing negative social image information (in the form of unattractive spokespeople) and attractive sensory arguments. We expected that if the social image directive instructions increased the degree to which subjects thought about the social image of the restaurant, they would respond more negatively to the restaurant after completing the directive thought listing, whereas those receiving the sensory directive instructions would respond more favorably, and that this would be reflected by changes in attitudes after the directive task. Because subjects' attitudes did not change after completing the directive task, it appears that the directive thought-listing procedures did not alter the way in which subjects thought about the ad, but instead encouraged them to report the social image or sensory thoughts they had already generated.

were told to write down all of the thoughts they recalled in the order that they came to mind. After some other measures, subjects completed the 25-item Self-Monitoring Scale (Snyder, 1974).

Results

A number of issues were of interest in this study: (a) How well the thoughts that subjects listed after advertising exposure predicted their attitudes after a 1-week delay, (b) what types of thoughts were recalled at a delay, and (c) how well those thoughts that subjects recalled correlated with their delayed attitudes. In each case, we examined the role that product type, self-monitoring level, and thought type would play in these relationships.

The thoughts that subjects listed were coded to assess the functions they reflected using the coding scheme described earlier. Two trained judges independently coded all the thoughts (including those from directive instructions), agreeing on 87% of their classifications. The thoughts that elicited disagreements were approximately evenly distributed between the major thought categories, and meanings were discussed and negotiated between the judges until agreement was reached. In addition, the accuracy of recalled thoughts was assessed by one judge according to a "gist" criterion.

Subjects were classified as high or low self-monitors on the basis of a median split of their responses on the Self-Monitoring Scale (Snyder, 1974).

Predictiveness of Cognitive Responses.   First, we examined all of the thoughts subjects listed after exposure to the ads in order to determine how well their listed thoughts predicted attitudes at a 1-week delay. Overall, the favorability of the thoughts that low self-monitors listed was more highly correlated with delayed attitudes ($r = .67$) than was the favorability of high self-monitors' thoughts ($r = .59$), although this difference was not statistically significant. This finding appears consistent with past research that has shown the attitudes of low self-monitors to be more accessible in memory (Kardes, Sanbonmatsu, Voss, & Fazio, 1986) and more predictive of behavior (Snyder & Tanke, 1976) than the attitudes of high self-monitors. The present findings suggest that low self-monitors' listed thoughts may have somewhat more predictive validity than high self-monitors' listed thoughts in forecasting commercial persuasion.

Interestingly, however, the pattern we observed appeared to depend on the type of product advertised and the type of thought being used as a predictor. Refer to Table 9.1 for correlations as a function of thought type, product type, and self-monitoring level. Although correlations for low self-monitors tended to be higher than those of high self-monitors throughout, the one exception was for social identity thoughts within the social identity product category. In this case, high self-monitors' thoughts were more predictive of their attitudes ($r = .52$) than low self-monitors' ($r = .35$), although the difference was not statistically significant. This finding suggests that when the product is particularly relevant to the goals of high self-monitoring consumers (i.e., social identity

TABLE 9.1
Correlations Between Favorability of Listed Thoughts (Time 1) and Attitude Toward
Brand (Time 2) as a Function of Thought Type, Product Type, and Self-Monitoring

	Utilitarian Thoughts[**]	Social Identity Thoughts
	Utilitarian Product	
Low SM	.73 (n = 25)	.63 (n = 24)
High SM	.29 (n = 26)	.48 (n = 25)
Overall	.54 (n = 51)	.53 (n = 49)
	Utilitarian Thoughts[**]	Social Identity Thoughts[*]
	Multiple-Function Product	
Low SM	.65 (n = 23)	.66 (n = 25)
High SM	.20 (n = 25)	.33 (n = 26)
Overall	.36 (n = 48)	.47 (n = 51)
	Utilitarian Thoughts	Social Identity Thoughts
	Social Identity Product	
Low SM[***]	.62 (n = 25)	.35 (n = 23)
High SM	.46 (n = 26)	.52 (n = 24)
Overall	.53 (n = 51)	.46 (n = 47)

Note. Subjects who did not provide any thoughts for a given thought type were not included in
the relevant thought index analyses.

[*]For this thought type within this product category, correlations for low and high self-monitors
differed at $p < .10$. [**]For this thought type within this product category, correlations for low
and high self-monitors differed at $p < .05$. [***]Within this self-monitoring level for this product
category, correlations for utilitarian thoughts and social identity thoughts differed at $p < .10$.

products such as flowers and banners), the goal-relevant thoughts they list may
be relatively good predictors of subsequent persuasion.

In addition, the data suggested that level of self-monitoring influenced which
type of thought was more predictive of persuasion. For low self-monitors, the
favorability of utilitarian thoughts appeared to be more predictive of long-term
persuasion than the favorability of social identity thoughts, although this
difference was statistically significant for social identity products only. In
contrast, for high self-monitors, the favorability of social identity thoughts was
more predictive of persuasion than the favorability of utilitarian thoughts
(although consistent across products, these differences were not statistically
significant for high self-monitors).

These differences in the predictiveness of listed thoughts for high and low
self-monitors fit well with the self-monitoring construct. Past research (e.g.,
Snyder & DeBono, 1985) has shown that low self-monitors are generally more
influenced by claims about the inherent qualities of a product and, therefore,
one would expect their utilitarian thoughts to be more predictive of their

attitudes. On the other hand, high self-monitors are more influenced by image arguments, so one might expect their social identity thoughts to be more predictive. These data point to the value of accounting for consumers' level of self-monitoring; when the data were collapsed across levels of self-monitoring (see overall numbers in Table 9.1), the correlations suggested no reliable differences in the predictiveness of utilitarian versus social identity thoughts.

Content of Recalled Thoughts.   Very few studies have examined the long-term recall of cognitive responses, or the factors that influence which thoughts are recalled. Therefore, it was difficult to predict how strongly personality and product type would affect the types of thoughts that would be recalled. Overall, very few differences emerged.

Consistently across all product types, however, we found that low self-monitors recalled a greater proportion of their listed thoughts (48%) than did high self-monitors (39%), although high self-monitors had listed more thoughts initially after advertising exposure. Differences in the proportion of thoughts recalled were significant only for social identity products, where low self-monitors recalled 50% and high self-monitors recalled 37% of their originally listed thoughts.

No significant differences emerged in the types of thoughts that were recalled, although both high and low self-monitors tended to recall a greater proportion of their utilitarian thoughts than their social identity thoughts. The only exception to this trend was found for high self-monitors in the social identity product category. In this case, high self-monitors recalled a greater proportion of their social identity thoughts (42%), than their utilitarian thoughts (37%), whereas low self-monitors recalled a greater proportion of their utilitarian thoughts (55% vs. 43%), although none of these differences were statistically significant.

Relation Between Recalled Thoughts and Attitudes.   Although it might be interesting to note what types of thoughts were recalled, it is perhaps more important for marketers to consider which of those recalled thoughts were most consistent with attitudes at a delay. This is another way of assessing the long-term significance of listed thoughts. In other words, which of the thoughts about the ad that consumers recalled actually related to long-term persuasion?

Overall, the favorability of the recalled thoughts of low self-monitors was more consistent with their attitudes ($r = .73$) than that of high self-monitors ($r = .57$), although the difference was not significant. However, self-monitoring differences were significant for social identity thoughts (Low SM: $r = .61$; High SM: $r = .15$; $p < .05$) and marginally significant for utilitarian thoughts (Low SM: $r = .56$; High SM: $r = .30$; $p = .12$). Again, this finding is consistent with past research on self-monitoring showing that low self-monitors have better access to their attitudes (Kardes et al., 1986). The results given here suggest that they also have better access in memory to the thoughts underlying their attitudes. This finding is also consistent with the results described earlier showing that low self-monitors' listed thoughts were somewhat more predictive of their attitudes than high self-monitors', and that their thoughts overall were generally better recalled.

However, once again, these differences seemed to depend on the type of product being advertised. For utilitarian and multiple-function products, the differences between low and high self-monitors were significant (for utilitarian products, Low SM: $r = .74$, High SM: $r = .44$; $p < .05$; and for multiple-function products, Low SM: $r = .81$, High SM: $r = .53$; $p < .05$), but for social identity products these differences disappeared (Low SM: $r = .62$, High SM: $r = .69$; ns). This indicates that both the personality of the consumer and the type of product matter when examining the relevance of recalled thoughts. It also suggests that when the type of product corresponds with the goals of the consumer—as with social identity products for high self-monitors—recalled thoughts may be more consistent with attitudes.

We also found a consistent trend for the predictive value of each thought type to vary with the type of product. For utilitarian products, recalled utilitarian thoughts were significantly more consistent with attitude ($r = .54$) than recalled social identity thoughts ($r = .14$; $p < .05$) and the opposite was the case, although not significantly, for social identity products (utilitarian thoughts: $r = .35$; and social identity thoughts: $r = .43$; ns). These findings are consistent with our assumptions about the role of these product categories, as the types of thoughts that were predictive corresponded with the ascribed functions of the product.

By examining the role of all three independent variables, we noted some additional patterns of interest (see Table 9.2). For example, for low self-monitors, recalled utilitarian thoughts were significantly more consistent with attitude for utilitarian products ($r = .74$) than for social identity products ($r = .28$, $p < .05$). The converse was true for high self-monitors, for whom recalled social identity thoughts were significantly more consistent with attitude for social identity products ($r = .28$) than for utilitarian products ($r = -.30$, $p = .06$). However, within-product comparisons did not support our assumptions about the role of thought type and personality type in the consistency of recalled thoughts and attitudes.

Discussion

This study emphasized the importance of testing the effects of advertising on consumers' thoughts and attitudes toward a brand over the long term. Obviously, consumers change their opinions of brands over time, so it is important to know which of their responses to the advertising message have enduring relevance to their attitudes. By examining the goal-relevant content of listed thoughts, we can gain a better understanding of the processes by which consumers form attitudes, and then apply these thought-listing measures effectively in an advertising copy testing arena to predict subsequent attitudes. This

TABLE 9.2
Correlations Between Favorability of Thoughts Recalled at a Delay (Time 2)
and AttitudeToward the Brand (Time 2) as a Function of Thought Type,
Product Type, and Level of Self-Monitoring

	Recalled Utilitarian Thoughts[**]	Recalled Social Identity Thoughts[**]
	Utilitarian Product	
Low SM	.74 (n = 16)	.50 (n = 14)
High SM	.33 (n = 16)	−.30 (n = 17)
Overall***	.54 (n = 32)	.14 (n = 31)
	Recalled Utilitarian Thoughts[*]	Recalled Social Identity Thoughts[**]
	Multiple-Function Product	
Low SM	.58 (n = 16)	.73 (n = 19)
High SM	.18 (n = 19)	.15 (n = 17)
Overall	.41 (n = 35)	.46 (n = 36)
	Recalled Utilitarian Thoughts	Recalled Social Identity Thoughts
	Social Identity Product	
Low SM	.28 (n = 18)	.58 (n = 14)
High SM	.38 (n = 12)	.28 (n = 15)
Overall	.35 (n = 30)	.43 (n = 29)

Note. Subjects who did not provide any thoughts for a given thought type were not included in the relevant thought index analyses.
[*]For this thought type within this product category, correlations for low and high self-monitors differed at $p < .10$. [**]For this thought type within this product category, correlations for low and high self-monitors differed at $p < .05$. [***]Within subjects for this product category, correlations for recalled utilitarian thoughts and recalled social identity thoughts differed at $p < .05$.

study also highlighted the importance of accounting for personality and type of product, in that the predictiveness of thoughts can differ depending on the functions of the advertised product and the personality of the consumer.

Specifically, the types of thoughts that tended to be more predictive of attitudes at a 1-week delay were those that were most relevant to the personality of the consumer and the function served by the product. This was depicted in correlations of listed thoughts and delayed attitude, as well as correlations of recalled thoughts and delayed attitude. Although low self-monitors appeared to be generally better at listing and recalling thoughts that were consistent with their attitudes, this difference did not emerge for social identity products (particularly with respect to social identity thoughts). Here, high self-monitors' thoughts appeared to be more predictive of their attitudes. Thus, although the attitudes of high self-monitors tend to be less stable according to previous research (Snyder & DeBono, 1985), our findings suggest that their listed social identity thoughts can be relatively good predictors of attitude toward social identity products.

The interactive effects we found for product and personality might be explained in terms of how well the functions of the product correspond to the goals of the individual. Generally, for utilitarian products, the thoughts that low self-monitors listed initially (as well as the thoughts they recalled) were more consistent with their attitudes than those of high self-monitors. Again, this might be because the functions of utilitarian products fit well with the quality-oriented goals of a low self-monitor. In contrast, for social identity products, high self-monitors' listed and recalled thoughts were at least as predictive of their attitudes as those of low self-monitors. Here, the image-based goals of the high self-monitor might be better fulfilled by social identity products.

Although one might have expected greater effects for multiple-function products (i.e., greater differences in the types of thoughts that predicted attitudes for high and low self-monitors), these results showed instead that differences mainly emerged for utilitarian and social identity product categories. This pattern appears to differ from the results of earlier studies described (Shavitt et al., 1992). A potential explanation lies in the advertising stimuli employed and the methodologies used. In the earlier studies, differences found between low and high self-monitors for multiple-function products may have been due to the opportunity such products afforded to focus on different functions. When writing ads for multiple-function products, those studies showed that high self-monitors tended to use image-based arguments and low self-monitors tended to use utilitarian claims. For utilitarian or social identity products (i.e., single-function products), no significant differences between high and low self-monitors emerged as both groups used claims that matched the product type (e.g., utilitarian claims for utilitarian products).

In this study, however, we presented subjects with stimulus ads that reflected a balance of claims. By including both utilitarian and social identity claims within each ad and across product categories, readers were given the opportunity to focus on different functions for all product types, thus perhaps prompting high and low self-monitors to focus on different goals when considering single-function products. This could have contributed to the differences for utilitarian and social identity product categories. It should be noted that such a balancing of claims is probably more realistic in terms of application to advertising, as many advertisements contain multiple types of claims.

Evaluating the Technique of Directive Thought Elicitation

This study employed new thought-listing techniques designed to elicit thoughts in specific function-relevant categories. These directive instructions encouraged subjects to report more of their existing function-relevant thoughts than did the general thought-listing instructions alone. The directive instructions increased the average number of utilitarian thoughts reported by 112% and the average number of social identity thoughts reported by 108%. Moreover, pretest data suggested that our directive instructions did not change the thoughts subjects had about the ad, but instead increased the likelihood that the relevant functional thoughts would be reported (see footnote 2).

Other consumer researchers have begun using similar instructions to "encourage a greater sensitivity . . . by framing or intensifying one's processing of an ad" (Wansink, Ray, & Batra, 1994, p. 66). By focusing on certain dimensions of the product, directive instructions enable subjects to retrieve and write down those specific, function-oriented thoughts that are relevant to their attitude. In their study, Wansink et al. (1994) used preexposure elicitation exercises (such as practice tests or examples) or directed postexposure instructions. In both cases, they were able to increase the number of thoughts about a target issue compared to using general instructions alone.

As Ericsson and Simon (1984) suggested, the more general the elicitation instructions, the greater the opportunity for irrelevant responses. Indeed, across a number of studies, we have found that whereas subjects often spontaneously list thoughts that reflect function-relevant goals, many thoughts are also listed about the structure of the ad itself (e.g., "the font size on the headline is too small"). Perhaps this is due, in part, to the nature of the ad evaluation task or to the "advertising study" context, which leads subjects to focus on irrelevant ad features in the absence of directive instructions.

Importantly, the use of directive instructions did not appear to reduce the predictive validity of the listed thoughts. The overall mean thought favorability (which was calculated based on all thoughts listed by a subject to a given ad) correlated with brand attitude at a delay ($r = .63$) as strongly as did the initial thought-list favorability (no directives, $r = .59$) or the directive thought favorability (only directives, $r = .57$). These correlations did not differ significantly.

The fact that the directive thought index was as predictive of attitudes as the initial thought list is also noteworthy because the directive index is often based on fewer thoughts than the initial list, and thus one might expect it to be less reliable. However, it may derive its predictive validity, in part, from the fact that it contains more function-relevant thoughts. Such thoughts are likely to relate more directly to the basis for one's product evaluation than do ad-structure thoughts or other thoughts in the initial thought list that may be less relevant to the goals of the consumer.

Our use of directive instructions is part of a growing effort by cognitive response researchers to explore dimension-specific elicitation methods (Wansink et al., 1994; Wright, 1980; Wright & Rip, 1980). These new methodologies seem to enhance the relevance of cognitive responses and may also aid in the prediction of attitudes.

SELF-SCORING THE IMPORTANCE OF THOUGHTS: A NEW COGNITIVE RESPONSE TECHNIQUE

A separate series of studies examined a new and simplified method of using listed thoughts for predicting persuasion. Our other efforts have focused on identifying a priori the types of thoughts most likely to predict persuasion.

However, in these studies, rather than trying to discern which thoughts were most important in determining persuasion, we asked subjects themselves to tell us which of their thoughts contributed the most to their attitudes. Then, we examined the degree to which these thoughts corresponded with subjects' attitudes.

In the first such study, subjects listed thoughts toward a print ad for a fictitious campus restaurant, rated their thoughts (on the +2 to –2 favorability scale), and completed an attitude measure. Then, they were instructed to review the thoughts they had listed and draw a circle around the one thought that they felt contributed the most to their attitude, that is, to choose the one that was "the most important in determining your attitude toward the restaurant."

This circle-a-thought task is different from any other self-scoring method used to date in cognitive response research. Although it is common to ask respondents to score their own thoughts for favorability, and occasionally respondents are asked to rate their thoughts along other dimensions, none of those judgments require subjects to have insight into what influenced their attitudes.

In fact, it is generally assumed that respondents do not have such insight into the bases of their attitudes. In an extensive review of literature comparing verbal reports and behavior, Nisbett and Wilson (1977) questioned individuals' introspective ability and concluded that, "people often cannot report accurately on the effects of particular stimuli on higher order, inference-based responses" (p. 233). They sought to discover why individuals are so poor at discerning the difference between private facts that "can be known with near certainty" (attitudes) and "mental processes to which there may be no access at all" (p. 255). Nisbett and Wilson (1977) showed that individuals often have difficulty verbalizing the reasons they feel the way they do about objects or situations. Further, they claimed that the reasons that subjects gave were ones that were most accessible in memory and sounded reasonable, but may not have been accurate. As such, they concluded by questioning the validity of cognitive response methods in general. However, Ericsson and Simon (1980) suggested that cognitive response methods can nevertheless be valid because they do not require the individual's insight into the psychological processes underlying one's attitude formation.

More recently, in an interesting line of research, Wilson and his colleagues have set out to deconstruct the introspection process. They demonstrated that two types of introspection, analyzing reasons for attitudes versus focusing on feelings, have different effects (Wilson, Dunn, Kraft, & Lisle, 1989). Whereas "focusing" has been shown to increase the accessibility of attitudes (Wilson et al., 1989), which had previously been shown to increase the degree to which those attitudes predict behavior (Fazio, Chen, McDonel, & Sherman, 1982), the other type of introspection—analyzing reasons for one's attitude—has been shown to reduce attitude–behavior correlations (Wilson & Dunn, 1986). Wilson and LaFleur (1995) suggested that when subjects are asked to explain their attitudes, they focus on those thoughts that are the most accessible, plausible, and easy to verbalize (e.g., "I like milk mostly because it is good for me"). Although these reasons may not correspond closely to the underlying attitudes, people assume that the reasons they report do reflect their feelings, and modify their attitudes or behaviors, at least temporarily, in the direction of those reasons. This weakens the correlation between one's initial attitude and subsequent attitudes or behavior. Apparently, then, people's insight into the real reasons or thoughts that underlie their attitudes is often flawed.

Our studies, using the circle-a-thought task described earlier, also require subjects to introspect into the bases for their attitude. Rather than analyzing reasons, however, subjects in this task focus their attention on their original cognitive responses. How much insight do subjects have into the significance of their cognitive responses? Are they able to gauge the relevance of their thoughts to their attitudes? This study explored these questions. If, indeed, subjects are able to identify their most important thought among their many listed thoughts, that could greatly simplify existing procedures for using cognitive responses to test the persuasiveness of ads.

Self-Scoring Study 1: Using Circled Thoughts to Predict Attitudes

This exploratory experiment focused on subjects' thoughts and attitudes to a fictitious campus restaurant for which they had seen a print ad. The correlations between subjects' attitudes and (a) their overall thought list, and (b) their circled thought were examined.

Method

Ninety-two subjects from an introductory advertising class viewed a set of 10 print ads in which the target ad for a restaurant appeared in the third position. Subjects were told that a local advertising agency was copy testing these mock-up ads before placing them in student publications. After viewing the ads, subjects were instructed to list their thoughts and feelings toward the restaurant according to standard directions. Subjects also responded to the two forms of directive thought-listing instructions (see earlier descriptions) in counterbalanced order. These instructions were adapted to be relevant to restaurants.

Next, subjects rated each of their thoughts on the +2 to –2 favorability scale and indicated their attitudes according to three semantic differential scales (anchored by *bad–good*, *undesirable–desirable*, and *unfavorable–favorable*). Finally, subjects responded to the "circle-a-thought" instructions, which read:

> You have just finished rating your attitude toward Brady's restaurant. We are now interested in which one of the thoughts you listed *contributed the most* to your attitude. Please look back at your three thought-box sheets and circle the ONE thought that you feel was most important in determining your attitude toward Brady's.

It is important to note that subjects did not seem to have any difficulty with this task and were readily able to circle a thought.

Results and Discussion

Three different thought favorability indices were calculated for each subject: (a) the mean favorability of subjects' initial thoughts, elicited from the general thought-listing instructions; (b) the mean favorability of subjects' thoughts from the directive instructions only; and (c) the mean favorability of all thoughts, combining those from the general and the directive thought-listing instructions. Each of these thought favorability indices, as well as the favorability of each subject's circled thought, was then correlated with subjects' attitudes toward the restaurant to determine the degree to which each thought measure corresponded with persuasion.

Interestingly, the favorability of the circled thought selected by subjects correlated with attitudes a little more strongly ($r = .74$) than the mean favorability index based on the initial thought list ($r = .69$, difference is *ns*) or directive-only thought list ($r = .61$, difference is *ns*). In addition, the favorability of the circled thought correlated just as strongly with attitude as did the mean favorability index for all thoughts ($r = .74$), which was based on as many as 12 thoughts. This suggests that subjects do have some insight into the bases of their attitudes, at least insofar as being able to discern the significance of their listed thoughts.

The fact that the cognitive response–attitude correlation for the circled thought was as high as those for the multiple-thought indices suggests some interesting possibilities for copy testing. Presently, thought indices based on multiple thoughts are standardly used in a variety of consumer research tests, yet our preliminary results showed that a single circled thought can perform just as well as multiple thoughts in predicting persuasion in this context. Importantly, this was true despite the fact that the other thought indices were based on a much greater number of thoughts and therefore could be expected to be more reliable as well as more representative of the multiple beliefs and attributes underlying attitudes. If researchers could rely on the introspective ability of subjects to identify their most relevant thoughts, they might eliminate the need to code and compile several thoughts for predicting attitudes.

Self-Scoring Study 2: Using Circled Thoughts to Predict Attitude at a Delay

The potential of this new self-scoring, circle-a-thought technique for predicting attitudes was examined in a second, two-session study using the same target advertisement.

Method

Seventy-seven subjects from an introductory advertising course participated in this study. For this experiment, however, attitudes were measured not only during the first session (as described earlier) but also at a week's delay.

During the first session, subjects listed their thoughts toward the restaurant ad, reported their attitudes toward the restaurant along three semantic differential scales (anchored by *good–bad*, *desirable–undesirable*, and *favorable–unfavorable*), and then circled the one thought that contributed the most to their attitudes. Subjects returned to the lab a week later and their attitudes were measured again along the three semantic differential scales.

Results and Discussion

The favorability of the circled thought again correlated with attitudes as strongly as did the three thought favorability indices, as shown in Table 9.3. Interestingly, the correlations for thoughts and attitudes were consistently higher for the second (delayed) attitude measure, although the differences were not always significant. Perhaps the extra processing of the thoughts and the act of circling the "thought that contributed the most" during the first session made that thought more salient to subjects when reporting their attitudes at a week's delay. That is, rather than simply retrieving their initial attitude from the earlier session, subjects might have been guided by the salience of the circled thought at a delay in formulating a new attitude at that time.

Indeed, the salience of the circled thought could also be a factor in the high correlations between circled thought favorability and attitudes during the first session. Because subjects circled their thought immediately after reporting their attitude (and rating the favorability of each thought), their attitudes would likely still be salient at the time of the circle-a-thought task. In this context, with the thought favorability ratings in front of them on the thought-listing sheets, subjects may have been guided in their selection of the circled thought

TABLE 9.3
Correlations Between the Favorability of Listed Thought Indices
and Subsequent Attitude Measures in the Second Circle-a-Thought Study

	Attitude Time 1	Attitude Time 2
General Thought Index (Thoughts 1–6 only)	.54 (n = 81)	.64 (n = 81)
Directive Thought Index (Thoughts 7–12 only)[**]	.43 (n = 71)	.68 (n = 71)
Overall Thought Index[*] (Thoughts 1–12)	.51 (n = 81)	.67 (n = 81)
Circled Thought[*] (Subjects selected one thought)	.52 (n = 81)	.67 (n = 81)

Note. Subjects who did not provide any thoughts for a given thought type were not included in the relevant thought index analyses. Attitude Time 1 indicates attitude measured at the first session. Attitude Time 2 indicates attitude measured at a 1-week delay.

[*]Within subjects for this thought index, correlations for Attitude Time 1 and Attitude Time 2 differed at $p < .10$. [**]Within subjects for this thought index, correlations for Attitude Time 1 and Attitude Time 2 differed at $p < .05$.

by the consistency of the favorability ratings with their attitude rating. Further research, in which attitudes are measured separately, is needed to address this possibility.

Implications of the Self-Scoring Methodology

Results from the two studies utilizing the circle-a-thought methodology offer preliminary evidence that subjects are able to discern which cognitive responses played an important role in their attitude formation. This new circle-a-thought technique holds both methodological and theoretical relevance for the evaluation of advertisements in the cognitive response paradigm. For methodological purposes in copy testing, this single-thought identification may offer a viable alternative to scoring and compiling several thoughts. Consumers (or at least those under the conditions we tested) could readily and accurately judge the relevance of their thoughts to their attitudes. Therefore, in copy testing, advertisers could utilize the circled thought as a simple tool to evaluate the persuasiveness of the ad over the long term. In addition, it might be of interest to examine the content of subjects' circled thoughts systematically to discern what criteria distinguish them from other thoughts.

It is also interesting to note that in each circle-a-thought study, the thought that subjects circled appeared most often in the first or second position on the initial thought-listing form (almost 50% of the thoughts selected as most important were the first or second thought). This seems to imply that the very first thoughts subjects list may be their most important for attitude formation. Again, rather than compiling several thoughts for predicting ad persuasion, results of these preliminary studies suggest that copy test researchers could potentially rely on the content of the first few thoughts. Further research is needed to determine the reliability of this order effect and the processes underlying it.

On a theoretical level, we find evidence that people seem to have better access to the bases of their attitudes than might have been thought. Although studies using "reasons analysis" procedures have shown that people lack insight into the factors underlying their attitudes (e.g., Wilson & Dunn, 1986; Wilson et al., 1989), subjects in our studies appeared to have some insight into the reasons for their attitudes, at least insofar as gauging the relevance of their listed thoughts to their attitudes. The favorability of the thought circled as being the most important in determining their attitudes correlated at least as highly, if not more so, with attitude as did more conventional thought-favorability indices based on multiple thoughts.

The circle-a-thought task we employed is different from any other self-scoring method used to date in cognitive response research. The preliminary results obtained here suggest a broader potential for utilizing self-scoring methods in which subjects' interpretations and insights into their thoughts are used, along with the thoughts themselves, as evidence in testing the effectiveness of advertisements.

SUMMARY AND CONCLUSIONS

The results reported here are part of a program of research that examines the processes of attitude formation through cognitive response measures. The most recent studies have investigated new cognitive response techniques involving (a) directive thought elicitation and (b) self-scoring circle-a-thought tasks. The application of these methodologies in cognitive response research has potential for creating more effective and efficient methods to gauge advertising persuasiveness.

In addition, results from these techniques and examination of personality factors and product factors have contributed to a conceptual framework for understanding antecedents of attitude formation. Future research could consider the roles of self-monitoring and product differences in the ability to discern the significance of one's listed thoughts, and could apply this knowledge to copy testing situations. For example, would low self-monitors (who seem to have better access to their attitudes) have better insight than high self-monitors into the bases of their attitudes, using the circle-a-thought task? Would the types of thoughts circled differ for high versus low self-monitors? What types of thoughts would be circled the most for different types of products? By examining such issues, we can gain a better understanding of the processes involved in attitude formation and utilize the most efficient and effective methods for predicting advertising effectiveness.

ACKNOWLEDGMENTS

We gratefully acknowledge the support of the James Webb Young Fund, Department of Advertising, University of Illinois. Thanks are also due to Linnea Wentzel and Shannon Reese for their assistance in data collection and coding. We wish to thank Timothy C. Brock, Curt Haugtvedt, Tom O'Guinn, and Bill Wells for helpful comments on this research.

REFERENCES

Batra, R., & Ray, M. L. (1986). Affective responses mediating acceptance of advertising. *Journal of Consumer Research, 13*(2), 234–249.

Brannon, L. A., & Brock, T. C. (1994). Test of schema correspondence theory of persuasion: Effects of matching an appeal to actual, ideal, and product "selves." In E. M. Clark, T. C. Brock, & D. W. Steward (Eds.), *Attention, attitude, and affect in response to advertising* (pp. 169–188). Hillsdale, NJ: Lawrence Erlbaum Associates.

Cacioppo, J. T., & Petty, R. E. (1981). Social psychological procedures for cognitive response assessment: The thought-listing technique. In T. Merluzzi, C. Glass, & M. Genest (Eds.), *Cognitive assessment* (pp. 309–342). New York: Guilford.

Chattopadhyay, A., & Alba, J. W. (1988). The situational importance of recall and inference in consumer decision making. *Journal of Consumer Research*, 15(1), 1–12.

Ericsson, K. A., & Simon, H. A. (1980). Verbal reports as data. *Psychological Review*, 87(3), 215–251.

Ericsson, K. A., & Simon, H. A. (1984). *Protocol analysis: Verbal reports as data*. Cambridge, MA: MIT Press.

Fazio, R. H., Chen, J., McDonel, E., & Sherman, S. J. (1982). Attitude accessibility, attitude–behavior consistency, and the strength of the object-evaluation association. *Journal of Experimental Social Psychology*, 18, 339–357.

Johar, J. S., & Sirgy, M. J. (1991). Value-expressive versus utilitarian advertising appeals: When and why to use which appeal. *Journal of Advertising*, 20, 23–33.

Kardes, F. R., Sanbonmatsu, D. M., Voss, R. T., & Fazio, R. H. (1986). Self-monitoring and attitude accessibility. *Personality and Social Psychology Bulletin*, 12, 468–474.

Katz, D. (1960). The functional approach to the study of attitudes. *Public Opinion Quarterly*, 24(2), 163–204.

Kelman, H. C. (1958). Compliance, identification, and internalization: Three processes of attitude change. *Journal of Conflict Resolution*, 2, 51–60.

Kelman, H. C. (1961). Processes of opinion change. *Public Opinion Quarterly*, 25, 57–78.

Leavitt, C., Waddell, C., & Wells, W. (1970). Improving day-after recall techniques. *Journal of Advertising Research*, 10(3), 13–17.

Lutz, J., & MacKenzie, S. B. (1982). Construction of a diagnostic cognitive response model for use in commercial pretesting. In M. J. Naples & J. S. Chasin (Eds.), *Straight talk about attitude research* (pp. 145–156). Chicago: American Marketing Association.

McDonald, C. (1993, September–October). Point of view: The key is to understand consumer response. *Journal of Advertising Research*, 63–69.

Nisbett, R. E., & Wilson, T. D. (1977). Telling more than we know: Verbal reports on mental processes. *Psychological Review*, 84, 231–259.

Petty, R. E., Ostrom, M., & Brock, T. C. (1981). *Cognitive responses in persuasion*. Hillsdale, NJ: Lawrence Erlbaum Associates.

Sawyer, A., & Ward, S. (1979). Carry-over effects in advertising communication. *Research in Marketing*, 2, 259–314.

Shavitt, S. (1989). Operationalizing functional theories of attitude. In A. R. Pratkanis, S. J. Breckler, & A. G. Greenwald (Eds.), *Attitude structure and function* (pp. 311–337). Hillsdale, NJ: Lawrence Erlbaum Associates.

Shavitt, S. (1990). The role of attitude objects in attitude functions. *Journal of Experimental Social Psychology*, 26, 124–148.

Shavitt, S., & Brock, T. C. (1986). Self-relevant responses in commercial persuasion: Field and experimental tests. In K. Sentis & J. Olson (Eds.), *Advertising and consumer psychology* (Vol. 3, pp. 149–171). New York: Praeger.

Shavitt, S., & Brock, T. C. (1990). Delayed recall of copytest responses: The temporal stability of listed thoughts. *Journal of Advertising*, 19(4), 6–17.

Shavitt, S., & Fazio, R. H. (1991). Effects of attribute salience on the consistency between attitudes and behavior predictions. *Personality and Social Psychology Bulletin*, 17, 507–516.

Shavitt, S., Lowrey, T. M., & Han, S. (1992). Attitude functions in advertising: The interactive role of products and self-monitoring. *Journal of Consumer Psychology*, 1(4), 337–364.

Smith, M. B., Bruner, J. S., & White, R. W. (1956). *Opinions and personality*. New York: Wiley.

Snyder, M. (1974). Self-monitoring of expressive behavior. *Journal of Personality and Social Psychology*, 30, 526–537.

Snyder, M. (1987). *Public appearances, private realities: The psychology of self-monitoring.* New York: Freeman.

Snyder, M., & DeBono, K. G. (1985). Appeals to image and claims about quality: Understanding the psychology of advertising. *Journal of Personality and Social Psychology, 49,* 586–597.

Snyder, M., & Tanke, E. D. (1976). Behavior and attitude: Some people are more consistent than others. *Journal of Personality, 44,* 510–517.

Wansink, B., Ray, M., & Batra, R. (1994). Increasing cognitive response sensitivity. *Journal of Advertising, 23*(2), 65–75.

Wilson, T. D., & Dunn, D. S. (1986). Effects of introspection on attitude–behavior consistency: Analyzing reasons versus focusing on feelings. *Journal of Experimental Social Psychology, 22,* 249–263.

Wilson, T. D., Dunn, D. S., Kraft, D., & Lisle, D. J. (1989). Introspection, attitude change, and attitude–behavior consistency: The disruptive effects of explaining why we feel the way we do. In L. Berkowitz (Ed.), *Advances in Experimental Social Psychology* (Vol. 22, pp. 287–343). San Diego, CA: Academic Press.

Wilson, T. D., & LaFleur, S. J. (1995). Knowing what you'll do: Effects of analyzing reasons on self-prediction. *Journal of Personality and Social Psychology, 68*(1), 21–35.

Wright, P. (1980). Message-evoked thoughts: Persuasion research using thought verbalizations. *Journal of Consumer Research, 7,* 151–175.

Wright, P., & Rip, P. (1980). Retrospective reports on consumer decision processes. In J. Olson (Ed.), *Advances in consumer research* (Vol. 7, pp. 146–147). Ann Arbor, MI: Association for Consumer Research.

10

Extensions of the Cognitive Response Approach to Predicting Postadvertisement Attitudes

Debra L. Stephens
Villanova University

J. Edward Russo
Cornell University

Postexposure attitudes are widely used measures of advertisement effectiveness, and attempts to explain them have played an important role in research on advertising.[1] The most common framework for explaining these attitudes focuses on an individual's internal responses during exposure to an ad (e.g., MacInnis & Jaworski, 1989). We adopt this framework in its broadest sense—for instance, including emotional as well as cognitive responses.

This chapter reports an initial attempt to supplement current cognitive response methods. Our goal is purely methodological. We want to improve the information base (of internal responses) that supports the subsequent explanation of postexposure attitudes. Our focus is the relative efficacy of different techniques for revealing information about internal responses, where efficacy will be assessed by the ability to predict postexposure attitudes.

Our effort to extend and refine the cognitive response approach is two-pronged. First, we consider how to extract more information from the standard retrospective verbal report or thought listing. Second, we test two techniques

---

[1] We would have preferred to assess ad effectiveness with a behavioral measure like brand choice, but this proved impractical (although see, e.g., Wansink & Ray, chap. 20, this volume). Also, we acknowledge long-standing disagreements over the definition and nature of attitudes, such as whether they are always learned (or whether some might have a genetic component), and for how long they endure. (For an authoritative discussion, see Eagly & Chaiken, 1993; see also Krosnick, Boninger, Chuang, Berent, & Carnot, 1993). In addition, like all measurement, the explicit assessment of an attitude risks reactivity, for instance by encouraging subjects to formulate or elaborate their reasons for an attitude (e.g., see Wilson & Hodges, 1992). We adopt the position that, despite these legitimate concerns, for our purposes attitudes are efficient and sufficiently valid measures of the overall evaluative response to an advertisement.

for extending the database itself, namely ad-specific emotional responses and a tactic for increasing the completeness of the retrospective report.

COGNITIVE RESPONSES

The cognitive response framework was developed as part of the research on persuasion in social psychology (Brock, 1967; Greenwald, 1968; see also Petty, Ostrom, & Brock, 1981). This work has two distinct streams, cognitive response analysis and cognitive response theory (see Fiske & Taylor, 1991). The former is a technique to measure the internal responses that mediate attitude formation or change. The latter posits specific mediating relations between particular internal responses and resultant attitudes. The work reported here focuses on cognitive response analysis. In keeping with our limited goal, we establish the relative efficacy of different responses in predicting postexposure attitudes. It is our hope that these results may stimulate and provide material for the construction of theory-based explanations of attitude formation and change.

Application of the cognitive response approach to advertising was successful from the beginning. All three internal responses coded from a thought listing had significant predictive impact on postexposure attitude: agreement with message content, or support argument; disagreement or counterargument; and critical reaction to the source of the message, or source derogation (Wright, 1973). Advertising researchers then expanded this taxonomy by incorporating additional internal responses pertinent to advertisements. When investigators discovered that attitude toward the ad itself is an important predictor of brand attitude (Holbrook, 1978; Mitchell & Olson, 1981), they launched a search for cognitive responses that directly mediate ad attitude (e.g., Lutz & MacKenzie, 1982; Lutz, MacKenzie, & Belch, 1983; see MacKenzie & Lutz, 1989, for a review). For instance, Lutz and MacKenzie (1982) added categories for responses to ad execution (execution bolstering and derogation). Batra and Ray (1986) moved beyond "cognition" by adding positive affective responses, "moods and internal reactions evoked by the ad which are not evaluative of the ad execution itself" (p. 4). These two major extensions of the cognitive response taxonomy have contributed significantly to improving the prediction of brand attitude.

VALENCE AS A REFINEMENT

Although attitude is a ubiquitous construct, it lacks a generally agreed-on definition. There is, however, substantial agreement that attitude connotes an evaluation of the attitude object, even if only a valenced (positive, neutral, or negative) feeling (Churchill, 1987; Eagly & Chaiken, 1993). If attitude is a valenced construct, we might expect the valence of each statement in the retrospective verbal report to contribute to the prediction of overall brand attitude. This is not a new idea. Several investigators have coded statements in terms of "polarity," defined as "the degree to which the response is in favor of or opposed to the referent (attitude object)" (Cacioppo & Petty, 1981, p. 319); and the "favorableness" of statements has been shown to be related to the overall evaluation of a communication (e.g., Greenwald, 1968; Wright, 1974; see also Nelson, Shavitt, Schennum, & Barkmeier, chap. 9, this volume).

Although past uses of valenced predictors have been confined to rational arguments (the type of message typically used in social psychology), there is good reason to expect that the valence of ad-evoked reactions will predict the resultant attitude. TV commercials in particular seem to encourage direct affective responses as opposed to extensive cognitive elaboration. They usually contain evocative visual scenes, music, or moving vignettes in addition to, and often instead of, rational arguments (Calder & Gruder, 1989). Finally, valence already plays a prominent role in the most common cognitive response taxonomies. Arguments are either support (positive) or counter (negative); and execution-related responses either bolster (positive) or derogate (negative). The question that we raise is whether valence should be made explicit and then treated in a more sensitive way, specifically by assessing its intensity as well as direction. Any measurement of valence's intensity would refine the most common cognitive response taxonomies.

DIRECT VERSUS INTENDED VALENCE

We can distinguish between two ways of defining and, therefore, measuring the valence of any particular response. The most obvious is subjects' perceptions of their internal responses. We call this *direct valence*. It differs from the valence implicit in the cognitive response framework. The latter is defined in terms of the impact of the advertiser's intent. Hence we call it *intended valence*.[2]

An example may help clarify the distinction between direct and intended valence. One of the commercials we tested advertises a restaurant (Del Taco) as a different place to go for a weekday lunch. It begins with clonelike office workers leaving for the lunch place where they always eat. It then portrays Del Taco's novel menu and fun atmosphere. Subjects' responses to this ad included "sounds like my [dull] lunches" and "I am into too many ruts." From each subject's perspective at the time, these statements were negative. Consequently, they would be assigned a negative direct valence. In the cognitive response

---

[2]The notion of an intended response plays a critical role in reader response theory, which explicitly deals with the relation between a writer's intended response and a reader's actual response (Davis & Schleifer, 1989; Tompkins, 1980). This theory of literary criticism has been applied to advertising, but without the empirical base typical of studies in the cognitive response framework (e.g., see Scott, 1992).

framework, however, they are support arguments indicating agreement with the advertising message. Thus, their intended valence is positive.

Whether direct or intended valence better predicts attitudes requires an empirical answer. On the one hand, a strong argument can be made for intended valence because it captures part of the intended effect. In this example, the negative image that begins the ad and elicits the responses quoted is transformed by later ad elements into a reason for eating at the advertised restaurant. On the other hand, the intended transformation of direct valence by the subsequent elements of the ad may not always succeed, or may do so only partially. Even if the transformation does occur, there may still be some residual effect of the direct valence. Thus, there is no conclusive argument a priori to hypothesize that either type of valence will better predict attitudes.

AUGMENTATION OF VERBAL REPORTS BY AD-SPECIFIC INTERNAL RESPONSES

Among the intended responses to many ads are ad-specific internal responses. For example, internal responses of warmth and pride are presumably among the intended responses to the Rainer Bank commercial described in Table 10.1. Past advertising researchers have assessed emotion as a general affective response (e.g., the warmth measure of Aaker, Stayman, & Hagerty, 1986) or developed typologies of emotional responses to ads (e.g., Batra & Holbrook, 1990; Batra

TABLE 10.1
Synopsis of a Representative Advertisement: Rainer Bank

A Black boy (3 years old) is building structures out of toy blocks, sticks, and so on, as his father watches attentively. The little boy explains proudly, "It's a skyscraper, daddy." "Yes it is, son," the delighted father replies.

The same boy (10 years old) is constructing a tree house in his backyard. His father calls lovingly, "Kenny, it's time for supper." The boy keeps banging nails, happily engrossed in his work/play.

The boy is now a college student reading a book (with an intent but happy facial expression) while serving as a short-order cook in a small restaurant. A waitress interrupts his reading with an order. She is impatient but understanding.

The same young man, now an architect, visits a bank with his plans for a building. He walks through the door and says "thank you" as someone holds it open for him. He meets with a young, pleasant White loan officer, and unfurls a set of plans on a table. The plans are for a warehouse for which the young Black architect is seeking financing. The voice-over says that the young man has a "good idea that needed a little help."

The man/architect returning to the bank encounters the same officer in the lobby. "I just called your office," the banker says. "You got the loan!" "Great," says the man/architect, with a direct gaze and long handshake.

Father (obviously older, with some gray hair) and son walk past a construction project. "It's only two stories, dad; but it's a beginning." "Son, it looks like a skyscraper to me."

Bank logo is shown with announcer extolling, "If you've got a goal, we'll help you get there."

& Ray, 1986; Edell & Burke, 1987; Holbrook & Westwood, 1989). Our belief that intensities of intended, ad-specific internal responses may contribute to the prediction of attitudes requires a different approach. Rather than developing a universal typology of internal responses that applies to all ads, we identify those responses specific to each ad.

EXPERIMENTS 1 AND 2

Rationale

In the two studies described in the following, the cognitive response framework and the additional constructs of intended valence and direct valence provide the basis for two coding schemes designed to extract information from postexposure verbal reports. We compare the power of these two coding schemes to predict brand attitude, and also of ad attitude because of the latter's demonstrated relevance (e.g., Batra & Stephens, 1987). Experiment 2 is essentially a replication of Experiment 1. Although their different ads and subjects require separate reporting of results, the findings should be considered as a whole.

METHOD OF EXPERIMENT 1

Stimuli

The stimuli were TV commercials for regional brands not distributed in the subjects' residential area. We chose unfamiliar brands to observe each commercial's impact on attitudes undiluted by prior brand knowledge. The ads were selected from reels of Ad Age and Clio award winners, and were pretested for homogeneity of perceived professional quality.

Fifty-two individuals from our subject population rated a sample of ads on two measures of professional quality: overall impact and professionalism. Averaging over the two 1-to-7 scales, the median rating of the six ads was 5.5 (range 5.0–6.0). The same 52 pretest subjects described in writing each of the emotions they felt during the ad. The three most frequently listed were used as target feelings. We also selected as a distractor one feeling that none of the pretest subjects had listed and that seemed unrelated to the ad. In the experiment, the intensity of arousal of both the target and distractor feelings was measured as described in the following.

Subjects

Eighty-one undergraduate students drawn from two classes in a large Eastern university served as subjects. The experiment was conducted during one class period.

Procedure

Participants were instructed to watch the commercials as people naturally do at home, in a relaxed, nonanalytical manner. Two practice ads were followed by four test ads. All analyses are based on the test ads only. Immediately after each ad, we went through the following procedure:

1. Verbal report—Subjects were instructed, "Write down whatever went through your mind while you were watching the ad."

2. Intensity of internal reactions—Intensity of three internal reactions evoked by the ad and one distractor feeling, were measured by unipolar scales anchored at 1 (*not at all*) and 7 (*very strongly*). The question "How strongly are you experiencing the following feelings?" preceded the four scales. For half of the subjects, intensity ratings were collected prior to the written report.

3. Brand attitude—Three 1-to-7 semantic differential scales were used: *good–bad, like–dislike,* and *positive–negative.* The measure of brand attitude used in all analyses was the mean rating on these three scales.

4. Ad attitude—The following four 1-to-7 scales were employed: *like–dislike, good–bad, interesting–uninteresting,* and *not irritating–irritating.* Ad attitude was the mean of these four responses. At the end of the session, we measured brand familiarity and noted the age and gender of the subject.

METHOD OF EXPERIMENT 2

The second experiment replicated the first, using the same design and procedure but increasing the number of test ads to six.[3] The pretest used 37 subjects, whereas the experiment proper had 48 participants. As in Experiment 1, the pretest subjects rated a sample of Ad Age and Clio award winners on professional quality. Averaging over the two scales described earlier, the median rating of the six experimental ads was 5.9 (range 5.0–6.0).

Coding of the Verbal Reports

One of the authors segmented the verbal reports into the smallest coherent phrases. Then two judges, working independently and uninformed about the purpose of the study, coded each statement using the two coding schemes described later. A judge used a given scheme to code all statements before moving on to the next one.

---

[3]Two of these six were also used in Experiment 1. The main constraint on ad selection was homogeneity of perceived quality. The ads for Experiment 2 were selected from a larger pool, and it was coincidental that two ads from Experiment 1 were chosen again.

The cognitive response coding scheme was a modification of Batra and Ray's (1986) taxonomy. Each statement was assigned to one of 14 categories: support argument and counterargument; execution bolstering, execution discounting, execution curiosity, execution nonreaction, and execution neutral; emotion positive and emotion negative; personal association positive, personal association neutral, and personal association negative; ad replay; and other.

The coders assigned a valence to each statement on a 7-point scale anchored at −3 (*very negative*) and +3 (*very positive*). In making these (direct) valence judgments, the coders were instructed to try to take the perspective of the subject, and assign a number on the basis of how it would feel to utter the given phrase. These instructions treated each recalled response separately and were designed to assess direct valence rather than any subsequent transformed valence's impact on attitudes.

Table 10.2 contains a sample of verbal responses to the commercial described in Table 10.1, with accompanying codes from the two coding schemes. To determine the reliability of each coding scheme, we compared the two coders' classifications and observed the following interrater agreements for Experiments 1 and 2, respectively: cognitive responses, 64% and 69%; valence (scale values exactly equal), 59% and 48%; and valence (scale values within 1 unit), 93% and 94%. The reliabilities for cognitive responses are lower than those in many studies. For instance, Chattopadhyay and Basu (1990) reported a 95% agreement between coders. However, we used 14 categories rather than the standard six or seven or the four used by Chattopadhyay and Basu. Collapsing to seven categories increased our reliabilities but not their predictive power. Therefore, we report results using all 14 categories.

Pretest data indicated that the brands in the test ads would be unfamiliar to the vast majority of our subjects. For Experiment 1, the familiarity question revealed that in 45 of 324 cases (81 subjects × 4 ads), the viewer was familiar with the brand; that is the viewer had heard about it prior to the experiment.

TABLE 10.2
Sample Responses and Codes for the Rainer Bank Commercial

	Coding Scheme	
Sample Statement	*Cognitive Response*	*Valence*
I thought of my son's tree house.	Personal association, positive	+2
I was thinking how a Black man was the aspiring architect. How appropriate.	Execution bolstering	+2
Feeling that I'm getting respect and help.	Support argument	+1
It made me sad	Emotion, negative	−2
How friendly are banks really?	Counterargument	−1
Don't trivialize working your way through school like that.	Execution discounting	−2

Of the 288 retrospective reports in Experiment 2 (48 subjects × 6 ads), 125 were from subjects familiar with the advertised brand. Because familiarity should reduce the impact of an ad exposure on brand attitude (e.g., Machleit & Wilson, 1988) and thereby blur our comparisons among different predictive models, we eliminated these 170 cases (28%) from all analyses.

RESULTS

Validity Checks

We checked whether the three target emotions were indeed given higher intensity ratings than the distractor. For each of the 10 test ads (four in Experiment 1 and six in Experiment 2), a one-way analysis of variance (ANOVA) was performed with rated intensity as the dependent variable and the four emotions as the independent variable. A Tukey studentized range test was used to compare the distractor to each target feeling. The distractor was rated significantly lower than all target emotions ($p < .05$) with two exceptions. For one ad, the distractor was rated lower than all target emotions, but not significantly so. For another ad, the distractor was rated higher than one of the three target emotions, again not significantly so.

We also checked whether the collection order of the retrospective verbal report and the emotional intensity ratings affected either the attitudes or the emotional responses themselves. For the 10 ads and for each of the four emotions and two attitudes, a t test was performed comparing subjects who recorded emotional intensity ratings first and verbal reports second with individuals performing these tasks in the reverse order. Only 3 unrelated tests out of 60 yielded a significant difference at $p < .05$, a rate no different from the expected proportion of false alarms. Thus, the order of retrospective report and emotional intensities was ignored in all further analyses.

Predicting Ad and Brand Attitudes
from Retrospective Reports Alone

Table 10.3 displays the adjusted R^2s for the OLS regressions of ad and brand attitude on each coding scheme. These regressions treat each ad × subject combination as an independent case. We chose not to analyze these data in a repeated measures design, although this would have removed any systematic effects of subject and increased our statistical power. Instead, we followed a rather strict interpretation of the cognitive response framework: The specific internal responses should produce (and, therefore, predict) the observed attitudes, completely capturing any systematic effects of subject and ad.

TABLE 10.3
Adjusted R^2s of Models Predicting Postexposure Attitudes

Coding Scheme	Attitude Toward the Ad		Attitude Toward the Brand	
	Exp. 1	Exp. 2	Exp. 1	Exp. 2
Cognitive responses	.35	.28	.26	.28
Intended valence	.30	.24	.22	.19
Valence	.32	.34	.23	.25
Valence (3 levels)	.24	.32	.17	.24

Cognitive Responses

For Experiment 1 the full 14-predictor cognitive response model yielded R^2s of .35 and .26 for ad and brand attitude, respectively (for brevity we drop the qualifier "adjusted"; all reported R^2s are adjusted for the number of parameters in the model). For Experiment 2, the corresponding R^2s are 0.28 and 0.28.

Valence

The (direct) valence factor was modeled as six dummy variables, with zero valence corresponding to the null value. Thus, we did not presume a linear relation between the intensity of valence and its impact on attitude, but permitted full flexibility in this relation. For Experiment 1, the R^2s for ad and brand attitude are .32 and .23, respectively; the corresponding values for Experiment 2 are .34 and .25. Differences between the R^2s of the cognitive response and valence models were tested for statistical significance using the J statistic of Davidson and MacKinnon (1981).[4] All four comparisons (two experiments and two attitudes) showed no significant difference. That is, in each case the estimate of the valence model had a beta coefficient significantly different from zero ($p < .01$) when added to the cognitive response model, and the reverse was also true. If one viewed the cognitive response and valence models as competitors (which we do not), these results yield a tie. Neither is reliably superior to the other. The conclusion that we draw, however, is that the single attribute of valence can extract as much predictive value from a retrospective verbal report as a much larger and more complex cognitive response scheme.

---

[4]This test is conducted as follows. First, one of the two models to be compared is estimated. That estimate is then included as a predictor in the other model. The J test is essentially a t test of the significance of the null hypothesis that the beta coefficient for that predictor equals zero. If this hypothesis can be rejected, the first model (the one that was estimated and whose estimates are included in the other model) must be accepted and the second model is rejected. As Davidson and MacKinnon (1981) pointed out, however, "It is conceivable that both hypotheses may be rejected or that neither may be rejected" (p. 783). For this reason, we performed all estimations bidirectionally.

Does intended valence, the version implicit in the cognitive response framework, account for a large portion of that model's predictive ability? To answer this question the 14 cognitive response categories were aggregated into three valences: support arguments, execution bolstering, positive emotions, and positive personal associations are positive; counterarguments, execution discounting, negative emotions, and negative personal associations are negative; and the other six statements are neutral.

A two-parameter model with neutral valence as the null level was used to predict ad and brand attitude. As reported in Table 10.3, for Experiment 1 the R^2 is .30 for ad attitude and .22 for brand attitude. For Experiment 2, the corresponding values are .24 and .19. Using partial F tests, we found that all four intended valence models have lower R^2s than their corresponding full cognitive response models. For three models, $p < .05$; ad attitude for Experiment 2 yields only a marginally significant effect, $p < .10$. Although the loss of predictive power is statistically reliable, it is not large. A comparison of the proportion of variance accounted for by the full model (14 parameters) and by the reduced model (2 parameters) shows that the latter accounts for about 72% of the former. The exact values are: for Experiment 1, 80% for ad attitude and 77% for brand attitude, and for Experiment 2, 73% (ad) and 57% (brand). Thus, by itself the valence of recalled internal responses accounts for most of the predictive power in the cognitive response framework.

Direct Versus Indirect Valence

We now turn to the question posed earlier: Which is superior in predicting attitudes, direct or intended valence? To answer this question we constructed a comparable three-category (two-parameter) model of direct valence by ignoring all distinctions in the magnitude of positive and negative valence. The R^2s of this model are .24 and .17 for ad and brand attitude, respectively, in Experiment 1; and .32 and .24 for the same attitudes in Experiment 2. When compared to the corresponding values for intended valence, the results are mixed. J tests with $p = .05$ indicate that for Experiment 1, the intended valence model should be accepted and the direct valence model rejected for both ad and brand attitude. The reverse is true for Experiment 2. The direct valence model is accepted for both attitudes, and the intended valence model rejected.

Because we could find no compelling reason for this pattern, we conclude only that both types of valence capture valuable predictive power. We note, however, that Experiments 1 and 2 were not designed to discriminate between these two closely related constructs. A conclusive comparison would require an adequate sample of ads that attempt to transform direct to intended valence. We did not narrow our pool of ads by adopting this very restrictive selection criterion.

Emotional Intensity

We measured the intensity of several ad-specific emotions in an attempt to augment the power of the recalled internal responses to predict ad and brand attitude. To test whether these ratings of emotions contributed significantly, we added them to the cognitive response model and the (direct) valence model. Twelve predictors (three internal reactions for each of four ads) were created for Experiment 1, and 18 (three internal reactions for each of six ads) for Experiment 2.

The results, reported in Table 10.4, show a uniformly large increase in R^2 caused by the addition of the feeling scales. For Experiment 1, when the 12 predictors are added to the 14-predictor cognitive response model, the R^2 for ad attitude increases from .35 to .59, whereas that for brand attitude rises from .26 to .46. The pattern is similar for Experiment 2: R^2 for ad attitude increases from .28 to .62, and R^2 for brand attitude rises from .28 to .55.

The results are similar for the valence model. In Experiment 1, the addition of the 12 feeling scales increases the R^2 for ad attitude from .32 to .59 and the R^2 for brand attitude from .23 to .46. For Experiment 2, the 18 emotions increased R^2 from .34 to .62 for ad attitude, and from .25 to .50 for brand attitude. It hardly needs to be added that all eight of these shifts in R^2 are statistically significant.

Adding Attitude Toward the Ad as a Predictor

We also consider the value of ad attitude as a predictor of brand attitude (e.g., Gardner, 1985; MacKenzie, Lutz, & Belch, 1986; Mitchell & Olson, 1981). As reported in Table 10.4, ad attitude substantially increases the R^2 based on coded phrases and feeling intensities from around .50 to about .65. For each of the four cases (two experiments × two coding schemes) the partial F test is statistically significant.

TABLE 10.4
Adjusted R^2s of Models Containing Emotional Intensity

| Model | Attitude Toward the Advertisement | | | |
| | Cognitive response | | Coding scheme Valence | |
	Exp. 1	Exp. 2	Exp. 1	Exp. 2
Coded phrases only	.35	.28	.32	.34
Add emotional intensities	.59	.62	.59	.62
	Attitude Toward the Brand			
Coded phrases only	.26	.28	.23	.25
Add emotional intensities	.46	.55	.46	.50
Also add ad attitude	.64	.68	.65	.65

DISCUSSION

Our overall goal was to investigate ways to extend the ability of the cognitive response approach to predict postadvertisement attitudes. The results for ad-specific emotions are unambiguously positive and parallel other work finding that specific measures of internal responses add significantly to the predictive power of general verbal reports (e.g., Edell & Burke, 1987, 1989). What our experiments have not done is address the question of whether ad-specific emotions are any more effective than a set of universal feeling scales designed to apply to all ads. A first step in answering this important question has been pursued elsewhere (Russo & Stephens, 1990).

The results for more effective use of the statements in a retrospective verbal report are encouraging as well. The predictive ability of direct valence was about equal to that of a full cognitive response approach. Moreover, intended valence was shown to account for most of the effect of cognitive responses.

In Experiment 3 we continue to ask what can be done to improve the predictive power of a retrospective verbal report of the internal responses evoked during the viewing of a television commercial. We consider two possibilities: a better database of recalled responses and better coding of the responses that are available.

EXPERIMENT 3

Experiment 3 investigates two ways of improving the predictive value of retrospective verbal reports: prompting the recall of internal responses through a replay of the ad itself and having subjects code their own protocols for the valence of each statement or phrase. First, replaying the ad should improve the retrospective verbal report by providing a more effective prompt or cue to the memory trace of the original internal responses to the ad. This database may provide superior prediction of ad and brand attitude in two ways. A greater number of responses may be recalled, and each recalled response may be more valid (as reflected by its greater power to predict attitudes). One form of this prompting tactic has been used by Clucas (1993) in a practitioner context for many years.

Second, we explore the possibility that subjects may be more accurate than experimenters in coding their own reports for valence. Subjects may have access to private knowledge that allows them to clarify or interpret statements that others cannot. For instance, brief statements like "pun, ha, ha" or "different" can be ambiguous to experimenters even with the surrounding context of the ad and other verbalizations.

METHOD

Stimuli

Subjects watched 13 TV commercials, each for a different product or service. Four were practice and nine were test ads. As in the earlier experiments, all advertised goods were available only regionally.

In this study, however, we included ads that showed more variation in professional quality as perceived by our subject population. An initial set of 51 ads was divided into two groups, which were rated on professional quality by 28 and 31 pretest subjects, respectively. Averaging over the two 1-to-7 scales of overall impact and professionalism used earlier, as well as the scale "moving people to purchase," the median rating of the nine test ads was 4.0 (range 1.9–5.3). These nine ads were comprised of a single ad of low quality, and four each of medium and high quality. The quality mean and range for each block was: 1.9 for low quality, 3.1 for medium quality (range 2.8–3.2); and 5.1 for high quality (range: 4.7–5.3). The low- and medium-quality ads were nonaward winners, whereas the high quality ads had won awards. This increased diversity in quality should make whatever results emerge more generalizable. Recall that Experiments 1 and 2 used only high-quality, award-winning ads.

Subjects

The subjects were 10 undergraduate students enrolled in the adult education program of a large Eastern university. Their mean age was 29, nearer to that of the national population of television viewers than that of typical undergraduate samples, including those used in Experiments 1 and 2. Subjects participated individually in a single session lasting between 4 and 8 hours, with a break about every hour.[5]

Procedure

Subjects were instructed to watch the commercials as they naturally would at home, namely, in a relaxed nonanalytical manner. The nine test ads were preceded by four practice ads, none of which were used in any data analysis. The nine test ads were shown in two blocks, the first beginning with the one ad of low quality followed by the four medium-quality ads. The second block

---

[5]We explored two additional ways of analyzing verbal reports: advertiser intent and response origin (Greenwald, 1968). Low reliabilities and predictive power, coupled with the need for brevity, led us to omit from this chapter any discussion of those taxonomies. A complete report may be obtained from either of the authors. We mention these additional findings here because they contributed to subjects' unusually long participation time in the experiment, primarily through subject coding of response origin.

was comprised of the four high-quality ads. This order was chosen because any carryover effects of increasing quality were expected to be small relative to a mixed or decreasing order. In particular, if a high quality ad was followed by one of lower quality we expected subjects would notice the quality variable more than if the order were reversed.

Immediately after each ad had been shown, it was replayed in segments of 5- to 9-second duration. Subjects were instructed to write down, after each segment, everything that had come to mind when they first watched that portion of the ad. Thus, we obtained a retrospective verbal report prompted by a segmented replay of the ad.

After the first five test ads, brand and then ad attitude were measured with the same seven bipolar scales used in the first two studies. Similarly, attitudes for the last four ads were measured after they had all been shown.

Coding of the Verbal Protocols

After all retrospective protocols and attitude ratings had been collected, subjects were required to segment their protocols into individual phrases that reflected separate thoughts or feelings. The subject and the experimenter, working independently but simultaneously, then coded these phrases for (direct) valence. Subjects were trained to use private knowledge in making coding judgments through the presentation of sample responses and a commentary on the internal knowledge that might accompany them. The coding guidelines seemed quite simple for subjects to learn. It is worth noting that experimenter- and subject-codings of valence had opposite signs for only 22 of the 508 total phrases. Thus, any substantial difference in the predictive ability of subject versus experimenter coding cannot be attributed to such gross discrepancies as sign reversals. Furthermore, of the 508 phrases, 388 (76%) received experimenter and subject codings within one unit of each other; 201 of these were assigned precisely the same valence.

After the experimental session, two judges working independently coded each subject's reports for cognitive responses. The judges agreed on 77% of the cognitive response codings. The coders resolved any discrepancies through discussion.

RESULTS

The Value of Verbal Protocols

Our first question was whether an alternate method of collecting retrospective reports, namely prompting by a segmented replay of the ad, would yield a database with increased power to predict ad and brand attitudes. The R^2s for the cognitive response and (direct) valence models are shown in Table 10.5 for both ad and brand attitudes. All four values are far superior to those from Experiments 1 and 2 (Table 10.3). Thus, the answer to our first question is that the prompted replay technique does yield a superior verbal report. Note that this conclusion must be qualified by the use of different ads and different subjects in Experiment 3 compared to the two earlier studies. Although the results conform to our expectations, they must be considered tentative.

The Value of Self-Coding

We turn to our second question, namely whether self-coding of valence increases predictive power. As reported in Table 10.3, self-coding of valence yielded a further increase in this factor's ability to predict attitude. The difference between self-coding and experimenter coding is significant for both ad and brand attitude. Using the J test, the coefficients of the estimates for both self-coding models are significantly different from zero ($p < .01$). Thus, the coding of this factor benefits significantly from subjects' private knowledge.

Quality Versus Quantity

Given that a prompted protocol provides a superior verbal report, is its advantage due to quantity or quality? That is, does it yield more recalled responses or are the individual responses on average better predictors?

The issue of quantity is straightforward. The prompted verbal protocols of Experiment 3 contain more phrases, a mean of 5.6, than the (unprompted) verbal reports of Experiments 1 and 2 (3.2 and 2.1 phrases per report, respectively). Thus, the crucial question becomes whether there is any increase in quality or whether the impact of a prompted protocol is attributed solely to a greater number of reported responses.

This question is not answerable by the standard tactic of controlling for quantity (the number of phrases in a retrospective report), because the marginal

TABLE 10.5
Adjusted R^2s of Models Predicting Postexposure, Attitudes in Experiment 3

Coding Scheme	Attitude Toward the Ad		Attitude Toward the Brand	
	Experimenter Coded	Subject Coded	Experimenter Coded	Subject Coded
Cognitive responses[a]	.49	—	.50	—
Intended valence	.45	—	.44	—
Valence (direct)[a]	.49	.69	.53	.65
Valence (3 levels)	.47	.58	.48	.58

[a]J tests indicate here, as for Experiments 1 and 2, that the cognitive response model and the full direct valence model do not differ in their predictive ability.

predictive contribution of each phrase can be expected to decline as their number increases. The additional impact of the last, say, support argument on brand attitude would typically be less than that of the first such phrase. If all phrases were included in the analysis then the observed result would be less predictive value per phrase (a smaller absolute beta coefficient) for the cases with longer verbal reports. This amounts to an inherent bias against quality whenever quantity is greater.

To obviate this bias we used a Monte Carlo strategy to equate all retrospective reports on quantity, and test these for any remaining difference of quality. Specifically, all reports were reduced to the same number of phrases by random trimming. Such trimming was done to produce one, two, three, or four phrases per report. Note that not every report had at least four phrases to begin with (some had only one), so sample sizes decreased as the number of phrases increased. The result of this Monte Carlo pruning of "excess" phrases is a database of (trimmed) reports that are equated at four different numbers of phrases per report (one, two, three, and four) across the three experiments. This 4 × 3 design was reproduced in 50 Monte Carlo runs; that is, 50 random prunings of excess phrases. For each of these 600 sets of phrases, ad and brand attitude were regressed on both the cognitive response and (direct) valence models. The resulting 2,400 R^2s were subjected to a 4 × 3 × 2 × 2 fully factorial ANOVA. Figure 10.1 displays the results for the two main factors, quality as reflected in the difference between Experiment 3 and Experiments 1 and 2, and quantity as captured by the number of phrases per verbal report. As before, we note that because of differences in ads and subjects between Experiments 1 and 2 and Experiment 3, the results of this analysis are viewed as tentative.

The data reveal the clear superiority of the prompted protocols of Experiment 3 over the (unprompted) verbal reports of Experiments 1 and 2. Figure 10.1 shows a substantially higher R^2 for prompted protocols over all levels of phrases per protocol. The apparent pattern of Fig. 10.1 is confirmed by the planned contrast between Experiment 3 and the combination of Experiments 1 and 2, $F(1, 2352) = 4726.16, p < .001$. The magnitude of the improvement in quality is better conveyed by the percentage of variance accounted for by this contrast, 43.6% of the total variance.

It is worth noting that the increase in R^2 with quantity as shown in Fig. 10.1 is also significant, $F(93, 2352) = 243.08, p < .001$. Of more interest is the fan-shaped interaction between experiment (quality) and quantity. This is also significant, $F(6, 2352) = 150.25, p < .0001$, and accounts for more variance (8.3%) than the main effect of quality (6.7%). This interaction reflects an expected increase in predictive power as the superior quality of the individual phrases in Experiment 3 cumulates over a greater number of phrases per report.

Predictive Power Revisited

For completeness, we add the results of Experiment 3 to two earlier conclusions. First, again we find that the single construct of valence (experimenter-coded)

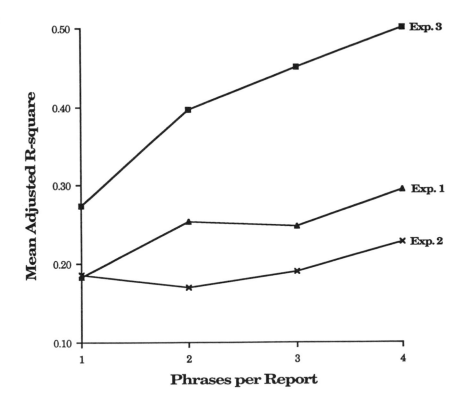

FIG. 10.1. The predictive power of verbal reports controlled for the number of phrases in each report.

predicts about as well as a cognitive response model (see Table 10.5). Of course, when valence is self-coded, its R^2s are substantially superior to those from the cognitive response framework.

Second, we can compare direct and intended valence as before by creating three-category models for each. As the adjusted R^2s reported in Table 10.5 reveal, direct valence is superior for both ad attitude (.47 vs. .45 for intended valence) and brand attitude (.48 vs. .44). J tests reveal that the corresponding beta coefficients for the direct valence estimates are significantly different from zero ($p < .01$). This replicates the finding of Experiment 2. However, because the opposite result was obtained in Experiment 1, and because the differences in R^2 are small, we draw only the conservative conclusion that neither type of valence is clearly superior. We believe, however, that direct valence has performed better than might have been expected.

GENERAL DISCUSSION

Our major findings on improving the information base of internal responses on which explanations of postadvertisement attitudes can be built are as follows.

1. The valence of the reported internal responses, although only a single construct, contains about as much power to predict attitudes as a full cognitive response model.
2. When subjects code their own responses for valence, information value increases substantially, even exceeding that of a full cognitive response model (whose categories are coded by an experimenter).
3. Prompting a subject's retrospective report by a replay of the ad increases both the number of reported responses and the predictive accuracy of each individual response. (This result awaits a replication controlling for ad and subject differences.)
4. Finally, reported intensities of ad-specific emotions contribute substantially to the predictive accuracy of verbal reports.

Unanswered Questions

Like many initial efforts, we leave many questions unanswered.

1. The distinction between direct and indirect valence requires the focused test we could not provide in these more general studies.

2. Can self-coding be extended to other taxonomic categories? Hastak and Olson (1989) applied it to a simple version of the cognitive response taxonomy. Dave (1993) used self-coding to categorize recalled responses as thoughts, feelings, or inferences.

3. The use of ad-specific emotions (and their intensities) raises at least two questions. First, what is the best combination of ad-specific and general emotion scales? Second, what is the best combination of cognitive and emotional measures? This question echoes Edell and Moore's (1991) claim, "It is not feelings *or* cognitions, but feelings *and* cognitions" (p. 34, emphasis in original).

4. Are there other, even better coding schemes for extracting information from a retrospective verbal report? As already mentioned, Dave (1993) coded for thoughts, feelings, and inferences. Chattopadhyay and Alba (1988) coded for relative abstractness, a construct that captures memorability of the internal responses.

5. Might other measures of the internal response to an ad be used? These might include: (a) manually recording, on a more or less continuous basis, the overall positive or negative affect (Baumgartner, Sujan, & Padgett, 1994; Pham, Hughes, & Cohen, 1993; Polfuss & Hess, 1990; Thorson, 1991) or only one particular affective component such as warmth (Aaker & Stayman, 1990; Vanden Abeele & MacLachlan, 1994); (b) attention to the ad (Thorson & Zhao, chapter 13, this volume); and (c) electrodermal responses.

6. Finally, we note that a retrospective verbal report might be prompted by replaying separate components of the ad such as video, music, and spoken words (Clucas, 1993) or by the continuously recorded affect measures described earlier.

Limitations

We want to acknowledge several specific and one general limitation of this work. First, our results must be qualified by our subject population (students) and the relatively few ads selected. Also with the exception of varying quality in Experiment 3, even the ads used were not chosen as part of a representative design. Finally, and maybe most important of all, the ads were viewed under forced exposure. Although we carefully instructed subjects to simulate home viewing, we doubt that this was uniformly achieved.

Beyond these specific limitations is the general concern that all measurement risks reactivity. The more measures we take or the more deeply we probe to obtain any one measure, the more we risk changing the phenomenon we are trying to measure. If subjects provide a prompted protocol after one ad, even only a practice ad to learn the technique, they are likely to expect a request for such a protocol after the next ad. This might alter their viewing (Russo, Johnson, & Stephens, 1989). More importantly, whenever attitudes are assessed after a replay of the ad, they may be distorted either by internal responses recalled solely as a result of the replay (and which would otherwise have had a lesser impact, if any at all, on attitudes) or by internal responses generated only during the replay itself (Wilson & Hodges, 1992).[6] There will always be a delicate trade-off between the extent of measurement and the risk of invalidity due to reactivity.

ACKNOWLEDGMENTS

This research was supported by grants from the Marketing Science Institute, the Johnson Graduate School of Management of Cornell University, and the College of Business and Management at the University of Maryland. The Computer Science Center at the University of Maryland provided financial and software support for the primary data analyses.

The authors thank Rajeev Batra and Richard Durand for helpful comments on a previous draft of this manuscript. We also wish to acknowledge Silvana Accame, Sally Bourgeois, Gabby Daley, Alka Desai, Dolly Kumar, and Laurie Murphy for their assistance with data collection and coding. We are grateful to Chip Denman and Scott Lathrop for their assistance with data analyses. Finally, we thank Silvana Accame, Alka Desai, Michael Mazis, Larry Percy, and the University of Maryland libraries for supplying us with television commercials.

---

[6]We thank Anand Kumar for pointing out this potential threat to validity in his oral discussion of this chapter.

REFERENCES

Aaker, D. A., & Stayman, D. M. (1990). A micro approach to feelings in advertising. In S. Agres, J. Edell, & T. Dubitsky (Eds.), *Emotion in advertising: Theoretical and practical explorations* (pp. 53–68). Westport, CT: Quorum Books.

Aaker, D. A., Stayman, D. M., & Hagerty, M. R. (1986). Warmth in advertising: Measurement, impact, and sequence effects. *Journal of Consumer Research, 12*, 365–381.

Batra, R., & Holbrook, M. B. (1990). Developing a typology of affective responses to advertising: A test of validity and reliability. *Psychology and Marketing, 7*, 11–25.

Batra, R., & Ray, M. L. (1986). Affective responses mediating acceptance of advertising. *Journal of Consumer Research, 13*, 234–249.

Batra, R., & Stephens, D. L. (1987). Attitudinal effects of ad-evoked moods and emotions: The moderating role of motivation. *Psychology and Marketing, 11*, 199–215.

Baumgartner, H., Sujan, M., & Padgett, D. (1994). *Patterns of affective reactions to ads: The integration of moment-to-moment response into overall judgements* (Working paper). State College: Pennsylvania State University.

Brock, T. C. (1967). Communication discrepancy and intent to persuade as determinants of counterargument production. *Journal of Experimental Social Psychology, 3*, 269–309.

Cacioppo, J. T., & Petty, R. E. (1981). Social psychological procedures for cognitive response assessment: The thought-listing technique. In C. R. Glass & M. Ganest (Eds.), *Cognitive Assessment* (pp. 309–342). New York: Guilford.

Calder, B. J., & Gruder, C. L. (1989). Emotional advertising appeals. In P. Cafferata & A. M. Tybout (Eds.), *Cognitive and affective responses to advertising* (pp. 277–285). Lexington, MA: D.C. Heath.

Chattopadhyay, A., & Alba, J. W. (1988). The situational importance of recall and inference in consumer decision making. *Journal of Consumer Research, 15*, 1–12.

Chattopadhyay, A., & Basu, K. (1990). Humor in advertising: The moderating role of prior brand evaluation. *Journal of Marketing Research, 27*, 466–476.

Churchill, G. A. (1987). *Marketing research: Methodological foundations* (4th ed.). Chicago: Dryden.

Clucas, E. (1993, August). *Digging the ego state for communication data.* Paper presented at the American Psychological Association Convention, Toronto, Canada.

Dave, A. (1993). *The impact of advertising on brand choice.* Unpublished doctoral dissertation, Cornell University, Ithaca, NY.

Davidson, R., & MacKinnon, J. G. (1981). Several tests for model specification in the presence of alternative hypotheses. *Econometrica, 49*, 781–793.

Davis, R. C., & Schleifer, R. (Eds.). (1989). *Contemporary literary criticism: Literary and cultural studies.* New York: Longman.

Eagly, A. H., & Chaiken, S. (1993). The nature of attitudes. In A. H. Eagly & S. Chaiken (Eds.), *The psychology of attitudes* (pp. 1–21). Ft. Worth, TX: Harcourt Brace Jovanovich.

Edell, J. A., & Burke, M. C. (1987). The power of feelings in understanding advertising effects. *Journal of Consumer Research, 14*, 421–433.

Edell, J. A., & Burke, M. C. (1989). The impact of feelings on ad-based affect and cognition. *Journal of Marketing Research, 26*, 69–83.

Edell, J. A., & Moore, M. C. (1991). The effects of feelings on attitude toward the ad. In C. Yoon (Ed.), *Tears, cheers, and fears: The role of emotions in advertising* (Rep. No. 91-112, pp. 32–34). Cambridge, MA: Marketing Science Institute.

Fiske, S. T., & Taylor, S. (1991). *Social cognition* (2nd ed.). New York: McGraw-Hill.

Gardner, M. P. (1985). Does attitude toward the ad affect brand attitude under a brand evaluation set? *Journal of Marketing Research, 12*, 192–198.

Greenwald, A. G. (1968). Cognitive learning, cognitive response to persuasion, and attitude change. In A. C. Greenwald, T. C. Brock, & T. C. Ostrom (Eds.), *Psychological foundations of attitudes* (pp. 147–156). New York: Academic Press.

Hastak, M., & Olson, J. C. (1989). Assessing the role of brand-related cognitive responses as mediators of communication effects on cognitive structure. *Journal of Consumer Research, 15,* 444–456.

Holbrook, M. B. (1978). Beyond attitude structure: Toward the informational determinants of attitude. *Journal of Marketing Research, 15,* 9–15.

Holbrook, M. B., & Westwood, R. A. (1989). The role of emotion in advertising revisited: Testing a typology of emotional responses. In P. Cafferata & A. M. Tybout (Eds.), *Cognitive and affective responses to advertising* (pp. 353–371). Lexington, MA: D.C. Heath.

Krosnick, J. A., Boninger, D. S., Chuang, Y. C., Berent, M. K., & Carnot, C. G. (1993). Attitude strength: One construct or many related constructs. *Journal of Personality and Social Psychology, 65,* 1132–1151.

Lutz, R. J., & MacKenzie, S. B. (1982). Construction of a diagnostic cognitive response model for use in commercial pretesting. In M. J. Naples & J. S. Chasin (Eds.), *Straight talk about attitude research* (pp. 145–156). Chicago: American Marketing Association.

Lutz, R. J., MacKenzie, S. B., & Belch, G. E. (1983). Attitude toward the ad as a mediator of advertising effectiveness: Determinants and consequences. In R. P. Bagozzi & A. M. Tybout (Eds.), *Advances in consumer research* (Vol. 10, pp. 532–539). Ann Arbor, MI: Association for Consumer Research.

Machleit, K. A., & Wilson, R. D. (1988). Emotional feelings and attitude toward the advertisement: The roles of brand familiarity and repetition. *Journal of Advertising, 17,* 27–35.

MacInnis, D. J., & Jaworski, B. J. (1989). Information processing from advertisements: Towards an integrative framework. *Journal of Marketing, 53,* 1–23.

MacKenzie, S. B., & Lutz, R. J. (1989). An empirical examination of affective and cognitive antecedents of attitude toward the ad. *Journal of Marketing, 53,* 48–65.

MacKenzie, S. B., Lutz, R. J., & Belch, G. E. (1986). The role of attitude toward the ad as a mediator of advertising effectiveness: A test of competing explanations. *Journal of Marketing Research, 23,* 130–143.

Mitchell, A. A., & Olson, J. C. (1981). Are product attribute beliefs the only mediator of advertising effects on brand attitude? *Journal of Marketing Research, 18,* 318–332.

Petty, R. E., Ostrom, T. M., & Brock, T. C. (Eds.). (1981). *Cognitive responses to persuasion.* Hillsdale, NJ: Lawrence Erlbaum Associates.

Pham, M. T., Hughes, G. D., & Cohen, J. B. (1993). *Validating a dial-turning instrument for real-time measurement of affective and evaluative responses to advertising* (Rep. No. 93-116). Cambridge, MA: Marketing Science Institute.

Polsfuss, M., & Hess, M. (1991). "Liking" through moment-to-moment evaluation: Identifying key selling arguments in advertising. In R. Holman & M. R. Soloman (Eds.), *Advances in consumer research* (Vol. 18, pp. 540–544). Provo, UT: Association for Consumer Research.

Russo, J. E., Johnson, E. J., & Stephens, D. L. (1989). The validity of verbal protocols. *Memory and Cognition, 17,* 759–769.

Russo, J. E., & Stephens, D. L. (1990). Ad-specific emotional responses to advertising. In S. Agres, J. A. Edell, & T. M. Dubitsky (Eds.), *Emotion in advertising: Theoretical and practical explorations* (pp. 113–123). Westport, CT: Quorum Books.

Scott, L. M. (1992). For the rest of us: A reader-oriented interpretation of Apple's 1984 commercial. *Journal of Popular Culture, 25,* 67.

Thorson, E. (1991). Emotional flow during commercials. In C. Yoon (Ed.), *Tears, cheers, and fears: The role of emotions in advertising* (Rep. No. 91-112, pp. 17–19). Cambridge, MA: Marketing Science Institute.

Tompkins, J. P. (Ed.). (1980). *Reader response criticism: From formalism to post-structuralism.* Baltimore, MD: Johns Hopkins.

Vanden Abeele, P., & MacLachlan, D. L. (1994). Process tracing of emotional responses to TV ads: Revisiting the warmth monitor. *Journal of Consumer Research, 20,* 586–600.

Wilson, T. D., & Hodges, S. D. (1992). Attitudes as temporary constructions. In L. L. Martin & A. Tesser (Eds.), *The construction of social judgments* (pp. 37–65). Hillsdale, NJ: Lawrence Erlbaum Associates.

Wright, P. (1973). The cognitive processes mediating acceptance of advertising. *Journal of Marketing Research, 10,* 53–62.

Wright, P. (1974). Analyzing media effects on advertising responses. *Public Opinion Quarterly, 38,* 192–205.

Comments on Chapters 1 Through 10

William D. Wells
University of Minnesota

In the first section of this volume, authors and discussants stressed differences between academic and applied approaches to measuring advertising's diverse effects. They emphasized conceptual and operational distinctions, and they analyzed disagreements as to the meanings of success. The chapters that followed took a somewhat different tack. They suggested that academic and applied researchers learn useful lessons when they cross paths.

For instance, preattentive processing, the priming effect, and the "truth effect"—all mainly of "academic" interest—have potentially important practical implications, as practitioners' comments on those topics point out. Transferring those topics from academic laboratories to more realistic environments is a highly desirable next step.

Chapters 6 and 7 show that transfer process at work. Haugtvedt and Priester's chapter reviews (largely) academic research on cognitive processing of persuasive messages with special reference to conditions that render persuasion-based attitudes predictive of behavior and resistant to attack. Crimmins' chapter transfers those findings to real evaluations of real ads.

In addition to verifying many of the distinctions between central and peripheral processing, chapter 7 says, "Now wait a minute, there's something else. Beyond central and peripheral processing, a meaningful difference between self-conscious and unself-conscious processing deserves further thought and careful work." If academic researchers pay attention to the implications of that observation, they are likely to improve the validity of whatever they do next.

Chapters 8, 9, and 10 continue to demonstrate the contributions of reiterated feedback. Chapter 8 provides real-world support for many of the academic conceptualizations reviewed in earlier chapters, and it presents two critical distinctions: the distinction between package goods on one hand and durables and services on the other, and distinctions among brand, call-to-action and feel-good effects. Both observations seem likely to change the outcomes of all thought-listing research.

Chapter 9 documents important differences between instrumental and social identity products; and, in its exposition of the circle-a-thought technique, demonstrates a methodological refinement that can simplify and enhance thought-listing projects. Chapter 10 adds to the researcher's art. In demonstrating the value of improved procedures, it shows how to increase sensitivity and precision in both academic and applied analysis of cognitive responses.

In these chapters, academic and applied concepts and methods support, validate, correct, and refine one another. Collectively, they provide strong evidence that synergies between the academic world and the applied world are likely to be more than worth the cost of creating them.

V

Context

The chapters in this section continue the dialogue between academicians and practitioners. In chapter 11, Jennifer Gregan-Paxton and Barbara Loken—of Washington State University and the University of Minnesota, respectively—present the Wyer–Srull model of information processing and derive implications that have the capacity to enrich both academic and applied research. They take particular account of two determinants of advertising's consequences: multiple exposures of the same advertisement, and interference from competing ads.

In chapter 12, V. Carter Broach of the University of Delaware, Thomas J. Page, Jr. of Michigan State University, and R. Dale Wilson of Michigan State University present two laboratory experiments that demonstrate some of the ways television program content mediates consumers' reactions to advertisements. The discussions that follow that chapter—one by Brian Wansink of the University of Illinois, Urbana–Champaign, the others by Abhilasha Mehta of Gallup & Robinson Inc. and Christine Wright-Isak of Young & Rubicam, Advertising—build methodological and substantive bridges between the laboratory and the real world.

Chapter 13, by Esther Thorson of the University of Missouri–Columbia and Xinshu Zhao of the University of North Carolina, takes an important and informative step away from the artificial conditions that limit most laboratory investigations. Although retaining the advantages of strict stimulus control, it examines reactions to TV commercials in a setting that resembles the environment in which television advertisements are normally received. This transition was made possible through collaboration with real-world researchers at DDB Needham Worldwide.

Chapter 14, by Pirjo Vuokko—of the Turku School of Economics and Business Administration, Turku, Finland—completes the transition from the laboratory to the outside world. It reports a large-scale field study in which the conditions that mediate effectiveness change naturally, in response to strategic marketing considerations and common marketing events. Although this "experiment" is realistic in all respects, it enriches our understanding of constructs that predate Lucas and Britt.

11

Understanding Consumer Memory For Ads: A Process View

Jennifer Gregan-Paxton
Washington State University

Barbara Loken
University of Minnesota

It has long been assumed that measures of memory, such as recall and recognition, provide valuable insight into the effectiveness of advertisements (e.g., Barlow & Wogalter, 1993; R. A. Kent, 1993; Stewart, 1989). Research relying on memory measures has been successful in isolating two key factors thought to inhibit advertising effectiveness. First, the greater the amount of time that has elapsed since consumers viewed an ad, the less likely they are to remember information presented in the ad. Second, the more interference consumers experience from information external to the ad (e.g., "clutter"), the less likely they are to recall features of the ad. Because these two factors represent critical determinants of consumer memory, they also impact an ad's effectiveness.

Despite the central role that time and interference play in determining an ad's effectiveness, surprisingly little is known about how these factors affect our ability to remember. This represents an important gap in our knowledge because it places limits on our ability to predict the likely impact of advertising. Armed with an understanding of the processes by which time and interference factors impact memory for an ad's contents (e.g., brand name, ad claim), it should be easier to design, place, and schedule ads such that they will be "on strategy" (Percy & Rossiter, chap. 15, this volume).

Addressing this issue, the purpose of this chapter is to illustrate the ability of a process model, developed by Wyer and Srull (1986, 1989), to integrate the empirical findings in the advertising literature on the roles of time and interference, such that useful propositions emerge regarding the processes underlying consumer memory for advertisements. Toward that goal, this chapter begins with a brief summary of the findings obtained in the advertising literature on the role of time and interference in memory loss. We then provide an overview of the social psychological model of human cognition, developed by Wyer and Srull (1986, 1989), which provides a useful framework for understanding the processes underlying memory loss due to time delays and interfering information. Finally, we develop propositions and discuss their implications with respect to recent research on advertising effectiveness.

TIME AND INTERFERENCE EFFECTS

Forgetting as a Function of Time

It is generally agreed that memory loss occurs as a function of the passage of time since viewing the ad (Hutchinson & Moore, 1984; R. J. Kent, 1993). This time effect has been observed over a wide variety of time delays and contexts. For instance, examining memory for statements similar to those found in ads (e.g., Red Lobster serves seafood), Hawkins and Hoch (1992) found that subjects' recognition accuracy was significantly better after a 20-minute time delay than after a 1-week time delay. In a study of the impact of expansion advertising on brand usage frequency, Wansink and Ray (1993) uncovered a similar decline in memory over time. That is, 3 months after reading transcripts for a television commercial, the percentage of subjects who could recall the target brand varied from 70% to 45%, depending on the type of commercial to which they were exposed. As another example, in the context of a study of the effects of comparative advertising on memory for the comparison brand, Pechmann and Stewart (1990) uncovered tremendous variance in the degree of memory decay in a condition with no delay as well as a condition with a 24-hour delay. Specifically, they reported brand recall proportions as low as .12 and as high as 1.0, depending on the market share of the comparison brand and the type of ad. Similar findings were obtained by Meyers-Levy and Maheswaran (1991) in a study of gender differences in ad processing style. In that study, subjects read an ad for a news program and then were asked to recall the ad as completely as possible. The proportion of message items recalled varied between .34 and .87, depending on the subject's gender and whether the item was congruent or incongruent with the message.

Thus, it is apparent that memory for advertising declines over time. Much less apparent is how time impacts memory. Understanding the processes underlying time effects is critical because it represents an important step toward specifying how to combat the negative effects of time on memory for advertising.

Forgetting as a Function of Interference

Memory loss can also occur as the result of interference from information external to the ad (Stewart, 1989). Nowhere is this more evident than in research on the adverse impact of television clutter on ad effectiveness. As ad length has declined, and the number of nonprogram elements on TV has increased (R. J. Kent, 1993), clutter has become an increasingly important issue for advertisers. Advertising research lends evidence that recall suffers when clutter increases (Bogart & Lehman, 1983; Webb & Ray, 1979).

Of particular interest to many researchers is the extent to which ads for competitive brands (vs. advertising in general) impact ad effectiveness. Examining this issue in an experimental context, Keller (1991) found that providing an ad retrieval cue (the ad photo and headline) facilitated recall of target ad claims when the ads were viewed in the context of competitive advertising, but not when they were viewed in the context of no competitive advertising. The fact that the ad retrieval cue improved recall only when competitive ads were present suggests that the competitive ads were indeed interfering with subjects' memory for the target ad. Further support for this interpretation comes from the finding that ad claim recall declined as the amount of competitive advertising increased. Specifically, ad claim recall was best in the context of no competitive advertising and worst in the context of three competitive ads. Other experimental studies have turned up similar findings. For example, Costley and Brucks (1992) found that competitive ads can inhibit the recall of attributes featured in previously presented ads. These findings are particularly alarming in light of a recent study that revealed that during prime time television, 32% of ads were shown within an hour of an ad for a competing brand (R.J. Kent, 1993).

The findings of Burke and Srull (1988, Experiment 1) lend further support to the idea that the presence of competitive ads compromises an ad's effectiveness. Comparing ad recall in a varied product context (ads for unrelated products and brands) to ad recall in a competitive context (different brands of the same product), they found significantly lower recall levels in the competitive context. Notably, their study found that, compared to the varied product context, recall was also significantly hindered by exposure to an ad for the same brand (but different model). A similar pattern of findings was observed when they looked at the incidence of cued confusions (i.e., attributing information from one ad to another ad). That is, compared to the varied-product context, there were more cued confusions for ads occurring in both the competitive-brand context and the same-brand context. Indicating the complex nature of clutter effects, this study suggests that the general clutter effects reported earlier may be largely driven by ads placed by the brand's competitors and, ironically, by the brand's other ads.

In summary, research on the effects of clutter on the memorability of an ad indicates that interference plays an important role in advertising effectiveness. Given the continued movement toward more clutter (Ray & Webb, 1986), the importance of this issue cannot be overstated. That being the case, it is important that we obtain a more thorough understanding of the process by which interference impacts memory for an ad. Doing so should put us in a better position to make recommendations regarding ways to reduce the negative impact of interference on the effectiveness of ads.

THE WYER–SRULL MODEL

The Wyer–Srull model is a model of human information processing and represents a useful framework for understanding how interference affects people's abilities to remember advertising information. In this section, we provide a brief overview of the Wyer–Srull model and its individual components and postulates (for a more complete description, see Wyer & Srull, 1989), paying particular attention to those features that are important for understanding advertising effectiveness.

Overview of Model Components

The Wyer–Srull model can be broken down into two main units—storage and processing. These units are made up of several individual components, each of which is responsible for a distinct task within the system. As shown in Fig. 11.1, the storage unit is made up of four components or functions: the sensory store, work space, permanent storage, and the goal specification box. The processing unit includes five components or functions: the executor, comprehender, encoder/organizer, integrator, and response selector.

Storage Units. All information about the external environment, including information from advertisements, enters the system by means of the *sensory store*, the first storage unit. The information in this unit does not undergo any processing and only remains here a few seconds.

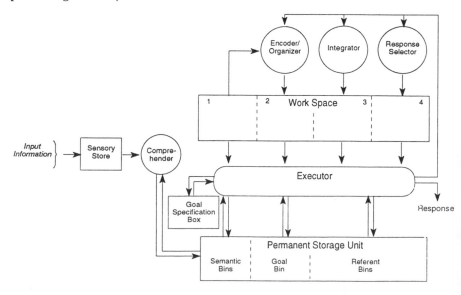

FIG. 11.1. The Wyer–Srull model of the human cognitive system. From: Wyer, R. S., Jr., & Srull, T. K. (1986). Human cognition in its social context. *Psychological Review, 93*(3), 322–359. Reprinted with permission.

A longer lasting, yet still temporary, storage area is the *work space*. Analogous to working memory (Bower, 1975), the compartments of this unit serve as layover areas for pieces of information as they complete their journey through the different processing units. The work space is designed to store both input material (to be processed) as well as output material (the results of processing). Advertising information is retained in this unit only as long as it is needed for the pursuit of processing objectives. When the objectives relevant to a piece of information are achieved, the material is cleared away. Any information that is not transferred to permanent storage before clearing occurs will be lost forever. Therefore, if a consumer views an ad with the objective of purchasing an economy car, any information that reaches the work space and is relevant to this objective will be transferred to permanent storage, and all other irrelevant information will be lost forever. Wyer and Srull formulated several specific postulates to govern the operation of the work space, and they are summarized in the Appendix.

Material that is to be kept indefinitely in memory is deposited in *permanent storage*. Wyer and Srull conceptualized permanent storage as being made up of content-addressable bins into which pieces of information are deposited and, analogous to others' conceptualization of long-term storage (e.g., Norman, 1968), are never erased. The pieces of information in each bin are assumed to be stored and retrieved independently. Each bin is identified by a header that classifies the contents of the bin. Wyer and Srull presented a summary of postulates pertaining to the structure and content of permanent storage and they are presented in the Appendix.

There are three general types of bins found in permanent storage and each performs a unique function within the system. Of particular interest is a special type of bin called the *goal bin*. This bin contains specific goal schemata that outline the cognitive steps necessary for achievement of particular objectives. Wyer and Srull paid particular attention to the roles of the hypothesized bins in the storage and retrieval of information. The specific postulates that detail these aspects of information processing are summarized in the Appendix.

The final storage unit, the *goal specification box*, contains the currently active processing objectives and the procedures (goal schemata) for attaining them. It is to this storage area that the executor refers for instructions on how to direct the flow of information within the system and to find out which procedures to tell the processing units to activate. The goal specification box can contain more than one processing objective at a time, but it does not have unlimited capacity. The number of objectives that can be pursued simultaneously is a function of the complexity of the individual procedures they require. For example, a consumer may be able to process advertising information with the goal of buying an economy car and, at the same time, plan dinner with the objective of planning nutritious meals, as long as neither goal is so complex that the system becomes overloaded.

Processing Units.   Although the five processing units serve different purposes within the model, they do share a common feature: Each unit has its own library of procedures. An active processing objective guides the selection of a procedure, and that procedure in turn guides processing within the unit.

The *executor* is responsible for directing the flow of information between processing and storage units. The executor is active at all times. When a processing objective is activated, the executor's actions are regulated by a relevant goal schema from the goal specification box. This goal schema directs the executor to retrieve information from permanent storage, send information to the work space, transmit instructions to the other processing units, and transmit newly acquired information to permanent storage.

A second processing unit, the *comprehender*, operates as a low-level processor of raw stimulus information. This unit assigns meaning to all pieces of data that the organism receives. It does so automatically and independently of specific processing objectives. The comprehender interprets incoming stimuli by reference to concepts the organism has previously acquired and stored in permanent storage. In other words, all clarifications are made in terms of prior information. Therefore, if a consumer had extensive knowledge about economy cars, the comprehender would interpret incoming advertising information with respect to this prior knowledge.

When higher level interpretation of information is required, the *encoder/organizer* is utilized. This unit is invoked whenever information sent to the work space from the comprehender or permanent storage lacks the type of higher order encoding demanded by the currently active processing objective. The output of this unit is determined solely by this active processing objective and, in contrast to the comprehender, may differ substantially from the input on which it is based.

The *integrator* is employed when a judgment or decision based on more than one piece of information is required. As the name suggests, this unit specializes in combining different and often contradictory pieces of information together so that a single conclusion can be drawn. Using our same example, if an advertisement provides information about price and miles per gallon that suggest a car is low priced and fuel efficient (economy car attributes), but the car has previously been classified by the consumer as a luxury car, the encoder/organizer might be relied on to determine whether the miles per gallon information is, indeed, consistent with most economy cars. If so, the integrator might be used to resolve the apparent contradictions that arise when trying to classify a luxury car that has economy car attributes.

Finally, when a judgment or decision needs to be translated into an overt behavior, the *response selector* is invoked. Rules for the conversion are found in the unit's library and depend on the type of mental process and the type of response required.

Importance of the Model

The Wyer and Srull model (1986, 1989) was developed to describe how the human cognitive system operates in its natural social context. The appeal of the model lies primarily in its comprehensiveness. Within this one framework, it is possible to conceptualize a wide range of phenomena with a relatively small set of propositions and a single unified group of cognitive mechanisms. Further, because the model encompasses all aspects of information processing (e.g., storage, retrieval, judgment), it can incorporate other models of cognitive functioning (e.g., the availability-valence hypothesis of Kisielius & Sternthal, 1986; the accessibility-diagnosticity model of Feldman & Lynch, 1988).

The Wyer–Srull model is also appealing for its explicit recognition that the encoding, organizing, storing, and retrieving of information all depend greatly on the objective being pursued at the time information is processed. Consumer researchers have become increasingly aware of the influence of goals on all aspects of processing activities (e.g., Brown & Stayman, 1992; Hastak & Olson, 1989; Huffman & Houston, 1993). However, the associative network models of memory that currently dominate memory research in consumer behavior do not incorporate goals into their conceptualizations (for a review of these models see Raaijmakers & Shiffrin, 1992).

WYER–SRULL CONCEPTUALIZATION OF TIME EFFECTS

Negative Impact of Time

Permanent Storage Effects. The passage of time may impact memory functioning in the Wyer and Srull conceptualization in several ways. The first of these considers how items are stored and retrieved from the bins of permanent storage. Information created as the result of a processing objective is transmitted and stored in the order in which it is generated (Postulate B5). The longer information is held in permanent storage without being used, the less likely it is to be located near the top of a bin. Because the search for information within a bin proceeds in a top-down fashion (Postulate C9) and exhaustive searches for information are rarely undertaken (Postulate C11), the importance of being located near the top of a bin is obvious. That is, if a bin is identified as appropriate for a search, the search will continue until a sufficient amount of information is obtained to achieve the objective. If a piece of information is far down in the bin there is a better chance that the search will end before it is reached. Notice, however, that in order for a piece of information to descend to a lower position in a bin it is necessary that the executor subsequently transfer additional material to that bin. That is, the system must experience interference from similar (i.e., bin-relevant) information. This point is explored later.

Given the nature of the advertising environment, it is easy to see how ad information might sink down in a bin, thus decreasing its availability over time. The point at which a consumer is exposed to an advertisement for a product is generally separated temporally from the context of making a purchase decision. Similarly, the consumer may gather information from many different sources (e.g., stores, other people) over a period of time before making a purchase decision. The present conceptualization suggests that in such cases, the probability that consumers will be able to retrieve an item of information they have gathered declines as the interval between information gathering and information use increases. In addition to extensive anecdotal evidence for this proposition, research has also confirmed the existence of the negative impact of time (e.g., Hawkins & Hoch, 1992; Wansink & Ray, 1993).

This discussion leads to the following proposition regarding the effects of time on memory for advertising:

P_1: Other things being equal, memory for advertising information will decrease over time.

Work Space Effects.   As just described, the passage of time can adversely impact memory via the processes by which information is stored and retrieved from the bins in permanent storage. However, that analysis only applies to information that has been around long enough to be processed in the pursuit of an objective, and has consequently been stashed away in permanent storage. Although it is certainly useful to understand how these memories are forgotten over time, it is also useful to understand how information might be acquired and lost in a matter of minutes. To understand loss of this nature it is necessary to examine the impact of time on the functioning of the work space.

The passage of time is not beneficial to information in the work space because, unlike permanent storage, the work space is of limited capacity (Postulate A1). When that limit is reached, the work space is automatically cleared of information that has not been recently used (Postulate A3). Unless the cleared material was transferred to permanent storage prior to removal, it will be lost forever. Thus, information not used in pursuit of a processing objective is likely to be available in the short run (while it is still held in the work space), but is unlikely to be available in the long run (because it never made it to permanent storage).

This process is likely to be in operation in many laboratory studies of ad effectiveness. For example, in their investigation of the impact of between-brand and within-brand processing on memory for ads, Kent and Machleit (1990) exposed subjects to a videotape containing 16 consecutive ads and then immediately administered brand recall and recognition measures. Importantly, prior to being shown the videotape, subjects were not told that recall and recognition tests would be administered. Instead, they were simply told that they were filling out a questionnaire to aid the instructor in preparing a set of measures of ad content. Thus, there was no processing objective that would motivate the transfer of brand name information to permanent storage.[1] As

---

[1] In fact, the focal manipulation of the study centered on processing objectives. Subjects were either told to "list the main benefits" of the brand featured in the ad or to list the ways in which the advertised brand was similar to another brand's product. In either case, some information may have been transferred to permanent storage. The main point here is that there was no processing objective specifically related to providing the information needed for the recall and recognition tasks. It is important to keep this in mind when interpreting the results of this and other studies using this approach.

spelled out earlier, in such a scenario, one would have to rely on whatever information was available in the work space when responding to the recall and recognition measures. However, with so many ads, much of the information contained in the earlier ads may have been lost due to the automatic clearance of the work space. Unfortunately, the experiment did not test this possibility.

In addition to the automatic clearance of the work space described already, it is possible for information to be removed from the work space purposely (Postulate A2). This occurs when the individual does not anticipate any immediate need for the information (e.g., Srull & Wyer, 1983). The longer material resides in the work space without being used, the more likely it is to be willfully removed. Because only information used in pursuit of a processing objective is transferred to permanent storage, this displaced information will be lost from the system.

The operation of such a process raises serious concerns about the use of distractor tasks, which are so common in studies of consumer memory for advertising. In a typical experiment, subjects first receive the target information (e.g., print ads) and then are asked to perform a task such as filling out a questionnaire (unrelated to the experimental manipulation) or solving an arithmetic problem. After completing the distractor task, the subjects' memory for the target information is assessed.

Applying the process connected with the willful clearance of the work space, the Wyer–Srull framework provides a unique perspective on this tactic. In a typical consumer setting, the delay between information acquisition and use is such that the consumer must rely on material retrieved from the bins in permanent storage, rather than the compartments of the work space, for performing consumption-related tasks. In studies employing the distractor task technique it is assumed that the information introduced by the task will displace the target information from the work space (Postulates A1 through A3), thus forcing the subject to use what they can retrieve from permanent storage to respond to subsequent memory measures. Recall, however, that only information that is used in pursuit of a processing objective is deposited in the bins of permanent storage (Postulate B2), and further, that information that is displaced from the work space before being transferred to permanent storage is lost from the system (Postulate A4). The implications of these two postulates for the use of a distractor task are clear. If subjects do not use the information in pursuit of a processing objective before performing the distractor task, the distractor task may cause this information to be cleared from the system, making it unavailable for future retrieval. Thus, in some cases, failure to remember an ad and/or its contents may simply be an artifact of the experimental procedure.

Suggestive evidence of just such a process is provided in a study by Burke and Srull (1988, Experiment 1) mentioned earlier. The subjects in this study were encouraged to view ads with the objective of either purchasing the advertised product or rating the interest value of the ad itself. Following a distractor task, subjects recalled almost twice as much information presented in the ad if they examined the ads with the intention of rating the advertised brands' purchase likelihood than if they rated the ads' inherent interest value. Presumably those in the purchase group had processed information related to the product and had transferred that information to permanent storage prior to the administration of the distractor task. In contrast, those in the interest group most likely processed information related to the ad execution and transferred that to permanent storage. Information picked up about the product was most likely not transferred to permanent storage and thus was unavailable for retrieval when the surprise recall test was administered. Support for this explanation of distractor task effects would also be obtained if subjects with the interest rating objective recalled significantly more ad execution information than the purchase subjects. Unfortunately, recall of ad execution elements was not assessed in this study.

Findings similar to those obtained by Burke and Srull (1988) have been found when the actual passage of time, rather than a distractor task, is part of the experimental design. For example, Gardial, Schumann, Petkus, and Smith (1993) examined differences in the total amount of information retrieved from an ad 1 week after exposure. In their study, subjects differed only in the processing objective active at the time of ad exposure. Prior to viewing the ad, half the subjects were told to evaluate the style of the ad and the other half were told to evaluate the product featured in the ad. As the Wyer–Srull conceptualization would predict, more total information was retrieved after a week if the objective was to evaluate the product than if the objective was to evaluate the ad.

This analysis of the more immediate loss of memory for advertising information leads to the following proposition:

P2: Memory for advertising will be enhanced by ads that activate processing objectives that require evaluating the relevant features of the ad.

Positive Impact of Time. In another way the passage of time can actually increase the likelihood that a piece of information will be retrieved. Each time information within a bin is identified as necessary for a processing objective, a copy of it is transmitted to the work space (Postulate C10). However, the original remains in the bin in the same location. When the processing objective is completed, the copy is returned to the same bin and takes its place at the top (as explained earlier). This same procedure is followed each time information is retrieved from a bin. Thus, over time, repeated usage of a piece of information increases its likelihood of being retrieved on any given search by increasing its number of representations and improving its position in the bin.

This counterintuitive notion of the positive impact of time on memory for advertising information is supported by studies that demonstrate the effect of ad repetition on memory (Finlay, 1993). For example, in one study (Meyers-Levy, 1989), one group of subjects saw advertisements containing target brand names once, whereas a second group saw them three times. It was believed that the multiple exposure group would have greater access to the target brand names than the single exposure group. In terms of the Wyer–Srull framework, this should be the case because multiple usage of information should result in multiple copies of that material being deposited in permanent storage (Postulate C9). This, in turn, should result in an increased chance of retrieval. The findings support this expectation. Recall of the target brand names was significantly higher in the three-exposure condition than in the one-exposure condition after a 24-hour delay. Other research (e.g., Peracchio, 1992; Schumann, Petty, & Clemons, 1990) supports the notion that repetition enhances learning (as measured by performance on tests of recall or recognition).

The present conceptualization also suggests conditions under which repetition would not be expected to have beneficial effects. If information is not processed in the pursuit of a processing objective, it is not transferred to a bin in permanent storage (Postulate B2), and multiple copies will not be available to enhance retrieval. Because of this, simply repeating a marketing communication would not be sufficient to affect consumer memory. Consumers are exposed to hundreds of promotional messages a day and only a very small percentage of those generate any active processing (Hawkins & Hoch, 1992).

These ideas are summarized in the following proposition:

P3: Memory for advertising will be enhanced by the repeated usage of information contained in the ad.

WYER–SRULL CONCEPTUALIZATION
OF INTERFERENCE EFFECTS

Interference From Similar and Dissimilar Information

Interference effects are realized through the introduction of added information to the system. Within the present framework there are numerous ways in which this extra material, whether it is similar or dissimilar to the information in the ad, manifests its influence. First, consider the search process. When information is needed to pursue a processing objective, the work space is the first place to be searched (Postulate C2), and this search is conducted in a random fashion (Postulate C3). Interference caused by dissimilar information, such as evaluating a fountain pen in the Gardial et al. (1993) camera ad study, or similar information, such as viewing ads for a different model of the same brand in the Burke and Srull (1988) study, introduces added information to the work space. As the amount of information in the work space goes up, the probability of retrieving the sought-after information, if it is there, decreases.

The next step in the search process involves an inspection of permanent storage. In order to do this, the executor assembles a probe cue, consisting of a random sample of information taken from the first compartment of the work space (Postulate C7), and searches the bins for a matching header (Postulate C4). As noted earlier, sources of interference can add both similar and dissimilar information to the work space, but in either case their introduction increases the probability that irrelevant information will be contained in the probe cue. When such an event occurs, the executor may be led to search an inappropriate bin. For instance, in the study by Keller (1991), the decreased recall ability of subjects exposed to a competitive advertising environment, but not given an ad retrieval cue, could be explained in this way. That is, the competitive ads introduced information to the work space that interfered with the compilation of an effective probe cue. That being the case, the executor was more often led to the wrong bin in permanent storage. Conversely, the information contained in the ad retrieval cue, when provided, served as a very effective probe cue, and thus led to enhanced recall.

This analysis of interference via processes operating in the work space and permanent storage leads to the following general proposition:

> P4: Memory for advertising may be adversely affected by all information external to the ad (i.e., whether it is similar or dissimilar to the ad information).

Interference From Similar Information

As P_4 points out, up to this point in the search process all information external to the ad itself has the ability to cause interference. The devastating effects of television clutter clearly depict the outcome of such general interference effects (e.g., Bogart & Lehman, 1983; Webb & Ray, 1979). However, analyzing the interference issue within the processes proposed by the Wyer–Srull model suggests the importance of paying particular attention to the interference caused by external information that is similar to the ad information. That is, once a bin is identified as relevant and the search through that bin begins, material similar to that contained within the bin is capable of introducing additional interference effects.

Research on comparative advertising provides suggestive evidence for this type of interference (e.g., Rogers & Williams, 1989). One can think of the consumer as having numerous "brand bins" in permanent storage into which they deposit all types of information relevant to the brand. A direct comparative ad (i.e., one where the comparison brand is explicitly named) may prompt the formation of a more general "product category bin" into which all types of information about the product category are deposited (e.g., brands available, important attributes). However, because information is stored and retrieved independently from the bins in permanent storage (Postulate B3), this type of ad increases the potential for interference. That is, with brand information retrieved separately from attribute information, the potential for incorrect associations, or failed recall attempts, increases.

Supporting this idea, Pechmann and Stewart (1990) found that sponsor misidentification was significantly greater for direct comparative ads than for both indirect comparative ads (i.e., where the other brand is not named) and noncomparative ads. As described earlier, the direct comparative ad may have prompted the formation of a product category bin, into which the information from the ad was deposited. When later asked, "Who sponsored the ad?" an individual, according to the Wyer–Srull conceptualization, will conduct a top-down search of the bin for the required information (Postulate C9). Because information is stored and retrieved in the order in which it is generated (Postulate B5) and exhaustive searches rarely occur (Postulate C11), this top-down search process may proceed only until the first piece of brand information is encountered. This may be the actual sponsor of the ad or it may be the other brand mentioned in the ad. According to the Wyer–Srull conceptualization, the first piece of brand information encountered in the bin is likely to be the last brand mentioned in the ad. Thus, the Wyer–Srull model underscores the importance of ending a direct comparative ad with a prominent display of the sponsor's brand.

In contrast to the situation for direct comparative ads, neither the indirect nor the noncomparative ad is likely to prompt the formation of a product class bin because only one brand is explicitly mentioned in the ad. Thus, in both cases, the information contained in the ad is likely to be deposited in the sponsor brand's bin, where it can be readily retrieved later.

This analysis indicates the extent to which advertising effectiveness is impacted by within-bin interference, and its implications can be summarized in the following proposition:

P5: Information that is in some way related to the ad will have a greater adverse impact on memory for advertising information than information that is not related to the ad.

Interference From Simultaneous Objectives

As discussed so far, interference is conceptualized as the loss of memory for an item of information due to disruption caused by other items of information (Baddeley, 1990). Within the present framework, item interference effects operate in the work space and within the bins of permanent storage. Interference effects may also arise, however, within the goal specification box, when performance of one task is disrupted by the performance of another (i.e., task interference). Although more than one goal can be pursued simultaneously, there is a limit to the capacity of this unit (cf., MacInnis & Jaworski, 1989). Specifically, as the complexity of the active goals increases, the number of goals that can be concurrently pursued decreases.

Although the potential for task interference is substantial in the environment in which advertising operates, this type of interference has been largely ignored by researchers. However, Biehal and Chakravarti's (1986) work on consumers' use of memory and external information in choice situations provides evidence in support of the idea that task interference influences the accessibility of consumption-related information. In their study, subjects made choices with either (a) all information available externally or (b) some information available externally and the rest available in memory. Recall measures collected after all the subjects made their choices revealed that subjects who had all the brand and attribute information available externally during the choice phase were subsequently better able to recall that information than subjects who had to rely on their memory for some of the choice information.

One interpretation of these findings is that the processing tasks associated with (a) gathering and interpreting external information and (b) storing and retrieving memory information interfere with one another. Several pieces of evidence gleaned from verbal protocol data in the Biehal and Chakravarti study suggest that these tasks may have been interfering with one another. First, it was found that a greater number of processing operations were employed when some of the choice information had to be retrieved from memory than when it was all available externally. Also, a greater variety of processing operations were employed when some of the choice information had to be retrieved from memory. Taken together, these findings indicate the complexity of processing required when both tasks are pursued simultaneously. Given the drop in recall in the dual task situation, these findings also suggest that the complexity of processing in this situation may, in fact, exceed the limits of the goal specification box.

The type of task interference highlighted here is certainly common in an advertising context (e.g., Gardial et al., 1993). For instance, a consumer may view an ad for a product and later visit a store to gather more information about that product. At the second store the consumer must gather the new information and recall the information obtained from the ad (also referred to as a memory-based task). As seen earlier, the consumer's recall in this situation may be hindered. Other types of task interference are likely to arise in an advertising setting as well. For example, the task of driving may interfere with the task of processing the information on a billboard. Similarly, listening to the radio is generally accompanied by some other task, and that task has the potential to interfere with the processing and recollection of ads placed on the radio. It is clear that the issue of task interference warrants further investigation by advertising researchers.

This discussion leads to the following proposition regarding task interference:

P6: Memory for advertising will be hindered by the simultaneous performance of tasks unrelated to processing the ad's contents.

The Relationship Between Time and Interference Effects

Although examined separately in this chapter, the analysis here highlights the complex interaction of time and interference effects on memory for advertising.

For instance, earlier it was suggested that the longer information is held in permanent storage without being used, the weaker memory for the information will be. This time-effects explanation will only hold, however, if related information is added to the bin in which the information resides. If no new information is added, the item will remain at the top of the bin and memory for it will not weaken over time. In such a case, time simply increases the probability of interference effects (Burke & Srull, 1988).

It was also suggested earlier that, over time, repeated usage of a piece of information decreases its loss from memory by increasing its number of representations and improving its position in the bin. In such a case, time decreases the probability of interference effects by allowing new representations of old information to be deposited on top of any similar information that may have been subsequently added to the bin.

As a final example of the interaction of time and interference effects, it was previously argued that the inability to remember very recently presented information (e.g., the videotaped ads in the Kent & Machleit [1990] study) could be traced to the automatic clearance of information from the work space. Given that the automatic clearance process is guided by a first-in, first-out principle, time clearly drives that memory effect. However, notice that automatic clearance is only necessary when the volume of incoming information exceeds the capacity of the work space. Thus, this time effect depends on the introduction of interfering information.

SUMMARY AND CONCLUSION

Using the Wyer–Srull model as a guide, this chapter analyzed the processes underlying memory for advertising. In particular, the focus was on how two key factors, the passage of time since viewing the ad and interference from information external to the ad, impact memory for ads. This analysis led to several propositions relevant to understanding and improving the effectiveness of advertising. In this section, we present a summary of the analysis, paying particular attention to the implications of that analysis for increasing advertising effectiveness.

Time Effects

As one might expect, the evidence reviewed here suggests that the passage of time has an adverse effect on consumer memory for advertising. Focusing on the processes underlying the impact of time, however, provided insight into how to combat these negative effects. First, research demonstrating a relationship between the processing objective active at the time of ad exposure, and the amount and type of information retained from an ad, suggests that it is critical that ads be designed to encourage particular processing objectives (our Proposition 2). For example, if the communication objective of the advertisement is to convey concrete product benefit information, then the ad should activate a processing goal that focuses attention on the product itself, not on other extraneous factors in the ad (e.g., the endorser, the color scheme). More generally, our analysis suggests that the advertiser pay close attention to whether the ad's relative focus on "substance versus style" fits with the ad's communication objective (Gardial et al., 1993).

Our analysis of the processes underlying the decline in memory for advertising over time also revealed that an ad's effectiveness can be improved by the repeated usage of ad information (our Proposition 3). A particularly important point to take away from that discussion is that it is not sheer repetition that leads to enhanced memory, but repetitive usage. This raises an interesting question: How do we get consumers to pay attention to an ad they have already seen several times? A potent way to do that would be to vary particular aspects of the ad. Demonstrating the efficacy of such a strategy, Schumann et al. (1990) found beneficial effects of both cosmetic variations (e.g., graphics, color) and substantive variations (e.g., product benefits) for the effectiveness of a repeated ad (see also Unnava & Burnkrant, 1991).

Interference Effects

The literature reviewed earlier indicated that information external to the ad plays an important role in determining memory for the ad's contents (our Proposition 4). This suggests that advertisers need to assume quite a broad perspective when identifying the material likely to compete with their message. For example, our analysis suggests that clutter effects come not only from other television ads, but also from information presented in the television program, ads placed in other media vehicles, and any other source of information to which the consumer is exposed. Although it is impossible to eliminate these potential sources of interference, an advertiser can take steps to ensure that ad information is retrievable at critical points in the decision process. For instance, having key ad elements available at the point of purchase may reduce interference effects by providing the consumer with an effective probe cue (Keller, 1991).

Beyond these general interference effects, analyzing the processes by which interference from other material impedes memory revealed the unique effects that information closely related to the ad can have on memory for advertising (our Proposition 5). This analysis suggests why both ads for competitive brands and ads for a different model of the same brand result in such strong interference effects. The obvious implication of this proposition is that advertisers should avoid placing ads in programs cluttered with ads for competing products (R. J. Kent, 1993). This is a critical implication because, as R. J. Kent (1993) pointed out, this prescription runs counter to the traditional practice of placing ads according to demographics.

Comparative advertising has long been of interest to advertising practitioners and academic researchers alike. Despite a great deal of research on the subject, there is little agreement regarding the effectiveness of this advertising technique (Barry, 1993; Donthu, 1992; Rogers & Williams, 1989). Viewing this issue from the perspective of the Wyer–Srull model provided unique insights into the process by which comparative advertising works, and suggested methods to ensure its effectiveness (e.g., always end a direct comparative ad with salient restatement of the sponsor brand).

Examining the processes underlying interference effects within the Wyer–Srull model also highlighted the existence of task interference (our Proposition 6). This form of interference recognizes that the performance of one task often interferes with the performance of another. Despite the prevalence of multitask situations in the environment in which advertising operates, this form of interference was found to be an area largely untouched by advertising researchers. When designing ads, advertisers need to consider the complexity of the tasks likely to accompany ad exposure. For example, people generally perform some other task while listening to the radio (e.g., driving, working), which suggests that ads placed on the radio need to be relatively easy to process (i.e., not require a complex set of procedures). In contrast, people are much less inclined to perform other tasks while reading a magazine and thus, ads requiring complex processing are much more likely to be effective when placed in that medium.

APPENDIX: WYER–SRULL POSTULATES

Structure and Function of Work Space

A1[a] The work space is of limited capacity.

A2 The displacement of information from the work space may be either automatic or volitional.

A3 Under conditions of high information-processing load, the material that has been least recently involved in the processing (either as input to a processing unit or as output from a unit) is most likely to be displaced from the work space.

A4 When the work space is cleared, any material that has not been transmitted to a bin in permanent storage is irretrievably lost.

Structure and Content of Permanent Storage

B1 The permanent storage unit consists of a set of content-addressable storage bins. Each bin is identified by a header that defines and circumscribes its contents.

---

[a]Postulates in the Wyer–Srull model have been renumbered in the present context for ease of exposition. From: Wyer, R. S., Jr., & Srull, T. K. (1986). Human cognition in its social context. *Psychological Review, 93*(3), 322–359.

B2 Only the output of processing information in pursuit of a specific objective is transmitted to permanent storage.

B3 The output of processing at each stage is transmitted to and stored in a referent bin as a separate unit of information. The output of each stage is transmitted and stored in the order it is generated.

B4 Information is transmitted to the bin pertaining to the referent to which processing objectives are relevant. If no previously formed bin pertaining to the referent exists, a new bin is formed.

Search and Retrieval Processes

C1 (Heuristic postulate): No more information is retrieved for use in attaining a processing objective than is sufficient to allow the objective to be attained. When this minimal amount has been retrieved, the search terminates.

C2 When information relevant to a processing objective is required, the contents of the work space are searched first.

C3 The search for information in the work space is random. The probability of retrieving a given unit of information from it is increased with the extensiveness with which the information has been processed.

C4 The relevance of any referent bin to a particular processing objective is determined by a comparison of the features in its header with a set of probe cues compiled by the executor.

C5 When no bin is found that contains all of the features in a set of probe cues, the set is randomly subdivided into smaller subsets, and the search is repeated using these subsets as probe cues until a bin is found.

C6 The probe cues compiled by the executor to govern the search of permanent storage are a sample of the features contained in Compartment 1 of the work space at the time the information is sought.

C7 Once a bin is identified, the remaining features of its header are searched for information relevant to attaining processing objectives. If these features and their implications are sufficient to attain these objectives, they are used without retrieving any information in the bin itself.

C8 (Recency postulate): When the contents of a bin are searched for the purpose of attaining a processing objective, the search proceeds from the top down. A particular unit of information is identified as potentially relevant if its features include the probe cues governing the search. The probability of retrieving a unit of information from a bin, given that units stored on top of it have not been used, is a constant.

C9 (Copy postulate): When a unit of information in a bin is identified as relevant for attaining a processing objective, a copy of this information is transmitted to the work space. Thus, the original position of the information in the bin is preserved. However, when processing objectives are completed, a copy of the retrieved unit of information is returned to the top of the bin from which it was drawn.

C10 (Stopping rule): A referent bin will be searched for goal-relevant information until either (a) information sufficient to attain processing objectives is obtained, (b) a total of n successive units have been retrieved that are inapplicable for attaining the objective, or (c) a total of k identical units of information have been identified, whichever comes first.

ACKNOWLEDGMENT

The authors wish to thank Bob Wyer for his thoughtful comments on an earlier draft of this chapter.

REFERENCES

Baddeley, A. (1990). *Human memory: Theory and practice.* Needham Heights, MA: Allyn & Bacon.

Barlow, T., & Wogalter, M. (1993). Alcoholic beverage warnings in magazine and television advertisements. *Journal of Consumer Research, 20*(1), 147–156.

Barry, T. (1993, March–April). Comparative advertising: What have we learned in two decades? *Journal of Advertising Research,* 19–29.

Biehal, G., & Chakravarti, D. (1986). Consumers' use of memory and external information in choice: Macro and micro perspectives. *Journal of Consumer Research, 12,* 382–405.

Bogart, L., & Lehman, C. (1983). The case of the 30–second commercial. *Journal of Advertising Research, 23*(1), 11–19.

Bower, G. H. (1975). Cognitive psychology: An introduction. In W. K. Estes (Ed.), *Handbook of learning and cognitive processes* (pp. 25–80). Hillsdale, NJ: Lawrence Erlbaum Associates.

Brown, S., & Stayman, D. (1992). Antecedents and consequences of attitude toward the ad: A meta-analysis. *Journal of Consumer Research, 19*(1), 34–51.

Burke, R. R., & Srull, T. (1988). Competitive interference and consumer memory for advertising. *Journal of Consumer Research, 15,* 55–68.

Costley, C. L., & Brucks, M. (1992). Selective recall and information use in consumer preferences. *Journal of Consumer Research, 18,* 464–474.

Donthu, N. (1992, November–December). Comparative advertising intensity. *Journal of Advertising Research,* 53–58.

Feldman, J. M., & Lynch, J. G. (1988). Self-generated validity and other effects of measurement on belief, attitude, intention and behavior. *Journal of Applied Psychology, 73,* 421–435.

Finlay, K. (1993). A new perspective on the effects of advertising repetition: The mediating role of memory structure. In L. McAlister & M. Rothschild (Eds.), *Advances in consumer research* (Vol. 20, p. 26). Provo, UT: Association for Consumer Research.

Gardial, S. F., Schumann, D., Petkus, E., & Smith, R. (1993). Processing and retrieval of inferences and descriptive advertising information: The effects of message elaboration. *Journal of Advertising, 22*(1), 25–34.

Hastak, M., & Olson, J. C. (1989). Assessing the role of brand-related cognitive responses as mediators of communication effects on cognitive structure. *Journal of Consumer Research, 15,* 444–456.

Hawkins, S. A., & Hoch, S. J. (1992). Low involvement learning: Memory without evaluation. *Journal of Consumer Research, 19,* 212–225.

Huffman, C., & Houston, M. (1993). Goal-oriented experiences and the development of knowledge. *Journal of Consumer Research, 20*(2), 190–207.

Hutchinson, J. W., & Moore, D. (1984). Issues surrounding the examination of delay effects in advertising. In T. Kinnear (Ed.), *Advances in consumer research* (pp. 650–655). Provo, UT: Association for Consumer Research.

Keller, K. L. (1991). Memory and evaluation effects in competitive advertising environments. *Journal of Consumer Research, 17,* 463–476.

Kent, R., & Machleit, K. (1990). The differential effects of within-brand and between-brand processing on the recall and recognition of television commercials. *Journal of Advertising, 19*(2), 4–14.

Kent, R. A. (1993). *Marketing research in action.* London: Rutledge.

Kent, R. J. (1993, March–April). Competitive versus noncompetitive clutter in television advertising. *Journal of Advertising Research,* 40–46.

Kisielius, J., & Sternthal, B. (1986). Examining the vividness controversy: An availability-valence interpretation. *Journal of Consumer Research, 12,* 418–431.

MacInnis, D., & Jaworski, B. (1989). Information processing from advertisements: Toward an integrative framework. *Journal of Marketing, 53,* 1–23.

Meyers-Levy, J. (1989). The influence of a brand name's association set size and word frequency on brand memory. *Journal of Consumer Research, 16,* 197–207.

Meyers-Levy, J., & Maheswaran, D. (1991). Exploring differences in males' and females' processing strategies. *Journal of Consumer Research, 18*(1), 63–70.

Norman, D. A. (1968). Toward a theory of memory and attention. *Psychological Review, 75,* 522–536.

Pechmann, C., & Stewart, D. (1990). The effects of comparative advertising on attention, memory, and purchase intentions. *Journal of Consumer Research, 17*(2), 180–191.

Peracchio, L. (1992). How do young children learn to be consumers? A script processing approach. *Journal of Consumer Research, 18,* 425–440.

Raaijmakers, J. G., & Shiffrin, R. M. (1992). Models for recall and recognition. *Annual Review of Psychology, 43,* 205–234.

Rogers, J., & Williams, T. (1989, October–November). Comparative advertising effectiveness: Practitioners' perceptions versus academic research findings. *Journal of Advertising Research,* 22–36.

Schumann, D., Petty, R., & Clemons, S. D. (1990). Predicting the effectiveness of different strategies of advertising variation: A test of the repetition-variation hypothesis. *Journal of Consumer Research, 17*(2), 192–202.

Srull, T. K., & Wyer, R. S., Jr. (1983). The role of control processes and structural constraints in models of memory and social judgment. *Journal of Experimental Social Psychology, 19,* 497–521.

Stewart, D. (1989). Measures, methods, and models in advertising research. *Journal of Advertising Research, 29,* 54–60.

Unnava, H. R., & Burnkrant, R. E. (1991). Effect of repeating varied ad executions on brand name memory. *Journal of Marketing Research, 28,* 406–416.

Wansink, B., & Ray, M. (1993). *How expansion advertising affects brand usage frequency: A programmic evaluation.* (Marketing Science Working Paper No. 93–126). Cambridge, MA: Marketing Science Institute.

Webb, P., & Ray, M. (1979). Effects of TV clutter. *Journal of Advertising Research, 19,* 7–12.

Wyer, R. S., Jr., & Srull, T. K. (1986). Human cognition in its social context. *Psychological Review, 93,* 322–59.

Wyer, R., & Srull, T. (1989). *Memory and cognition in its social context.* Hillsdale, NJ: Lawrence Erlbaum Associates.

12

The Effects of Program Context on Advertising Effectiveness

V. Carter Broach
University of Delaware

Thomas J. Page, Jr.
Michigan State University

R. Dale Wilson
Michigan State University

Since the early 1970s, much research has been conducted on the effectiveness of television advertising messages. In the vast majority of studies, this research has centered on the measurement of the effectiveness of a single commercial. However, in the real world of television advertising, commercials are run in groups, or pods. The possibility that a commercial's position within the pod may influence its overall effectiveness has received very little attention in the literature.

Not only are commercials shown in a pod, but the pod is embedded in a program. Programs are likely to have an impact on the way viewers react to commercials, and this response may influence effectiveness. Numerous studies (e.g., Goldberg & Gorn, 1987; Kamins, Marks, & Skinner, 1991) have examined the effect of programs on commercials. However, as pointed out by Mundorf, Zillman, and Drew (1991), the theoretical rationales for these studies have been diverse and the findings have been inconsistent. Thus, additional research that addresses some of the issues dealing with the impact of program context could expand our understanding of advertising effectiveness.

One area neglected in the literature is context effects within the pod of commercials. This area is relevant not only from a conceptual perspective, but also from a practitioner's standpoint because, as noted by Aaker, Stayman, and Hagerty (1986), some advertisers buy entire blocks of commercial time. As a result, they are able to control the placement of commercials within the pod.

The objective of the research reported here is to examine the effects of program context on viewers' immediate response to commercials. Immediate responses are important because they serve as important antecedents of longer-term effects and because they offer practical insights for the placement of commercials in television programs.

This chapter presents the details of two experiments designed to examine viewers' immediate response to commercials. The first experiment uses emotionally neutral commercials, whereas the second experiment uses emotionally positive commercials. The chapter then concludes with a discussion of the results of the two experiments, their implications, limitations of the study, and directions for future research.

BACKGROUND AND HYPOTHESES

Although numerous studies have examined program context effects, most have looked at only one dimension. For example, Singh and Churchill (1987) reviewed the concept of arousal, and Goldberg and Gorn (1987) examined pleasantness. No known studies have examined both dimensions simultaneously. The research reported here examines the effects of both program-induced arousal and pleasantness.

The first hypothesis concerns the effect of program-induced arousal on viewers' emotional response to commercials. Zillman (1988) argued that as arousal dissipates, viewer response will be based less on the arousing stimulus (i.e., the program) and more on the current stimulus (i.e., the commercial). Mattes and Cantor (1982), using stimuli that were much more arousing than normal television programming, found that program-induced arousal does decrease as a function of commercial pod position. This decrease in arousal should lead to commercial evaluations that dissipate over the commercial pod. Thus, the first hypothesis is:

> H1: There will be a two-way interaction between program arousal and commercial pod position. The nature of the interaction will be such that the effects of high program arousal on emotional response to neutral commercials will decrease as the number of commercials increases. The low-arousal program will have no effect on emotional response to neutral commercials.

The second hypothesis concerns the effect of program-induced pleasantness on viewer response. Because pleasantness is a dimension of emotional response as defined by Mehrabian and Russell (1974), it is expected to produce the same type of effects as arousal. Mundorf et al. (1991) found that exposure to an unpleasant news story impaired the viewer's ability to acquire information, but this impairment decreased as the time between viewing and the measurement increased. Simply stated, it is expected that pleasant programs create pleasant reactions to neutral commercials at the beginning of the pod, and these reactions wear off for later commercials. Likewise, unpleasant programs create negative reactions to the commercials that wear off for later commercials. Thus, the second hypothesis is:

H2: There will be a two-way interaction between program pleasantness and commercial pod position. The nature of the interaction will be such that neutral commercials embedded in pleasant programs will be perceived as less pleasant as the number of commercials increases, and neutral commercials embedded in unpleasant programs will be perceived as more pleasant as the number of commercials increases.

METHOD

Overall Design and Covariates

The study used a $2 \times 2 \times 4$ design, with program arousal (low vs. high) and program pleasantness (pleasant vs. unpleasant) being between-subjects factors and commercial pod position (first, second, third, and fourth) being a within-subjects factor. Because there is no a priori theoretical rationale for predicting how many commercial pod positions might be influenced by program arousal or program pleasantness, four commercial pod positions were used to simulate a realistic "commercial break" from the programming. Order effects were controlled by rotating the sequence of commercials, with each commercial appearing equally often in every ordinal position.

The dependent variable was commercial pleasantness. Due to the expectation that a relatively high level of arousal or feeling of pleasantness prior to the experiment could serve as alternate explanations for the hypothesized effects, both were measured prior to the experiment and treated as covariates. A third covariate—subjects' prior familiarity with the commercials—was also measured. The measures for the covariates are discussed next.

Sample

The subjects were students enrolled in either an undergraduate principles of marketing course or an undergraduate communications course at a large midwestern university. They were told that a local TV station needed help in deciding what programs to rerun during the summer. The few subjects who guessed the true purpose of the study were dropped from the analysis. Subjects were paid a small amount of cash in return for their participation in the study. There were 20 subjects (10 male and 10 female) in each of the between-subjects cells, for a total of 80 subjects.

Variables

Measures of arousal and pleasantness, for both the covariates and the dependent variable, were selected from Averill's (1975) semantic atlas of emotional words. Prior arousal was measured by asking subjects to respond to the statement, "Presently, I feel:" followed by five adjectives. The five adjectives were active, excited, stimulated, lively, and activated. Subjects' responses were measured on a scale ranging from 0 (*not*) to 6 (*extremely*). When assessing program arousal, subjects responded to the statement, "Did the TV program as a whole make you feel:" followed by the five adjectives used for prior arousal. When measuring prior pleasantness, subjects responded to the statement, "At this time I feel:" followed by five adjectives. The five bipolar adjectives were positive–negative, good–bad, nice–awful, happy–sad, and pleasant–unpleasant. For program pleasantness, subjects responded to the statement, "Did the program as a whole make you feel:" followed by the same five adjectives. For commercial pleasantness, the dependent variable, subjects responded to the statement, "Did the commercial as a whole make you feel:" followed by the same five adjectives. For each of the three pleasantness measures, the scale ranged from +3 (*extremely pleasant*) to –3 (*extremely unpleasant*). For each scale, the summary measure was the mean of the five items.

For the measure of commercial familiarity, subjects were asked, "Have you seen this commercial before? (yes or no)." When a subject answered "yes," he or she was asked, "If yes, about how many times have you seen this commercial?" Each subject's response was then measured on a ratio scale ranging from 0 (*No*) to *n* (with *n* equal to the number of times each subject indicated that he or she had seen the commercial).

Selection of the TV Programs

The four program segments were pretested extensively. Real programs were used because it was extremely unlikely that artificial stimuli would create the levels of the independent variables needed for a valid test of the hypotheses. In addition, the external validity of a study using artificial programs would be quite low.

The subjects used to pretest the programs were enrolled in the same courses as subjects used in the main experiment. Respondents viewed 10-minute program segments and rated them using the arousal and pleasantness measures described earlier.

The programs used in the experiment were *Double Trouble* (the low arousing, pleasant program), *Cable Hearing* (the low arousing, unpleasant program), *Buddy Hackett* (the highly arousing, pleasant program), and *The Hitcher* (the highly arousing, unpleasant program). *Double Trouble* (DT), a situation comedy shown on the USA Network, featured two young, adult women who are identical twins. The segment portrayed a rather awkward situation that occurred when one of the twins dated an older man. *Cable Hearing* (CH), a segment shown by the C-SPAN channel, was testimony before a U.S. Senate subcommittee about the monopolistic tendencies of cable television. *Buddy Hackett* (BH) was a comedy routine that appeared on the Home Box Office (HBO) channel. The segment was a ribald account of Hackett's experiences on a skiing trip. *The Hitcher* (TH) was taken from a movie that also appeared on HBO. The segment showed a hitchhiker who was threatening to kill a young man with a knife.

Pretests assessed both the reliability of the measures and the extent to which program arousal and program pleasantness were manipulated as expected. Cronbach's α for the program arousal scales by program were: $\alpha_{DT} = .98$, $\alpha_{CH} = .95$, $\alpha_{BH} = .91$, and $\alpha_{TH} = .94$. Cronbach's α for the program pleasantness scales by program were: $\alpha_{DT} = .96$, $\alpha_{CH} = .93$, $\alpha_{BH} = .95$, and $\alpha_{TH} = .85$.

Pretest checks included two analyses of covariance (ANCOVAs) with program arousal and program pleasantness manipulations as independent variables. In the first analysis, the main effect of program arousal was significant at the .001 level, $F(1, 98) = 120.47, p < .001$. No other significant findings were present. In the high arousal condition, the mean was 5.54. In the low arousal condition, the mean was 2.36. Therefore, program arousal was manipulated as expected.

In the second analysis, the main effect of program pleasantness was significant, $F(1, 98) = 95.77, p < .001$. The mean was 1.32 in the pleasant program condition while the mean was -0.74 in the unpleasant program condition. The two-way interaction of pleasantness by arousal was also significant, $F(1, 98) = 22.92, p < .001$. There were no other significant effects. A hierarchical multiple regression indicated that the interaction accounted for a very small portion of the total variance. Because the interaction was ordinal, we concluded that pleasantness was manipulated as intended (Keppel, 1982).

Selection of the Commercials

As Aaker et al. (1986) advocated, real commercials were used to enhance external validity. To assure that the commercials were relatively neutral in pleasantness, they were pretested extensively with subjects enrolled in the same courses as subjects used in the main experiment.

The commercials were 30-second advertisements for Check-Up toothpaste, Crystal Ice Cream, McDonald's, and WLTI Radio. The Check-Up (CU) toothpaste commercial compared Check-Up to Crest and Colgate on ability to clean teeth and remove plaque. The Crystal Ice Cream (CI) commercial featured a Crystal factory foreman discussing how Crystal assured a high level of product quality. The McDonald's (MD) commercial described how McDonald's buys only fresh ingredients for its hamburgers. The WLTI Radio (WL) commercial presented the station's format. (WLTI was not available in the area where the data were collected).

Cronbach's αs for the commercial pleasantness scale by commercial were: $\alpha_{CU} = .91$, $\alpha_{CI} = .95$, $\alpha_{MD} = .90$, and $\alpha_{WL} = .96$. Commercial pleasantness was not significantly different from zero for the Check-Up Toothpaste commercial ($\bar{x}_{CU} = .27, t = 1.09, p = .290$) or the Crystal Ice Cream commercial ($\bar{x}_{CI} = .57, t = 1.68, p = .110$). However, commercial pleasantness was significantly different from zero for the McDonald's commercial ($\bar{x}_{MD} = .65, t = 2.31, p =$

.033) and the WLTI Radio commercial ($\bar{x}_{WL} = .80$, $t = 2.30$, $p = .033$). Thus, two of the commercials selected to be neutral in pleasantness were slightly positive. The average score for commercial familiarity was 0.74, indicating that subjects had seen the commercials on average less than one time each.

Procedure

The program and commercials were professionally edited together to replicate broadcast quality. For each cell in the experiment, subjects were shown the programs and commercials in a small classroom. Subjects were run in groups of 5 to 10 subjects per session.

Prior to being exposed to any stimuli, subjects filled out a questionnaire that measured their current levels of arousal and pleasantness. Then each group of subjects saw the videotape of a 10-minute program segment and four 30-second commercials. After viewing the videotape, subjects answered questions about the program (to confirm the guise of the study) and responded to the dependent variable measures. Finally, subjects were debriefed, thanked, and paid for their participation.

RESULTS OF EXPERIMENT 1

The results reported here are for the within-subjects factor of commercial position within the pod. The between-subjects factors are not relevant to this study. The results of Experiment 1 focus on the data generated by the emotionally neutral commercials described earlier. Experiment 2, to be discussed later in this chapter, focuses on emotionally positive commercials.

Reliability

Cronbach's α for each administration of all measures used in the study ranged from .85 to .98. Thus, the measures were reliable.

Manipulation Checks

Two ANCOVAs determined that program arousal and program pleasantness were manipulated as expected. In the first analysis, induced arousal was the dependent variable. In the second analysis, induced pleasantness was the dependent variable. In the first analysis, the effect of the set of covariates was significant, $F(2, 74) = 4.35$, $p = .016$, but only the effect of prior arousal was significant individually, $F(1, 74) = 5.20$, $p = .025$. The main effect of the program arousal manipulation was significant, $F(1, 74) = 53.24$, $p < .001$. There were no other significant findings. The program arousal means were 3.88

in the high arousal condition and 2.28 in the low arousal condition, respectively. Thus, program arousal was manipulated as expected.

In the second analysis, the main effect of program pleasantness was significant, $F(1, 74) = 68.41, p < .001$. The unpleasantness mean was 1.35 in the pleasant program condition and -0.67 in the unpleasant program condition. The two-way interaction of the program pleasantness manipulation by the program arousal manipulation was also significant, $F(1, 74) = 4.83, p = .031$. There were no other significant findings. A plot of the induced pleasantness means indicated an ordinal interaction, and a hierarchical multiple regression showed that the interaction accounted for only a small percentage of the total explained variance. Thus, even though there was a slight confounding between the independent variables, its magnitude was small and did not present a problem in allowing the hypotheses to be tested as intended (Keppel, 1982).

Effects Within the Pod of Commercials

A within-subjects ANCOVA with four repeated measures tested the hypotheses for all four commercial pod positions. H1 and H2 predicted two-way interactions of program arousal by commercial pod position and program pleasantness with commercial pod position, respectively. For the interaction of program arousal with commercial pod position (H1), the effect of the high-arousal programs was expected to decline over the series of commercials in the pod, but the effect of the low-arousal programs was expected to remain unchanged over pod position. For the interaction of program pleasantness with commercial pod position (H2), it was anticipated that in the pleasant program condition, the effect of the program would increase viewers' perception of commercial pleasantness for neutral commercials in the initial pod position; this effect would be expected to subside over the series of commercials in the pod. Within the unpleasant program condition, the effect of program pleasantness was expected to initially depress viewers' perception of commercial pleasantness for neutral commercials in the initial pod position, and this effect would diminish over pod position. The within-subjects repeated measures ANCOVA for all four commercial pod positions indicated that there were no significant results. Thus, H1 and H2 were not supported for four commercial pod positions. However, it is possible that any effects of program arousal or program pleasantness might have dissipated by the fourth commercial pod position.

Because it could not be predicted a priori how many commercial pod positions might be influenced by program arousal or program pleasantness, it was decided to test for the effect of the predicted two-way interactions by excluding the fourth commercial pod position. Thus, a within-subjects repeated measures ANCOVA was conducted to test H1 and H2 for the first three commercial pod positions. This ANCOVA indicated that the predicted two-way interaction of program pleasantness by commercial pod position (H2) was significant at $p = .06$, $F(2, 151) = 2.89$, as shown in Fig. 12.1.

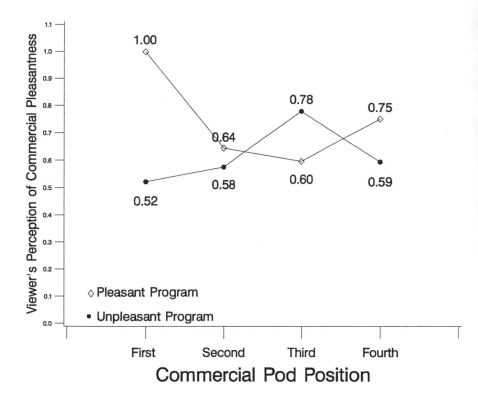

FIG. 12.1. Commercial pleasantness means—Effects of program pleasantness by pod position.

Simple contrasts were performed on the two-way interaction. For each program pleasantness condition, the simple contrasts compared the effect at each commercial pod position to the effect at the third commercial pod position. There was a significant effect between the first and third commercial pod position, $F(1, 77) = 4.16, p = .04$, for the pleasant program condition but not for the unpleasant program condition.

A plot of commercial pleasantness means by pod position indicated that commercial pleasantness declined between the first and third pod positions (see Fig. 12.1). Within the pleasant program condition, viewers' mean perception of commercial pleasantness for commercials in the third commercial pod position decreased relative to the first pod position. The commercial pleasantness mean for the commercials at the second and third pod positions in the pleasant program condition were not significantly different from the commercial pleasantness mean for their respective counterparts in the unpleasant program condition. Furthermore, the commercial pleasantness mean for commercials in the third pod position in either condition did not differ significantly, $t = 0.52$, $p = .604$, from the pretest commercial pleasantness mean for those commercials. Therefore, H2 was supported statistically for three commercial pod positions in the pleasant program condition. The effect of program-induced pleasantness, based on these results, appears to dissipate by the third position in a pod of four 30-second commercials. However, a close look at Fig. 12.1 indicates that most of this dissipation takes place between the first and second commercial positions.

The program arousal by commercial position interaction (H1), analyzed for the first three commercials, was marginally significant ($p = .081$), but it was not in the expected direction. That is, as shown in Fig. 12.2, perceived commercial pleasantness in the low program arousal condition was higher than perceived commercial pleasantness in the high program arousal condition. It was expected that commercial pleasantness would decline by commercial position in the high program arousal condition but would remain relatively flat in the low program arousal condition. However, mean commercial pleasantness for commercials in the first commercial pod position was higher in the low program arousal condition than it was in the high program arousal condition. By the second commercial pod position, this effect had dissipated and, for the remaining pod positions, perceived commercial pleasantness was equal for both program arousal conditions. Therefore, H2 is supported marginally for the first three commercial positions.

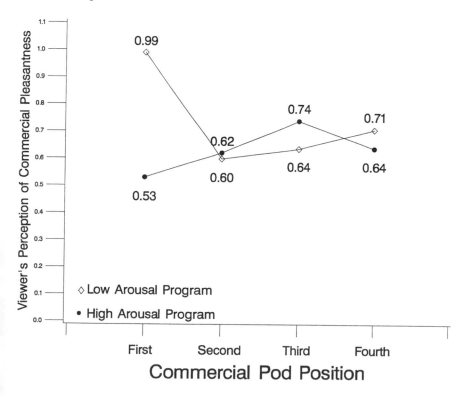

FIG. 12.2. Commercial pleasantness means—Effects of program arousal by pod position.

Experiment 2

The purpose of the second experiment was to determine whether program effects are negated when the commercials produce emotionally positive effects. Everything in the second experiment was the same as the first experiment except that emotionally positive commercials were used rather than emotionally neutral commercials. The same programs were used, but the commercials were again extensively pretested to ensure that they induced positive emotional responses in the viewers. The study of emotionally positive commercials was seen as a logical extension of Experiment 1 that would further investigate the impact of program context on advertising effectiveness.

The commercials used in Experiment 2 consisted of 30-second spots for Kodak, Wheaties, Tofutti, and the Beef Council. The Kodak commercial depicted a touching "photo opportunity" of two boys playing ice hockey. The Wheaties commercial featured baseball great Pete Rose breaking Ty Cobb's career hit record (the data were collected just prior to the disclosure of Pete Rose's alleged gambling and income tax problems). The Tofutti commercial was a parody of a board of directors meeting in which the directors sing about the good taste of Tofutti (a dessert product). The Beef Council commercial showed actor James Garner enjoying beef in a restaurant. As in Experiment 1, the scales used to measure the variables were found to be reliable (i.e., all of the Cronbach's αs were greater than .85), and the manipulation checks indicated that the programs and commercials were successful in creating the desired effects.

The repeated-measures ANCOVA showed no significant interactions for either program-induced arousal or pleasantness by commercial position when all four positions were included in the analysis. Furthermore, no significant interactions were found when only the first three or first two positions were included. Thus, positive emotional commercials appear to be capable of negating the program effects found in Experiment 1.

DISCUSSION

The results of the two experiments provide insight into the effects of program context on viewers' reactions to a series of commercials. In particular, the results of Experiment 1 show that, for neutral commercials, the effects of program pleasantness wear off fairly quickly. In fact, Fig. 12.1 indicates that, after the first commercial, the effects of commercial pleasantness have largely dissipated. Thus, it seems that a commercial that is run immediately following a pleasant program may benefit from a positive carryover effect. However, the carryover effect is not evident for commercials run immediately after unpleasant programs.

For program-induced arousal in Experiment 1, the effect also wears off quickly. The results of the study indicate that the low-arousal program produced more positive evaluations of the commercials than the high-arousal program, although this effect wears off rapidly after the first commercial in the pod. In fact, Fig. 12.2 shows that the first commercial run after a low-arousal program seems to benefit rather substantially. One possible explanation for this finding is a contrast effect. Subjects may have seen the low-arousal program as so boring that the commercials were seen as a welcome relief. In the high-arousal program condition, subjects may have disliked the interruption of the action so much that it was reflected in their negative evaluations of the commercials.

In Experiment 2, which used emotionally positive commercials, program-context effects were negated. Neither program pleasantness nor program arousal produced any effect on subjects' commercial pleasantness scores. Presumably, the program-context effects were negated because the commercials were strong enough to produce the desired effect themselves. In other words, emotionally positive commercials seem to generate a short-term response that is independent from either program pleasantness or program arousal.

These results have several implications for assessing advertising effectiveness. First, advertisers who use emotionally neutral commercials, such as factual or informational ads, should evaluate both the type of program and where in the pod the commercial is placed. For example, placing an emotionally neutral commercial immediately following a pleasant program segment may enhance the commercial's ability to communicate its information to the viewer. Because viewers will evaluate a commercial more positively, they may pay more attention to the commercial and thus absorb more of the information. On the other hand, placing an emotionally neutral commercial immediately following an unpleasant program may limit the effectiveness of that commercial. These implications are especially important for advertisers who can control the placement of commercials within the pod. Second, it would seem that advertisers who use emotionally positive commercials could depend on the strength of the commercial itself to generate a positive response without having to worry about program-context effects.

As with any research, limitations must be acknowledged. The main limitation concerns the use of real programs and commercials instead of artificially created stimuli. The use of real commercials undoubtedly increases the external validity of the experiments, but it also decreases the control over the manipulations. This is most likely why the manipulation of program pleasantness was slightly confounded with program arousal. It simply may not be possible to generate perfectly clean manipulations using real stimuli. However, this was seen as an acceptable trade-off in this study, especially because the confounding was relatively minor. Other limitations include the use of a sample consisting of university students and the artificial situation used to expose subjects to the experimental stimuli and collect the data. In future studies, improvement of these aspects of the research would help to enhance external validity.

Although this research provides some insight into the effects of program context on viewer response to commercials, several questions remain. Now that the short-term effects of program context have been demonstrated, research needs to examine how these effects interact with other, longer term measures of advertising effectiveness such as attitude toward the brand, attitude toward the ad, and purchase intention. Also, unpleasant commercials, such as some public service announcements, should be examined to see if they are capable of negating program effects in the same manner as positive commercials did in Experiment 2. One other issue to be investigated is the effect of varying length of program segments and commercial pods. Commercials in programs and pods of different lengths may have different emotional impact.

REFERENCES

Aaker, D. A., Stayman, D. M., & Hagerty, M. R. (1986). Warmth in advertising: Measurement, impact, and sequence effects. *Journal of Consumer Research, 12*, 365–381.

Averill, J. R. (1975). A semantic atlas of emotional concepts. *JSAS Catalogue of Selected Documents in Psychology*, 330.

Goldberg, M. E., & Gorn, G. J. (1987). Happy and sad TV programs: How they affect reactions to commercials. *Journal of Consumer Research, 14*, 387–403.

Kamins, M., Marks, L. J., & Skinner, D. (1991). Television commercial evaluation in the context of program induced mood. *Journal of Advertising, 20*, 1–14.

Keppel, G. (1982). *Design and analysis: A researcher's handbook*. Englewood Cliffs, NJ: Prentice-Hall.

Mattes, J., & Cantor, J. (1982). Enhancing responses to television advertisements via the transfer of residual arousal from prior programming. *Journal of Broadcasting, 26*, 553–566.

Mehrabian, A., & Russell, J. A. (1974). *An approach to environmental psychology*. Cambridge, MA: MIT Press.

Mundorf, N., Zillman, D., & Drew, D. (1991). Effects of disturbing televised events on the acquisition of information from subsequently presented commercials. *Journal of Advertising, 20*, 46–53.

Singh, S. N., & Churchill, G. A. (1987). Arousal and advertising effectiveness. *Journal of Advertising, 16*, 4–10, 40.

Zillman, D. (1988). Cognition-excitation interdependencies in aggressive behavior. *Aggressive Behavior, 14*, 51–64.

Comments on Chapter 12

Brian Wansink
University of Illinois, Urbana–Champaign

Chapter 12 has notable methodological implications for researchers, as well as practical "Monday-morning" implications for managers. A primary finding was that a neutral ad will be viewed more favorably if it follows a pleasant or an uninvolving TV program than if it follows an unpleasant or highly involving program. Such ads are not viewed more favorably, however, if (a) they are positive instead of neutral, or (b) they are preceded by one or more ads in the commercial pod.

METHODOLOGICAL CONTRIBUTIONS

The findings of Broach, Page, and Wilson suggest that null results found by some advertising researchers could be due to noise from program context effects. The important lesson that researchers can take from these studies is that subtle advertising effects can be overwhelmed by pod position and by program interference. If we are not interested in context effects, we may wish to avoid using highly valenced programming in our studies. Furthermore, we should think carefully about what the optimal position is in a commercial pod.

Similarly, if one is intentionally studying the impact of context effects (such as pod position and programming), it is important to note that a positive-valenced ad can wipe out any evidence of such effects. In such contexts, neutral ads should yield the greatest differences in processing and attitude formation. Imagine there are three ads in a pod. If studying advertising effectiveness, the target ad should be put in the third position. If studying program context effects, the target ad should be put in the first.

MANAGERIAL IMPLICATIONS

If a manager could control the position of his or her ads within a pod, the perfect placement would be the first ad following a pleasant or unarousing program, or the third ad following an unpleasant or arousing program. Unfortunately, managers have neither the luxury of choosing such placement, nor the luxury of prescreening all TV shows on which they advertise. What should a manager do? First, if feasible, broadcast only positive-valenced ads, because they appear to minimize program-context effects. Second, if positively valenced ads cannot be produced, ads should be placed on programs that are predicted to be pleasant and unarousing.

It is refreshing to read research that is rigorous and conclusive enough to offer direction to both academics and practitioners. A next step to take would be in a theoretical direction. It will be useful to determine the circumstances under which contrast effects might negate the affect referral process we appear to see here.

Comments on Chapter 12

Abhilasha Mehta
Gallup & Robinson, Inc.

The effect of program context on advertising effectiveness has been recognized as an important and relevant issue in evaluating advertising performance, and much research exists on the subject. Broach, Page, and Wilson, in this study, have taken the investigation further by focusing on studying context effects for different positions within a pod of commercials. The influence of pleasant or unpleasant and highly arousing or low-arousing programs were studied for emotionally positive and neutral commercials in four pod positions.

The dependent variable studied was commercial pleasantness. Results for the emotionally neutral commercial showed an influence of the pleasant program for the first pod position; this effect of the commercial being perceived as significantly more pleasant declined over the second and third positions. A similar trend was found for the arousing program conditions, although not in the expected direction. Only the first pod position was influenced, but contrary to expectations, commercial pleasantness was higher for the low-arousing program. No effect for the unpleasant program condition was found. Results for the same experiments with emotionally pleasant commercials showed no effects of the pleasant or unpleasant or high- and low-arousing programs on any pod positions.

The study results have relevance for media planners in the real world. It seems that when emotionally pleasant commercials are used, advertisers need not be concerned about the position within the pod that their commercial will appear in—at least, not for commercial pleasantness effects. When emotionally neutral commercials are used, however, program effects are likely for the first pod position. These results, however, need to be substantiated in in-market tests with nonstudent samples.

The one important issue to explore is related to better understanding the dependent variable used in this study, namely commercial pleasantness. What is this construct? Is it a valid measure of advertising effectiveness? How does commercial pleasantness correlate with ad attitude or commercial liking—variables that have been shown to influence brand attitudes in previous research? Two important measures used extensively in evaluative and diagnostic advertising research in the industry relate to intrusiveness and persuasion. Although these concepts are operationalized in a variety of ways, they are generally accepted as valid and valuable measures of advertising effectiveness. How does commercial pleasantness relate to these variables, in the short term as well as long term? Further, it would be useful to study program context effects for different pod positions for the variables such as intrusiveness and persuasion.

Comments on Chapter 12

Christine Wright-Isak
Young & Rubicam, Advertising

PRACTICAL RELEVANCE OF THIS RESEARCH

The strengths of Broach, Page, and Wilson's work lie in the systematic effort they have made to call attention to the importance of identifying ways in which programming can enhance or diminish the impact of advertising. Their findings are directly relevant to two important aspects of the advertising process, namely the development of creative and the effective placement of that creative so it can do its work best. They focus on the emotional character of both ads and programs—which are the elements that keep people watching. Their subject is important because the intersection of program and ad has not been explored at all adequately. They are attempting to determine factors that define optimal positioning in pods, which is something client and agency managers would love to know.

Too often in evaluating advertising we fail to take into account the environment in which it must deliver its message. Chapter 12 focuses on television commercials and their unique 15 or 30 seconds of contact with viewers. However, consumers do not view advertising in the analytical way research scholars or business managers do. For those of us in academia, isolating effects and attributing their impact free of other variables is important and it is how we instinctively think about testing the effects of a commercial. For industry managers, knowing whether or not the creative we commissioned was the best use of the advertising budget and that our media placement was the most efficient possible are the most important issues that preoccupy us in judging its effectiveness.

For the consumer, however, ads are simply alternative and additional sets of stimuli that they watch on TV between attending to the story or sports event or news exposition that constitutes the program choice. In these days of VCRs and increased surfing of the channels offered by cable networks, the programs themselves are hard pressed to keep viewers watching. Advertising has an ever more difficult job to do to hold viewer interest in a very brief period of time. Some advertisers try to capture viewer attention by scheduling their messages as *roadblocks*. This is the practice of placing the same ad in the same time slot on all three main networks so that viewers cannot easily avoid being exposed to it. Additional strategies to hold viewer attention and increase the impact of advertising in today's different media environment are strongly desired by practitioners.

218

USEFULNESS OF THE FINDINGS

The usefulness of the findings in chapter 12 is limited by the nature of the research design. By examining the valence (positive, neutral, or negative) of affect, they make a useful contribution in systematically comparing the impact of program and commercial separately and together on viewers' felt reactions. However, by focusing on isolating psychological variables they do not address the impact of sociocultural variables that have a great deal to do with how messages are reacted to and interpreted.

To the consumer, a pod of ads is not a distinct unit of analysis; it is a series of interruptions. The first ad in a pod is the immediately antecedent context for the second, and both are context for the third. Except in the case of episodic pairs of ads designed to follow one another, ads in pods occur in disjunction. They concern different categories of products brought to us by different clients and labeled with different brand names, and are therefore interrupters of program continuity and of pod continuity as well. In actual commercial situations, control over the entire pod is unlikely. A pod is a very complicated perceptual situation for viewers, especially because their motivation for viewing is to pay attention to the program rather than the ads. Further complicating the research situation is the fact that emotions are so volatile, evanescent, and fleeting (often lasting only seconds before changing).

A considerable amount of work has been done regarding what I call the "happy halo" effect of how positive emotions generated by programming influence receptivity to the ads embedded within it. In attempting to extend this work to pods of ads, the authors do a service to our consideration of effectiveness. However, they suffer the same shortcomings most work on mood effects suffers, namely that the socially generated meanings contained in programs and the other ads that form the context for a given ad being tested are not adequately taken into account in either the design or interpretation of the research.

If we consider communication generally, we attend to and remember that which has meaning for us. The culture in which we are raised and the culture we operate in both have great impact in defining what is important, what is significant, and what is incomprehensible about any message we receive. Aspects of culture like social role, social status, customs, and normative speech and behavior all factor into our apprehension of an ad as well as its programming and advertising pod environment.

From an applied perspective, one also needs to be concerned with the characteristics of the viewers. Generalizability of this work is limited by the use of college students as subjects. College students are least likely to be regular TV viewers and do not resemble the majority of advertisers' target audiences with regard to life phase, social experience, or decision-making processes. The product categories in which they are the appropriate audience for advertising are similarly limited. As a result, both their emotional responses to the TV stimuli and their reactions to the ads is likely to be questioned in actual agency–client situations.

FUTURE RESEARCH POSSIBILITIES

Future work in several subject areas could build on understanding the consumers own experiences in watching television and how messages and other information is extracted from them. For example, some work has already been done that indicates consumer proactivity in grazing ads and programming for role models and socialization information among adolescents. Factoring some of those audience motivations into interpreting reaction to the content of ads and programming along with the impact of affect in reacting to them would make work on pod effects more specific and more useful.

Three existing streams of research could be synthesized and extended by focusing their theoretical issues into the design of future pod examinations. They include sociology of role and status effects on television usage, work on the impact of affect on advertising reception, and reader response work on the impact of contextual meaning on message interpretation by audiences. All three perspectives are richly informative about the process this work attempts to measure and could help refine hypotheses so that future measurement might uncover differences in response.

13

Television Viewing Behavior as an Indicator of Commercial Effectiveness

Esther Thorson
University of Missouri–Columbia

Xinshu Zhao
University of North Carolina

This chapter considers the notion that a critical measure of commercial effectiveness is the probability that a commercial will be watched when it occurs in a competitive television environment. In the United States, people generally watch television to experience the programming, not the commercials. There is therefore little positive motivation to expend effort to watch commercials. As leisure time decreases, people have more and more to accomplish and that likely means that time dedicated solely to watching—rather than watching interspersed with other activities—is lessened. Commercial "breaks" are just that, a break time during which people can do something else without missing the programming. Remote controls allow people to "channel surf" during commercials, and the increasing number of cable channels available increases the time spent "surfing." Videocassette players allow the prerecording of programming, making it possible for individuals to fast-forward through the ads. In addition, the environment in which people "watch" television is a busy one, and competing events no doubt distract attention from watching (e.g., see Krugman & Rust, 1993).

What all of this adds up to is competition for attention to commercials. Therefore, a commercial that can produce a high likelihood of being watched can be thought of as a highly "effective" message. Based on the assumption that commercial effectiveness includes "stopping" power and "holding" power, this chapter examines a series of analyses of people's watching of television commercials. The data discussed here come from a natural viewing experiment wherein people could either watch television or engage in a number of alternative activities including eating, reading, leaving the room, or talking to each other.

From the outset it should be noted that, in this experiment, respondents did not have the opportunity to change channels with a remote. This opportunity would have allowed a better replication of home viewing. In general, however, the approach taken here allows examination of the effectiveness of commercials in capturing attention, as indexed by viewer watching behavior (hereafter referred to as eyes on screen or EOS). Although EOS is not a perfect measure of attention, it can provide some interesting insights into what it is about commercials that motivates people to watch them and thereby influences subsequent aspects of effectiveness.

The organization of this chapter is as follows. First, we look at how people have tried to measure attention to television. Second, we examine the extent to which EOS can be considered a measure of attention, and compare EOS to other ways of measuring attention to television. Third, we describe an extensive study in which the data reported here were collected. Fourth, we examine the relationships among (a) watching, (b) learning the content of commercials, and (c) attitudinal response to them. This is necessary in order to demonstrate that "watching" is a reasonable index of commercial effectiveness, in that it predicts learning from and being swayed by commercials.

Finally, we look at five main barriers to viewing. The first concerns the impact of the programming in which a commercial occurs. The second concerns the creative qualities of the commercial, including its perceived relevance to the viewer, its originality, and its affective impact. The third concerns the location of a commercial's position in the programming. The fourth concerns the commercial's location within a particular break. The fifth concerns the intrinsic loss of viewing to which commercials in general are subject. As we show, each of these types of "barriers" to watching provides a major challenge to the impact of a commercial. If a commercial can overcome these challenges, its effectiveness, at least in an immediate viewing sense, can be considered high.

EOS AS A MEASURE OF THE ATTENTIONAL IMPACT OF COMMERCIALS

Determining a satisfactory definition for attention and then operationalizing its measurement has long presented a challenge to psychologists, media, and consumer researchers.

In the experimental literature on television viewing, watching is often measured online. For example, eye gaze in children or adults is sometimes measured while they watch (Anderson, 1987; Collett, 1987; Horn & Atkin, 1987). Sometimes, after viewing, people are simply asked how much attention they paid to various components of the viewing materials (Friestad & Thorson, 1993). Which measure is used probably determines to a large degree the relationship between watching and remembering.

In the survey literature, Chaffee and Schleuder (1986) reported that the correlations between exposure measures and knowledge tend to be small, or sometimes even negative. Chaffee and Schleuder, in their discussion of the lack of relationship between watching and memory, noted that it is important to distinguish between asking people about exposure levels and asking them to rate how much attention they have paid to news stories of various types. Indeed, Chaffee and Choe (1979) showed that whereas the number of stories reported predicts political knowledge for newspapers, attention paid to the stories predicts political knowledge for television. Chaffee and Schleuder (1986) showed that general news knowledge gain could be predicted by attentional self-report, even after exposure levels were covaried out. This was particularly true for television.

Asking survey respondents how much attention they paid to specific exemplars of television messages, which demonstrates a stronger relationship between watching and memory, then, becomes more consistent with the results of experimental research. In fact, experiments usually demonstrate that people learn from watching television (Drew & Reeves, 1980; Gunter, 1987; Lemert, Elliott, Nestvold, & Rarick, 1983).

It is becoming clear, then, that self-reported exposure to television, particularly when time estimates alone are involved, measures a different kind of "watching" than do attention estimates, or actual measurements of viewing behavior. In a now classic study, Bechtel, Achelpohl, and Akers (1972) found that correlations between self-reported viewing behavior and measures of television viewing derived from filming people watching television in their own homes were less than .5.

A number of researchers have examined experimentally the relationship between watching television and remembering its content. Lorch, Anderson, and Levin (1979) examined the relationship in children. They found no differences between learning in children who half the time played with toys rather than looking at the television screen, and children who watched throughout the viewing period. In adults, Stauffer, Frost, and Rybolt (1980) compared memory for a news broadcast among people warned in advance to watch the news show and those unwarned. Warned individuals performed at much higher memory levels. Robinson and Sahin (1984) had small groups of people watch television news, occasionally switched the program off, and asked the subjects about their thoughts at that moment. They found that people were actually thinking of the news item on the screen less than 50 percent of the time.

In television research, attention has been inferred from the quality of memory for televised content (see review in Reeves, Thorson, & Schleuder, 1986). Attention has been operationalized as the selecting of television content to watch (Schumann & Thorson, 1990). Some researchers have attempted to reach inside people and use psychophysiologic measures of attention; for example, the orienting response pattern of heartbeats (Thorson & Lang, 1992), or the EEG pattern of brain waves (Reeves et al., 1985; Rothschild et al., 1988). Many researchers have asked for self-report of attention (e.g., Chaffee & Schleuder, 1986). Although none of these measures tells the whole story, studies of attention to television provide evidence that each of the measures adds something to our understanding of the process of attending to some stimuli to the exclusion of others.

WHAT EOS TELLS US ABOUT
ATTENTION TO COMMERCIALS

To make the argument that EOS is an appropriate index of commercial effectiveness, we need to look first at situations in which the measure fails. There are at least two such situations.

In the first situation, we observe that sometimes people have their eyes on the screen throughout a commercial. However, when these same subjects are tested for their recall and recognition of the commercial, they score low. Thus, on occasion, people produce high EOS scores, but fail to remember information that they are known to have seen. Here it seems likely that although the orienting response to the screen is present, "attention" is actually elsewhere. Thus, although overt orienting of the eyes toward the screen is usually associated with the "internal" operations of human attention, this relationship is not perfect. People can look at the television screen, but fail to have the content of commercials enter their consciousness. It may alternatively be that some irrelevant aspect of the commercial takes attention away from the product being sold, and although people paid attention to something, it was not what was contained in the memory test.

In a second situation, we observe that sometimes people do not have their eyes on screen during a commercial, and yet they score well on recall and recognition of its content. EOS is clearly a visual measure, but television also provides much of its information via the audio channel. Therefore, one can "attend" to television without looking at it. One can learn from the audio channel, and in fact, there is no doubt that people use that channel extensively. However, when they use the audio channel without looking at the screen, EOS is not predictive of memory.

Fortunately, however, these examples are exceptions. Most of the time when people look at the television screen, they later remember what they have seen, and report that they paid attention to the material. In other words, orienting toward the visual stimulus of television is highly correlated with the internal processes of conscious attention and with memory for television content. Furthermore, the attentional processing of the audio and video stimulation that occur together in television are also usually highly correlated. Certainly the high correlation of audio and video attention to television is a fortunate occurrence for those who study television viewing because, of course, the ears do not orient toward audio stimuli as the eyes do toward video stimuli, and thus we have no analogous measure of "ears to sound."

WHAT EOS TELLS US ABOUT
COMMERCIAL EFFECTIVENESS

In the research reported here, EOS data were collected in a fairly natural, although relatively short (90-minute) viewing session (see also Zhao, 1989). Subjects watched programs with commercial breaks interspersed in them according to television scheduling patterns present in the late 1980s.

The analyses reported here include four kinds of questions that EOS was used to answer. First, we asked how EOS was related to other dependent variables that have been used as indices of commercial effectiveness: recall and recognition of commercials, and attitudes toward the commercials and the brands they advertised. Second, we asked how EOS was related to measures of how high the "impact" of individual commercials was—another measure, of course, of effectiveness. Third, we examined how commercials fared as a function of attention to the programming in which they were embedded, the break in which they were located, and finally in their location within the break.

METHOD

The Study

Two hundred men and women between 18 and 54 years of age served as participants in the basic study. All participants reported that they watched approximately 2 hours of television each evening at home. Participants were paid $75 for their participation.

Half the participants were shown a half-hour situation comedy followed by a 1-hour mystery. The other half viewed a different situation comedy and a mystery, also for a total of 90 minutes of viewing. Commercials, a news break, and network promotions were dubbed into the programming in various counterbalanced orders. All analyses are reported for the data collapsed over the 32 conditions used and for all 200 participants.

Participants were tested in groups of five to seven individuals. They watched television in a comfortable living room setting furnished with couches, chairs, a coffee table, newspapers and magazines, carpeting, lamps, and a television. At the back of the room was a bar furnished with soft drinks, sandwiches, and snacks.

After viewing was completed, the participants were asked for free recall of any commercials they could remember, regardless of whether they could recall product category or brand name. Participants were then asked to recognize a sample of the commercials.

Attitude toward the commercials was measured with three items anchored with 0 (*strongly agree*) and 6 (*strongly disagree*) on 7- point scales: (a) the enthusiasm of the commercial is catching; it picks you up; (b) the commercial was lots of fun to watch and listen to; and (c) the commercial irritated me; it was annoying.

To look at how EOS related to other measures of the creative impact of the commercials, we presented the commercials to a separate sample of 230 individuals who then evaluated each one on 17 statements. These items were part of a copy testing system called ROI (Relevance, Originality, and Impact; Wells, 1989). Factor analysis identified nine items as measuring relevance, four measuring originality, and four as measures of impact. These items are shown in Table 13.1.

TABLE 13.1
Scales for Relevance, Originality, and Impact

Relevance

The message in the commercial said something important to me.

The commercial gave me a good reason to buy the brand.

It was meaningful for me.

The commercial did not show me anything that would make me want to use their product/service.

The ad didn't have anything to do with me or my needs.

The commercial made me think about buying the brand that was advertised.

The commercial made me want the brand that was advertised.

The ad talked about something that concerns me, personally.

During the commercial I thought how the product/service might be useful to me.

Originality

It was just like most other commercials.

It was typical of most ads you see today.

You see ads like that all the time—it's the same old thing.

I've seen a lot of ads like this before.

Impact

I found myself responding strongly to this ad.

I got involved with the feelings of this ad.

I got emotionally involved in this ad.

I experienced emotion while watching this ad.

Describing the EOS Data

The EOS data from the videotaped viewers were initially coded simply as watching or not watching. It was eventually necessary to add a "probably watching" category because sometimes the grain in the tape simply did not allow certainty about whether the individual was looking at the screen or slightly above or to the side of it. When viewers were not watching, their behavior was coded as reading, sitting or standing, talking to someone, out of the room, or at the snack bar at the back of the room.

RESULTS AND DISCUSSION

EOS, Memory, and Attitudinal Response to the Commercials

We are now in a position to examine the relationships among (a) EOS, (b) remembering the content of commercials, and (c) attitudinal responses to them.

Figure 13.1 shows the effects of EOS during a commercial on recall and recognition of that commercial. Analyses of variance (ANOVAs) showed a significant effect of EOS on both measures (p < .0001; unless otherwise specified, all statistics were ANOVAs and only the p values are reported). This result demonstrates that the more likely people were to be watching an ad, the more likely they were to remember it.

Figure 13.2 shows the relation of EOS during commercials and attitude toward the commercials. Again, there was an effect of EOS on attitude toward the ad (p < .03). Selecting to watch an ad did, therefore, improve its chances of being liked. This seems reasonable in that ads are designed to make people

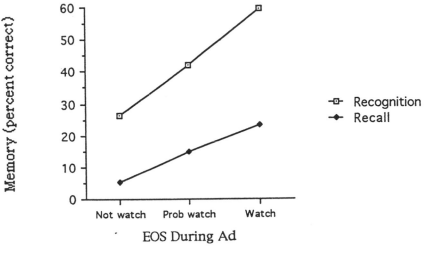

FIG. 13.1. EOS, recall, and recognition.

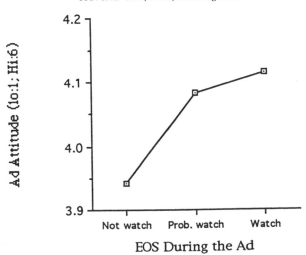

FIG. 13.2. EOS and attitude toward the ad.

like them—and whether they succeed in accomplishing that, at least watching them is better than not watching at all. Thus it is clear that EOS is a good index of commercial effectiveness, not only because it likely indicates "attention," but because it predicts how well the commercial will be remembered and the degree of positive attitudinal response to it.

Barriers to Watching Commercials

We are now ready to examine the five barriers to watching a commercial. The first barrier we look at is the watching response to the programming in which the commercial is placed. In the advertising literature, the impact of programming on commercial effectiveness is termed *context effect*. Many aspects of programming affect commercial viewing, and it is clear that there are many puzzles and complications in this area (e.g., Schumann & Thorson, 1990). Here, however, we simplify the issue, and consider only whether the programming leads people to watch or not, particularly in the seconds before a commercial break begins.

To test the impact of watching programming on whether people watch succeeding commercials, we first compared EOS data during the programming at 60, 10, and 5 seconds before ad breaks began. Fortunately, all three of these measures were highly correlated (.9 or above), so all treatment of attention before the ad was based on the 5-seconds-before-an-ad data.

Figures 13.3 and 13.4 show the effects of attention 5 seconds before the ad, attention to the ad, and recall and recognition of the ad. Three one-way ANOVAs showed that attention before the ad had a significant effect on all three measures ($p < .0001$). The most straightforward interpretation of this result is that attention to programming (and other material preceding an ad)

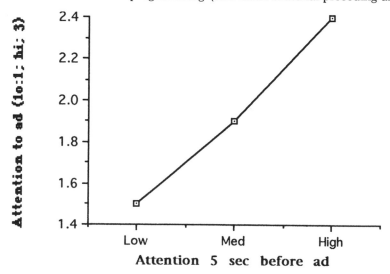

FIG. 13.3. EOS before the ad and attention.

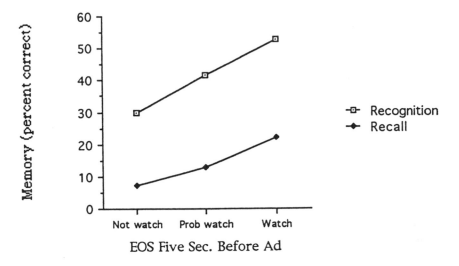

FIG. 13.4. Effects of EOS before ad on memory for the ad.

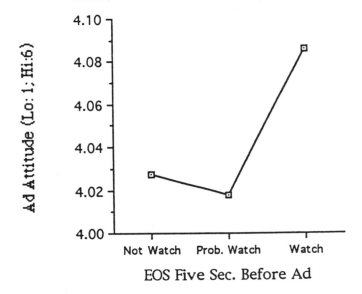

FIG. 13.5. EOS before ad and attitude toward the ad.

enhances attention to ads, and enhances ad memory. The other side of the coin, however, is that nonattention to programming will serve as a barrier to ad EOS, as well as to memory.

Figure 13.5 shows the relation between EOS 5 seconds before a commercial and attitude toward the commercial. A one-way ANOVA showed a significant effect of EOS before the commercial on attitude toward the ad ($p < .03$), with a more positive attitude occurring for ads following watched programming than for those following not-watched programming. Thus not watching the program-ming right before an ad break can be considered a barrier to an ad's positive impact on attitude. This result is consistent with the common finding of "attentional inertia" (Anderson, 1987), a phenomenon in which the likelihood of continuing to watch television at a moment in time is higher if the individual has been watching in the previous moment in time. In other words, inertia of watching grows over time.

In general, then, for ads at the beginning of a break, nonwatching of the programming immediately before the ad can damage EOS to the ad, remem-bering the ad, and showing a positive attitudinal response to it.

A second barrier to being watched is creative impact. As noted earlier, three measures of creative quality—relevance, originality, and impact (Wells, 1989)—were used to test how commercial creative qualities would relate to EOS. The ROI data were collected as described earlier. In general, we expected that the more relevant, original, and high impact (emotion inducing) a com-mercial was, the more likely it would be watched. On the other hand, the less relevant, original, and high impact a commercial was, the greater would be the barriers to watching it.

Basically, then, we wanted to look at the impact of R, O, and I on EOS for all of the commercials in the study. In addition, we wanted to look at the impact of R, O, and I on recall, recognition, and attitude, so we could test the assumption that variables that hurt EOS would also damage these other effectiveness measures. The analysis strategy called for multiple regression. To account for having repeated measures from individual subjects, a "subject mean" variable was computed by taking each subject's average score on each dependent variable and entering this mean into each regression equation before any other independent variable(s) (see Pedhazur, 1982, for a description of regressions with repeated measure designs). Because recall and recognition were dichotomously coded, their distribution would violate the normal assumption on which ANOVA or least square regression techniques are based (Wonnacott & Wonnacott, 1981). Further, because curvilin-ear relations among EOS, memory and attitude, and R, O, and I were possible, hierarchical polynomial regression was employed. Unlike linear regression equa-tions in which only the original independent variables (linear terms) are used to predict a dependent variable, a polynomial regression equation may also contain the independent variables' square (quadratic term), cube (cubic term), or higher order polynomial, which are entered consecutively. Significance tests for incre-mental r^2 at the .05 level were used as the criterion to decide when to stop entering higher order polynomials (Cohen & Cohen, 1983).

Therefore, the first task was to determine whether each of the three inde-pendent variables—that is, relevance, originality, and impact—separately could predict EOS. Three linear regression equations were estimated, one for each independent variable. As shown in Table 13.2, after each subject's mean for the dependent variable in question was entered into an equation, each relevance originality or impact score added a statistically significant power to predict EOS. The incremental r^2s were all significant at the .01 level.

TABLE 13.2
Incremental R^2 in Regressions Predicting the Dependent Variables
as a Function of Relevance, Originality, and Impact

	Dependent Variables								
	Relevance			Originality			Impact		
Independent	Atten	Recog	Recall	Atten	Recog	Recall	Atten	Recog	Recall
Variables									
Subject mean of dependent variables	.30	.25	.10	.30	.25	.10	.10	.25	.10
Relevance	.0018	.0093	.0059						
	(.003)		(.008)						
Originality				.003	.01	.003			
Impact							.003	.012	.009
							(.004)	(0.12)	(.014)
Total R2	.30	.26	.11	.30	.26	.10	.30	.26	.11
	(.30)		(.11)	(.30)	(.27)	(.11)	(.30)	(.27)	(.113)

Note. The entries for relevance, originality, and impact show the incremental R^2 to the effects of the subject means. The entries in parentheses are the incremental R^2 for the polynominal terms of the independent variables. All R reported are significant different from zero at the .05 or the .01 level.

Figure 13.6 displays the predicted level of attention as polynomial functions of relevance. When relevance increased from 25 to 35, EOS showed almost no change. When relevance increased from 35 to 50, EOS showed an increase. As relevance exceeded 50, EOS rose significantly.

Figure 13.7 displays the predicted EOS as a polynomial function of original-ity. High originality predicted high EOS. When originality increased from 25 to 45, EOS decreased slightly. When originality increased from 55 to 70, EOS tended to increase significantly.

Figure 13.8 displays predicted EOS as polynomial function of impact. When impact was low, EOS showed a decrease. When impact increased from 25 to 50, EOS increased slowly. When impact exceeded 50, EOS showed a higher rate of increase.

The curvilinear relationship of R, O, and I to EOS provides an interesting and important commentary on these "commercial creativity" measures as barriers to watching commercials. If R, O, or I is too low, commercials are less likely to be watched than when they are of intermediate levels. Of course, when R, O, or I are high, watching is also high.

Figures 13.6, 13.7, and 13.8 also show the impact of R, O, and I on recall and recognition (R, O, or I were not significantly related to attitude). For relevance, the patterning of impact on recall and recognition is similar to the impact on EOS. Generally, more relevance is better.

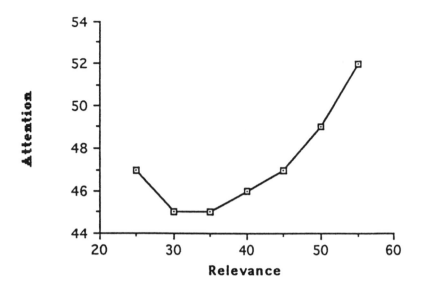

FIG. 13.6. Attention as a function of relevance.

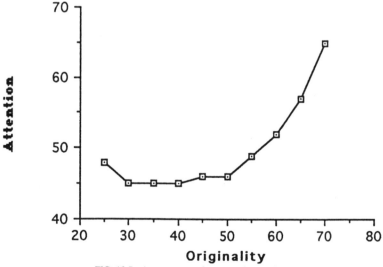

FIG. 13.7. Attention as a function of originality.

As can also be seen, however, the patterning of impact on memory as a function of originality and impact does not match that of EOS. If originality or impact is low, memory is poor. When originality or impact is intermediate, memory is strong. However, when either originality or impact become too high, memory again drops off. Both too much and too little creativity can therefore be thought of as a barrier to remembering—even when people are watching. In contrast, however, within the limits of the ads tested here, there cannot be too much relevance, regardless of whether one is concerned with watching or with memory.

A third barrier to a commercial being watched is the location of the break in the program. Figure 13.9 shows EOS as a function of break location. As noted, in the study reported here there were two half-hour and two full-hour programs, which were varied across participants. The results from the four programs were collapsed and in Fig. 13.9 we see the mean response to commercials across three breaks in the half-hour program, the EOS between the programs, the four breaks in the full-hour program, and EOS after the hour program. As can be seen, not

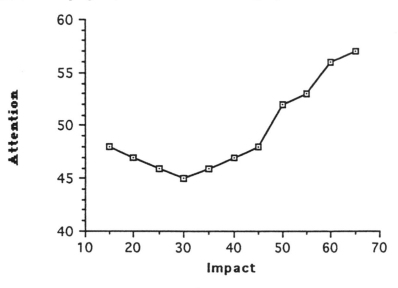

FIG. 13.8. Attention as a function of impact.

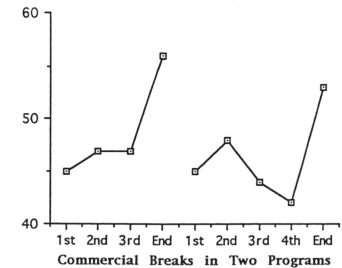

FIG. 13.9. Percentage EOS for each commercial break.

all breaks are equally likely to be watched. Postprogram breaks showed the highest levels of EOS. The last two breaks in the hour program were particularly low in EOS. Although it would be difficult to argue that all half-hour and full-hour programs would show exactly these patterns, they are at least general guides. In addition, the variations in EOS show quite clearly that being located in the middle of an hour program is a barrier to obtaining high levels of viewing.

A fourth barrier to viewing is location within breaks. Figure 13.10 shows EOS across 3 minutes of break time. This figure represents all of the breaks shown in all of the viewing conditions superimposed on each other. As can be seen, there is a clear pattern of "cycling" in the EOS pattern across the break. EOS starts high, then drops, then rises again, repeating this cycle in each 60-second time period. It is not clear what is causing the cycling. The fact that the cycle is 60 seconds in length may implicate learning on the part of the viewers. If their goal is to avoid commercials but not miss the programming, they may check back every 60 seconds or so to see whether the break is over. On the other hand, cycling may result from some intrinsic psychophysiology of attention. Regardless of its cause, however, the cycling presents a potential barrier to being watched. Being located midway in a 60-second unit clearly drags down viewing levels.

A fifth barrier to viewing can be observed in Fig. 13.11. This figure shows the mean EOS level for each 5-second period of each 60- and 30-second commercial, again with all commercials from all positions superimposed. The bottom line here is that throughout commercials, watching levels decrease. The most obvious explanation for this is that people are not motivated in general to watch commercials, and therefore other activities increasingly win out over the watching of the commercial as time goes on. Thus it can be argued that an

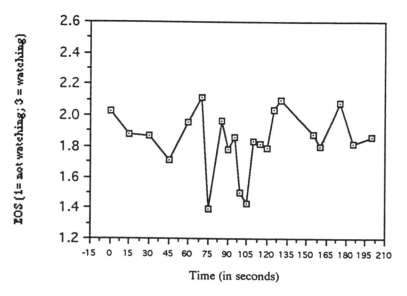

FIG. 13.10. EOS over time within breaks.

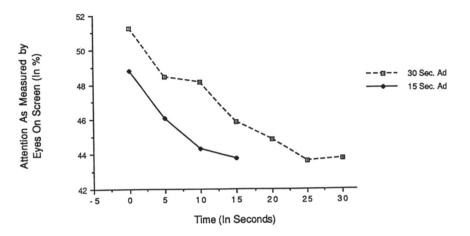

FIG. 13.11. Over-time EOS to 30- and 15-second commercials.

intrinsic barrier to EOS is the fact that the message is a commercial and thereby encourages "not watching." In other words, commercials, by being commercials, carry their own barriers to scoring high EOS levels.

SUMMARY AND GENERAL DISCUSSION

In general, the use of EOS as an index of commercial effectiveness would seem to have considerable potential. The extent to which a commercial commands extensive watching is highly predictive of learning the content of the commercial, and is related to whether the attitudinal response to it is more or less positive. Thus EOS as an index of commercial effectiveness is reasonably related to other such indices.

EOS is also helpful when we think about it as reflecting barriers that can damage viewing and thereby effectiveness. Even when a commercial measures extremely well on copy testing indicators of commercial effectiveness (such as originality and impact), EOS shows that there can be too much of a good thing. When originality and impact are quite high, likelihood of viewing actually decreases—and along with that decrease there is lowered memory and positive attitudinal response.

A commercial's effectiveness, as measured by EOS, can also be threatened by being located in a less advantageous break. Likewise, EOS can be threatened by a disadvantageous location within a break.

Finally, EOS across a variety of different ads in different locations shows that the propensity of the audience overall is to quit watching. Therefore due to the simple fact that a message is an ad, there are barriers to achieving a high level of being watched.

The important message here is that ad effectiveness is clearly not just a function of the ad by itself. Instead, it is a complex function of attributes of the ad, attributes of the environment in which the ad appears, and also a function of the audience and the viewing situation. This in turn suggests that copy testing alone is not sufficient to determine or predict how well an ad will perform. What also needs to be explored is how the ad performs in its media environment. As we become more knowledgeable about critical features of television commercials and their impact on people, we also need to understand critical features of the television viewing environment, and how a particular ad's characteristics lead it to perform when pitted against the "barriers to watching" that we know it will face.

REFERENCES

Anderson, D. (1987, October). *Now you see them—Now you don't: Frequency and duration of exiting behavior in a home viewing environment.* Paper presented at the Association for Consumer Research, Boston.

Bechtel, R., Achelpohl, C., & Akers, R. (1971). Correlations between observed behavior and questionnaire responses on television viewing. In E. Rubinstein, G. Comstock, & J. Murray (Eds.), *Television and social behavior: Vol. 4. Television in day-to-day life: Patterns of use.* Washington, DC: U.S. Government Printing Office.

Chaffee, S. H., & Choe, S. Y. (1979, September). *Communication measurement in the March 1979 NES pilot study.* Paper presented at the meeting of the American Political Science Association, Washington, DC.

Chaffee, S. H., & Schleuder, J. (1986). Measurement and effects of attention to media news. *Human Communication Research, 13*(1), 76–107.

Cohen, J., & Cohen, P. (1983). *Applied multiple regression/correlation analysis for the behavioral sciences.* Hillsdale, NJ: Lawrence Erlbaum Associates.

Collett, P. (1987, October). *The scientific analysis of commercial breaks.* Paper presented at the Association for Consumer Research, Boston.

Drew, D., & Reeves, B. (1980). Learning from a television news story. *Communication Research, 7,* 95–120.

Friestad, M. F., & Thorson, E. (1993). Remembering ads: The effects of encoding strategies, retrieval cues, and emotional response. *Journal of Consumer Psychology, 2*(1), 1–24.

Gunter, B. (1987). *Poor reception.* Hillsdale, NJ: Lawrence Erlbaum Associates.

Horn, M. I., & Atkin, M. (1987, October). *The changing commercial environment: Preserving the power of television.* Paper presented at the Association for Consumer Research, Boston, MA.

Krugman, D. M., & Rust, R. T. (1993, January–February). The impact of cable and VCR penetration on network viewing: Assessing the decade. *Journal of Advertising Research,* 67–73.

Lemert, J., Elliott, W., Nestvold, K., & Rarick, G. (1983). Effects of viewing a presidential primary debate: An experiment. *Communication Research, 10,* 155–174.

Lorch, E. P., Anderson, D. R., & Levin, S. R. (1979). The relationship of visual attention to children's comprehension of television. *Child Development, 50,* 722–727.

Pedhazur, E. J. (1982). *Multiple regression in behavioral research.* New York: Holt, Rinehart & Winston.

Reeves, B., Thorson, E., Rothschild, M. L., McDonald, D., Goldstein, R., & Hirsch, J. (1985). Attention to television: Intrastimulus effects of movement and scene changes on alpha variation over time. *International Journal of Neuroscience, 27,* 241–255.

Reeves, B., Thorson, E., & Schleuder, J. (1986). Attention to television: Psychological theories and chronometric measures. In J. Bryant & D. Zillman (Eds.), *Perspectives on media effects* (pp. 251–280). Hillsdale, NJ: Lawrence Erlbaum Associates.

Robinson, J. P., & Sahin, H. (1984). *Audience comprehension of television news: Results from some exploratory research.* London: British Broadcasting Corporation Research Department.

Rothschild, M. L., Hyun, Y. J., Reeves, B., Thorson, E., & Goldstein, R. (1988). Hemispherically lateralized EEG as a response to television commercials. *Communication Research, 15*(2), 185–198.

Schumann, D., & Thorson, E. (1990). The influence of viewing context on commercial effectiveness: An intensity-affect response model. In J. H. Leigh & C. R. Martin, Jr. (Eds.), *Current issues and research in advertising* (Vol. 12, pp. 1–24). Ann Arbor: Division of Research, Graduate School of Business Administration, University of Michigan.

Stauffer, J., Frost, R., & Rybolt, W. (1980). The attention factor in recalling network television news. *Journal of Communication, 33,* 29–37.

Thorson, E., & Lang, A. (1992). The effects of television videographics and lecture familiarity on adult cardiac orienting responses and memory. *Communication Research, 19*(3), 346–369.

Wells, W. D. (1989). *Planning for R.O.I.: Effective advertising strategy.* Englewood Cliffs, NJ: Prentice-Hall.

Wonnacott, T. H., & Wonnacott, R. J. (1981). *Regression: A second course in statistics.* New York: Wiley.

Zhao, X. (1989). *Eyes-on-screen, memory, and attitudes toward television commercials.* Unpublished doctoral dissertation, University of Wisconsin–Madison.

14

The Determinants of Advertising Repetition Effects

Pirjo Vuokko
*The Turku School of Economics
and Business Administration, Finland*

How many times should we repeat a commercial in order to increase the brand awareness of a newly launched brand to a satisfactory level? Last time we repeated our message 10 times without reaching our campaign objectives; should we now increase the number of repetitions in order to guarantee the effects? Our competitor seems to use fewer repetitions in its campaign; how can it be more successful than ours? Tell me, what is the optimal amount of repetition?

Questions such as these have been addressed to media managers, agencies, and researchers. The need to reduce the uncertainty connected to the effective use of repetition is considerable (Cacioppo & Petty, 1980; Elliot, 1985; Geis, 1981; Leckenby & Boyd, 1984; Ostrow, 1981; Schultz, 1979), especially in light of high media costs. In many cases, the use of repetition is a necessity; it is even regarded as the basis of a successful campaign. Repetition can help cut through the noise and implant the message (e.g., Axelrod, 1980; Krugman, 1972; Leckenby & Wedding, 1982; McQuail, 1983; Ray, 1982; Sawyer, 1973; Singh & Rothschild, 1983; Sissors, 1982–1983; Sternthal & Craig, 1982; Swinyard, 1979). Advertisers can, consciously or otherwise, even repeat more than is necessary in order to guarantee effects (Aaker & Carman, 1982; Aykac, Corstjens, & Gautschi, 1984). In this way it is possible to utilize the benefits of overlearning (see Britt, 1978; Ebbinghaus, 1964; Ray, 1973; Stephens & Warrens, 1983–1984) and save on production costs. Overspending can also be used as a competitive maneuver, that is, as noise over competitors' messages (Rothschild, 1987). Saturation point may be reached and exceeded, however, which leads to advertising wearout and negative effects (Axelrod, 1980; Sternthal & Craig, 1982). Too little repetition, on the other hand, may lead to advertising having no effects. Thus, what is the right amount of repetition—neither too much nor too little?

Determining the optimal amount of repetition is said to be the greatest problem in media strategy (Leckenby & Kishi, 1982; Sissors, 1982–1983; Sissors

& Surmanek, 1982; Swinyard, 1979). Krugman (1972) said that the essential problem is not, however, the amount of repetition but the question of when to repeat. When advertising is directed at the right time, three exposures should be enough. However, there still exists a question about the properties of the right time. Krugman, in a way, moved the topic of discussion from the optimal amount of repetition to the optimal situation for repetition.

Situationality is also seen in the scheduling of repetition. The studies by Zielske and Henry (1980) show that it is possible to discover the most effective way of scheduling, both in the long-term and the short-term. It is always the objective of the campaign that directs the scheduling plan, however (cf. Bettman, 1979; Ray, 1982; Rothschild, 1987; Simon, 1982; Zielske & Henry, 1980).

Advertising repetition effects are often represented via advertising response curves that show what effect is produced with different amounts of repetition. The right shape of the advertising response curve is under continuous debate. The two alternatives most often supported are the same as for learning curves, that is, a concave curve or an s-curve (Albion & Farris, 1981; Ray, 1982; Simon & Arndt, 1980). In fact, these two curves differ from each other only at the beginning of each: The concave curve shows diminishing returns, whereas the typical feature of the s-curve is that there are increasing marginal returns at the beginning of the curve. In all probability, both curve shapes are relevant. They simply describe the advertising response function in different situations. The situation represented by the concave curve is in a way more favorable to the advertiser, because more effects are produced with a small amount of repetition than in a situation represented by an s-curve. This again indicates that repetition may not have the same kind of impact in all situations.

The basic assumption in this study is that repetition effects are situational, and that there is no single amount of repetition that is optimal in general and in all situations. Thus there are factors that have an impact on repetition effects and that should, therefore, also be considered when making advertising decisions concerning the use of repetition. Knowledge about these factors or determinants and their impact helps in understanding repetition effects, as well as in making repetition decisions in different situations.

The purpose of this study is to discover what the determinants of advertising repetition are, and what their impact is on repetition effects. A contingency approach is employed (see Zeithaml, Varadarajan, & Zeithaml, 1988). Emphasis is placed on discovering the determinants, and thereby identifying different kinds of situations or settings in which different kinds of repetition effects are produced—and in which different kinds of repetition strategies should thus be employed. To this end, the conceptual framework is first constructed and second examined to see whether empirical evidence exists for the determinants and their impact on repetition effects.

CONCEPTUAL FRAMEWORK

The Function of Repetition in the Advertising Response Process

In order to produce a response, advertising stimuli must proceed through three stages: exposure, attention, and processing (cf. Mitchell, 1986). Repetition is at its most significant in the attention and processing stages, although it may also have a part to play at the exposure stage by increasing the probability of exposure to the advertising message.

The importance of repetition at the attention stage is due to two factors: receiver selectivity and communication noise. Repetition of a stimulus increases the probability that attention will, on at least one occasion, be centered toward that stimulus, in this case an advertisement. Further, repeating the stimulus offers the opportunity that the stimulus will be available in the environment at a silent or at least less noisy moment, or that the message will be one of the stimuli to which attention is paid in a noisy environment.

At the processing stage, the function of advertising repetition (a method of external reinforcement) is similar to the function of reinforcement in learning processes (see Crane, 1965; Hull, 1958; McGuire, 1969). External reinforcement, such as advertising repetition, is a way to produce and maintain deep memory traces, those that play the most active role in a consumer's decision-making situation (see the following about the role of information stored in long-term memory: Keller, 1987; Kellermann, 1985; Mitchell, 1983; Nedungadi, 1990). Repetition does not, as such, increase learning but provides an opportunity for repetitive reinforcement (Cacioppo & Petty, 1979; Nelson, 1977; Rethans, Swasy, & Marks, 1986). In short, repetition by:

1. Repeated exposure increases the probability of attention to the message (attention function).
2. Repetitive processing helps the message to enter one's long-term memory (storage function).
3. Repetitive processing can also be used to increase the probability of retrieval (retention function).

The effects of repetition are strongest on cognitive effects such as attention, awareness, knowledge, or comprehension (Batra & Ray, 1983a; Ray & Sawyer, 1971; Robertson, 1976). These effects can be produced by creating opportunities for processing the stimulus more completely, more deeply, or just more than once. Only by mere rote repetition (i.e., repetitive sensory level processing) is it possible to increase brand awareness, too (Bettman, 1979). Further, as people may also form preferences on the basis of familiarity, such repetition may also produce affective level effects, for example as follows: "I have seen this brand more often than other brands. It must sell well. It must be good. I'll try it." The opportunity for advertising repetition to form or change higher order beliefs is limited, however, because in many cases advertising stimuli are processed only unconsciously and shallowly. This is also the case for conative effects in general. By repetitive advertising of well-established brands, it is nevertheless possible to reinforce repetitious purchasing habits and compete against brand switching.

In addition to the already-mentioned positive effects, repetition may also cause negative effects (Aaker & Carman, 1982; Batra, 1984; Lewin, 1951). Too much repetition, the amount of which is not fixed, irritates the audience, produces boredom, satiation, fatigue, or even attempts by the subject to avoid the advertisement. This may also lead to negative effects toward the advertised brand itself. The attitude toward the brand is then conditioned by the attitude toward the advertisement (Mitchell & Olson, 1981).

The Determinants of Advertising Repetition Effects

In his Field Theory, Lewin (1951) stated that all reactions are functions of the person and the person's environment. Further, Keller (1987) said that the nature and formation of memory traces and associative links depend on the stimulus, one's goals, and the environment. Accordingly, the factors that have an impact on repetition effects are classified into two groups, the endogenous and exogenous determinants of repetition effects.

When examining the issue from the receiver's perspective, the endogenous determinant is the receiver. The exogenous determinant consists of two factors: the advertising stimulus that is repeated and the communication environment in which the receiver is exposed to the repeated stimulus. In short, what impact advertising repetition will produce is affected by the receiver, advertising stimulus, and communication environment. The setting with its determinants is seen in Fig. 14.1, which represents a total description of the advertising response process and factors affecting the process.

The advertising stimulus includes the message and the media, both of which have an impact on the advertising response process. The qualities of the advertising message with its attention and processing values affect only the attention and processing stages of the process. The qualities of the advertising media with its exposure, attention, and processing values affect all three stages in that process. The other exogenous determinant, the communication environment, includes factors that may either be supportive to or interfere with a brand's advertising. Depending on the values of these determinants and their elements, the repetition setting may be more or less demanding in terms of the amount of repetition needed. Each determinant is first analyzed separately here, and then the group is analyzed as a whole.

The Endogenous Determinant

The endogenous determinant consists of factors that, as receiver qualities, affect the entire advertising response process, that is, the receiver's motivation,

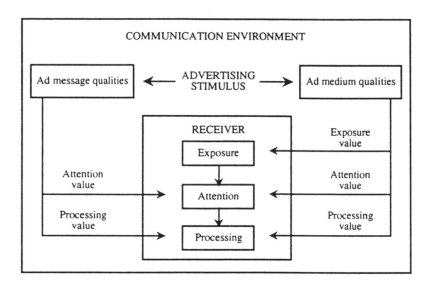

FIG. 14.1. The advertising response process and factors affecting the process.

opportunity, and ability to attend and process the advertisement. These three factors are the antecedents of the receiver's involvement level (Batra, 1984; Batra & Ray, 1983b; cf. Alba & Hutchinson, 1987; Moorman, 1990). Therefore, the endogenous determinant of advertising repetition effects is dealt with in this study as the concept of "involvement."

In a high-involvement situation, the receiver is an active subject in the response process, because the issue (e.g., the product category) is of personal relevance. By using simple stimulus–organism–reaction symbols, the advertising response process can be described as follows: s–O–r (cf. cognitive learning). The importance of the receiver is emphasized as the determinant of the effects. In a low-involvement situation the process is described as follows: S–o–r (cf. classical conditioning). In this case the importance of a strong stimulus is emphasized. As a managerial implication, this means that if the receiver is not pulling the stimulus (low-involvement situation) the stimulus should be pushed toward (capital S) the receiver, by using higher amounts of repetition in a campaign, for example. When the receiver is active, on the other hand, there is no similar need for a strong stimulus and/or great amounts of repetition.

The influence of the receiver's involvement level on repetition effects is, however, dependent on the level of the effects in question. The impact of the endogenous determinant in low- and high-involvement situations as well as in cognitive and conative level effects is described in Table 14.1. Different kinds of settings are described in the table, with the concepts *demanding* and *nonde-manding* referring respectively to high or low amounts of repetition needed. The response curve symbols, an s-curve and a concave curve, are also applied here to describe the way the effects are developed in different settings as the amount

TABLE 14.1
The Impact of the Receiver's Involvement Level on Cognitive
and Conative Effects of Repetition (From Vuokko, 1992)

	Advertising Effect	
	Cognitive	Conative
Involvement level		
Low	Demanding (s-curve)	Nondemanding (concave curve)
High	Nondemanding (concave curve)	Demanding (s-curve)

of repetition increases. Affective effects are excluded in the table because in some cases, especially in low-involvement situations, these effects are the results of brand experiences and not of advertising at all (cf. Ray, 1982).

Cognitive effects are produced more easily—that is, with a smaller amount of repetition—in people whose involvement is high rather than low. Because of the personal relevance of the issue, the receiver is interested in all information concerning the issue, whether seeking it actively or not. Thus cognitive effects are easier to produce in a high-involvement situation than in a low-involvement situation, the latter requiring greater amounts of repetition in order to get the stimulus through (cf. Batra & Ray, 1983a).

The situation is reversed where conative effects are concerned. Once the cognitive effects are produced in a low-involvement receiver, it is much easier to reach the conative level as well. Brand advertisements and awareness can directly create a brand trial—provided that the receiver has the ability to make a purchase. One can even consciously try the brand just to gather more information and to form affective responses about it: Is the brand worth further consideration? In a high-involvement situation, however, it is not easy to carry the receiver to the conative level by just repeating the advertisement or even with advertising alone.

The Exogenous Determinants

Advertising Stimulus. As stated earlier, advertising stimulus, as one exogenous determinant, consists of the qualities of advertising message and media. The qualities of a stimulus that make it easy or difficult to get that stimulus through the response process are also the factors that make the need of repetition low or high, respectively.

When planning an advertising message, an advertiser has to make a decision about what to say (message content or argumentation) to its audience and how to say it (message format or execution style). These decisions (i.e., the values of a stimulus determinant) have an impact on how much repetition is needed in order to get this stimulus through. If the values are highly positive, the need for repetition is small; where the advertising message and/or media do not have enough power as such, more repetitions are needed. What, then, are the qualities that make the stimulus more or less prominent and effective?

The argumentation should be relevant, important, and salient to the receiver so that it offers "something to think about," consciously or unconsciously. Message content should also be fitted to the receiver's frame and existing schemas so that the receiver can decode it (Moore, Reardon, & Durso, 1986).

Each advertisement with its execution style is not equally likely to receive high attention rates or to be comprehended. We pay attention to those stimuli whose dimensions appear out of the ordinary or as Berlyne (1960) stated, whose perceived dimensions are overestimated. Novel or surprising stimuli are arresting because they "have not yet had a chance to lose effects that all stimuli originally possess" (p. 20). Repetition of the same stimulus is, of course, a way to rob the message of its novelty. This means that it might be more effective not to repeat the same advertisement, but rather to vary its message format so that both the power of novelty and repetition are utilized. This procedure is consistent with the "unity in diversity" principle (cf. Berlyne, 1960). The campaign and a single advertisement should contain sufficient variety to make them arresting and interesting, but also sufficient unity for the different elements of the campaign or advertisement to be organizable into an entity in one's memory. Accordingly, if the advertising stimulus is complex it should be repeated several times to achieve order in the elements; the risk of wearout is smaller, too.

If the stimulus is really arresting, unique, and grabbing, there is no need to use the amounts of repetition that should be used in situations in which the stimulus is not arresting or perceived as something new. The advertising message should, however, contain both attention and processing value. Berlyne (1970) stated that although a high degree of novelty implies a high potential for arousal, both pleasantness and interest also appear to increase with novelty.

The qualities of advertising media are analyzed here using the quantitative and qualitative values of that media. The higher these values are, the smaller is the need for repetition. The quantitative value of media consists of reach and frequency. Reach, as an exposure stage in general, is only marginally connected to the use of repetition. On the contrary, there is an obvious connection between frequency and repetition, as repetition is a way to produce opportunities for repetitive exposure. It is possible, however, by using only one medium once to have a frequency higher than one. The way consumers "use" media, for example, by reading or leafing through the same magazine more than once, also produces repetitive exposures to all advertisements in the magazine. If a medium possesses this property, it has a higher quantitative value than media that do not. Print media have higher quantitative values than broadcast media because a receiver can control the message pace and the number of exposures (cf. Batra & Ray, 1986).

The qualitative value of a medium is the total increment that the medium contributes to the advertising message effect. The things that the medium may carry with it and that may have an impact on the attention or processing value of an advertising stimulus are medium image, medium environment or editorial/programming context, and medium involvement (i.e., the importance and relevance of the medium to a receiver; cf. Appel, 1987; Ostrow, 1981; Sissors

& Surmanek, 1982). A positive medium image, an appropriate medium environment to the message, and high medium involvement create favorable conditions for a message to get through the attention and processing stages by supporting and reinforcing the advertising message. This leads to a smaller need for repetition.

Communication Environment.   The communication environment includes the factors that can create favorable or unfavorable conditions for an advertising message to get through and be processed in the desired way. If the communication environment is unfavorable, that is, there are more interfering than supportive factors, repetition is needed in order to overcome at least some of the barriers. If favorable factors dominate, the need for repetition will be smaller.

Noise is a typical distractive factor that interferes with all communication situations. The main property of the noise, however, is the amount and nature of competitors' messages in the past, present, and future (Ray, 1982). Further, the toughness of competition is determined by the degree of equality, strength, the number, and the homogeneity of competing brands in consumers' minds (cf. Berlyne, 1960). Therefore, a brand's strong position, whether indicative of a high market share or simply a brand's established, unique image, offers the brand a better chance to win in the fight against newcomers or brands without any established position in consumers' minds.

Public atmosphere or the nature of publicity also affects the favorability of the communication environment, as does the state of primary demand. Positive publicity surrounding a brand or an issue and positive primary demand support the advertising of the brand whose advertising message appeals are consistent with these factors. If, for example, environmental factors are given a high value when making a choice between different brands in a product category, this kind of primary demand (and positive publicity) helps the advertising of those brands with environmental advertising appeal or execution.

To summarize, the need for repetition can be defined by the values of the two exogenous determinants. In this case, the greater the degree to which the following conditions are valid, the easier the advertising situation is, and the smaller the amount of repetition needed:

1. The advertising format is arresting and appeal appropriate and salient.
2. The advertising medium has a high qualitative and quantitative value.
3. The brand's market position is strong, and public atmosphere and primary demand are supportive for the brand.

The lesser the extent to which these conditions are valid, the more repetition is needed. As when analyzing the impact of a receiver's involvement level on repetition effects, we can also describe the impact of the exogenous determinants on the shape of the advertising response curve. The response curve is assumed to be concave in the situation just defined, and an s-curve when these conditions are not valid (cf. Ray, 1982).

After analyzing the endogenous and exogenous determinants separately, we can now put the determinants together and analyze their total impact on repetition effects. First, all determinants with their elements are represented in Fig. 14.2. It should be noted that there may also be important interactions between different determinants (cf. Mitchell, 1983).

Next, different kinds of repetition settings and a typology of advertising repetition effects are constructed. By identifying the advertising objective, a receiver's involvement level, and the values of the exogenous determinants, it is possible to define how demanding the setting is to the advertiser regarding the need for repetition. The settings and their impacts on the repetition effects are represented in Table 14.2, in which the two exogenous determinants are combined into one, called the "advertising situation." "Easy situation" refers to the favorability of the exogenous determinants (values mentioned earlier) and "difficult situation" refers to the lack of these favorable values. When combining the values of the endogenous determinant and the two exogenous determinants, we may also describe these combinations with stimulus–organism–response symbols. Whether the symbols are capitalized or not refers to the relative importance of the stimulus (or the exogenous determinants in general) and the particular receiver in the situation. The amount of repetition needed in a certain setting is described in the table by the concepts demanding and nondemanding,

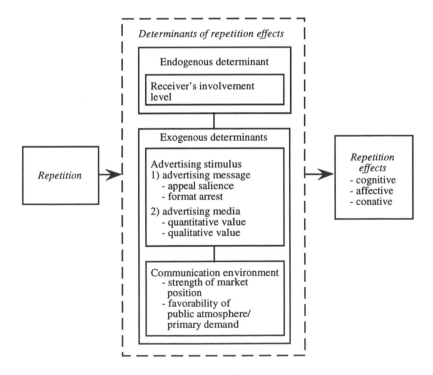

FIG. 14.2. The elements of repetition effect determinants.

TABLE 14.2
A Typology of Advertising Repetition Effects (From Vuokko, 1992)

Advertising Objective		Cognitive	Conative
Involvement level/Advertising situation			
Low	Easy (S–o–r)	Nondemanding (concave curve)	Nondemanding (concave curve)
	Difficult (s–o–r)	Demanding (s-curve)	Nondemanding (concave curve)
High	Easy (S–O–r)	Nondemanding (concave curve)	Demanding (s-curve)
	Difficult (s–O–r)	Demanding (s-curve)	Demanding (s-curve)

as well as the symbols of different response curve shapes, that is, the s-curve and concave curve, respectively.

There are four demanding and four nondemanding settings defined in Table 14.2. Greater amounts of repetition are needed if the receiver is highly involved and the advertising objective is conative. The setting is also demanding when cognitive effects are desired in such an audience, and the values of the exogenous determinants are unfavorable; for example, if there is a nonsupportive public atmosphere for the brand's advertising or if the audience does not regard the advertisement to be credible or sufficiently informative. Further, the demanding setting appears if the advertising objective is cognitive, the advertising situation is difficult, and there is a low-involvement receiver. The need for repetition in this situation is high because the passivity of the receiver is not compensated for by the "pushing" strong stimulus in the response process.

As can be seen, a difficult advertising situation usually causes a higher need for repetition than an easy advertising situation. When the stimulus is not strong and/or the communication environment is nonsupportive, repetition is needed in order to compensate for these weaknesses in the settings.

A typical feature of the settings described as nondemanding is an easy advertising situation, that is, favorable values of the two exogenous determinants. There is, however, one exception: a setting with a low-involvement receiver, conative effects as an advertising objective, and a difficult advertising situation. In the case of a low-involvement receiver, a cognitive stage is always the critical one. After reaching that stage, there may be only a low threshold to the conative stage because no deep elaboration is carried out before the purchase is activated.

METHOD

The purpose of the empirical study was to find out if there is empirical evidence for the determinants of advertising repetition effects and their impact as presented in the conceptual framework. When designing the empirical investigation for this study, the possibility of analyzing the impact of all determinants together was emphasized. Further, as such common real-world determinant values as a passive receiver or a noisy communication environment were also in focus, a field study was considered to guarantee higher ecological validity than experimental designs (cf. Allen & Madden, 1989; Gardner & Raj, 1983; Rothschild, 1987).

Two main problems in the research design were: how to create opportunities to analyze repetition effects in different types of settings and how to collect data from different types of variables. In order to exercise control over the whole variety of settings, several brands and product categories were judgmentally selected for the study. The four product categories under examination were chocolate bars, edible fats, passenger cars, and passenger voyages. Several brands with different kinds of market positions were included in the study within each product category, with 34 brand items analyzed in all.

As the contingency approach was applied in this study, it was important to examine all three types of variables typical to this kind of approach: contingency, response, and performance variables. The types and sources of data and the data collection methods in each case are presented in Table 14.3.

The empirical research design employed in this study may be termed "quasi-experimental." The way this quasi- experiment was conducted may be termed *interrupted time-series* design, in which multiple observations are made over time. The purpose of the analysis was to infer whether or not the treatment—in this case repetition of the advertising message and the whole setting with its determinant values—had any effect (see Cook & Campbell, 1979; Saxe & Fine, 1981). This means that data had to be collected about the amount of repetition used in the campaigns, the effects of these campaigns, and the values of the endogenous and exogenous determinants (see Appendix). Further, several sources of data were used: advertisers, consumers, and literature sources.

The research period chosen for the study was 7 months. During this period a tracking study (a monthly survey) was conducted with the help of a market research company, in order to collect data about repetition effects and about

TABLE 14.3
Types of Data Collection Methods (From Vuokko, 1992)

Variables Under Consideration	Sources of Data	Methods
I. Contingency variables a) exogenous determinants (advertising stimulus, communication environment)	Literature	Conceptual analysis
	Advertisers	Interview, questionnaire
b) endogenous determinant (involvement)	Consumers	Tracking study
II. Response variable (repetition strategies)	Advertisers	Interview, questionnaire
III. Performance variable (repetition effects)	Consumers	Tracking study

the endogenous determinant, that is, receivers' involvement levels. The total number of responses for each product category was around 2,000. Advertising recall, brand awareness, brand score, brand attributes, purchase interest, ad score, ad attributes, and brand experiences were all measured in the tracking study questionnaire as possible effects of repetition. In addition, information about brand sales was collected from inventory statistics and from the advertisers.

The data about repetition strategies and detailed data on all advertising for the research brands were collected from advertisers through personal interviews and self-report questionnaires. These procedures were also used in order to examine the values of the exogenous determinants, data about which were also collected from literature sources.

The basic research unit under examination in this study was a brand. Data analysis was conducted by combining the data collected through advertiser interviews and questionnaires, the consumer tracking study, and conceptual analysis. An examination was thus made of what effects were produced by which kind of strategies, and with what determinant values. The tracking study data was analyzed using a statistical computer program, SPSSX.

RESULTS

In all four product categories, the most distinctive effects of advertising repetition were found in recall rates, although—depending on the product category—other levels of effects also emerged (for a detailed description of the research findings in each product category, see Vuokko, 1992). Further, both the endogenous and exogenous determinants appeared to be relevant, in addition to all the individual elements of the exogenous determinants. Therefore, the receiver's involvement level, the advertisement format, advertisement appeal, advertising media, the brand's position, and public atmosphere or primary demand all had an impact on repetition effects. Which determinants (or their elements) had the highest impact on repetition effects was, however, dependent on the product category (see Table 14.4). The determinant values that in each product category form demanding and nondemanding settings, that is, high or low needs for repetition, are represented in the table. The determinants are categorized as endogenous or exogenous.

The primary factors influencing repetition effects for chocolate bars were advertisement format, the receiver's involvement level, and the brand's market position. For edible fats, corresponding factors were the consistency of advertisement appeal with primary demand trends, advertisement format, the receiver's involvement level, and the brand's market position. In passenger cars, the following factors emerged as determinants of advertising repetition effects: advertisement appeal, the brand's position, advertisement format, and the receiver's involvement level. In the fourth product category, passenger voyages,

TABLE 14.4
Repetition Settings for the Four Product Categories

Product Categories	Demanding Setting	Nondemanding Setting
Chocolate bars		
Endogenous determinant	• Low-involvement receiver	• High-involvement receiver
Exogenous determinants	• Nondistinctive ad format	• Distinctive ad format
	• Brand's weak position	• Brand's strong position
		• Emotional tone
		• Television as media
Edible fats		
Endogenous determinant		• High-involvement receiver
Exogenous determinants	• Brand's weak position	• Brand's strong position or brand is new
		• Arresting ad format
		• Ad appeal is consistent with primary demand
Passenger cars		
Endogenous determinant		• High-involvement receiver
Exogenous determinants	• Brand's weak position	• Brand's strong position
	• Pure image campaign	• Launch or premium appeal
		• Distinctive ad format
Voyages		
Endogenous determinant	• Low-involvement receiver	• High-involvement receiver
Exogenous determinants	• Pure image campaign	• Price of premium appeal
		• High primary demand

Note. From Vuokko (1992).

the primary determinant factors were the receiver's involvement level, temporary variations in primary demand, and advertisement appeal.

As is seen in the product category results, the receiver's involvement level (i.e., the endogenous determinant) had an impact on repetition effects in all product categories under examination. Of particular importance was its impact in product categories in which emotional criteria (e.g., pleasure, enjoyment) are primary—in this study, chocolate bars and passenger voyages. In Fig. 14.3 the impact of the receiver's involvement level on advertising recall is, as an example, represented for four chocolate bars. The asterisks indicate the significant differences between the recall rates of the two groups. The width of the rectangles on the vertical media lines indicates the duration of the campaign

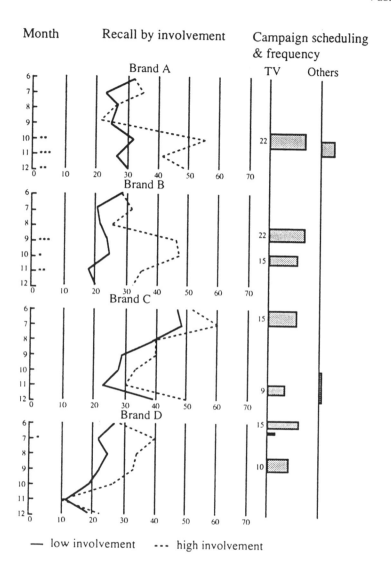

FIG. 14.3. Recall rates of people with high and low involvement for four chocolate bar brands.

and the height (from left to right) and/or the figures indicate the amount of repetition used.

It can be seen, especially in the recall curves of two strong position brands, A and B, that there was a statistically significant dependence between recall and involvement in the campaign periods. Distinct recall peaks appeared among the highly involved. This is also seen in Brand D, which was not categorized as a strong brand. In Brand C, which was categorized as a strong position brand, the two curves are nevertheless very much alike; the brand's advertising was well recalled despite lower repetition figures. The reason for these findings, most probably, was the distinctive and highly entertaining style of execution of Brand C's advertisements. They were more arresting, even with a smaller amount of repetition, than traditional chocolate bar advertising carried out by other brands.

The impact of the advertisement format or execution style as well as the impact of market position also emerged in all product categories (in passenger voyages it was not possible to analyze their impact because of the highly homogenous style of execution and market positions). These findings emphasize the importance of both advertising format planning and building a competitively strong and unique position for the brand. A strong brand's advertising campaign with an arresting advertising format needs less repetition than the nonarresting campaign of a weak position brand.

If the importance of advertisement format emerged in cases with emotional purchase criteria, salience of advertisement appeal was, on the contrary, an important factor determining advertising repetition effects in product categories where rational criteria were emphasized, that is, in edible fats and passenger cars, but also in passenger voyages. Advertising with launch or premium appeal was in all cases more effective than, for example, pure image campaigns; effective also means here that the need for repetition was smaller. As an example, Fig. 14.4 represents the impact of the message appeal and format on repetition effects for five passenger car makes, two of which (A and B) were categorized as strong position car makes, and the other three (C, D, and E) as weak position makes.

In the two strong position car makes, there are recall peaks in October and November when both introduced a new model. The amounts of repetition used in these campaigns were, on average, lower than in other makes' campaigns (the campaigns of 13 car makes were analyzed in all). There were probably two reasons for the success of the autumn campaigns of A and B: the strong positions of the brands and launch appeal. For Brand C, two peaks appeared in the recall curve. The first peak occurred in the summer, when Brand C conducted a campaign in which the primary appeal was a car test success. In October, Brand C launched a new model with a new name, not just a "facelift." In addition, teaser commercials (with an arresting execution style, too) were used in the campaign, which was most exceptional in this product category. Brand D, on the contrary, carried out only pure image campaigns during the research period, with a traditional car advertising format. Although the amount of repetition was much like Brand C, the responses were not. Having a salient appeal and an arresting advertising format reduces the need for repetition. Similar findings were seen for Brand E, a weak position brand, whose advertising campaigns had two specialties: sales promotion activities and a launch.

The impact of public atmosphere or the state of primary demand emerged in edible fats and passenger voyages. Brands whose advertising appeals (or executions) are consistent with public atmosphere need less repetition. During the research period, there was a lot of public discussion in the mass media about

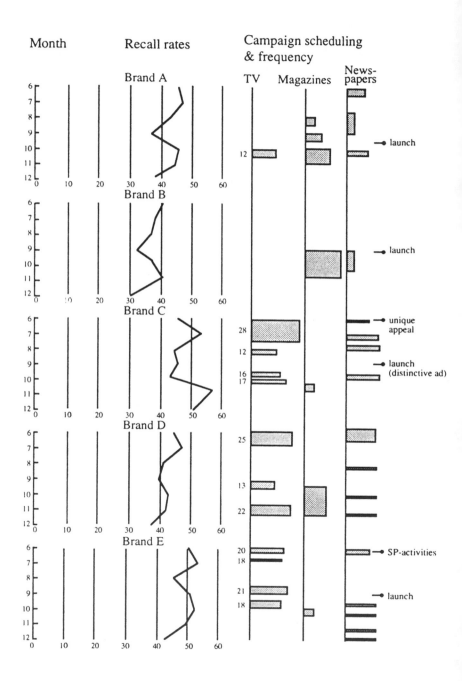

FIG. 14.4. Recall rates of five car makes.

the effects of different kinds of edible fats on one's health. The brands whose advertising appeals were consistent with "the new trend" (i.e., vegetable fat) were more easily able to get the message through—with a lower amount of repetition—as the communication environment was supportive to them. For passenger voyages this supportive impact was seen in the summer, when the primary demand for voyages was high: During the summer months, with people in the "voyage mood," receivers are also more open to small advertisements, which were seen after only a few exposures, that did not occur during the wintertime.

DISCUSSION

There was distinct empirical evidence that effects produced by repetition are dependent on the setting and, therefore, on the values of the endogenous and exogenous determinants. Empirical investigation also showed that there is, in general, no such thing as an optimal amount of repetition. These findings imply that repetition should always be examined by considering the context or setting in which it is used. This concerns both repetition decisions and repetition effects.

An advertiser, when deliberating about how much repetition to use, should first analyze the setting and then make decisions according to situational needs. The importance of the situation analysis and of target group knowledge in the advertising planning process emerged. The effects of repetition, which might differ greatly in different campaigns or studies, should also be evaluated against the setting in which these repetition effects were produced. The fact that the impact of a certain amount of repetition may be very impressive or alternatively insignificant could be explained by different values of the determinants in those situations.

By examining the research findings from yet another perspective, we can say that the study clearly showed that increasing the amount of repetition is not the only way to create more effective campaigns. Repetition can be used to compensate (e.g., the nonarrest of an advertisement), but this is not always the best strategy to be applied or selected. In many cases it might be more effective (and cheaper) to use an advertiser's resources, for instance, to design arresting advertisement formats or salient advertisement appeals, than to use them to attain a high amount of repetition. This emphasizes the importance of what to say and how over how many times to say it. Accordingly, the share of mind should be regarded as more important than the share of voice.

It is, however, important to keep in mind that there are situations in which even the power of the most arresting message can be of benefit only through its repetition, at least a few times. People's selectivity and the noise in the communication environment are facts that will always sustain repetition as a relevant means of increasing the impact of advertising campaigns. Repetition should not, however, be considered as a sufficient condition for an effective campaign; it is not. The best way to utilize the power of repetition is first to analyze the communication environment and the target group. The second step is to use one's resources in order to make the most effective message and media decisions possible. The third step is then to deliberate as to the amount of repetition that might still be needed in order to benefit the total power of the advertising stimulus in the target group and communication environment.

As presented earlier, both theoretical and managerial implications can be derived from the research findings of this study, but methodological implications can also be found. The contingency approach was applied, repetition effects and their determinants were examined by a quasi-experimental field study, and empirical data was collected from several sources using several methods. Although this kind of research design took time and resources, it also offered opportunities to elicit valuable information about repetition effects in real-life situations where conditions for natural exposure exist. Because of the field study design, there was a lack of *ceteris paribus* control over variables under examination, but there was a better view of the whole setting and its impact on repetition effects. Further, the judgmental selection of the product categories and brands was conducted using criteria that were supposed to gain control over the whole range of the variables. This way, it was possible to examine both the impact of different determinants and also that of different values of each determinant on repetition effects.

APPENDIX: VARIABLES MEASURED
AND TYPES OF OPERATIONAL MEASURES

Theoretical Concepts	Variables Measured	Type of Operational Measure
A. Endogenous Determinant		
Involvement	• General importance	
	• Thinking dimension	5-point scales (CS)
	• Feeling dimension	
B. Exogenous Determinants		
a) Advertising stimulus		
Ad message	• Appeal salience	Open-ended questions (AI)
	• Ad format arrest	Open-ended questions (AI, AQ)
Ad medium	• Qualitative and quantitative value of ad media	Open-ended questions (AI, AQ)
b) Communication environment		

Theoretical Concepts	Variables Measured	Type of Operational Measure
Market position of the brand	• Target groups	
	• Brand age	
	• Special qualities	Open-ended questions (AI)
	• Market share	
	• Competitive situation	
	• Campaign qualities	
Public atmosphere or primary demand	• Supporting and nonsupporting elements in the environment	Open-ended questions (AI), articles
C. Repetition Strategies		
Amount and scheduling of repetition	• Amount and scheduling of repetition in	
	(a) campaigns	Open-ended questions (AI, AQ)
	(b) different situations	
	(c) different media	
D. Repetition Effects		
Cognitive	• Attention	Yes/no recall test (CS)
	• Brand awareness	3-point scale (CS)
Affective	• Brand-score	Scale 4-10 (CS)
	• Brand attributes	+/– dichotomy (CS)
	• Purchase interest	3-point scale (CS)
	• Ad score	Scale 4–10 (CS)
	• Ad attributes (entertaining, irritating, informative)	Dichotomies (CS)
Conative	• Brand experiences	3-point scale (CS)
	• Sales	Inventory statistics

Note. AI = Advertiser interview; AQ = Subsequent advertiser questionnaire; CS = Consumer surveys in the tracking study.

REFERENCES

Aaker, D. A., & Carman, J. M. (1982). Are you overadvertising? *Journal of Advertising Research, 22,* 57–70.

Alba, J. W., & Hutchinson, J. W. (1987). Dimensions of consumer expertise. *Journal of Consumer Research, 14,* 411–454.

Albion, M. S., & Farris, P. W. (1981). *The advertising controversy: Evidence on the economic effects of advertising.* Boston: Auburn House.

Allen, C. T., & Madden, T. J. (1989). Gauging and explaining advertising effects: Emergent concerns regarding construct and ecological validity. In P. Cafferata & A. Tybout (Eds.), *Cognitive and affective responses to advertising* (pp. 327–351). Lexington, MA: Lexington Books.

Appel, V. (1987). Editorial environment and advertising effectiveness. *Journal of Advertising Research, 27,* 11–16.

Axelrod, J. N. (1980). Advertising wearout. *Journal of Advertising Research, 20,* 13–18.

Aykac, A., Corstjens, M., & Gautschi, D. (1984). Is there a kink in your advertising? *Journal of Advertising Research, 24,* 27–36.

Batra, R. (1984). *"Low-involvement" message reception processes and advertising implications.* Doctoral dissertation. Ann Arbor, MI: University Microfilms International.

Batra, R., & Ray, M. L. (1983a). Advertising situations: The implications of differential involvement and accompanying affect responses. In R. J. Harris (Ed.), *Information processing research in advertising* (pp. 127–151). Hillsdale, NJ: Lawrence Erlbaum Associates.

Batra, R., & Ray, M. L. (1983b). Operationalizing involvement as depth and quality of cognitive response. In R. P. Bazoggi & A. M. Tybout (Eds.), *Advances in consumer research* (Vol. 10, pp. 309–311). Ann Arbor, MI: Association for Consumer Research.

Batra, R., & Ray, M. L. (1986). Situational effects of advertising repetition: The moderating influence of motivation, ability, and opportunity to respond. *Journal of Consumer Research, 13,* 432–445.

Berlyne, D. E. (1960). *Conflict, arousal, and curiosity.* New York: McGraw-Hill.

Berlyne, D. E. (1970). Novelty, complexity, and hedonic value. *Perception & Psychophysics, 8,* 279–285.

Bettman, J. R. (1979). Memory factors in consumer choice: A review. *Journal of Marketing, 43,* 37–53.

Britt, S. H. (1978). *Psychological principles of marketing and consumer behavior* (2nd ed.). Lexington, MA: Lexington Books.

Cacioppo, J. T., & Petty, R. E. (1979). Effects of message repetition and position on cognitive response, recall, and persuasion. *Journal of Personality and Social Psychology, 37,* 97–109.

Cacioppo, J. T., & Petty, R. E. (1980). Persuasiveness of communications is affected by exposure frequency and message quality: A theoretical and empirical analysis of persisting attitude change. In J. H. Leigh & C. R. Martin, Jr. (Eds.), *Current issues and research in advertising 1980* (pp. 97–122). Ann Arbor: University of Michigan, Division of Research, School of Business Administration.

Cook, T. D., & Campbell, D. T. (1979). *Quasi-experimentation: Design & analysis issues for field settings.* Chicago: Houghton Mifflin.

Crane, E. (1965). *Marketing communications.* New York: Books Demand.

Ebbinghaus, H. (1964). *Memory.* New York: Dover.

Elliot, J. (1985, October). How advertising frequency affects advertising effectiveness: Indications of change. *ADMAP, 512–515.*

Gardner, M. P., & Raj, S. P. (1983). Responses to commercials in laboratory versus natural setting: A conceptual framework. In R. P. Bagozzi & A. M. Tybout (Eds.), *Advances in consumer research* (Vol. 10, pp. 142–146). Ann Arbor, MI: Association for Consumer Research.

Geis, R. H. (1981). Media commentary: How much we know. *Advertising Age, 52,* 58.

Hull, C. L. (1958). *A behavior system: An introduction to behavior theory concerning the individual organism.* New Haven, CT: Yale University Press.

Keller, K. L. (1987). Memory factors in advertising: The effect of advertising retrieval cues on brand evaluations. *Journal of Consumer Research, 14,* 316–333.

Kellermann, K. (1985). Memory processes in media effects. *Communication Research, 12,* 83–131.

Krugman, H. (1972). Why three exposures may be enough. *Journal of Advertising Research, 12,* 11–14.

Leckenby, J. D., & Boyd, M. M. (1984). How media directors view reach/frequency model evaluation standards. *Journal of Advertising Research, 24,* 43–51.

Leckenby, J. D., & Kishi, S. (1982). How media directors view reach/frequency estimation. *Journal of Advertising Research, 22,* 64–69.

Leckenby, J. D., & Wedding, N. (1982). *Advertising management.* New York: Wiley.

Lewin, K. (1951). *Field theory in social science.* New York: University of Chicago Press.

McGuire, W. J. (1969) The nature of attitudes and attitude change. In G. Lindzey & E. Aronson (Eds.), *The handbook of social psychology* (Vol. 3, pp. 136–314). Reading, MA: Addison-Wesley.

McQuail, D. (1983). *Mass communication theory.* London: Sage.

Mitchell, A. A. (1983). Cognitive processes initiated by exposure to advertising. In R. J. Harris (Ed.), *Information processing research in advertising* (pp. 13–42). Hillsdale, NJ: Lawrence Erlbaum Associates.

Mitchell, A. A. (1986). Theoretical and methodological issues in developing an individual level model of advertising effects. In J. Olson & K. Sentis (Eds.), *Advertising and consumer psychology* (Vol. 3, pp. 172–196). New York: Praeger.

Mitchell, A. A., & Olson, J. C. (1981). Are product attribute beliefs the only mediators of advertising effects on brand attitude? *Journal of Marketing Research, 18,* 318–332.

Moore, D. J., Reardon, R., & Durso, F. T. (1986). The generation effect in advertising appeals. In R. J. Lutz (Ed.), *Advances in consumer research* (Vol. 13, pp. 117–120). Ann Arbor, MI: Association for Consumer Research.

Moorman, C. (1990). The effects of stimulus and consumer characteristics on the utilization of nutrition information. *Journal of Consumer Research, 17,* 362–374.

Nedungadi, P. (1990). Recall and consumer consideration sets: Influencing choice without altering brand evaluations. *Journal of Consumer Research, 17,* 263–276.

Nelson, T. O. (1977). Repetition and depth of processing. *Journal of Verbal Learning and Verbal Behavior, 16,* 151–171.

Ostrow, J. W. (1981). What level frequency? *Advertising Age, 52,* 4, 6, 8.

Ray, M. (1973). Psychological theories and interpretations of learning. In S. Ward & T. S. Robertson (Eds.), *Consumer behavior: Theoretical sources* (pp. 45–117). Englewood Cliffs, NJ: Prentice-Hall.

Ray, M. (1982). *Advertising and communication management.* Englewood Cliffs, NJ: Prentice-Hall.

Ray, M. L., & Sawyer, A. G. (1971). Repetition in media models: A laboratory technique. *Journal of Marketing Research, 8,* 20–29.

Rethans, A. J., Swasy, J. L., & Marks, L. J. (1986). Effects of television commercial repetition, receiver knowledge, and commercial length: A test of the two-factor model. *Journal of Marketing Research, 23,* 50–61.

Robertson, T. S. (1976). Low-commitment consumer behavior. *Journal of Advertising Research, 16,* 19–24.

Rothschild, M. L. (1987). *Advertising: From fundamentals to strategies.* Lexington, MA: Heath.

Sawyer, A. G. (1973). The effects of repetition of refutational and supportive advertising appeals. *Journal of Marketing Research, 10,* 23–33.

Saxe, L., & Fine, M. (1981). *Social experiments: Methods for design and evaluation.* Beverly Hills, CA: Sage.

Schultz, D. E. (1979). Media research users want. *Journal of Advertising Research, 19,* 13–17.

Simon, H. (1982). ADPULS: An advertising model with wearout and pulsation. *Journal of Marketing Research, 19,* 352–363.

Simon, J. L., & Arndt, J. (1980). The shape of the advertising response function. *Journal of Advertising Research, 20,* 11–28.

Singh, S. N., & Rothschild, M. L. (1983). Recognition as a measure of learning from television commercial. *Journal of Marketing Research, 20,* 235–248.

Sissors, J. Z. (1982–1983). Confusions about effective frequency. *Journal of Advertising Research, 22,* 33–37.

Sissors, J. Z., & Surmanek, J. (1982). *Advertising media planning* (2nd ed.). Chicago: Crain Books.

Stephens, N., & Warrens, R. A. (1983–1984). Advertising frequency requirements for older adults. *Journal of Advertising Research, 23,* 23–32.

Sternthal, B., & Craig, S. C. (1982). *Consumer behavior: An information processing perspective.* Englewood Cliffs, NJ: Prentice-Hall.

Swinyard, W. R. (1979). How many ad exposures is a sales call worth? *Journal of Advertising Research, 19,* 17–21.

Vuokko, P. (1992). Advertising repetition effects. Conceptual framework and field study in four product categories. *Publications of the Turku School of Economics and Business Administration* (Series A-1:1992). Turku, Finland.

Zeithaml, V. A., Varadarajan, P. R., & Zeithaml, C. P. (1988). The contingency approach: Its foundations and relevance to theory building and research in marketing. *European Journal of Marketing, 22,* 37–64.

Zielske, H. A., & Henry, W. A. (1980). Remembering and forgetting television ads. *Journal of Advertising Research, 20,* 7–13.

Comments on Chapter 14

Christine Wright-Isak
Young & Rubicam, Advertising

PRACTICAL RELEVANCE OF THIS RESEARCH

This chapter is of direct relevance to practitioners because of its subject, its manner of discussion, and the thorough research design that uses approaches that practitioners themselves use. The methods of data definition and collection are particularly comprehensive. Taking the trouble to ascertain the actual intended targets of the messages in the ads is of particular value to academic scholars and advertising researchers alike. Moreover, Vuokko carefully distinguishes between relevance and salience of messages and then examines the importance of each concept.

Conducting research with samples of respondents chosen to resemble actual message target audiences is a critical issue for managers who would consider using academic research results to improve creative work. In today's business environment, few if any advertisers can afford to afford to waste money advertising to people who are not prospects for their brand. In industry we always specify particular targets—we would be unable to make a media plan without doing so. Yet for reasons of feasibility and cost, many academic efforts to isolate effects of specific components of an ad creative use student samples who differ from real consumer targets. Additionally, most academic studies test only a limited number of brands and executions. These conditions limit generalizability. Happily this study is an exception to this norm, utilizing actual consumers in enough different situations (four categories and 34 brands) to allow meaningful generalizations to be made.

USEFULNESS OF THE FINDINGS

When industry researchers need to explain the usefulness of academic research findings to our management, we are called on to give "rules" that can be used over and over again. Principles that arise from research findings are what actually get used. The strength of this chapter for managers and their research professionals is that it explicitly refers to situations and problems encountered by those involved in development and placement of advertising and explicitly describes the ramifications of the findings for them.

The utility of the findings themselves begins with the fact that they can help us think about how to evaluate creative performance more accurately by including not only the likely effect of its format but also the other key factors. These include the message recipient's involvement level, consequent likely appeal, the nature of its media, and the ingoing advantage or disadvantage of the brand's position against the messages of the current competition. Most importantly, the social environment that will influence individual judgment about the credibility, appropriateness, and therefore appeal of the message is explicitly considered. It lays out the elements of what a good evidence chain can consist of for a fair and practical evaluation of campaign performance.

In addition, the ramifications of this evaluation are directly applied to a key cost consideration, the impact of several key variables on the need for frequency. Much management debate between agencies and their clients regarding how much to spend and where to spend it could be clarified by understanding the implications of Vuokko's findings.

FUTURE RESEARCH POSSIBILITIES

Ideally this research would be conducted in even more categories across more brands and perhaps linked to other worldwide brand diagnostic research being conducted by clients and agencies. By doing so, the long-term impact of the cumulative outcomes of message, reach and frequency, could be linked to actual brand building.

Comments on Chapters 11 Through 14

William D. Wells
University of Minnesota

Two themes unite the diverse observations in chapters 11 through 14. The first is the importance of context. All four of these chapters, and all of the comments associated with them, suggest that the effects of advertisements depend to a very large degree on stimuli that come from the environment: other advertisements (especially similar advertisements), the media, and broader economic and social events.

This theme explains some of the tensions between academicians and practitioners. In their completely understandable efforts to minimize the clamor of context, academicians "control away" influences that have exceedingly important influences in the real world. Having controlled away those influences, they fall prey to the assumption that their findings are universal. When practitioners become aware of these decontextualizations, they wonder whether academicians are really interested in how advertisements really work.

A second theme that unites these four chapters is segmentation. In chapter 14—after a detailed real-world examination—Vuokko concluded that "there is, in general, no such thing as 'the optimal amount of repetition'" (p. 255). Instead, she concluded, the optimal amount of repetition depends on "the receiver, the advertising stimuli, and the communication environment" (p. 255). Different kinds of receivers, different kinds of stimuli, different kinds of environmental situations, and all the interactions among those differences, produce sharply different effects.

Similarly, the Wyer–Srull theory—recounted in chapter 11—predicts that an advertisement's place in its receiver's memory depends on the receiver's processing goals, which in turn depend on how the product fits into the receiver's purposes and the advertisement's competitive mission in the real world. Thus, types products, types of competitive situations, and types of receivers are major segmenting variables. As previous chapters have demonstrated, advertisements produce one effect for one kind of product in one kind of situation, a different effect for a different kind of product in a different kind of situation, and so on.

The experiment reported in chapter 12 shows that context mediates the effects of positively valenced advertisements but not the effects of neutrally valenced advertisements—another form of segmentation. The experiment reported in chapter 13 indicates that even positive valence should be segmented. An advertisement can have too much originality and too much emotional impact, but not too much relevance. With that many critical contingencies, high-level general propositions—propositions that cross products, environments, processing goals, consumers, advertisements, and responses—are not likely to provide valid predictions in the specific case.

These two themes—context and segmentation—show why academicians and practitioners need each other. Academicians need practitioners to remind them that the results of individual experiments are necessarily limited, no matter how artfully designed the experiment, no matter how much effort the experiment required, and no matter how much the experimenter would like to have discovered general truth. When academicians begin to believe they have discovered verity they need skeptical practitioners to remind them of the ground-level facts of life.

On the other hand, practitioners need academicians to save them from the tyranny of limited experience. Whereas useful universal generalizations are exceedingly rare, useful low-level generalizations are common. Chapters 11 through 14 provide useful low-level generalizations about messages, receivers, and environments. With careful attention to those findings, neither practitioners nor academicians need to start each time from scratch.

VI

Copy Testing

We now turn to overtly applied considerations. In chapter 15, two veterans present a practical cookbook that summarizes many years of copy testing experience. As the discussant of this chapter notes, it contains "many helpful hints for pretesting short-term effectiveness." As the discussant also notes, not everyone will agree with all these prescriptions. The authors are Larry Percy, formerly Research Director at Lintas and now proprietor of his own consulting firm, and John Rossiter, coauthor with Percy of a well-known advertising textbook, and faculty member at the Australian Graduate School of Management. The discussant is Esther Thorson of the University of Missouri–Columbia.

In chapter 16, two academicians challenge many popular copy testing methods by proposing alternatives to key assumptions. In commenting on this challenge, two practitioners acknowledge that, in principle, the academicians might be right. The authors, Richard W. Olshavsky and Anand Kumar, are based at the University of Indiana. The practitioners are Larry Percy, coauthor of the preceding chapter, and Abhilasha Mehta of Gallup & Robinson, Inc.

Chapter 17 summarizes a large collection of real evaluations of real advertisements. It presents substantial evidence that the difference between preexposure intention and postexposure intention is the single most valid predictor of sales effectiveness, and that the relationship between day-after recall and sales effectiveness is at best extremely weak. It also provides substantial evidence that whether consumers like an advertisement has no bearing on its effectiveness, that bare-bones renditions of sales propositions predict the sales effectiveness of finished ads, that executional differences have measurable effects on sales, and that wear-out with repeated exposure follows a predictable course. Allen Kuse, the author of this chapter, is an executive at research systems corporation, a firm that specializes in pretests of rough and finished advertisements. The discussant of this chapter, Brian Wansink of the University of Illinois, Urbana–Champaign, identifies implications of Kuse's methods and conclusions for academic advertising research.

Chapter 18 presents a case history in which an "informational" advertisement and a "transformational" advertisement reached their communications objective through different routes, and it details the process through which that outcome came about. Abhilasha Mehta and Scott C. Purvis, the authors, are executives at Gallup & Robinson, Inc. Brian Wansink commented on this chapter as well. In his comments, Wansink links Mehta and Purvis' real-world concepts and findings to concepts and findings in more theoretical academic work.

Chapter 19 describes a quite different case. Here, the contrast is between more traditional methods of measuring advertising effectiveness and a method that examines a chain of relationships that leads from perceptions of product attributes to beliefs that the product will contribute to important aspects of the perceiver's life. The authors, like the content, blend academic and industry affiliations. Thomas J. Reynolds, a former academician, is an executive at Richmond Partners, Inc. Jerry C. Olson is an academic researcher at Pennsylvania State University. John P. Rochon is an executive at Richmont Partners, Inc. The discussant, Christine Wright-Isak of Young & Rubicam, Advertising, fits means–end chain analysis into the more general context of measuring advertising's broader, medium to long-range effects.

Chapter 20 examines an important exception to the common assumption that advertisements are intended to elicit purchase rather than use. The products featured in chapter 20 are already in inventory in many of their users' homes, and the object of the advertising is to move the product off the pantry shelf. As chapter 20 shows, that situation requires a unique approach to measuring effect. The authors of chapter 20 are both academicians—Brian Wansink at University of Illinois, Urbana–Champaign and Michael Ray at Stanford.

Chapter 21 focuses on another important exception to standard copy testing tasks. It reminds us that an important segment of marketing communication is not distributed through electronic and print media, but rather reaches the purchaser at the point of sale. It describes the assets of "place-based" media, and outlines a procedure through which the effectiveness of such media can be assessed. Like the authors of chapter 19, the authors of this chapter blend industry and academic posts. James Lucas is a research executive at Frankel & Company, a prominent promotions firm. David Prensky, formerly an advertising agency researcher, is on the faculty at Trenton State University.

15

A Theory-Based Approach to Pretesting Advertising

Larry Percy
Marketing Communications Consultant

John R. Rossiter
Australian Graduate School of Management

The job of evaluating the likely success of any particular advertising execution requires original primary research custom tailored to each particular circumstance, but executed within strict theoretical guidelines. Accordingly, we caution against sole reliance on the standardized procedures offered by any one particular supplier or syndicated service. Flexible procedures based on the brand's advertising communication objectives provide a better fit and more valid results.

The purpose of pretesting is to improve the chances that advertising will work as planned when placed in media. Whether it will work as planned, however, depends on three factors:

- The creative content of the executions.
- The correct media placement and scheduling.
- Competitive advertising activity.

Pretesting deals with the first factor only. Campaign tracking over time evaluates all three factors. We pretest advertising to ensure it is "on strategy"—that it is capable of achieving the communication objectives desired for the brand, to be able to correct and revise the executions if necessary, and then to predict how it will work in the market.

METHODS UNSUITED FOR PRETESTING ADVERTISING

Before we begin to examine the best ways to pretest advertising, however, we want to point out three ways not to go about it, even though the first two are often used. The methods about which we hold strong reservations are focus groups, recall, and physiological measures.

Focus Groups

Whereas focus groups are essential for formulating the advertising strategy prior to the campaign, they are inappropriate for testing ads (Rossiter & Donovan, 1983). There are at least three compelling reasons. Focus groups vastly overexpose advertisements. In a group setting, advertisements are thoroughly discussed, a far cry from the 30 seconds, more or less, that broadcast advertising has available to communicate in the real world and the 1 to 2 seconds that a print or outdoor ad has to gain attention. This overexposure leads respondents in focus groups to exaggerate positive and negative aspects of the advertisement, as well as to focus on elements in the execution that would never get processed in the real world, generating a serious validity problem.

This validity problem follows from the group setting itself, which produces group interactions that largely prevent reactions from occurring as they would normally. Normally, people process advertising as individuals, even if they are watching TV with others.

The third problem is the lack of reliable projection. Even if the focus group methodology itself were valid, there would remain a serious reliability problem, owing to the small overall sample size. It would be a rare (as well as inefficient and expensive) test in which 100 respondents were exposed to the test advertising.

Recall

The most that can be said about advertising recall measures, especially day-after-recall (DAR) testing, is that they may be a rough measure of attention to the advertising. However, the fundamental flaw with recall testing, especially DAR, is that it is ad recall based, not brand recall based. Most DAR measures are initially and prejudicially tied to a particular media vehicle as a memory cue, and to a particular insertion, at a particular time. Such a measure cannot be generalized (Gibson, 1983; Percy, 1978). A similar problem applies to the "recall" measures used by leading pretesting services, such as RSC's ARS Recall[SM] and MSW's Clutter Awareness[SM], which have not been shown to be valid measures of advertising effectiveness even in these firm's own studies (Blair, 1988; Klien & Tainiter, 1983; see also Young & Robinson, 1992). No pretest measure of advertising recall has ever been shown to predict advertising effectiveness. This is because media vehicle (as in DAR) and the test situation (as in the case of most syndicated recall measures) are cues that are irrelevant to the consumer's decision process.

Physiological Measures

Physiological measures provide a measure of attention only. EEG or brain-wave measures record electrical response to executions, but the interpretation of this response is not clear (Olson & Ray, 1989; Rothschild, Hyun, Reeves, Thorson, & Goldstein, 1988; Stewart & Furse, 1982). Eye-movement measures (Kroeber-Riel, 1984; Weinblatt, 1985, 1987) exhibit some relationship with brand recognition, but not with brand recall or brand attitude.

THEORETICAL BACKGROUND

We believe that advertising pretesting must be based on the communication objectives for the advertised brand (or company or service) and that these, in turn, depend on the buyer decision process that the advertising is intended to influence. The five primary communication effects for advertising are outlined in the following, and it is from this set of effects that the objectives for a particular execution will come (Rossiter & Percy, 1987):

1. Category need: The consumer's realization of "need to purchase" with regard to the product or service category overall.
2. Brand awareness: The consumer's ability to recognize or recall the brand, within the product category, in sufficient detail to make a purchase.
3. Brand attitude: The consumer's overall evaluation of how well the brand can satisfy a relevant motive (the evaluation is based on benefit beliefs or affective feelings produced by the brand).
4. Brand purchase intention: The consumer's deliberate decision to purchase the brand or take purchase-related action within a given time period.
5. Brand purchase facilitation: The consumer's assurance that other marketing factors, such as availability and ease of payment, will not hinder purchase of the brand.

Although not all of the five communication effects may be objectives for a particular execution, brand awareness and brand attitude will always be objectives (Percy & Rossiter, 1992; Rossiter, Percy, & Donovan, 1991). All advertising is aimed at maintaining or increasing brand awareness, and at conveying information or creating an emotional response to form or change brand attitude. These two communication objectives differ greatly according to the type of buyer decision process, and these differences vitally affect the validity of advertising pretests.

Brand awareness divides into two types, depending on the consumer's decision process: brand recognition, where the brand name or package is to be recognized at the point of purchase, and brand recall, where the brand name is to be remembered prior to the point of purchase, when the need arises. These different types of brand awareness mean that different measures must be used in pretesting, as we see later.

Brand attitude strategies divide into four types, depending on the consumer's decision process. The four types (quadrants) are based on the main two dimensions of the decision: type of motivation and level of involvement, as outlined in the following and shown by the grid in Fig. 15.1 (Rossiter & Percy, 1987; Rossiter et al., 1991).

The brand attitude objective is met through either an "informational" or "transformational" advertising message appeal depending on whether purchase motivation for the brand is positive or negative. Negative motivations include problem removal ("quench thirst fast"), problem avoidance ("prevents bad breath"), incomplete satisfaction ("a better way to bank"), mixed approach avoidance ("less tar than other brands"), and normal depletion (a "restocking" motive for brand loyals only). When negative motives drive behavior in a product category for the target audience, an informational advertising appeal should be used. Positive motivations include sensory gratification ("tastes great"), intellectual stimulation ("challenge your mind"), and social approval ("friends will admire you"). When they drive behavior, a transformational advertising appeal should be used.

A second component affecting a brand attitude objective is whether the purchase decision is low involvement or high involvement. We define involvement in terms of economic or psychological risk. Involvement, or perceived risk, depends on the type of product and on the target audience's familiarity with the brand. Regular buyers of a brand are usually making a low-involvement decision in deciding to purchase it next time, regardless of how highly involving their initial decision may have been.

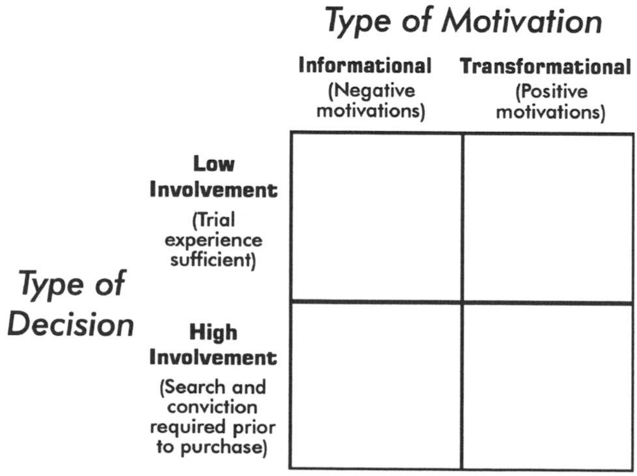

FIG. 15.1. Rossiter and Percy brand attitude quadrants.

The two types of brand awareness, brand recognition and brand recall, and the four "quadrants" of brand attitude strategies combine to provide a framework for evaluating the effectiveness of advertising executions.

RECOMMENDED PRETEST METHODOLOGY

An advertising pretest is an "experiment" in which the purpose is to measure the effects of the execution. This means that ideally we have test versus control samples. Each test cell should be exposed to only one test execution. This means that there must be as many test cells as there are executions. One execution per subject is really the only valid design, and attempts to save money by having each person in the test exposed to two (or worse, more) executions in "counterbalanced" or rotated order are misguided because the first test execution a subject sees will always bias responses to any subsequent test executions.

An alternative to the test versus control group design is to use a pre–post design with no control group; effectively, the premeasures substitute for the control group and the postmeasures are, of course, the test group. Although this design may save on field costs, it requires elaborate disguise to avoid sensitization and a reasonably long interval (up to an hour or two) before the postmeasures to minimize memory of the premeasure results. Although this type of design will work quite well for measures of brand purchase intention, (e.g. Rossiter & Eagleson, 1994), it is time consuming and difficult for measures of brand awareness and brand attitude. As a result, we do not recommend a pre–post design.

Rough Versus Finished Executions

The general purpose of pretesting advertising is to assess how well the finished executions will work, but pretesting usually is conducted with rough executions. Just how rough depends on whether the advertising is informational (addressing a negative purchase motivation) or transformational (addressing a positive purchase motivation).

For informational advertising, fairly rough executions in the form of black-and-white sketches of print ads with typed copy (also for informational direct mail ads and outdoor ads) or of "animatics" (sketches placed on videotape, with audio) of TV commercials may often be sufficient. Nevertheless, if more finished executions are possible, they should be used, because better finish will increase predictive validity (Schlinger & Green, 1980). Rougher executions are sufficient here because the informational ("reason why") message should be apparent regardless of the quality of the execution tested.

Transformational advertising is quite different. Its reliance on positive appeals means that its effectiveness depends greatly on production values. Accordingly, for transformational executions, and illustrated direct mail ads and outdoor ads, a higher quality of finish is required. Rough sketches in storyboards (animatics) should never be used for pretesting transformational advertising

(Greene & McCullough, 1985). Storyboards per se are suitable for presenting on videotape as long as the color and finish of the storyboards are very good (e.g., photomatics). When the audio portion (especially with music) contributes significantly to the feeling of the advertising, photomatics are required with professional voice-overs or music.

Cutting across both types of TV commercials is the commercial that depends on movement for its essential message, such as a "demonstration" informational commercial as seen in many direct-response TV ads or an "experiential" transformational commercial as seen in some new car advertising. For these, a "live-action rough" should be used.

It should go without saying that to make valid comparisons between test executions, they should all be tested in an equivalent degree of finish. Although equivalent degree of finish is easy to accomplish when all the executions are new, the problem arises in testing new (test) advertising against existing or earlier (finished) advertising. If the previous advertising has not been used in media for a considerable time (a year or more), the best solution is to "break it down" to the same degree of finish as the new advertising. This can be done by retrieving the storyboards or by preparing new storyboards based on the finished ads. If, however, the finished executions are currently in the media, then it is pointless to break them down, because the target audience already is seeing the finished advertising outside the test setting. Again, the type of advertising dictates the decision: For informational advertising, it should not matter too much if rough executions are tested against current finished advertising, although a better finish than normal would be advisable. For transformational advertising, the test executions must be of near-finished quality and, ideally, finished versions of the winning executions should be further tested.

Number of Exposures

Newspaper and magazine advertising should be given an attention, or "stopping power," test first. This consists of one competitive "portfolio" exposure, as explained in the measures section later. Newspaper and magazine advertising (thereafter) and direct mail should be given one exposure, without a time limit. In the real world, the target audience decision maker can control the exposure duration, spending as little or as much time with the advertising as interest dictates. This should be simulated in the pretest with a single unrestricted exposure. The usual instruction here is, "Just look at this ad as you would normally."

Broadcast advertising requires two or three exposures to provide sufficient opportunity for processing. Informational commercials should be exposed twice. The message in informational TV and radio commercials should be apparent quickly, thus suggesting one exposure. However, as described by Krugman (1972), because broadcast commercial exposure duration is fleeting, the respondents should be allowed a first exposure to begin to comprehend the commercial, then a second exposure for the execution to work. The communication effectiveness of most commercials changes and improves with two exposures (Klein, 1991) and commercials usually get two or more exposures in the real world.

Transformational commercials should be shown or played three times. As we just noted, broadcast media presentation means at least two exposures will be necessary for receivers to process the commercial. Thereafter, transformational commercials should continue to increase brand attitude beyond two exposures. However, four or five successive exposures in a single test might begin to induce either attentional wear-out or attitudinal wear-out (Rossiter & Percy, 1987). Therefore, for transformational commercials, three exposures should represent the best compromise between giving this softer sell type of advertising an opportunity and not subjecting it to forced-exposure wear-out.

PRETEST MEASURES

We now first, briefly, look at the correct order of the measures to be used in pretesting advertising, and then discuss in some detail their content. The correct sequence of measures for the control group is as follows:

1. Category need (if an objective).
2. Brand awareness.
3. Brand purchase intention (if an objective).
4. Brand attitude.
5. Brand benefit beliefs.

The following is the order for the test groups:

1. Attention (if newspaper or magazine ad).
2. Processing measures.
   a. Acceptance (if high involvement)
   b. Learning
   c. Adjective checklist
3. Other communication effects.
   a. Category need (if an objective)
   b. Brand purchase intention (if an objective)
   c. Brand attitude
   d. Brand benefit belief
   e. Brand awareness: delayed
4. Attention diagnostics (all other types of ads, if required).

Basically, the measures are ordered so as to be least sensitizing. For instance, brand purchase intention (if an objective) and brand attitude are measured before brand benefit beliefs because to measure the beliefs first may lead the subject to form a "new" or revised attitude or intention based on the experimentally provided beliefs (Sandelands & Larson, 1985). In the test group, brand awareness is measured on a delayed basis because to measure this communication effect immediately after exposure to the test execution would produce spuriously high awareness (see Rossiter & Percy, 1987, for further details). In the control group, however, the brand awareness measure is taken immediately because there is no advertising exposure.

The measures used in pretesting advertising are discussed in the order used for the test group. One will note that, apart from the attention measures, the processing and communication effects measures are not standardized (as is the practice in most syndicated pretesting services). Rather, in our approach, these measures are selected to fit the communication objectives for the brand.

Attention Test (Newspaper and Magazine Ads Only)

Advertising in newspapers and magazines must "stop" the reader from turning the page before it can communicate (this is not the case in broadcast media where reflexive attention can be relied on). Data from the Starch/INRA Hooper testing service's "Noted" score indicate that about 50% of all newspaper and magazine ads fail to stop the reader (Rossiter, 1988). Eye-tracking experiments by Kroeber-Riel (1988) and Von Keitz (1988) show that it takes about 1.75 seconds to process an illustration in a print ad and about 0.25 seconds to process each word in a headline—the illustration and headline being the minimum input to get the message.

To account for this, when pretesting print advertising one could compute the time necessary for minimally processing the test execution and then construct a timed portfolio test as the first measure. We recommend that about 10 other "distractor" pages, some advertising, some editorial, go into the portfolio. It does not matter too much what these distractor pages contain as long as there are enough of them to simulate a reading situation (Weinblatt, 1987). The time spent looking at the test execution, compared with likely minimum processing times for the headline and illustration (following the Kroeber-Riel and Von Keitz results), will provide a measure of the number of people exposed to the execution who are likely to process it. The communication effects results from the subsequent exposure can then be corrected for the proportion of attention achieved by the text execution. One simple way to do this is to analyze only those people who took at least the minimum time looking at the executions. If a large number of people fail to take enough time, it will be important to compare their responses with those that do. In any event, it is important to have some idea of the number of people likely to process a test execution sufficiently to achieve its objective.

Processing Measures

Processing reflects the consumer's immediate responses to the advertising. These responses are transient, so they must be measured immediately. To measure them when they actually occur would of course disrupt processing, so they must be measured immediately afterward. This immediate retrospective measurement of reactions to the executions does not affect the subsequent brand-related measures (Hastak, 1990). The two types of processing measures taken at this stage are acceptance (for high-involvement brand attitude) and learning (for low-involvement brand attitude).

Acceptance. If the brand attitude strategy is high involvement, then the consumer must agree with (accept) the claims about the brand. What matters in high-involvement strategies is the extent to which the consumer willingly agrees with message points. The most valid measure of high-involvement processing is cognitive response measurement (Petty, Ostrom, & Brock, 1981), which requires coding the respondent's open-ended comments. The best procedure is subject self-scoring (Cacioppo, Harkins, & Petty, 1981; Stephens & Russo, chap. 10, this volume), where the interviewer reads back the subjects' comments and asks whether each comment is good, bad, or neutral. Mention of the brand should also be recorded because the comments should reflect opinions about the brand. Failure to mention the brand could indicate a possible brand awareness problem with the ad.

Learning. With low-involvement brand attitude strategies, we are looking for "rote" learning response (learning is also necessary for brand awareness, but is measured later). In low-involvement strategies, what counts is the perceived message about the brand. It does not matter whether the target audience fully accepts, or is convinced by, the message during processing, as long as it is perceived correctly (Maloney, 1962; Petty & Cacioppo, 1983). A successfully registered low-involvement attitude shift will show up on the communication effect measure of intention to try the brand (low involvement/informational advertising) or brand attitude "image" benefit increases (low involvement/transformational advertising). However, we must remember this assumes we are dealing with category users. Trial of almost any product for someone new to the category, unless the decision is all but trivial, will be high involvement for that person, and they would need to accept the message as well.

The processing measure for low-involvement attitudinal learning is straightforward. It consists of the following type of question: "In this ad, aside from trying to convince you to try the brand, what do you think the advertiser is trying to tell you?" Verbatim playback or accurate paraphrases of the ad-proposed brand benefit are scored as successful learning during processing, with one important qualification: If the brand name has not yet been mentioned, the interviewer should ask: "What was the brand advertised?" The association to be learned is between the brand (awareness) and the benefit (attitude) and not the benefit in isolation.

After the open-ended acceptance (high-involvement) or learning (low-involvement) measures, for diagnostic purposes we recommend a closed-end adjective checklist (ACL) measure to gauge specific, immediate reactions to the execution. Whereas general ACLs are widely used (Aaker & Bruzzone, 1981; Schlinger, 1979; Wells, Leavitt, & McConville, 1971; Zinkhan & Burton, 1989), we recommend a customized ACL for each execution designed to reflect its communication tactics and to pick up reactions to special executional devices, such as music or a presenter. For example, the ACL for a low-involvement/informational execution would include "curious disbelief" statements (Maloney, 1962), whereas for a low-involvement/transformational execution the ACL would include "ad liking" statements (Madden & Ajzen, 1991; McCollum Spielman Worldwide, 1992; Rossiter, 1993). An ad with a celebrity presenter would have in its ACL selected statements that reflect characteristics associated with presenter effectiveness (Percy & Rossiter, 1980).

Communication Effects Measures

When category need is a communication objective, the measure to be used is category purchase intention. If the category need communication objective is to "sell" the category, two other measures are required: category benefit beliefs, and a delayed measure of category awareness. The addition of a category benefit beliefs measure is to assess whether, indeed, the advertisement has "sold" the prospect on the need to buy this product category. The addition of the category awareness measure is required to ensure that the prospect "remains sold" by remembering the product category; this category-level awareness occurs within the context of competing purchase categories. Once these category measures are secured, the brand measures follow.

Brand Purchase Intentions.   Brand purchase intention is not a useful measure for executions following a low-involvement/transformational brand attitude strategy. The attitude that such executions address takes time to build. In a pretest situation, it is not reasonable to expect an immediate effect on purchase intention. Indeed, the effect may be largely subconscious (Krugman, 1966–1967). However, one can get an idea of the likely success by looking for increases in brand benefit beliefs (in a tracking study, on the other hand, brand purchase intention is an appropriate measure because the transformational advertising has now had time—i.e., a sufficient number of exposures—to work).

Measures of brand purchase intention require three considerations: the wording of the intention question in terms of "try" or "use," a time frame for intention, and the response options in the measure. Paying attention to the wording of questions should go without saying, but too often important distinctions are ignored. For example, with new product categories (and brands), consumers are more willing to state intention to "try" a brand, which implies less commitment, than they are to state intentions to "buy" it. Similarly, purchase versus usage may be relevant, depending on the specific action objective of the advertising (Eastlack, 1984; Wansink & Ray, 1991). For example, many consumers own power tools, or dangerous chemical fertilizers, or drugs, but for a number of reasons are not really classifiable as "users," because they own them but rarely or never use them. The wording of the intention measure should reflect the purchase or purchase-related action objective precisely.

The second consideration, time frame for the brand purchase intention measure, is satisfied by making the intention conditional on category need. For example:

- If you were going to buy more life insurance, how likely is it that you would consider National Life?
- Next time you buy a cola, how likely is it that you will buy Pepsi?

Finally, a good measure to deal with the response option is the well-known unipolar 4-point scale of will not buy/might buy/probably will buy/definitely will buy (for low-involvement brand choice) or Juster's (1966) 11-point probability scale (for high-involvement brand choice). A reason for using these response measures is that weighting multipliers have been developed for converting intentions to purchase or usage incidence prediction. For instance, weights for the low involvement intention scale are 0, .1, .4, and .9 (Kalwani & Silk, 1982; Urban & Hauser, 1980), and for the Juster scale, they increase from 0 to 0.5 in increments of 0.05 (Infosino, 1986; Juster, 1966; Kalwani & Silk, 1983; Morrison, 1979).

Brand Attitude. Next comes the overall measure of brand attitude (this measure is omitted only when testing low-involvement/transformational executions as already explained). Brand attitude measurement helps to interpret the ultimate pretest criterion measure, brand purchase intention (given brand awareness). Whereas in brand purchase intention we measure how likely the subject is to buy, try, or use the brand, in overall brand attitude we measure how favorably the brand is evaluated relative to other brands, regardless of whether the subject would buy or consider it at the next purchase opportunity. The main thing to remember in preparing the brand attitude measure, as with the intention measure previously, is to specify the "situation" for which the brand is to be purchased or used (which in turn relates to the purchase motivation dimension of brand attitude). For instance, attitude toward a prepared food brand may differ depending on whether it is being considered for family consumption or for serving to guests. A suitable measure of overall situational brand attitude for the latter situation might be: "For serving to guests, Test Brand is: my single preferred brand/one of several preferred brands/an average brand that I would only serve if none of my preferred brands was available/a below-average brand I would never serve." This attitude measure is situation-specific and it provides the opportunity to evaluate one brand relative to competing brands.

Having people rate a brand's perceived delivery of the specific benefit or benefits employed in the advertisement serves as a diagnostic measure for the overall brand attitude result, as well as serving as the sole measure of brand attitude when the attitude strategy is low involvement/transformational. The brand benefit beliefs measures follow the overall brand attitude rating so as to again help minimize contamination. The advertiser does not want the subject forming a spurious attitude based on benefits suggested in the measures rather than on benefits spontaneously processed in the advertising. Hence, the diagnostic measures follow the overall attitude measure.

We recommend a one-step or two-step questioning sequence here. First, a simple dichotomy: "Is this statement (reflecting the specific beliefs implied by the advertising) likely to be true or unlikely to be true?" For low-involvement/informational advertising, this "yes/no" type of question is all that is needed because the brand is perceived to either have or not have the particular attribute. For low-involvement/transformational and high-involvement advertising, however, we must go on to ask how likely or unlikely the statement is to be true, using a balanced likelihood scale. Benefit beliefs for these two types of advertising are "softer" and more probabilistic rather than sharply yes–no. For high-involvement/informational advertising, we recommended graduated "benefit possession" scales, such as "the brand is not at all/slightly/moderately/very" in possession of the benefit.

If brand purchase facilitation is a communication objective, then its attainment should be measured in the list of brand benefit beliefs. For instance, if a distribution problem is perceived, add "not/widely available;" if a price problem, a benefit possession sale related to price can be added to the benefit beliefs list.

Brand Awareness.   Why is the measure of brand awareness delayed until the end of the pretest? Brand awareness is the linchpin communication effect that must result from advertising. It forms a gatekeeping role to the other communication effects (and thus purchase of the brand). If the prospective buyer does not recognize or recall the brand, it will not be purchased—regardless of how well-established or how favorable the other communication effects for the brand are in the prospective buyer's mind.

Only in the special case of direct-response broadcast advertising—such as the "call or write now" type of advertising that appears on TV or radio—should brand awareness be measured initially. In all other types of advertising, there will be a delay between advertising exposure and the next purchase decision opportunity. This may range from an hour or so for "same-day" retail advertising, to a week or more for other products.

Unfortunately, brand awareness measures taken within the pretesting session itself do not provide a reliable measure of the execution's ability to create or increase awareness for the brand. Short-interval measures should never be interpreted as absolute measures of an execution's ability to create or increase brand awareness, particularly brand recall, which declines drastically with time (due to other advertising's competitive interference in memory). The only reliable way to estimate brand awareness is to administer a delayed test:

- For brand recall, a delayed test can be administered by phone: An interviewer calls the subjects back at an appropriate interval and asks what brands in the product category they recall.
- For brand recognition, the measure is more difficult, because it requires a personal re-interview in which the subjects are shown a photograph of brand packages and asked which brands they recognize at a glance. Two-way TV methodologies should eventually facilitate brand recognition measurement, but at present, a personal follow-up interview is required.

This is perhaps a good place to underscore what should be, but frequently is not, obvious. The important measure here is brand awareness, not advertising awareness. Hence, in almost all cases, typical recall procedures (e.g., DAR as discussed earlier) that are based on advertising awareness are of no real value in understanding the communication effectiveness of one's advertising. As we have pointed out, most recall procedures of this kind have a number of theoretical and methodological problems attached to them.

SUMMARY

As the chapters in this volume attest, "evaluating advertising" is far from a settled question. It is our firm belief that the main reason for the controversy that continues to swirl around pretesting is that most advertisers and advertising research suppliers have been all too willing to take shortcuts by relying on single, often syndicated, measures that cannot possibly have good validity for all the advertising situations in which they are applied. So, is there a "right" way to pretest advertising? We think so, and have recommended using a set of measures that fit the consumer's decision process and accurately reflect the advertising's communication objectives for the brand. This approach to pretesting may be more expensive (because of semicustomized or tailored measures) and could be seen as more difficult (because managers and researchers have to devote more time to prior strategy research and to thinking about what they are measuring and why) than most currently employed approaches. However, in our view, this approach represents the only way one can be sure they are measuring those responses to the advertising that are most likely to reflect its communication objective.

REFERENCES

Aaker, D. A., & Bruzzone, D. E. (1981). Viewer perceptions of prime-time television advertising. *Journal of Advertising Research, 21,* 15–23.

Blair, M. H. (1988). An empirical investigation of advertising wearin and wearout. *Journal of Advertising Research, 28,* 45–50.

Cacioppo, J. T., Harkins, S. G., & Petty, R. E. (1981). The nature of attitudes and cognitive responses and their relationship to behavior. In R. E. Petty, T. M. Ostrom, & T. C. Brock (Eds.), *Cognitive responses in persuasion* (pp. 31–54). Hillsdale, NJ: Lawrence Erlbaum Associates.

Eastlack, J. O., Jr. (1984). Point of view: How to take the controversy out of TV copy testing. *Journal of Advertising Research, 24,* 37–39.

Gibson, L. D. (1983). Not recall. *Journal of Advertising Research, 23,* 39–46.

Greene, W. F., & McCullough, J. E. (1985). Animatic, photomatic to live-action rough pre-testing predictability vs. production cost tradeoffs. In *Copy research* (pp. 97–117). New York: Advertising Research Foundation.

Hastak, M. (1990). Does retrospective thought measurement influence subsequent measures of cognitive structure in advertising context? *Journal of Advertising, 19,* 3–13.

Infosino, W. J. (1986). Forecasting new product sales from likelihood of purchase ratings. *Marketing Science, 5,* 372–373.

Juster, T. F. (1966). Consumer buying intentions and purchase probability: An experiment in survey design. *Journal of the American Statistical Association, 61*(3), 658–696.

Kalwani, M. U., & Silk, A. J. (1983). On the reliability and predictive validity of purchase intention measures. *Marketing Science, 1*(3), 243–286.

Klein, P. R. (1991). *Image/mood television advertising and the multiple exposure of test stimuli: A philosophical and empirical overview.* Great Neck, NY: McCollum Spielman Worldwide.

Klein, P. R., & Tainiter, M. (1983). Copy research validation: The advertiser's perspective. *Journal of Advertising Research, 23,* 9–17.

Kroeber-Riel, W. (1984). Effects of emotional pictorial elements in ads analyzed by means of eye movement monitoring. In T. Kinnear (Ed.), *Advances in consumer research* (Vol. 11, pp. 591–597). Ann Arbor, MI: Association for Consumer Research.

Kroeber-Riel, W. (1988). *Advertising on saturated markets* (Working paper). Saarbrucken, Germany: Institute for Consumer and Behavioral Research, University of the Saarland.

Krugman, H. E. (1966–1967). The measurement of advertising involvement. *Public Opinion Quarterly, 30,* 583–596.

Krugman, H. E. (1972). Why three exposures may be enough. *Journal of Advertising Research, 12,* 11–14.

Madden, T. J., & Ajzen, L. (1991). Affective cues in persuasion: An assessment of causal mediation. *Marketing Letters, 2,* 359–366.

Maloney, J. C. (1962). Curiosity versus disbelief in advertising. *Journal of Advertising Research, 2,* 2–8.

McCollum Spielman Worldwide. (1992). Does commercial liking matter? *Topline, 36*(2).

Morrison, D. G. (1979). Purchase intentions and purchase behavior. *Journal of Marketing, 43,* 65–74.

Olson, J., & Ray, W. (1989). *Exploring the usefulness of brain waves as measures of advertising response.* (Report No. 89-116, pp. 1–60). Cambridge, MA: Marketing Science Institute.

Percy, L. (1978). Some questions on the validity of recall testing as a measure of advertising effectiveness. In J. Leigh & C. R. Martin, Jr. (Eds.), *Current issues & research in advertising* (pp. 121–130). Ann Arbor: University of Michigan, Graduate School of Business Administration.

Percy, L., & Rossiter, J. R. (1980). *Advertising strategy: A communication theory approach.* New York: Praeger.

Percy, L., & Rossiter, J. R. (1992). *Measuring advertising effectiveness: Copy testing (pre-testing) ads and tracking (post-testing) the campaign* (Working paper No. 92-0201). Sydney: Australian Graduate School of Management.

Petty, R. E., & Cacioppo, J. T. (1983). Central and peripheral routes to persuasion. In L. Percy & A. G. Woodside (Eds.), *Advertising and consumer psychology* (pp. 3–23). Lexington, MA: Lexington Books.

Petty, R. E., Ostrom, T. M., & Brock, T. C. (Eds.). (1981). *Cognitive responses in persuasion*. Hillsdale, NJ: Lawrence Erlbaum Associates.

Rossiter, J. R. (1988). The increase in magazine ad readership. *Journal of Advertising Research, 28,* 35–39.

Rossiter, J. R. (1993). *The limited effect of likable ads* (Working paper No. 93-021). Sydney: Australian Graduate School of Management.

Rossiter, J. R., & Donovan, R. J. (1983). Why you shouldn't test ads in focus groups. *Australian Marketing Researcher, 7,* 43–48.

Rossiter, J. R., & Eagleson, G. (1994). Conclusions from the ARF copy research validity project. *Journal of Advertising Research, 34*(3), 19–32.

Rossiter, J. R., & Percy, L. (1987). *Advertising and promotion management*. New York: McGraw-Hill.

Rossiter, J. R., Percy, L., & Donovan, R. J. (1991). A better advertising planning grid. *Journal of Advertising Research, 31,* 11–21.

Rothschild, M. L., Hyun, Y. J., Reeves, B., Thorson, E., & Goldstein, R. (1988). Hemispherically lateralised EEG as a response to television commercials. *Journal of Consumer Research, 15,* 185–198.

Sandelands, L. E., & Larson, J. R., Jr. (1985). When measurement causes task attitudes: A note from the laboratory. *Journal of Applied Psychology, 70,* 116–121.

Schlinger, M. J. (1979). A profile of responses to commercials. *Journal of Advertising Research, 19,* 37–46.

Schlinger, M. J., & Green, L. (1980). Art-work storyboards versus finished commercials. *Journal of Advertising Research, 20,* 19–23.

Stewart, D. W., & Furse, D. H. (1982). Applying psychophysiological measures to marketing and advertising research problems. In J. H. Leigh & C. R. Martin (Eds.), *Current issues and research in advertising* (pp. 1–38). Ann Arbor: University of Michigan, Graduate School of Business Administration.

Urban, G. L., & Hauser, J. R. (1980). *Design and marketing of new products*. Englewood Cliffs, NJ: Prentice-Hall.

Von Keitz, B. (1988). Eye movement research: Do consumers use the information they are offered? *European Research, 16,* 217–224.

Wansink, B., & Ray, M. L. (1991). *Estimating an advertisement's impact on a consumer's usage rate of a brand* (Working paper). Hanover, NH: Dartmouth College, Amos Tuck School of Business Administration.

Weinblatt, L. (1985). New research technology for today and tomorrow. In *Copy research* (pp. 180–192). New York: Advertising Research Foundation.

Weinblatt, L. (1987). Eye movement testing. *Marketing News,* June 5, 1.

Wells, W. D., Leavitt, C., & McConville, M. (1971). A reaction profile for TV commercials. *Journal of Advertising Research, 11,* 11–17.

Young, C. E., & Robinson, M. (1992). Visual connectedness and persuasion. *Journal of Advertising Research, 32,* 51–59.

Zinkhan, G. M., & Burton, S. (1989). An examination of three multidimensional profiles for assessing consumer reactions to advertisements. *Journal of Advertising, 18,* 6–14.

Comments on Chapter 15

Esther Thorson
University of Missouri–Columbia

This chapter contains many helpful hints and ideas for pretesting the short-term effectiveness of ads. There should be a warning label on this chapter, however, because although the authors recommend that procedures for pretesting should be "flexible," they present their suggestions as iron-clad dos and don'ts. And many of the suggestions, it must be admitted, are simply not as clear-cut and necessary as the authors assert. We look here at some helpful suggestions made in the chapter, and question a number of the "rules" that deserve a long hard look before they are adopted as the best and only way to pretest advertising effectiveness.

The most useful feature of the chapter is that it incorporates academic theory and research in its discussion of how to "pretest" ads. The theory specifies what communication effects advertising can accomplish: communication of category need, brand awareness, brand attitude, brand purchase intention, and brand purchase facilitation. The types of outcomes an ad can have are useful as ways of thinking through what the researcher should be trying to index in the evaluation process.

Claiming that the pretest must be an experiment is a good example of inappropriate stringency. An experimental format seems just as likely to "over-expose" an ad as are the much-maligned focus groups. When you instruct someone to "watch as you would normally," you are clearly creating a much more focused level of attention than an ad would get in "real life." It is like telling someone not to think about elephants. The very instruction necessitates the wrong response. Compounding the undesired effects of that instruction with showing a television commercial several times seems a practice that should be questioned as well. Equally, our knowledge of how transformational and informational ads operate is probably not sufficiently developed for us to trust the rules about how many times each kind of ad should be presented during pretesting. Finally, there are other ways to test ads besides comparing them to controls. For example, it would make sense to embed the ad of interest in an environment of a number of ads or of programming to lessen the intensity of attention that will be paid to it.

The suggestions about the order of questions to ask in a pretest are helpful, although, again, not to be followed blindly. It seems reasonable to ask for brand attitude and intention to purchase before having participants start to analyze all the brand characteristics. Although it is claimed that asking for immediate retrospective measurement of reactions does not affect subsequent brand-related measures, there is evidence that any measurement immediately following stimulus exposure can affect subsequent responses (e.g., Srull, 1989).

The authors also set out rules about how to ask about intention to purchase. What they fail to consider is whether the social requirements of providing the "right" answer render this measure meaningless. Again, it might be important to examine comparative levels of brand purchase intentions when participants have seen ads for a number of competing brands. Or, it may be that liking for the ad is actually a better predictor of purchase (Dubow, 1991).

The rule about testing brand awareness on a delayed basis must also be considered carefully before relying on the advice offered here. Another way to lower the measured level of brand awareness is to present people with a large number of brands within the product category. The task of recalling various brands then becomes more difficult and perhaps the confusability of brands takes on a more ecologically valid character. Brand recognition is probably not even a particularly interesting question to ask, except for new brands or brands that have not previously been heavily advertised.

This chapter is useful because it presents a wide array of issues to think about when deciding how and when to pretest. Its emphasis on basing the pretest on the goals of the advertising is consistent with the assertion in chapter 1, and subsequent chapters of this volume, that advertising effectiveness depends in a foundational way on what the ad is meant to do.

REFERENCES

Dubow, J. S. (Ed.). (1991). *Copy research: The new evidence.* New York: Advertising Research Foundation.

Srull, T. K. (1989). Advertising product evaluation: The relation between consumer memory and judgment. In P. Cafferata & A. Tybout (Eds.), *Cognitive and affective responses to advertising* (pp. 121–134). Lexington, MA: Lexington Books.

16

Top-Down, Stimulus-Based, and Bottom-Up Processes in Brand Choice: Some Implications for the Measurement of Advertising Effectiveness

Richard W. Olshavsky
Indiana University

Anand Kumar
Vanderbilt University

In discussing the problems with current methods for measuring advertising effectiveness, Belch and Belch (1993) stated that:

> The best starting point is principle 4 (of Positioning Advertising Copy Testing, a set of principles established by 21 of the largest U.S. advertising agencies) which states the research should be guided by and based on a model of human response to communications and this model must consider a number of responses including reception, comprehension, and behavioral response. . . . To have an effective measure, some relationship to the communication process must be included. (p. 706)

Belch and Belch were critical of the fact that most copy testing methods do not address all of the stages of traditional models of the communication process. They were referring to models such as AIDA, the Hierarchy of Effects, the Innovation Adoption Model, and the Information Processing Model (see Table 16.1). The purpose of this chapter is not to make a similar criticism of current measures of advertising effectiveness, but to propose that all of the traditional models may be inadequate for certain types of consumer and choice situations; consequently we agree with Belch and Belch but we argue that an appropriate model must first be selected.

Consumers can adopt at least three distinct approaches to brand choice—top-down, stimulus-based, or bottom-up. This chapter first demonstrates that all current theories of how advertising influences brand choice are

TABLE 16.1
Models of the Response Process

AIDA Model	Hierarchy of Effects Model	Innovation Adoption Model	Information Processing Model
Attention	Awareness	Awareness	Presentation
➤	➤	➤	➤
Interest	Knowledge	Interest	Attention
➤	➤	➤	➤
Desire	Liking	Evaluation	Comprehension
➤	➤	➤	➤
Action	Preference	Trial	Retention
	➤	➤	➤
	Conviction	Adoption	Behavior
	➤		
	Purchase		

based on the assumption that consumers adopt a stimulus-based approach to brand choice. It then considers all three possible approaches to choice, makes some suggestions concerning ways currently used advertising effectiveness measures could be modified to accommodate these three approaches, and presents some initial ideas concerning the conditions under which consumers are likely to adopt each of the three approaches. Finally, some additional implications for practice and some directions for future research and theory development are discussed.

THREE APPROACHES TO BRAND CHOICE

We assume that choice precedes and is an important determinant of intention to buy, and that intention to buy, in turn, precedes and is an important determinant of purchase. As described in the following, we assume that choice takes place in a *choice space*, which consists of the consumer's choice criteria, the consideration set, the image of alternatives contained within the consideration set, and the choice strategy.

The Top-Down Approach

Top-down processing (Bettman, 1979; Gutman, 1982; Johnson, 1984; Park & Smith, 1989) refers to a set of integrated processes that begins with a specification of a consumer's goal (e.g., a desire to take good photographs of the family).

Then the consumer derives positive and negative consequences of this goal (e.g., a desire for good pictures implies a desire for sharp images and a desire to avoid double exposures). Then the consumer specifies the attributes of a product or service believed to be instrumental in achieving or avoiding these consequences (e.g., automatic focus produces sharp images, automatic advance avoids double exposures). In this manner, the consumer forms choice criteria.

At about the same time that the choice criteria are being formed, the consumer assesses various categories of products and services from various sources; for example, several types of 35-mm cameras (such as compact, SLR manual, SLR automatic) and "instant" cameras may be retrieved from long-term memory or may be obtained from sources such as advertising, friends, visits to retail outlets, and product-testing organizations' reports. This initial group of categories may be goal derived (Barsalou, 1983) and/or it may include categories that are inappropriate to the goal. One or more categories in this initial set of alternatives may then be specified further at the level of available brands and models within types (e.g., SLR automatics may be specified as including specific models such as the Canon EOS A2E and the Pentax PZ-1). In this manner, the set of brands or models to be evaluated or the consumer's consideration set is formed (Olshavsky, 1994).

Next, the consumer forms the image of each brand or model within the consideration set. *Image* refers to beliefs about each alternative in the consideration set on each of the choice criteria or to the perception of the overall brand. A belief about an attribute may be formed by learning, judgment, or inference. For example, a consumer may learn that the Pentax PZ-1 has a shutter speed that ranges from 30 to 1/4000 seconds. In effect the consumer forms a brand-by-attribute matrix with a specific belief for each of the cells of the matrix. This matrix may be incomplete and it may be erroneous.

The consumer also selects a choice strategy for evaluating the alternatives within the consideration set. The selection of a choice strategy is determined by a consideration of the relative benefits and costs of alternative choice strategies (Payne, 1982; Payne, Bettman, & Johnson, 1992). This means that the specific choice strategy selected is contingent on the consumer's assessment of the perceived benefits of a strategy (e.g., the likelihood of identifying the best brand) and the perceived costs of that strategy (e.g., the time to implement).

The Choice Space

Taken together, the choice criteria, the consideration set, the images of alternatives, and the choice strategy form the consumer's choice space (Newell & Simon, 1972). All choice processes take place within this choice space. The outcome of the choice process (i.e., a preference for a specific brand) is determined by the interaction that occurs over time between characteristics of the consumer and characteristics of the task environment as the consumer attempts to execute the selected choice strategy (Olshavsky, 1985).

The information used to form a choice space in this top-down manner may be obtained from several sources. It may be retrieved from the consumer's long-term memory, from various external memory aids (e.g., past issues of *Consumer Reports*), from the marketplace (e.g., brands available at retailers), from the social environment (e.g., advertising), or from the physical environment (e.g., climate).

The Stimulus-Based Approach

In the top-down approach, the consumer "frames" the choice space. In contrast, in the stimulus-based approach, someone else (e.g., the advertiser, a salesperson, a friend, a product-testing agency) frames the choice space. For example, in a comparative ad, the advertiser presents the choice criteria, the consideration set, the image of alternatives, and the choice strategy. Even in a noncomparative ad, the advertiser may frame the choice space by presenting the choice criteria, the image of the brand, the choice strategy, and an image of the other alternatives in the consideration set by alluding to the competition and their attributes (e.g., "With These Important Essentials Most AF SLRs Leave Out," "And Add These Exclusives").

Most of the empirical research on the effects of advertising takes this approach. It assumes that consumers form an attitude toward a brand based on the information presented in a single ad (e.g., Belch & Belch, 1993; Brown & Stayman, 1992; MacInnis & Jaworski, 1989), and that attitude toward the brand, in turn, forms the basis for an intention to buy the advertised brand. The stimulus-based approach is also represented in laboratory studies of choice that use the information display board or similar devices (e.g., Lussier & Olshavsky, 1979).

The Bottom-Up Approach

Top-down and stimulus-based processing represent two extremes of a continuum. It is possible (and likely) that a stimulus-based processor begins with a source of information such as an ad but then modifies the proposed choice criteria, the proposed image of alternatives, the proposed alternative brands, or the proposed choice strategy. Consumers who start in a stimulus-based manner but then modify or embellish the provided information with information retrieved from memory to form a more complex choice space are referred to as bottom-up processors. It is important to emphasize that the embellishments are not goal-derived; for example, a presented brand simply cues the retrieval of another brand (e.g., Nikon ➡ Pentax). Hence, goals do not serve as cues for retrieval. (If goals are activated and serve as cues for retrieval, then the consumer has adopted the top-down approach, not the bottom-up approach.)

Evidence for the bottom-up approach to choice is provided by laboratory studies in which consumers are instructed to recall alternatives memorized earlier (e.g., Biehal & Chakravarti, 1986; Lynch, Marmorstein, & Weigold, 1988; Lynch & Srull, 1982). Also, the bottom-up approach to choice is represented by laboratory studies that use computer-generated displays in an attempt to prevent the occurrence of purely stimulus-based choice processes (e.g., Brucks, 1985).

Consumers who start in a stimulus-based manner may also embellish the choice space by transforming information to a higher level of abstraction. For example, if a camera ad presents attribute-level information about automatic focus then the consumer may transform this to the benefit level (i.e., automatic focus implies sharp images). Or, if an ad presents benefit-level information about sharp images then the consumer may transform this to the goal level (i.e., sharp images imply "good photographs of the family"). (Note that even though the bottom-up processor may end this transformation process with a goal or goals, the bottom-up process is very different from the top-down process in that the top-down process begins with a goal. If a consumer has difficulty in moving up and down the means–end chain, i.e., attributes-to-benefits-to-values or vice-versa, the choice outcomes may be different for the two processes.) Evidence for this type of abstraction process has been presented by Bettman and Sujan (1987), Johnson (1984, 1988), MacInnis and Jaworski (1989, Levels 5 & 6), Mick (1992, Levels 3 & 4), and Park and Smith (1989).

HOW ADVERTISING AFFECTS CHOICE

Traditional Models

Belch and Belch (1993) listed the four major models of how advertising influences choice: the AIDA model, the hierarchy of effects model, the innovation adoption model, and the information processing model (see Table 16.1). Although these models differ in important ways, they all assume that consumers adopt a stimulus-based approach to choice; that is, the consumer is always reacting to an ad and the ad is the primary (if not the only) source of information. MacInnis and Jawrowski (1989) recently presented a much more detailed model of the communication process. Their model also adopts a stimulus-based approach to choice, but at the deepest levels of processing (i.e., their Levels 4 and 5) bottom-up processes are also captured.

The Top-Down Approach

In the top-down approach the consumer's goal plays a central role in forming the choice space. Importantly, the consumer's goal also plays a central role in determining the desire for information. The types of information desired, the amount of information, the types of sources desired, and the criteria used to evaluate sources (e.g., expertise, trustworthiness, timeliness) are all determined in a top-down, goal-driven manner. Nelson, Shavitt, Schennum, and Barkmeier (chap. 9, this volume) provide empirical evidence for this chain. They found that, for low self-monitors, utilitarian cognitive responses are better predictors of brand attitudes than social identity responses. The reverse was true for high self-monitors.

This implies that for some top-down consumers, advertising—as a source of information—may not be desired at all; for others advertising will be desired and processed but will be processed in the context of information from other sources (such as friends, product-testing organizations, salespeople, and other ads). Hence, for top-down processing, the possible outcomes can range from complete rejection of the ad to processing the ad in the context of information from several other sources.

The Bottom-Up Approach

In the bottom-up approach, memory processes play a major role. Information from the ad is processed in the context of information retrieved from long-term memory. This implies that the effectiveness of an ad depends on the specific choice space formed after relevant information is accessed.

Hence, for bottom-up processing, the possible outcomes can range from complete dependence on the information presented in the ad to little or no impact due to the other information retrieved from long-term memory.

IMPLICATIONS FOR MEASURING
ADVERTISING EFFECTIVENESS

The overall goal of most advertising is to influence brand purchase (or store patronage). Consequently, measures of advertising effectiveness should be at the level of purchase. Because measuring purchase is difficult and costly, researchers often measure some proxy for purchase—such as intentions to purchase, or choice instead of intentions or purchase. Using this reasoning, arguments can and have been made that it is even appropriate to measure factors that are intimately involved in the choice process rather than choice itself (e.g., attitude toward the brand, recognition of the brand, and recall of the brand). It may even be appropriate to measure responses to the ad itself (e.g., attitudes toward the ad, recognition of an ad, recall of an ad, and recall of copy points contained within the ad). It has been argued that measures at this level are especially appropriate when they are interpreted in a relative manner (e.g., relative to competing ads or relative to a baseline established by prior ads for the same brand).

The key question then becomes, "What are the circumstances that make these various measures of ad effectiveness appropriate or inappropriate?" We believe that the three approaches to choice just described provide some important answers to this question. Specifically, we believe that the way the choice space is framed determines the appropriateness of the assumption that measures of attitude toward the ad, or recognition or recall of the ad, are valid indices of effects on choice (and on intentions and ultimately on purchase).

The Traditional Models and The Stimulus-Based Approach

Belch and Belch (1993) criticized existing measures of ad effectiveness because those measures did not take into account all of the stages described by the various models of advertising effects. We are making the more basic criticism that all existing models of advertising effects assume that consumers adopt a stimulus-based approach to choice. That is, all existing models are predicated on the assumption that the consumer is exposed to and actually processes the ad of interest. We believe that this assumption is correct for some but not all consumer and choice situations.

If consumers do make choices in a stimulus-based manner, then most if not all of the traditional measures of advertising effectiveness are appropriate. The procedures or measures employed more or less force the consumer to attend to and to process the ad (e.g., theater testing, focus group). Similarly, when only "qualified" audiences are used (e.g., Starch Readership, Burke Day-After) respondents have probably been exposed to the ad.

The Top-Down Approach

However, if consumers adopt the top-down approach, information from ads may not be desired. If the consumer happens to be exposed to an ad, the ad may be ignored. Even if information from an ad is desired and this information is processed, information from other sources is also likely to be processed. For example, in forming a choice space for cars, the consumer may have first obtained information about all available brands from *Consumer Reports*. To be effective, an ad for any particular brand of car must exert influence in the "context" of this other information, not just in isolation. This implies that any effectiveness measure that fails to allow for or fails to encourage a top-down approach to choice may be invalid for such consumers in such choice situations.

It follows that, in these situations, effectiveness can be measured only if procedures are adopted that ensure that the consumer has the motivation and the opportunity to obtain information needed to frame the type of choice space that would be framed prior to actual choice. For example, a question (such as "As you read this ad, think about any goals or objectives you want a camera to satisfy") should be asked that evokes each respondent's goal or goals for the relevant choice task. If necessary, information should be provided to enable the consumer to frame a choice space. Only after the choice space has been framed can the effectiveness of an ad be measured meaningfully.

In conducting these tests, one critical issue is whether consumers have framed their choice spaces before they enter the testing situation. If the product category is old (e.g., cars), consumers are experienced, and the information search process is ongoing, consumers may already have framed their choice spaces before entering the testing situation. In this case it may not be necessary to provide additional information as part of the procedure for the test; it may be sufficient to ask questions that evoke goals and already-formed choice spaces. When the product category is new (i.e., an innovation) and ad effectiveness measures are taken early in the life cycle of the product, the choice space is likely to be poorly formed and special procedural steps must be taken to enable the respondent to frame his or her own choice space. That is, the respondent must be provided with the time and opportunity to form a choice space prior to entering the testing situation or as part of the testing procedure.

This analysis also suggests that top-down consumers who really do not desire information from ads of any type should be screened from studies of ad effectiveness. Including such consumers, especially if they constitute a significant percentage of the respondents, could seriously bias the results. As respondents, they may be quite willing to view the ad and respond to questions posed about it, but as consumers in more natural conditions they may not be willing to view the ad, hence it will have little impact. The percentage of respondents who actively reject information from ads will vary considerably with characteristics of the consumer and characteristics of the product or service involved.

The Bottom-Up Approach

If the ad is the stimulus that precipitates processing and if consumers adopt the bottom-up approach, then by definition the ad plays a central role. However, after embellishing the choice space, the information presented in the ad may be less effective than if processed in isolation. What then is an appropriate measure of advertising effectiveness for consumers who adopt the bottom-up approach to choice? Because the choice space is different from that framed by the ad alone, procedures must be used that motivate and provide opportunities for the consumer to engage in the embellishment processes that would occur in more natural conditions. This may be accomplished by simply instructing respondents to react to the ad as they would under more typical conditions. Although such instructions are somewhat artificial and may involve reactivity, these problems are reduced by the use of relative as opposed to absolute measures.

As with the top-down approach, a critical issue concerns how far along consumers are in developing knowledge about the product category and the brands available. If the product category is old but the consumer still engages in some type of choice task, then it should be a relatively simple matter to instruct consumers to retrieve relevant information. (It should be noted that for certain product categories repeat purchase may become habitual. Then, the top-down, stimulus-based, or bottom-up approaches to choice are not relevant.) If the product category is new, however, then respondents must be provided with the time, the motivation, and explicit instructions to embellish the ad as they would under natural conditions, prior to testing the ad.

A THEORETICAL FRAMEWORK FOR SPECIFYING THE EFFECTS OF SELECTED FACTORS ON THE APPROACH TO CHOICE

Olshavsky and Kumar's (1993) review of past research and theory identified two variables as likely determinants of the three approaches to choice. These two variables are involvement and prior knowledge. Using Payne's (1982) cost–benefit framework, the direction of the effect of these variables on the approach to choice can be predicted.

Involvement

Following Krugman (1965) and Zaichkowsky (1985), involvement is high if the consumer has made several strong connections between his or her needs and values and the product being advertised. Higher involvement implies higher benefits. If involvement is high, consumers will engage in top-down or bottom-up processes. Otherwise, they will engage in stimulus-based processes.

Prior Knowledge

Higher knowledge consumers have the ability to process the required information (Alba & Hutchinson, 1987). They know their own goals, the related consequences, and the related attributes. Unambiguous goals permit more focused and efficient accessing of goal-appropriate alternatives from long-term memory (during retrieval), from the marketplace (during search), and from external memory aids (during search of these sources). Higher knowledge also implies that consumers are more capable of evaluating the accessed alternatives. This implies that extended decision making is likely to have higher benefits and lower (information processing) costs. Consumers with high prior knowledge are therefore more likely to engage in top-down or bottom-up processing than are low-knowledge consumers. As might be expected, consumers who are high in both involvement and knowledge are most likely to engage in top-down processing.

DISCUSSION

We believe that a better understanding of the approaches consumers may take to choice can help us to evaluate the appropriateness of the measures and procedures used to assess advertising effectiveness. Whenever it can be assumed that consumers will adopt a stimulus-based approach to choice, the traditional measures and procedures of ad effectiveness are defensible. However, if there is reason to believe that consumers engage in a top-down or a bottom-up approach to choice, then the traditional measures and procedures are probably not appropriate. For example, when consumer involvement and expertise are high, we would expect top-down processing. When such consumers serve as respondents in studies employing traditional measures of ad effectiveness, the studies will overestimate the effectiveness of the tested ads.

We suggest that consumers who are likely to engage in top-down processing should be tested with methods that ensure that their goals have been activated and that they have had sufficient motivation and opportunity to frame their choice spaces. Only then can the effectiveness of advertising be properly assessed. Likewise, we suggest that for consumers who are likely to adopt the bottom-up approach, sufficient motivation and opportunity must be provided to embellish the choice space as they normally would. We have made some suggestions as to how top-down and bottom-up processes might be initiated in a testing situation prior to the actual test of the ad; obviously, many different procedures must be tried before a really practical solution to this difficult but important problem will be found.

It may be possible to classify consumers on the basis of prior knowledge and involvement or on the basis of direct measures of brand choice processes (i.e., using process tracing procedures such as protocol analysis). Then, once classified, separate tests of advertising effectiveness could be administered to the different segments. At a minimum, such a segmentation would allow more accurate interpretations of standard measures of ad effectiveness.

Implications for Research and Theory Development

We presented a preliminary theory that identified two factors (prior knowledge and involvement) that may influence approach to brand choice. For certain types of consumer or choice situations (e.g., low knowledge, low involvement) the assumption of a stimulus-based choice process may be valid. For certain other types of consumer or choice situations (e.g., high knowledge, high involvement), top-down processing may occur.

Although this theory is based on a review of prior theory and related empirical studies, there is a need for more empirical research to identify and evaluate other consumer and environmental factors that may determine which one of the three possible approaches to choice will be adopted.

REFERENCES

Alba, J. W., & Hutchinson, J. W. (1987). Dimensions of consumer expertise. *Journal of Consumer Research, 13,* 441–454.

Barsalou, L. W. (1983). Ad hoc categories. *Memory and Cognition, 11,* 211–227.

Belch, G. E., & Belch, M. A. (1993). *Introduction to advertising and promotion—An integrated marketing communications perspective*. Homewood, IL: Irwin.

Bettman, J. R. (1979). *An information processing theory of consumer choice*. Reading, MA: Addison-Wesley.

Bettman, J. R., & Sujan, M. (1987). Effects of framing on evaluation of comparable and noncomparable alternatives by expert and novice consumers. *Journal of Consumer Research, 14*, 141–154.

Biehal, G., & Chakravarti, D. (1986). Consumers use of memory and external information in choice: Macro and micro perspectives. *Journal of Consumer Research, 12*, 382–405.

Brown, S. P., & Stayman, D. M. (1992). Antecedents and consequences of attitude toward the ad: A meta analysis. *Journal of Consumer Research, 19*, 34–51.

Brucks, M. (1985). The effects of product class knowledge on information search behavior. *Journal of Consumer Research, 12*, 1–16.

Gutman, J. (1982). A means–end chain model based on consumer categorization processes. *Journal of Marketing, 46*, 60–72.

Johnson, M. D. (1984). Consumer choice strategies for comparing noncomparable alternatives. *Journal of Consumer Research, 11*, 741–753.

Johnson, M. D. (1988). Comparability and hierarchical processing in multialternative choice. *Journal of Consumer Research, 15*, 303–314.

Krugman, H. (1965). The impact of television advertising: Learning without involvement. *Public Opinion Quarterly, 29*, 349–356.

Lussier, D. A., & Olshavsky, R. W. (1979). Task complexity and contingent processing in brand choice. *Journal of Consumer Research, 6*, 154–165.

Lynch, J. G., Marmorstein, H., & Weigold, M. (1988). Choices from sets including remembered brands: Use of recalled attributes and prior overall evaluations. *Journal of Consumer Research, 15*, 169–184.

Lynch, J. G., Jr., & Srull, T. (1982). Memory and attentional factors in consumer choice: Concepts and research methods. *Journal of Consumer Research, 9*, 18–37.

MacInnis, D. J., & Jaworski, B. J. (1989). Information processing from advertisements: Toward an integrated framework. *Journal of Marketing, 53*, 1–23.

Mick, D. G. (1992). Levels of subjective comprehension in advertising processing and their relations to ad perceptions, attitudes, and memory. *Journal of Consumer Research, 18*, 411–424.

Newell, A., & Simon, H. A. (1972). *Human problem solving*. Englewood Cliffs, NJ: Prentice-Hall.

Olshavsky, R. W. (1985). Toward a comprehensive theory of choice. In E. Hirschman & M. B. Holbrook (Eds.), *Advances in consumer research* (Vol. 12, pp. 465–470). Provo, UT: Association for Consumer Research.

Olshavsky, R. W. (1994). Top-down, stimulus-based, and bottom-up processes: Implications for consideration set formation in brand choice. In J. A. Cote & S. M. Leong (Eds.), *Advances in consumer research* (Vol. 1, pp. 4–9). Provo, UT: Association for Consumer Research.

Olshavsky, R. W., & Kumar, A. (1993). Top-down vs. bottom-up processes: Some implications for the study of brand choice. In K. Finlay, A. Mitchell, & F. C. Cummings (Eds.), *Proceedings of the Society for Consumer Psychology* (pp. 170–175). Clemson, SC: CtC Press.

Payne, J. W., Bettman, J. R., & Johnson, E. J. (1992). Behavior decision research: A constructive processing perspective. *Annual Review of Psychology, 43*, 87–131.

Payne, J. W. (1982). Continent decision behavior. *Psychological Bulletin, 92*, 382–402.

Park, C. W., & Smith, D. C. (1989). Product-level choice: A top-down or bottom-up process. *Journal of Consumer Research, 16*, 289–299.

Zaichkowsky, J. L. (1985). Measuring the involvement construct. *Journal of Consumer Research, 12*, 341–352.

Comments on Chapter 16

Larry Percy
Marketing Communications Consultant

In chapter 16, we are reminded again, and cannot be reminded too often, that a great deal of attention must be paid to what is likely going on in consumer decision making if one is to influence it effectively. By extension, this also means that measures of effectiveness must also be congruent with the decision-making process involved. The authors state in the chapter that "We believe that a better understanding of the various approaches consumers may take to choice can help us to evaluate the appropriateness of the measures and procedures used to assess advertising effectiveness" (p. 293). They are quite correct, but more often than not choice processes are long forgotten (if they were ever attended to) when the time comes to create advertising.

The thrust of the chapter involves the introduction by the authors of top-down and bottom-up processes in brand choice, and the warning that if consumers use either of these processes when making choices in an advertised product category, traditional measures of advertising under such circumstances may not be appropriate. They could be right, but for the average practitioner there is much to learn before those particular concerns are likely to be recognized. We agree with the authors that one litmus test for alerting advertisers that such decision processes may be operating is when the brand decision is likely to be high rather than low involving. However, we would be more inclined to define involvement in terms of risk (following, e.g., Bauer, 1967), rather than the definitions of Krugman (1965) or Zaichkowsky (1985). Their definitions are certainly compatible with the notion of risk, but they are not quite the same in terms of their overall implication for advertising strategy.

The explanation of top-down processing offered by the authors is rather involved, but might briefly be described as occurring in situations where consumers are goal directed and seek out information to help them better "frame" or understand the choice alternatives. Clearly this is unlikely to occur with most low involving brand or product choices. The bottom-up approach, too, seems to require consumers to modify or embellish information that has been provided to them. Again, this would seem to be most relevant to high-involvement decisions.

So, when confronted with the likelihood of a high-involvement decision, the advertiser should be alert to the possibility of a top-down or bottom-up process mediating brand choice. What then? How should the advertiser proceed in creating and then in evaluating advertising in light of possible top-down or bottom-up processing? Certainly, reasonable questions can and should be asked about why traditional measures of advertising effectiveness may not be appropriate. Unfortunately, the arguments offered in the chapter are not likely to seem compelling to the practitioner. The practitioner is likely to be left asking himself or herself a number of questions.

Let us put ourselves in the role of an advertiser of a product where a high-involvement decision is obvious, and see if we can work this out. The authors, in fact, offer a good illustration in the chapter. They present the problem a consumer is likely to have in framing a choice for a new car. Buying a new car involves a high-involvement brand choice, and even the best car advertising is unlikely to be the sole source of information driving choice. Certainly it will be playing a role, will it not? Could traditional measures of advertising effectiveness evaluate that role? We would argue yes, and can hear the practitioner saying "See, who needs this complicated stuff?" For example, with automotive advertising, much of it is designed to stimulate positive affect, not to affect choice (one must "like" a car before one can seriously begin to consider it).

Much of what the authors argue could be true in any particular case (note that they do say "*may* be involved"—our emphasis). This does not mean that the particular prescriptions offered are necessarily what is called for. In fact, most of their recommendations tend to lie outside of the effects generally attributed to advertising, and encourage measuring more peripheral issues related to choice.

If a choice set is poorly framed, traditional measures are measuring exactly what the advertising is likely to accomplish under those circumstances. It should not be necessary to create a test situation that takes into account every possible peripheral likelihood, especially if all one is looking for is a "read" on the likely effectiveness of an ad. For example, is it really necessary to prime a person to think about "goals" associated with a high-involvement product? Probably not, because those goals are going to be a part of the cognitive activity cued by the product via the advertising.

The real point is that given a particular product purchase decision, especially a high-involving one, advertising is only one part of the search for, and evaluation of, information. As advertisers approach the problem of evaluating their advertising in high-involvement situations, it is even more important than usual to consider where and how advertising will fit in the overall processing of information leading to choice. Chapter 16 notes two processes that could significantly mediate the role of advertising in high-involvement choice situations, and advertisers should give them serious consideration. Although the prescriptions offered in the chapter are open to debate, it is just such debate that leads to thinking about one's advertising and its likely effectiveness.

REFERENCES

Bauer, R. S. (1967). Several papers in B. F. Cox (Ed.), *Risk taking and information handling in consumer behavior* (pp. 469–486). Boston: Graduate School of Business Administration, Harvard University.

Krugman, H. (1965). The impact of television advertising: Learning without involvement. *Public Opinion Quarterly, 29,* 349–356.

Zaichkowsky, J. L. (1985). Measuring the incoherent construct. *Journal of Consumer Research, 12,* 341–352.

Comments on Chapter 16

Abhilasha Mehta
Gallup & Robinson, Inc.

Chapter 16 is an interesting presentation of three alternative advertising response strategies. As noted by the authors, an understanding of how consumers process brand-related information should help in improving advertising effectiveness techniques and methods.

The authors are correct in pointing out that traditional hierarchy of effects models assumed that communication processing is purely stimulus based. Consumers were assumed to be reacting to the message only. Although advertising testing systems and procedures were generally based on this premise, the idea that stimulus-based processing always occurs in all current testing systems is probably an overgeneralization. The authors acknowledge that consumers who start in a stimulus-based manner may "modify/embellish the provided information with information retrieved from memory" (p. 288) and move into what is termed the bottom-up approach. In highly involved respondents, it seems like an ad may trigger a top-down processing approach. Extensive work done by the cognitive response theorists using models like the Elaboration Likelihood Model (ELM) have shown that involvement levels moderate the extent of processing. Under low involvement conditions as well as when knowledge levels are low, individuals are less inclined to fully process the message. As suggested by the authors, measures of involvement and knowledge should provide help in evaluating advertising responses.

Testing situations that are context-based, that is, those that test the commercials in-program or ads in-magazine with invitations to participate in program viewership or magazine readership studies, may be more likely to encourage free choice in selecting the processing mode most appropriate for the consumer in any particular situation. The challenge is to obtain a measure of the type of processing that was used by a respondent. In addition to obtaining knowledge and involvement levels, can thought listings be used to indicate processing approaches? The suggestions that different measures may be needed for the different approaches sounds interesting: Clearly, empirical research is needed to investigate if that may be appropriate and valuable. Research is also needed to establish the outcomes of each of the different approaches and, consequently, explore the measures that would be most suitable in each case for use in evaluating advertising. Closely related is the issue of selecting the right audience for the advertising test. Should advertisers be more interested in some selected segment of the target

298

audience—for example, those who are highly involved or interested? Or should they be concerned about all others who may be potential customers, but are at the time relatively less involved or interested? Empirical research in the academe and industry along these avenues should help in better understanding how to evaluate advertising.

17

The Measurement
of Advertising Effectiveness:
Empirical Learning and Application

Allan R. Kuse
rsc THE QUALITY MEASUREMENT COMPANY

The marketplaces of the world have become increasingly competitive, making it harder for marketers to increase revenues and profits. Population growth and inflation, which helped revenue and profit growth in the past, have slowed. Most of the profit increases from efficiencies in manufacturing, distribution, and consolidation have been realized. The challenge that remains in the 1990s and beyond is achieving profitable growth through marketing.

Looking at how marketing investments are currently allocated, we find that consumer and trade promotion represent three fourths of the marketing activity, whereas media advertising is only one fourth (Donnelley Marketing Inc., 1994).

At the same time, recent studies of scanner-panel data by Information Resources, Inc. (IRI) have shown the profit limitations of heavy couponing and trade dealing. In IRI's analysis of payout track records, only 11% of coupon activity and 16% of trade-promotion activity are profitable (Baldinger, 1989; Fulgoni, 1990). Thus, the heavy investments in these price-related allocations appear to have a low likelihood of contributing to profitable growth.

The same type of scanner-panel data indicate that the advertising track record is a little better than promotion (at 20% profitable), but not high enough to depend on for meeting financial objectives. The fact is, most marketers have not been able to make promotion or advertising work consistently. The old Wanamaker saying that "half my advertising is wasted, and the trouble is I do not know which half" (or, as IRI's data indicate, which 80%), is as true today as it was at the turn of the century. Addressing this opportunity for improvement, a series of empirically based advertising measurement and management tools have been developed.

APPROPRIATE MEASUREMENT FEEDBACK

The opportunity for achieving more consistent advertising success can be learned from Total Quality Management (TQM), which has revolutionized

301

many businesses. The process of continuous improvement has, as a key component, appropriate measurement feedback at appropriate points in the process.

Advertising measurement is normally developed in the context of a theory on how advertising ought to work. The operating model of research systems corporation (rsc) is very simple: To create preference for the advertised brand in a manner that will be reflected in business results, worth the investment.

Perhaps the most important issue in determining what measurement feedback is appropriate lies in the validity of the criterion measurement on which advertising decisions are made.

In a 1964 study (Dodd, 1964; Kelly, 1964), advertising effectiveness was shown to account for 31% of the total variation in the brands' market-share changes (using Nielsen bimonthly audits), with ad weight accounting for just 8% (all other marketing variables accounted for the remainder; see Fig. 17.1).

This study, using 23 established brands for 67 sales waves, was the first study to document the importance of advertising quality over advertising weight. The study was replicated in Germany in 1968 with similar findings: Advertising effectiveness accounted for 24% of the brands' changes in market share, whereas ad weight accounted for just 7% (see Fig. 17.2).

In the 1970s, when many marketers were emphasizing new-product introductions as a means for achieving growth, the relationship of the ARS *Persuasion*[®] measure[1] to Awareness, Trial, and Usage (ATU) trial rate was found to be strong and quite straightforward—the higher the absolute ARS *Persuasion* level, the higher the trial rate (see Fig. 17.3).

In the 1980s, advertisers began using split-cable delivery and electronic scanner panels to measure the sales effects of advertising. From 1987 through 1991, rsc published studies that used 27 established-brand split-cable advertising weight and copy test cases to analyze several specific measures of advertising effectiveness (Blair, 1987; Kuse, 1991).

In 1990, the Advertising Research Foundation (ARF) published a study that also used split-cable results. The ARF study used 46 measures of advertising effectiveness and just five split-cable cases (Haley & Baldinger, 1991). The rsc studies were extended to include the two principal measures in the ARF study that were reported to relate to split-cable results.

Looking first at the seven rsc split-cable copy tests (different ads, same media weight), differences in Related Recall were usually unrelated to differences in sales effectiveness. Recall was predictive in only two out of seven cases. In fact, in two cases, Recall indicated an opposite outcome to that observed in the marketplace (see Fig. 17.4).

Although identified as related to sales in the ARF study, brand-name recall from a category cue (a component of related recall) was not strongly related to sales effectiveness in these cases. It correctly predicted sales differences only two of seven times and is also counterindicative in two cases (see Fig. 17.5).

---

[1]ARS *Persuasion* is a registered mark of rsc.

1964 Study
Change in Market Share
(Nielsen Bimonthly Audits)

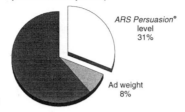

ARS Persuasion®
level
31%

Ad weight
8%

23 established brands
67 sales waves

Source: Dodd (1964); Kelly (1964).

FIG. 17.1

1968 Study
Change in Market Share
(Germany)

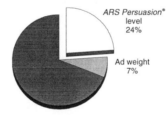

ARS Persuasion®
level
24%

Ad weight
7%

24 established brands
71 sales waves*

* This time the sales waves were six months long, perhaps accounting for the lower variance
  explained for advertising versus all other marketing variables in the "unexplained" portion
  (versus the 1964 study).
Source: Murphy (1968).

FIG. 17.2.

1970s Study
New-Brand (Reported) Trial
(Advertising-Only ATU Test Markets)

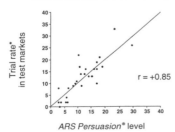

Trial rate*
in test markets

r = +0.85

ARS Persuasion® level

* Reported trial/reported awareness.
Source: **rsc** (1983).

FIG.17.3.

Related Recall
(1980s Split-Cable Copy Tests)

Related Recall score			Actual split-cable result	
Commercial A		Commercial B	Cable A	Cable B
22%	=	23%	>	
17	=	13	>	
32	=	29	=	
25	<	59	>	
14	<	21	=	
34	<	56	>	
48	>	35	>	

Source: Kuse (1991).

FIG.17.4.

Brand-Name Recall
(1980s Split-Cable Copy Tests)

Brand-name recall score			Actual split-cable result	
Commercial A		Commercial B	Cable A	Cable B
16%	=	16%	>	
9	=	10	=	
13	=	11	=	
42	=	45	>	
30	=	23	>	
13	<	24	>	
28	<	41	>	

Source: Kuse (1991).

FIG. 17.5.

Of the 46 measures included in the ARF study, commercial-liking reportedly showed the strongest statistical association to their five split-cable test outcomes. Ads from five rsc split-cable copy tests were available for later measurement of commercial liking. In none of the five cases did the commercial-liking measure used in the ARF study predict the sales outcome. In three cases, the liking results were opposite to sales results (see Fig. 17.6). In short, these split-cable cases did not replicate the findings reported by the ARF for commercial liking or brand-name recall. Thus, these measures do not appear to be as strongly predictive of in-market sales outcomes as the ARF results alone suggest.

When evaluating split-cable results against the ARS *Persuasion* measure, the accurate outcome was predicted seven out of seven times. None of the measures in the ARF study showed as strong a result (see Fig. 17.7).

Now turning to the split-cable media-weight tests (same ads, different weight), the first measurement examined was advertising weight (see Fig. 17.8). As Fig. 17.8 shows, weight alone was not enough to explain the sales outcomes. That is, the significant in-market results (shaded bars) do not cluster among the high weight differences. Nor did related recall provide direct, useful feedback for these established-brand tests. Assuming high recall would relate to sales, 60% of the sales/no sales outcomes were correctly predicted with the recall measure, not a great improvement over tossing a coin (see Fig. 17.9).

When brand-name recall was examined across the set of 20 spend tests, no predictive relationship to split-cable outcomes was observed. A correct prediction of sales results is found 50% of the time (see Fig. 17.10).

In addition, the liking measure used in the ARF study was administered on 19 of the spend-test cases. This measure did not appear to be a good indicator of advertising effectiveness, with liking scores correctly identifying 47% of sales outcomes (see Fig. 17.11).

Liking
(1980s Split-Cable Copy Tests)

| Liking score | | | Actual split-cable result | |
Commercial A		Commercial B	Cable A	Cable B
3.08	>	2.95	=	
3.33	<	3.95	=	
3.55	<	3.95	>	
3.11	<	3.80	>	
3.27	<	3.75	>	

Source: Kuse (1991).

FIG. 17.6.

ARS Persuasion® Measure
(1980s Split-Cable Copy Tests)

| ARS Persuasion® score | | | Actual split-cable result | |
Commercial A		Commercial B	Cable A	Cable B
4.6	>	1.1	>	
3.8	>	2.0	>	
5.0	=	4.4	=	
9.0	>	2.6	>	
2.8	=	2.0	=	
7.0	>	2.8	>	
15.9	>	11.1	>	

Source: Kuse (1991).

FIG. 17.7.

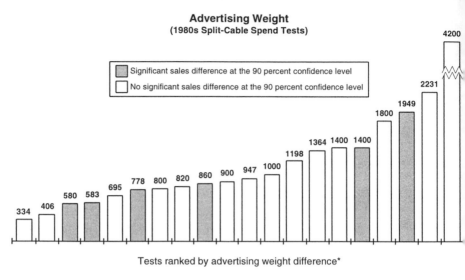

Advertising Weight
(1980s Split-Cable Spend Tests)

Significant sales difference at the 90 percent confidence level

No significant sales difference at the 90 percent confidence level

Tests ranked by advertising weight difference*

* As measured by Gross Rating Points (GRPs).
Source: Blair (1987).

FIG. 17.8.

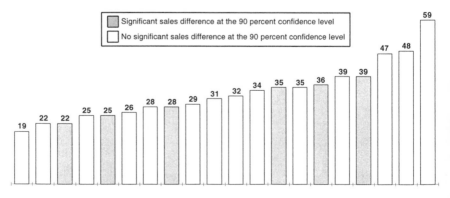

Related Recall
(1980s Split-Cable Spend Tests)

Significant sales difference at the 90 percent confidence level

No significant sales difference at the 90 percent confidence level

Tests ranked by Related Recall score

Source: Kuse (1991).

FIG. 17.9.

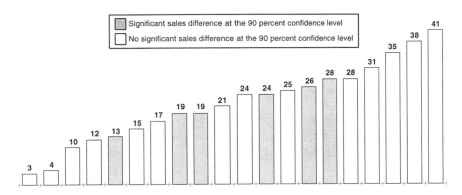

Brand-Name Recall
(1980s Split-Cable Spend Tests)

Tests ranked by brand-name recall score

Source: Kuse (1991).

FIG. 17.10.

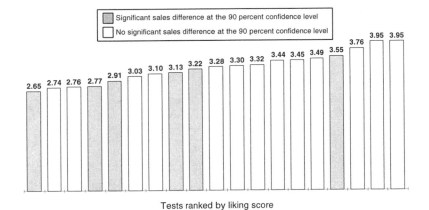

Liking
(1980s Split-Cable Spend Tests)

Tests ranked by liking score

Source: Kuse (1991).

FIG. 17.11.

However, as found in previous studies, the *ARS Persuasion* measure was found to be a reliable indicator of sales and was very straightforward—the higher the score, the greater the likelihood of sales effects—regardless of the weight invested (see Fig. 17.12).

In 1990, IRI provided 17 additional cases from their "How Advertising Works" study (Lodish, 1991; Lubetkin, 1991; McQueen, 1991). After adding these cases to the 20 original spend tests, the predictive value of the measure remained evident—the higher the absolute score, the higher the likelihood of sales/share change (see Fig. 17.13).

For split-cable environments (normally 9–12-month tests) the specific interpretation would be:

- An ad scoring +7.0 or better produces a sales effect large enough to be measurable at the end of a split-cable test.
- The sales effect from an ad scoring +5.0 and under is not by itself large enough to be measurable at the split-cable-test end.
- Between +5.0 and +7.0, there is a 50% probability that the sales effect will be large enough to be measurable at the split-cable-test end point (depending on the weight, split-cable sample size, purchase occasions during tests, competitive stress, etc.).

Although IRI stated "significance" in the relationship between the copy-test measures of brand preference and in-market sales effects, the predictability of the *ARS Persuasion* cases in the "How Advertising Works" database was not as strong as prior studies had suggested.

rsc approached IRI "How Advertising Works" sponsors to get a fuller understanding of the cases submitted. In 1992, it was learned and confirmed by

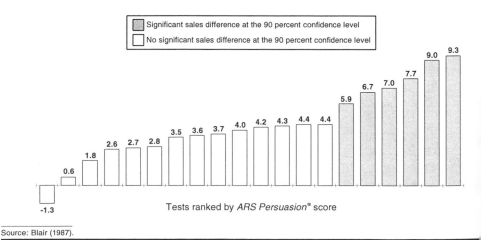

ARS Persuasion® Measure
(1980s Split-Cable Spend Tests)

Tests ranked by *ARS Persuasion®* score

Source: Blair (1987).

FIG. 17.12.

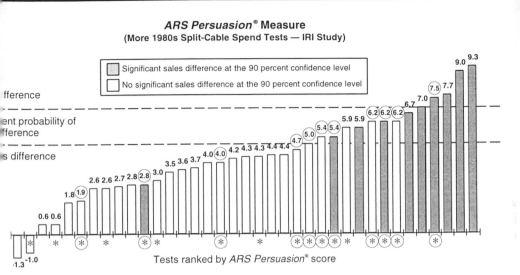

FIG. 17.13.

IRI that the 17 *ARS Persuasion* cases did not necessarily represent ads that actually aired in the BehaviorScan® markets.[2] For instance, at least 11 cases were submitted as "rough" commercial test scores—not those of the ads that actually aired (rsc Basic Research Study, 1992; see Fig. 17.13—circled numbers). It is therefore intriguing that IRI found any relationship at all, given their "apples to oranges" data set. The cleaner the data sets, the clearer the convergence.

Across 30 years of validation work (including studies performed by rsc, IRI, and the ARF), the *ARS Persuasion* measurement has the best predictive track record of any measure evaluated in published large-scale validation studies. Liking, related recall, and brand-name recall have fared no better than the 50–50 coin toss, hit-or-miss odds (see Fig. 17.14). Across all split-cable studies, the *ARS Persuasion* measure has shown a 91% track record. This evidence (added to the previous evidence) supports the use of this measurement as the primary source of feedback during the advertising development and management process.

ARS[3] data are collected using a laboratory environment to obtain respondent product choices in simulated purchase occasions before and after advertising exposure. The *ARS Persuasion* measure is calculated by subtracting the percentage choosing the advertised product before exposure from the percent-

---

[2]BehaviorScan is a registered trademark of Information Resources, Inc.

[3]ARS is a service mark of rsc.

1980s Split-Cable Environments
(Overview)

	Spend test		Copy test				
Measurement	rsc[1]	IRI[2]	rsc[1]	ARF[3]	IRI[2]	ASI[4]	Track record
Liking	9/19	NA	0/5	3/5	NA	NA	12/29 = 41%
Brand-name recall	10/20	NA	2/7	2/5	NA	NA	14/32 = 44%
Recall	12/20	27/41	2/7	1/5	6/16	7/10	55/99 = 56%
Advertising weight	12/20	NA	NA	NA	NA	NA	12/20 = 60%
ARS Persuasion* measure	20/20	13/17	7/7	NA	NA	NA	40/44 = 91%

Sources:
[1] Kuse (1991).
[2] McQueen (1991).
[3] Haley and Baldinger (1991).
[4] Walker (1990).

FIG. 17.14.

age choosing the advertised product after exposure—the net effect of retention and attraction as a result of the advertising stimulus. The most recent data from an ongoing test–retest program have shown this measure to be reliable (see Fig. 17.15).

Although this measurement has been found to be the best overall predictor of business results, additional measures (diagnostics) are important for understanding what elements contribute to or detract from an ad's effectiveness. So far, factors accounting for 86% of the variation in ARS Persuasion levels have been identified, providing a foundation for improving advertising (a diagnostic approach; see Fig. 17.16).

APPLICATION AT APPROPRIATE STAGES
IN THE ADVERTISING PROCESS

The real payout for valid measurement lies in its application at key stages in the advertising process, to assure success at each stage.

Selling Proposition

The first step in this process is evaluation of the basic selling proposition. The same method that is used to assess the ARS Persuasion level of television commercials can be used to evaluate selling propositions in a video format (i.e., "bare bones" videos containing minimal execution). Studies have indicated that the effectiveness of the basic selling proposition is the most powerful ingredient of advertising that sells.

For example, in two instances, several agencies worked exhaustively in attempts to find productive executions for a predetermined selling proposition. Brand A produced 14 executions and 1.3 was the highest result. On 11 tries, Brand B could only reach a 3.0 result.

Global Reliability of the *ARS Persuasion*® Measurement

	Canada	Mexico	U. K.	U. S.	France, Italy, the Netherlands, Belgium, and Germany
nber of test-retest pairs	75	82	64	104	82
t-retest variation observed[1]	±1.97	±2.05	±1.58	±1.43	±1.64
ation expected from dom samples[1]	±1.82	±2.04	±1.48	±1.40	±1.52
tio	1.16	1.01	1.13	1.05	1.16
clusion	Not significant[2]	Not significant[2]	Not significant[2]	Not significant[2]	Not significant[2]

standard deviation units. (Note: In Canada, Mexico, the United Kingdom, France, Italy, Belgium, the Netherlands, and Germany, ARSAR™
mples are about one-half as large as standard ARS™ tests in these countries. Variation reported is for full sample tests.)
the 95 percent confidence level.
rce: Crang (1995).

ARSAR is a service mark of rsc.

FIG. 17.15.

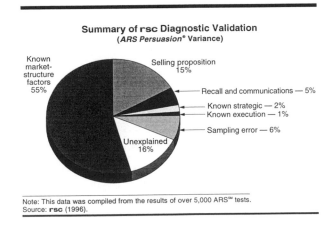

Summary of rsc Diagnostic Validation
(*ARS Persuasion*® Variance)

Known market-structure factors 55%
Selling proposition 15%
Recall and communications — 5%
Known strategic — 2%
Known execution — 1%
Sampling error — 6%
Unexplained 16%

Note: This data was compiled from the results of over 5,000 ARS™ tests.
Source: rsc (1996).

FIG. 17.16.

After the agencies failed to produce successful executions from the brands' existing strategies, a test of the bare-bones selling proposition was conducted for each brand, illustrating that all the creative talent in the world could not make a silk purse out of a sow's ear. In both cases, the underlying selling proposition was weak (see Fig. 17.17). Identifying an effective selling proposition before creative execution is a real opportunity for developing advertising that sells more consistently.

Experience in testing selling propositions before creative development has led to advertising improvement. To date, advertising executions developed from superior selling propositions have a 70% likelihood of superior results, whereas 78% of the executions developed from inferior propositions are inferior (see Fig. 17.18).

Weak Selling Propositions Lead to Weak Commercials

Brand	Number of commercials	Range in ARS Persuasion* scores	"Bare bones" selling proposition ARS Persuasion* score*
A	14	-0.4 to 1.3	0.1
B	11	0.2 to 3.0	2.0

* Service called *Firstep*.
Source: **rsc** (1994).

Firstep is a registered mark of rsc.

FIG. 17.17.

Superior Selling Propositions Lead to Superior-Selling Ads

Basic selling proposition*:	Resulting execution*		
	Inferior	Average	Superior
Inferior	78%	22%	0%
Average	24%	66%	10%
Superior	0%	30%	70%

* Selling propositions and executions are determined to be superior, average, or inferior based on their relationship to the market-structure "degree of difficulty" norm (*Fair Share*™).
Note: Based on 163 execution tests.
Source: **rsc** (1996).

Fair Share is a service mark of rsc.

FIG. 17.18.

Execution Can Enhance or Detract from Selling Proposition
(Examples)

Brand	ARS Persuasion* level		Number of executions
	Firstep	Executions	
M	9.3	7.9 to 16.3	4
P	10.6	5.9 to 10.9	5
K	14.8	7.7 to 27.7	2

Source: **rsc** (1994).

FIG. 17.19.

A more consistently successful advertising-development process, then, is dependent on establishing checkpoints for prevention of failures. Obtaining measurement feedback at the selling-proposition stage is the suggested first step in the rsc *T.Q. Process.*[4]

Execution

Although the track record is 70% superior executions from superior selling propositions, not all executions are equally strong; some enhance the selling proposition and some detract from it (see Fig. 17.19). Knowing which execu-

---

[4] rsc *T.Q. Process* is a service mark of rsc.

tions are more or less productive assures that the media dollars will be spent behind the more *sales-effective* ones.

In the Brand K case study, a selling-proposition test was conducted on a bare-bones video, achieving an *ARS Persuasion* score of 14.8. Then, the company tested Execution A, which obtained a 7.7 result. Because this result was disappointing, a diagnostic analysis of the commercial was undertaken in which executional elements validated to the *ARS Persuasion* measure were used to uncover the reason for the lower than expected results. This analysis helped guide the agency in producing a second execution (B) from the same selling proposition, this time with increased product focus and decreased executional distraction, and the ad attained a 27.7 result.

Both ads were later put on air in different regions, resulting in Execution B attaining nearly double the market share of the first ad, despite lower trade support and a higher price point (see Figs. 17.20 and 17.21).

Airing

Once productive ads are on air, what should be expected? Recent learning has challenged the traditional thinking that advertising works long term and should not be expected to have short-term sales effects. A study published in the *Journal of Advertising Research* (Blair, 1987) indicated that:

- "Ads which are *not* Persuasive do not increase sales and do not improve over time" (p. 50).
- "Ads which *are* Persuasive *do* increase sales" (p. 50).
- Persuasive advertising works quickly.

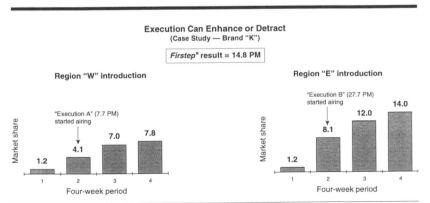

Execution Can Enhance or Detract
(Case Study — Brand "K")

Firstep° result = 14.8 PM

Note: The greater sales increase in Region "E" occurred despite the fact that distribution only reached 75 percent PSS versus 90 percent PSS in Region "W."
Source: Ashley (1993).

FIG. 17.20.

**Productive Advertising Performed Better than
Heavier Promotional Spending, Wider Distribution, and Lower Price**
(Case Study — Brand "K")

	Execution "B" index		Execution "A" indexed
BDI	100	←	121
Total GRPs	100	→	92
Average distribution	100	←	107
Average displays	100	←	227
Average retailer ads	100	←	114
Average selling price*	100	←	93
Total TV power (*PRP** delivery)	100	→	27
Sales gains (Dollar share)	100	→	55

* Versus category average in region.
Source: Ashley (1993).

FIG. 17.21.

Selling Power Is Delivered Quickly
(*ARS Persuasion** Wearout Curve)

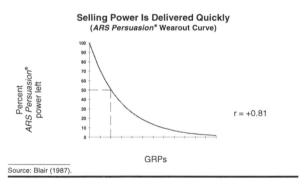

Source: Blair (1987).

FIG. 17.22.

IRI's study of over 300 split-cable tests yielded similar findings. In a *Harvard Business Review* article, it was noted that, "when a particular advertising weight or copy is effective, it works relatively rapidly. Incremental sales begin to occur within six months" (p. 51). And even more importantly, "if advertising changes do not show an effect in six months, then they will not have any impact, even if continued" (Abraham & Lodish, 1990, p. 51).

In 1984, rsc undertook a systematic tracking experiment to determine the effectiveness of advertising over time (Blair, 1987). After identifying cases in which the same execution had been on air for more than one measurement period, an interesting pattern emerged. As GRPs were spent behind the ads, the *ARS Persuasion* level declined, consistently. This relationship between spending and decline in *ARS Persuasion* power was very strong, with a correlation of +0.81 (see Fig. 17.22).

Because this discovery was so controversial at the time, most of our customers had to see if it was true for their specific brands, and consequently rsc's wearout database now includes over 100 commercial wearout verifications performed in the United States, Canada, Mexico, Germany, and Belgium. The original wearout curve fit these cases with remarkable precision (see Fig. 17.23).

At this stage, we can determine how long the advertising execution will be effective. ARS Persuasion outcomes are entered into the outlook® wearout model, a proprietary software package that projects commercial wearout based on ARS Persuasion levels and planned media spending (Rosenberg, 1988). This model is used to determine when the advertising's selling power will be delivered (i.e., when its effectiveness will be worn down) and, hence, when refreshment will be needed. We can also use this learning to decide how many executions will be necessary to attain a desired Persuasive Rating Point (PRP®)[5] level (PRPs are simply a combination of GRPs and the ARS Persuasion power of the executions on air during a particular period; the effectiveness of each ad declines from period to period when used in the plan). Given a media plan and ARS Persuasion objectives, this wearout model can be used to determine how many executions will be needed for the plan period.

Let us look at how this knowledge can be used to help deliver selling power to market, using a media plan calling for the greatest TV impact, or GRPs, during Periods 5, 6, and 7 (see Fig. 17.24). If we were to use only one commercial for the entire eight periods, the ad would have already delivered most of its selling power during Periods 1 through 4, leaving little ARS Persuasion power for Periods 5, 6, and 7, when we are spending the most and want the greatest impact. However, by planning ahead and refreshing with three additional effective executions, we can get the sales impact from advertising when we want it. Increased PRPs or selling power can be achieved through properly planned refreshment, where the PRP delivery matches the media or GRP pattern.

With the benefit of store scanner data, the impact of advertising short and long term can be tracked over time with greater sensitivity. Let us look at two case histories in which the brand-management and agency team have been using this Total Quality approach over an extended period of time.

In a published Campbell's case, the brand had a small impact with its initial ad, but the ad wore down, losing its effectiveness (see Fig. 17.25). The introduction of a brand-differentiating strategy produced two highly productive ads, as well as two not so productive ones that were not aired (Adams & Blair, 1992). Both productive ads had immediate impact when aired, resulting in significant share growth for the brand. Timely replenishment maintained the share momentum.

In addition, ad spending, promotion, and price did not explain the market-share change. The effectiveness of the Campbell's advertising made the difference in this share battle, with significantly lower marketing investment than its major competitor (see Fig. 17.26).

---

[5]PRP and outlook are registered marks of rsc.

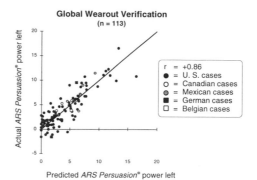

Source: Crang (1995).

FIG. 17.23.

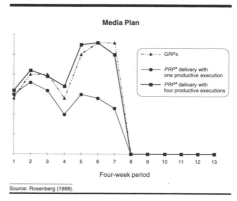

Source: Rosenberg (1988).

FIG. 17.24.

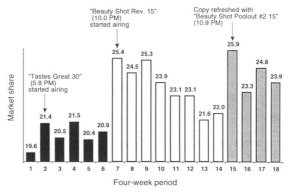

Source: Adams and Blair (1992).

FIG. 17.25.

In our nonfood example, the brand-management and agency team increased market share about 5 points in Period 6 with an effective 30-second ad; then using the same ad (with *ARS Persuasion* power left) increased share over 3 points in Period 19; and again with a fresh, highly effective ad, gained 7 share points in Period 21 (see Fig. 17.27).

Longer term (residual) effects are also evident in these cases, where the shares after the advertising waves remain higher than those before the particular wave. Note also that neither of these brands is small or new. They are both leading brands in their categories. The nonfood researcher said, "The most

Productive Advertising and Timely Refreshment
Overcame Heavier Competitive Spending and Lower Price
(Campbell's Published Case Study)

	Campbell's brand index		Major competitor indexed
Total GRPs	100	←	136
Average displays	100	←	170
Average retailer ads	100	←	141
Average selling price	100	←	92
Total TV power (*PRP** delivery)	100	→	19*
Sales gains (Units)	100	→	30

* *ARS Persuasion** scores for competitor's ads ranged from -1.0 to +1.0.
Source: Ashley (1993).

FIG. 17.26.

Nonfood Case Study

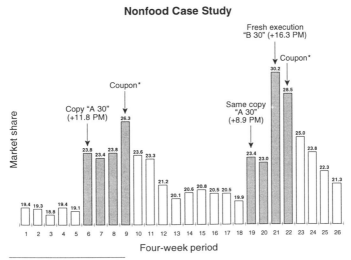

FIG. 17.27.

surprising thing we have learned is how fast commercials wear out. The initial response of our marketing department was disbelief. But a backup commercial was produced when sales started to slip. The new commercial began to air and sales picked up again."

Competition

The fifth and final stage in the currently suggested process incorporates the effects of competitive advertising. Once advertisers are able to develop and air productive advertising more consistently, the selling power of a competitor's advertising will need to be understood. Learning the selling power of competitors' new products, new strategies, line extensions, and so on, provides the direction for appropriate response.

A FIVE-YEAR CASE STUDY

This case study tracks the advertising success of major players in a large packaged-goods category. Over the 5-year period, there has been significant new-product activity in the category. New brands have gained about 25% of the market (see Fig. 17.28).

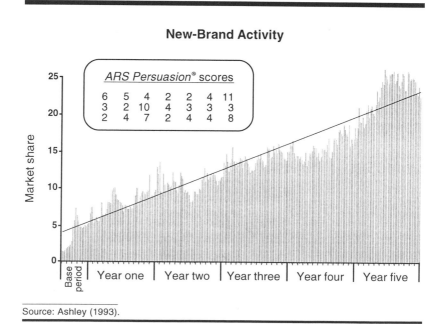

FIG. 17.28.

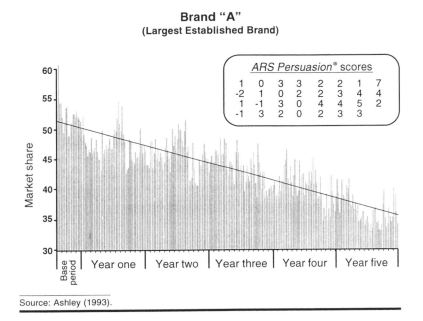

Brand "A"
(Largest Established Brand)

FIG. 17.29.

The largest established brand has lost roughly 19 share points operating under a "traditional advertising process." Although Brand A aired many executions, few were productive (see Fig. 17.29).

On the other hand, the second largest established brand (B) has gained share over these 5 years (despite the new-product activity) by having found an effective selling proposition and by continuing to refresh with productive executions (see Fig. 17.30). Brand B's share increase over 5 years was not explained by media expenditures, promotional activity, or pricing strategies (see Fig. 17.31). Although spending less, the brand sustained its success with effective advertising.

SUMMARY

Ample evidence indicates that advertising can help marketers meet both profit and revenue objectives quarter to quarter and over the long term. Achieving this result requires a commitment to obtaining sales-related feedback throughout the advertising development and management process. In the 1980s, the use of split-cable delivery and electronic scanner panels offered a means to evaluate the sales validity of advertising-effectiveness measures. Twenty-seven

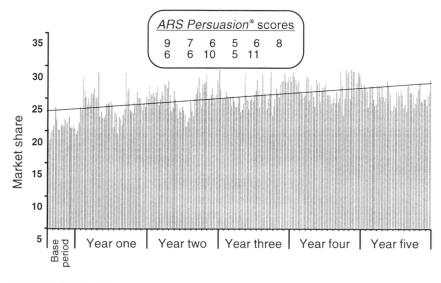

Brand "B"
(Second Largest Established Brand)

ARS Persuasion® scores

9	7	6	5	6	8
6	6	10	5	11	

Source: Ashley (1993).

FIG. 17.30.

Five-Year Overview

	Brand "A" index		Brand "B" indexed
Total GRPs	100	⟶	74
Average displays	100	⟶	51
Average retailer ads	100	⟶	78
Average selling price	100	⟶	110
Total TV power (*PRP*® delivery)	100	⟵	152
Sales gains (units)*	-19%	⟵	+22%

* Market share increase versus base period.
Source: Ashley (1993).

FIG. 17.31.

electronic-test-market cases (20 weight tests and seven copy tests) have been used to examine the relationship of advertising weight, related recall, brand-name recall, liking, and the ARS *Persuasion* measure to changes in market share. By examining the sales predictability of these measures, it has been determined that the ARS *Persuasion* measure has the greatest precision.

Furthermore, a Total Quality process has been identified for developing and managing advertising (see Fig. 17.32). Step one in this process is identification

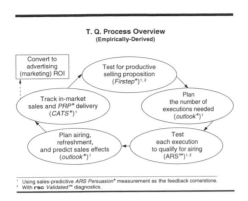

T. Q. Process Overview
(Empirically-Derived)

Convert to advertising (marketing) ROI

Test for productive selling proposition (*Firstep*[1,2])

Track in-market sales and *PRP* delivery (*CATS*[1])

Plan the number of executions needed (*outlook*[1])

Plan airing, refreshment, and predict sales effects (*outlook*[1])

Test each execution to qualify for airing (ARS[1,2])

[1] Using sales-predictive *ARS Persuasion* measurement as the feedback cornerstone.
[2] With **rsc** *Validated* diagnostics.

CATS is a registered mark of rsc. rsc *Validated* is a service mark of rsc.

FIG. 17.32.

of an effective selling proposition. Experience to date indicates that testing the selling proposition before beginning execution development leads to a dramatically higher advertising success rate. The second step is estimation of the number of executions needed for a given media plan. Given the ARS *Persuasion* level prior to airing, the number of GRPs that can be spent behind a commercial before it wears out can be modeled. The next step is to produce the number of productive commercials needed for the media plan. In addition, this process requires implementation of a refreshment schedule based on the commercials' ARS *Persuasion* levels, thereby maximizing the selling power delivered to market. This process allows advertisers to leverage media dollars behind the most productive executions and replace each when its power is depleted. The final step in this process requires gaining an understanding of the effects of competitors' advertising.

The empirical evidence suggests that the use of a reliable, sales-related measurement is essential to the advertising decision-making process. Furthermore, the use of the rsc *Total Quality Process* during advertising development can greatly increase the odds of achieving effective television advertising. As with many Total Quality approaches, the payout for following such a process is substantial return on investment.

REFERENCES

Abraham, M. M., & Lodish, L. M. (1990). Getting the most out of advertising and promotion. *Harvard Business Review, 68*(3), 50–60.

Adams, A. J., & Blair, M. H. (1992). Persuasive advertising and sales accountability: Past experience and forward validation. *Journal of Advertising Research, 32*(2), 20–25.

Ashley, S. R. (1993, October). *Measuring persuasion: Case studies.* Speech presented at the ESOMAR Teach-In on how to get the most out of research, Istanbul, Turkey.

Baldinger, A. L. (1989). Challenging the advertising and promotion myths: Is long-term vs. short-term the right issue? In *Proceedings of the Advertising and Promotion Effectiveness Workshop* (pp. 26–38). New York: Advertising Research Foundation.

Blair, M. H. (1987). An empirical investigation of advertising wearin and wearout. *Journal of Advertising Research, 27*(6), 45–50.

Blair, M. H. (1994). International to global: Another paradigm shift. In *Proceedings of the ARF 40th Annual Conference* (pp. 99–108). New York: Advertising Research Foundation.

Byers, L. M., & Gleason, M. D. (1993, May). Using measurement for more effective advertising. *Admap*, 31–35.

Dodd, A. R., Jr. (1964, May 8). New study tells TV advertisers how advertising builds sales and share of market. *Printers' Ink.*

Donnelley Marketing Inc. (1994). *The 16th annual survey of promotional practices.* Author.

Fulgoni, G. (1990). New knowledge regarding advertising & promotion effectiveness: Learning from IRI's historical data bases. In *Proceedings of the ARF 36th Annual Conference* (pp. 131–153). New York: Advertising Research Foundation.

Haley, R. I., & Baldinger, A. L. (1991). The ARF copy research validity project. *Journal of Advertising Research, 31*(2), 11–32.

Kelly, P. J. (1964, May 8). The Schwerin model: How you can use it to build your share of market. *Printers' Ink.*

Kuse, A. R. (1991). Measurement tools for ads that sell. In *Proceedings from the ARF Eighth Annual Copy Research Workshop* (pp. 127–139). New York: Advertising Research Foundation.

Lodish, L. M. (1991). Key findings from the "How Advertising Works" study. In *Proceedings from the ARF Marketplace Advertising Research Workshop* (pp. 23–33). New York: Advertising Research Foundation.

Lubetkin, B. (1991). Additional major findings from the "How Advertising Works" study. In *Proceedings from the ARF Marketplace Advertising Research Workshop* (pp. 35–51). New York: Advertising Research Foundation.

McQueen, J. (1991). Important learning about how advertising works in stimulating long-term brand growth. In *Proceedings from the ARF Marketplace Advertising Research Workshop* (pp. 53–73). New York: Advertising Research Foundation.

Murphy, M. P. (1968, October). *Empirical evidence of the effect of advertising on sales.* Speech presented at the Professional Market Research Society, Toronto.

Rosenberg, K. E. (1988). Managing advertising quality beyond copy testing: The role of ad quality vs. weight in generating sales. In *Proceedings from the ARF Fifth Annual Copy Research Workshop* (pp. 233–248). New York: Advertising Research Foundation.

rsc. (1983). *Advertising caused awareness and trial: ARS predictive validity for new brand advertising.* Evansville, IN: Author.

rsc. (1992). *Convergent findings: rsc and IRI "How Advertising Works" update.* Evansville, IN: Author.

rsc. (1993a). *ARS global reliability: 1993 report.* Evansville, IN: Author.

rsc. (1993b). *Summary of validated diagnostics for the ARS Persuasion measure.* Evansville, IN: Author.

rsc. (1994). *Firstep track record.* Evansville, IN: Author.

Comments on Chapter 17

Brian Wansink
University of Illinois, Urbana–Champaign

The consistency and thoughtfulness that have been used to collect this database enable one to develop important insights into the copy testing process. In the studies described by Kuse, there are lessons for both practitioners and researchers. After exploring the potential insights that can be gained from ad wear out data, I focus on the important implications and on the potential usefulness of the difference score that was used to measure ad persuasiveness.

WHAT ELSE INFLUENCES ADVERTISING WEAR-OUT?

An overwhelming conclusion of the studies described by Kuse confirms academic findings that an ad wears out if it is not alternated with other executions. Although wear-out varies across product categories and across ad executions, other important generalizations can be made. For instance, it may be possible to determine how effectiveness levels vary depending on prior usage habits or on ad processing involvement. It might be that the optimal number of exposures of a particular execution dramatically varies depending on whether the primary target of the campaign was loyal users or nonusers.

Furthermore, Broach, Page, and Wilson (chap. 12, this volume) suggest that wear-out may also be affected by media placement. One might argue, for instance, that an ad embedded in a highly involving drama would wear out more quickly than if the same ad was embedded in a situation comedy.

USING DIFFERENCE SCORES FOR INCREASED MEASUREMENT SENSITIVITY

The ad persuasion score is obtained by subtracting the percentage of people who select the target brand prior to ad exposure from the percentage who select it afterward. Such difference measures have some very attractive properties and are worth reconsideration for academic research. The within-subject design is more statistically powerful and requires fewer subjects than the more traditionally used between-subject designs. Concerns about reactivity and contamination are moderated by the positive correlation of these results with split-cable tests.

Because before–after difference scores can increase measurement sensitivity, it may be useful to reintroduce them to academic studies of advertising effectiveness by using control groups to determine if test–retest confounds exist. If scores from control groups are similar to those from treatment groups, we can be less concerned about potential confounding.

As marketing research advances and as we examine more subtle phenomena, it is critical that we develop the measurement tools that can enable us to do so. Regardless of whether we call them difference scores, test–retest scores, or before–after scores, revisiting the potential of these measures might keep us from trying to measure electrons with yardsticks.

18

Evaluating Advertising Effectiveness Through Advertising Response Modeling (ARM)

Abhilasha Mehta
Gallup & Robinson, Inc.

Scott C. Purvis
Gallup & Robinson, Inc.

It is well accepted today that in evaluating advertising effectiveness, multiple measures are required; no single measure is adequate. The recent Advertising Research Foundation (ARF) Copy Research Validity Study further endorsed the use of multiple measures (Haley & Baldinger, 1991). The inclusion of need for several measures in current copy research systems reflects the need to capture the various dimensions of persuasion. Consequently, researchers today are evaluating advertising performance on a variety of measures including memory-based intrusiveness levels of recall or recognition, brand rating, advertising liking, buying interest or intention, as well as diagnostics related to the advertised product or service and advertising execution. However, it is not clear which of these measures are more appropriate under certain conditions, or even how they relate to each other. The even greater challenge is in interpreting the sometimes conflicting results.

Advertising Response Modeling (ARM) is an attempt to provide a framework to assess advertising performance by means of integrating several measures. Based on past research on how advertising works, a conceptual model is derived that lends itself to empirical applications in a variety of advertising situations to help fully understand the processing of the advertising in question. Its application allows going beyond mere descriptives and helps evaluate whether or not the advertising being tested fulfills the marketing communications objectives set for it. Results of the modeling provide information for actionable decision making.

Although it is well recognized that an audience actively participates in the advertising process by going beyond the messages presented in the advertising itself and drawing conclusions about the brand, this inference process has received little attention in commercial copy testing. Understanding how the advertising was actually processed should help identify the strengths and weaknesses in the advertising. Application of ARM in copy testing is designed to do that.

Specifically, the objectives of this chapter are to present a conceptual model of ARM, and demonstrate through a case study how ARM adds insight gained toward a fuller understanding of the advertising process.

ARM: CONCEPTUAL MODEL

Researchers for the last five decades have attempted to understand how advertising works. From the early learning theories of persuasion (Hovland, Janis, & Kelly, 1953; McGuire, 1972) and the hierarchy of effects model, including Dagmar (Colley, 1961), to the more recent Elaboration Likelihood Model (ELM; Petty & Cacioppo, 1981, 1986), the extensive work on effects of ad attitudes on ad performance (Baker & Lutz, 1987; Batra & Ray, 1985; MacKenzie & Lutz, 1989; MacKenzie, Lutz, & Belch, 1986; Muehling, Laczniak, & Stoltman, 1991; Muehling, Stoltman, & Mishra, 1990), and the ARF Copy Research Validity Study (Haley & Baldinger, 1991), various pieces of the advertising effectiveness puzzle have been addressed. Based on these advances, and Gallup & Robinson's own empirical research, the ARM has been delineated (see Mehta, 1994).

As Fig. 18.1 shows, and consistent with past research, an ad needs to first break through the clutter and gain attention. If the advertising captures

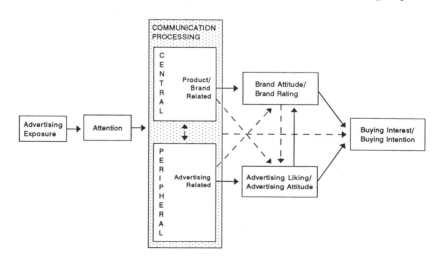

FIG. 18.1. Advertising Response Modeling (ARM) conceptual model.

attention, processing occurs along one or both routes: central and peripheral (Petty & Cacioppo, 1981, 1986). During central processing, the focus is on product and/or brand-related information, whereas ad/commercial-related issues are more dominant during peripheral processing.

The processing route is expected to be influenced by involvement levels. Under high involvement, respondents process information via a central route by elaborating on the brand-related information. Peripheral processing occurs under low-involvement conditions, and subjects typically rely on the available peripheral cues such as music, source or spokespersons, and so on.

Processing that occurs along the central route leads directly to brand attitude that, in turn, influences buying interest or buying intention. Peripheral cues may influence brand attitudes as well. Attitudes formed or changed as a result of central processing tend to be more permanent and resistant to change.

Peripheral processing leads directly to ad attitude/ad liking that, in turn, may influence brand attitude and buying interest. Ad attitude may be influenced by message-related issues as well (Greene, 1992). Attitudes formed or changed as a result of peripheral processing are apt to be more temporary in nature and may be lost as the peripheral cues influencing the attitudes cease to be present. It may thus be necessary to have repeated exposure of the same or similar advertising to reinforce the relationship between the peripheral cue and the brand in question.

Additionally, there is evidence suggesting that in cases of familiar, established brands, brand attitude may influence ad attitude (MacKenzie, Lutz, & Belch, 1986). However, Muehling, Stoltman, and Mishra (1990) found this relationship to exist for new, unfamiliar brands for low-involvement subjects as well.

Particular advertising executional styles may also influence the processing route that will be taken. For example, highly informational ads may promote central processing whereas affective ads may encourage the use of peripheral cues.

The distinction between central and peripheral route processing is useful when evaluating advertising performance and identifying the strengths and weaknesses in the advertising. By operationalizing central route factors as those related to the product or brand and message-related issues, and executional features as peripheral cues, it is possible to evaluate to what extent each works toward facilitating the advertising performance. Also, although in most cases simultaneous processing of the two routes occurs, one is usually dominant, and establishing the dominant route should be helpful because the consequences of each route are different.

Within this general conceptual model of ARM, adaptations are made for application to any particular testing situation. The choice of dependent variables, as well as the operationalizations of these variables are customized appropriately. For example, instead of buying interest or buying intention, intention to visit dealer was a more appropriate final dependent variable when studying automobile commercials. The communication processing variables—that is, the product-related and ad-related variables—are also changed from situation to situation as necessary; to measure these, we have variously used thought listings, scaled rating measures, and checklists. ARM offers this flexibility and works well in most situations. We have found that ARM adapts equally when studying TV commercials or print ads.

ARM: APPLICATIONS

Application of ARM to traditional copy testing results has yielded insight into fully understanding the advertising processes. It has helped identify whether what was intended by the advertising was actually achieved, and if the variables that were expected to be important in driving the advertising really are influencing the dependent measures of interest.

The following case study for two print beverage ads illustrates how ARM has been used in advertising effectiveness tests.

CASE STUDY: BACKGROUND AND OBJECTIVES

Two ads for the same leading brand of a nonalcoholic beverage were studied. Each ad introduced a new flavor for the brand, but differed significantly in content and execution. Ad A presented four different varieties of the sugar-free, low-calorie flavors by showing the various packages. It was basically an informational ad with the headline emphasizing the varieties and choices available. In Ad B, the style was transformational; The product was clearly shown in the ad by means of the package and an emotional and romantic atmosphere was created by suggestion of a couple, and the headline supported the romantic feelings.

METHOD

Sample

Regular readers of general interest magazines in 10 geographically dispersed U.S. markets were recruited to participate in, ostentatiously, a study of magazine readership habits. A total of 280 women participated in the study. Subjects saw only one of the two test ads.

Procedure

The two ads were tested in a contextual-based system: in-magazine, in-market, and at-home. The test magazines were placed at the home of the participant with the instructions to read the magazine that day as they naturally would read any magazine. A phone interview was scheduled for the following day. One of the test ads (Ad B) naturally appeared in the test issue. Ad A was tipped into another issue of the same magazine title that did not contain Ad B.

Interviewers called participants the day after exposure as scheduled and, after assuring magazine readership, administered advertising-related measures for the two test ads. After obtaining recall and idea communication measures, respondents (recallers and nonrecallers) were reexposed to the test ad and additional questions were administered to gauge reactions to the ad and attitudes toward the brand.

Measures

Recall was measured on a brand-aided basis. Idea communication is the playback of copy ideas obtained from recallers about the ad. Other major measures include buying interest, ad liking (5-point scale each), and brand rating (6-point scale). Diagnostics about the advertising in terms of ad statements and adjectives were measured on a yes–no basis. Other special questions included asking about product attributes of the brand in the ads on a yes–no basis as well. These special questions and response scales were selected for the descriptive value they held for the client and were not anticipated to be used for modeling.

RESULTS

Descriptive Measures

As shown in Table 18.1, the informational Ad A is the stronger of the two ads when recall and idea communication were the primary measures used to assess the advertising. Ad A was a more intrusive ad that more clearly communicated its sales messages of flavors, low calories, and being sugar free. Ad B, the transformational ad, is weaker than Ad A on memorability and communicated its ideas of flavors, taste, and making everyday experiences special at lower or generally low levels. It is interesting to note that although Ad B attempted to create a relaxing and romantic atmosphere, this idea was not verbalized or played back by any respondent.

In terms of the other major measures, there were no significant differences, although scores for ad liking and buying interest favor Ad B directionally. In terms of ad reactions, Ad B was considered more entertaining and Ad A was perceived as communicating a more important main idea. The two ads perform similarly on all other variables related to advertising reactions and product attributes and attitudes toward the brand. Further, although Ad B tried to portray the image of a "relaxing" product more than Ad A did, results for variables related to "treat" and "good to relax to" are at similar levels for both ads.

TABLE 18.1
Summary of Results for Nonalcoholic Beverage Ads

Measures	Ad A	Ad B
	%	%
Recall	26	20[*]
Ad liking	64	73
Brand rating	53	55
Buying interest	48	59
Idea communication (recallers only)		
Refer to flavors	75	67
Low in calories	67	N/A[*]
Sugar free	67	N/A[*]
New	31	27
Taste/appetite appeal	14	47[*]
Ad statements (yes–no)		
One of the best	46	53
Enjoyed reading	70	73
Like any other ad	49	38
Entertaining	41	58[*]
Main idea importance	46	27[*]
Makes me want to try	54	64
Product attributes (yes–no)		
For people like you	59	49
Rich taste	64	67
Good value	56	53
Everyday experiences special	45	33
Good to relax to	72	67
A treat	66	76
Perfect for everyday use	47	36
(Base: recallers/reexposure)	(101)	(45)

Note. Scaled measure reported top two boxes; yes–no items reported as the percentage saying yes.
[*]$p < .10$.

What do these findings say? It is clear that Ad A was a more intrusive ad and it communicated its sales messages of flavors, low calories, and being sugar free more successfully. It is not surprising that the more direct and informational Ad A is better remembered than the subtler and softer Ad B. News and information have historically been shown to be important drivers of recall.

Ad B was a transformational ad, and the objective for the ad therefore is to influence through affect rather than information. Affective measures do favor Ad B, which cues one to think there is strength in the ad. The question is, what? Can more analysis about how people react to and think about the Ad B identify this possible strength?

ARM

Application of ARM helped reveal the strength in the ad and helped in going beyond the descriptive data. It helped gain new insights about how the ads were working, and also helped examine the relationships that exist within the pattern of responses. The results of the modeling showed that processing of the two ads was quite different.

Diagnostic measures used in the study were factor analyzed for use in ARM. Pairwise deletion techniques were used to maintain sample size because there was some nonresponse for several of the diagnostic measures. Results of the modeling through LISREL VII (Joreskög & Sorböm, 1990) are presented in Figs. 18.2 and 18.3 for Ads A and B, respectively.

Ad A ARM Results.   In Ad A, reaction was driven by taste appeal, and by how important the idea of new flavor/sugar-free/low calories was to the respondent, as well as the perception that this product was for a special occasion; buying interest was more strongly influenced by brand rating than by ad liking.

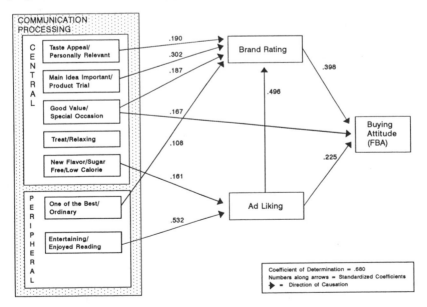

FIG. 18.2. Advertising Response Modeling (ARM) nonalcoholic beverage—Ad A.

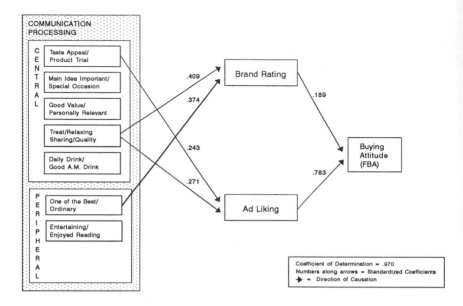

FIG. 18.3. Advertising Response Modeling (ARM) nonalcoholic beverage—Ad B.

Ad A was an informational ad, and it appears that the information provided in the ads was not only received by the respondent, but it also had an influence in driving the brand rating and, finally, the buying interest. This further establishes that the ad is strong and was processed in a way that was appropriate for the marketing communications objectives set for it.

Ad B ARM Results. In Ad B, taste appeal was again important, but reaction was strongly driven by whether the product was perceived as being a treat/relaxing/sharing/quality. Further, buying interest was much more influenced than brand rating by whether respondents liked the ad.

Ad B was transformational, and this aspect of a "relaxing" product was important in influencing persuasion, ad liking, and buying interest, particularly. It is interesting to note that although the idea of treat/relaxing/sharing/quality is virtually unmentioned in open-ended questions of idea communication and shows up in the diagnostics at levels that are descriptively the same as in the other ad, it is the single most significant influence on brand rating and ad liking in this ad.

From a marketing communications objectives point of view, Ad B works and was processed in an appropriate manner. Being an affective ad, recall scores were lower than for an informational ad. However, the message in the ad comes through. ARM clearly shows the strength in the ad and cautions that the ad should not be dismissed on the basis of lower recall.

ARM results reveal that both of the tested ads work well, although quite differently. Decisions regarding their use should be made in view of the larger marketing objectives, keeping in mind the strengths of each ad.

New Considerations.   Further, ARM offers three new considerations in this context beyond helping understand how the ads perform. First, it provides empirical evidence that ad liking can drive persuasion—specifically buying interest—in this product category, directly or indirectly through its influence on brand rating. Second, it demonstrates that copy points need not be verbalized at strong levels to have a significant influence on persuasion. As mentioned earlier, although the idea of treat/relaxing/sharing/quality was not mentioned in the open-ended questions, it is a strong influencing variable of brand rating and ad liking. Finally, it emphasizes the importance of reexamining measurement issues. In this case, it highlights a nonresponse problem with the yes–no questions, which suggests use of scaled measures in future tests.

Limitations and Future Applications

We have found that ARM has offered insights like these in different advertising situations, both TV and print. Nevertheless, we do need to be cautious as we interpret ARM results. It is important that the appropriate variables be selected for each testing situation, and that the operationalizations are meaningful and useful. Diagnostic measures used in this study were largely on a yes–no basis. More discriminating scales would yield better models. There was also some level of nonresponse in the data set that future studies should try to eliminate. Alternatively, sample size may be increased.

Further, although response to most advertising is at moderate to low involvement levels, we need to be concerned about how involvement rather than the advertising strategy and execution are influencing the results.

CONCLUSIONS

Nevertheless, it has been shown here that ARM application in advertising effectiveness testing has beneficial results.

- It leads to a better understanding of how the advertising is processed.
- It uncovers insights about advertising performance that can only be speculated upon within the confines of traditional descriptive data analysis.
- It evaluates if the advertising processing is appropriate in view of the marketing communications objectives set for it.

REFERENCES

Baker, W. E., & Lutz, R. J. (1987). The relevance-accessibility model of advertising effectiveness. In S. Hecker & D. Stewart (Eds.), *Nonverbal communication in advertising* (pp. 59–84). Lexington, MA: Lexington Books.

Batra, R., & Ray, M. L. (1985). How advertising works at contact. In L. F. Alwitt & A. A. Mitchell (Eds.), *Psychological processes and advertising effects: Theory, research and application* (pp. 13–44). Hillsdale, NJ: Lawrence Erlbaum Associates.

Colley, R. H. (1961). *Defining advertising goals for measured advertising results.* New York: Association of National Advertisers.

Greene, W. F. (1992). Observations: What drives commercial liking? *Journal of Advertising Research, 32*(2), 65–68.

Haley, R. I., & Baldinger, A. L. (1991). The ARF copy research project. *Journal of Advertising Research, 31*(2), 11–32.

Hovland, C. I., Janis, I. L., & Kelly, H. H. (1953). *Communication and persuasion.* New Haven, CT: Yale University Press.

Joreskög, K. G., & Sorböm, D. (1990). *LISREL VII: Estimation of linear structural equations system.* Mooresville, IN: Scientific Software, Inc.

MacKenzie, S. B., & Lutz, R. J. (1989). An empirical examination of the structural antecedents of attitude toward the ad in an advertising pretest context. *Journal of Marketing, 53,* 48–65.

MacKenzie, S. B., Lutz, R. J., & Belch, G. E. (1986). The role of attitude toward the ad as a mediator of advertising effectiveness: A test of competing explanations. *Journal of Marketing Research, 23*(2), 130–43.

McGuire, W. J. (1972). The information-processing paradigm. In C. G. McClintock (Ed.), *Experimental social psychology* (pp. 108–141). New York: Holt, Rinehart & Winston.

Mehta, A. (1994). How advertising response modeling (ARM) can increase ad effectiveness. *Journal of Advertising Research, 34*(3), 62–74.

Muehling, D. D., Laczniak, R. N., & Stoltman, J. J. (1991). The moderating effect of ad message involvement: A reassessment. *Journal of Advertising, 20*(2), 28–38.

Muehling, D. D., Stoltman, J. J., & Mishra, S. (1990). An examination of the cognitive antecedents of attitude-toward-the-ad. *Current Issues and Research in Advertising, 12*(1–2), 95–117.

Petty, R. E., & Cacioppo, J. T. (1981). *Attitude and persuasion: Classic and contemporary approaches.* Dubuque, IA: Brown.

Petty, R. E., & Cacioppo, J. T. (1986). *Communication and persuasion: Central and peripheral routes to attitude change.* New York: Springler-Verlag.

Comments on Chapter 18

Brian Wansink
University of Illinois, Urbana–Champaign

The work of Mehta and Pervis holds insights for both practitioners and academics. As additional data become available, there are further directions in which the model can be extended. These research directions can be viewed as either inputs, outputs, or moderators of the model they present in Fig. 18.1.

ARM INPUTS: HOW DOES INFORMATION PROCESSING DIFFER ACROSS VIEWERS?

We often assume a homogenous population when developing a parsimonious model. However, after parsimony has been achieved, it is important to consider whether the model should be adjusted to accommodate more heterogeneous groups of people. Consider the nonalcoholic beverages examined by Mehta and Pervis. It is known that heavy users of a consumer packaged good process ads for that product differently than light users. With heavy users, exposure to any ad might be sufficient to encourage repurchase or increases in usage frequency. Conversely, light users may be more influenced by central or peripheral processing, depending on why they were light users to begin with.

In refining this model, it is important to acknowledge that not all consumers respond similarly to a particular ad. The way ads influence buying attitudes might also depend on the knowledge, familiarity, usage patterns, and category involvement of a person prior to his or her exposure to the ad. Furthermore, the relative mix of central versus peripheral processing may need to shift as one moves through the various stages of the buying process.

ARM MODERATORS: BROADENING BEYOND BEVERAGES

The answer to any question about advertising effectiveness is, "It depends." The model by Mehta and Pervis has been tested with two ad executions for nonalcoholic beverages. To increase our confidence in the generalizability of this model, it is necessary to identify those brand- or product category-related factors that would moderate these results. Buying a soft drink is far different from buying a riding lawnmower. Perhaps these differences also influence how the respective ads are viewed, and how these ads influence attitudes.

In analyzing category differences, it will also be important—as implied earlier—to segment consumers based on where they are in their decision-making process. If a data set is dominated by subjects who are not in the market for the target brand, their responses will overwhelm the responses of those who are in the market. Collapsing all subjects into one group will obscure important potential differences.

ARM OUTPUTS: ARE THERE DIFFERENTIAL DECAY RATES OF THESE ADVERTISING EFFECTS?

The measure of "buying attitude" proved to be a robust dependent variable for this study. It has managerial relevance while also being sensitive enough to be influenced by one advertising exposure. Eventually, it would be valuable to have long-term impact measures of the processing stimulated by these ads. Although peripheral processing appears to have an immediate impact on attitude, its long-term impact might be less than that of a centrally processed ad. Depending on the marketing objectives of a campaign, differential decay rates would have drastically different marketing implications.

As mentioned earlier, this work holds insights for both practitioners and academics, and it provides a more useful framework than what many might currently use. Its value, however, will be further enhanced as it is modified to accommodate market heterogeneity, category differences, and the long-term effects of decay.

19

A Strategic Approach to Measuring Advertising Effectiveness

Thomas J. Reynolds
Richmont Partners, Inc.

Jerry C. Olson
The Pennsylvania State University

John P. Rochon
Richmont Partners, Inc.

We begin our discussion of advertising effectiveness by describing an advertising problem facing Royal Appliance Manufacturing, marketers of Dirt Devil vacuum cleaners. This business situation grounds our discussion of various approaches to measuring advertising effectiveness.

BACKGROUND

For many years, the U.S. vacuum cleaner industry avoided intense competition and seemed satisfied to maintain a consistent level of profitability. Their complacency was evidenced by relatively meager funding of research and development, lack of product innovation, and limited expenditures on consumer marketing. Then, beginning in 1988, Royal Appliance turned up the competitive heat.

In 1988, three companies—Maytag (34%), Electrolux AB (21%), and Electrolux Corporation (12%)—controlled two thirds of the U.S. vacuum cleaner market. Four years later, the same companies still held nearly two thirds of the market. However, Royal Appliance Manufacturing, once a niche player with its Dirt Devil brand of handheld vacuum cleaners, had increased its market share to 13%. In the process, Royal Appliance gained the attention of the industry giants.

The Dirt Devil Strategy: Channel Access Through Advertising

Royal Appliance's initial marketing strategy focused on gaining access to mass merchandisers, which were becoming a more important distribution channel for vacuum cleaners (mass merchandisers accounted for 37% of vacuum cleaner sales in 1991 and increased to 42% 1 year later). To achieve its growth objectives, Royal Appliance had to persuade mass merchants to carry the Dirt Devil brand.

Most companies find it difficult to gain shelf space from mass merchandisers without a recognized brand name or some other marketing clout. Royal Appliance's approach was to become the leading spender on national advertising. From 1988 to 1992, Royal increased its advertising and promotion expenditures at an average rate of nearly 80% per year. Royal's ad spending grew from $7 million in 1988 to $80 million in 1992. By 1992, Royal Appliance had more than a 50% share of voice in the vacuum cleaner category. The primary target of this advertising was the consumer market, but an important secondary target was the mass merchant. Presumably, retailers believed that Royal Appliance's high expenditures on advertising and sales promotions would add consumer traffic in their stores and generate increased sales for all vacuum cleaner brands, not just the Dirt Devil brand.

The Dirt Devil Brand

Royal Appliance manufactured several distinctive product lines with different brand names. The company targeted these brands at different markets and sold them through different channels.[1] Royal sold the Dirt Devil brand largely through mass merchandisers. Over time, Royal Appliance added other models of upright vacuum cleaners to the Dirt Devil line.

For a considerable time after its introduction, the handheld Dirt Devil vacuum held a unique place in the market. Consumers looking for a small but powerful vacuum compared it favorably with rechargeable, battery-powered vacuum cleaners. Other consumers looking for an inexpensive vacuum cleaner compared it favorably with canister and upright vacuum cleaners because of its low price. Because of its rotating brush, consumers perceived the Dirt Devil vacuum to deliver better cleaning power, particularly for carpeting. These desirable product features, plus the wide distribution provided by the mass merchandiser channel, resulted in rapid sales growth. The resulting profits provided additional funds for advertising. In turn, these media expenditures generated additional channel access and opportunities for product exposure, resulting in yet more sales. However, this favorable cycle came to an end in 1992.

---

[1]Royal sold the Signature Series through department stores and mail-order catalogs and another product line through warehouse clubs. The Pro-Series was a dealer-exclusive line, sold under the Royal brand name. Royal also sold a line of metal handheld canister and upright vacuum cleaners exclusively through a network of independent dealers.

Competitors' Reactions

Initially, when confronted by the dramatic charge of Royal Appliance into the marketplace, the industry leaders actually reduced their combined annual advertising and promotion expenditures by almost 50%, dropping from $70 million in 1988 to $36 million in 1990. Perhaps the market leaders believed Royal's expensive advertising campaign would increase category demand and benefit them as market share leaders. Actually, the market shares for Hoover and Electrolux/Regina, the two industry leaders, remained about the same during this time period. Undoubtedly, spending less to maintain their market position increased their profitability during these years.

No strategy works forever, of course. Eventually, Royal Appliance's intense marketing activity changed the nature of competition in the vacuum cleaner category. In 1991, the market leaders began to respond to Royal Appliance's competitive challenge with massive advertising and promotion campaigns of their own. By 1992, industrywide expenditures on advertising and promotion had increased to nearly $60 million and were growing at an annual rate of 25% to 30%.

The competitive response of Electrolux AB (makers of the Eureka brand) is representative. Although Royal Appliance gained most of its share points from second-tier brands, Eureka lost 5 share points from 1988 to 1992. This decrease corresponded roughly to $130 million in lost sales revenue and an estimated $50 million reduction in gross profit (assuming the cost of goods sold is 60%). In retaliation, Electrolux AB management responded with an aggressive product development and marketing plan to regain market share. Significant research and development expenditures resulted in several new products that came to market in 1994, which management supported with ad spending 300% greater than 1992 levels. Furthermore, Electrolux managers reduced prices on the full line of Eureka vacuum cleaners in 1993. They planned to offer the new 1994 models at the same price points.

The intensity of Eureka's marketing efforts reflected the industry's realization that increased marketing budgets were necessary to compete in the highly energized vacuum cleaner category. To remain competitive, vacuum manufacturers had to develop new product features and keep prices low. Most increased their advertising expenditures as companies fought for share of voice in the marketplace.

Royal Appliance's Advertising Problem

It began to appear that Royal Appliance had a serious problem with its advertising for the Dirt Devil brand. Even though Royal Appliance's ad spending in 1991 and 1992 accounted for over 50% of total industry spending, the Dirt Devil brand received only 13% of sales. Royal Appliance had used heavy advertising expenditures to achieve the dominant share of voice in the industry and successfully penetrate the mass merchandiser channel, but in 1991 this strategy was no longer relevant. Increases in sales for Dirt Devil stopped in 1992, and profits decreased in the face of continuing large advertising expenses.

Now, Royal Appliance had to consider the effectiveness of its Dirt Devil advertising campaign. Why was the current Dirt Devil advertising ineffective in driving sales? What, if anything, was wrong with the Dirt Devil advertising? Does the current Dirt Devil advertising create brand equity? Could Royal Appliance develop more effective advertising?

THINKING ABOUT ADVERTISING EFFECTIVENESS

Thinking about the effectiveness of the Dirt Devil advertising leads us to consider the purpose of advertising. We suggest that the fundamental purpose of (brand-oriented) advertising is to create, maintain, or leverage brand equity (Reynolds & Gutman, 1984). The core of brand equity is the brand image—the set of meanings the target group of consumers have about the product. The most important aspect of brand image is consumers' perceptions of personal relevance—"This brand is right for me. This brand will meet my needs."

Feelings of personal relevance are based on the perceived connection between the brand and the customer (Walker & Olson, 1991). Means–end chains are useful for modeling consumers' perceptions of a brand's personal relevance (Gutman, 1982). Means–end chains show how consumers link product attributes to their basic values and goals, through a sequence (or chain) of successively more abstract and more personal consequences:

Product Attributes (features, physical characteristics)	Functional → Consequences (tangible outcomes)	Psychosocial → Consequences (subjective outcomes)	Customer Values → (needs, goals, life desires)

The consequences consumers expect to occur during consumption are the key to understanding the perceived personal relevance of a product or brand (Walker & Olson, 1991). As the salient outcomes change from functional to psychosocial consequences to values, they become more abstract, more personally relevant, and more affective or emotional (Gutman, 1991). In general, higher levels of the means–end chain are more involving and have greater motivational power to drive and direct consumer behaviors such as purchase (cf. Perkins & Reynolds, 1988).

What Is Advertising Strategy?

We believe the essential objective of advertising is to create beliefs about the personally relevant consequences of brand use. Marketers can use means–end chains to model consumers' perceptions of personal relevance and to think about how to develop advertising strategies. We recommend that managers specify their advertising strategies in the consumer-based language of means–end chains (Reynolds & Rochon, 1991). The MECCAS model shown in Fig. 19.1 is a useful framework for specifying advertising strategies in consumer language (see Olson & Reynolds, 1983). The MECCAS format defines the strategic objectives of the ad and helps the advertising creative team focus on the key concepts to be communicated in the ad (Reynolds & Craddock, 1988).

The key elements of advertising strategy shown in the MECCAS model correspond to the four means–end levels described earlier. Message elements correspond to product attributes, and benefits refer to the functional consequences of product use. The leverage point of ad strategy is the psychosocial consequence level and the driving force refers to the values level. The MECCAS model emphasizes two aspects of advertising strategy. To help the target

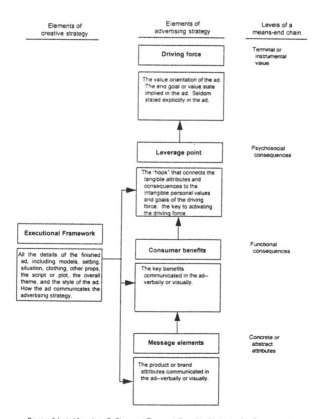

Source: Adapted from Jerry C. Olson and Thomas J. Reynolds, "Understanding Consumers' Cognitive Structures Implications for Advertising Strategies," in *Advertising and Consumer Psychology*, ed. Larry Percy and Arch Woodside (Lexington, Mass.: Lexington Books, 1983), pp. 77-90.

FIG. 19.1. The MECCAS Model of advertising strategy.

consumer create a coherent perception of the brand's personal relevance, the ad must strongly communicate each level of the strategy, from brand attributes to the driving force values of the customer. Moreover, the ad should communicate how those attributes and consequences are linked together in a way that is meaningful to the target consumer. Thus, an effective ad from a strategic perspective must communicate all the concepts in the specified strategy and create the connections between them (Gutman & Reynolds, 1987).

APPROACHES TO MEASURING
ADVERTISING EFFECTIVENESS

How should Royal Appliance measure the effectiveness of its advertising for the Dirt Devil brand? At the risk of oversimplifying, we can distinguish two approaches to measuring advertising effectiveness—the traditional and the strategic approaches.

Traditional Approaches

The traditional, copy testing approach to advertising effectiveness focuses on specific effects of the ad. Commonly used measures include recall (aided or unaided recall of the brand name or ad) and persuasion (beliefs, attitude change, purchase intentions). These measures are useful for answering simple questions about the ad. Did consumers recall the main copy point of the ad? Did they believe the main claim? Do consumers like the brand? Do consumers like the ad? Do consumers have a stronger intention to buy the product? Researchers have used such measures of advertising effectiveness for years, with few fundamental changes.

Strategic Approaches

The strategic approach, in contrast, takes a broader and more general view of advertising effectiveness (Reynolds & Rochon, 1991) by focusing on how well the ad communicates the strategy specified in the MECCAS framework. We need two types of measures to assess the effectiveness of the Dirt Devil advertising from a strategic specified perspective: (a) How well does the ad communicate the key means–end concepts in the strategy? (b) How well does the ad link these means–end concepts together to create a meaningful perception of personal relevance? An ad that communicates the key concepts of the ad strategy and links them together generates brand equity that influences the consumer to consume the advertised brand rather than competitive brands (Reynolds & Gutman, 1984).

What Type of Advertising Effectiveness Approach Should Royal Appliance Use?

We believe the advertising effectiveness issues facing Royal Appliance advertising go well beyond issues of copy testing. In our opinion, the fundamental issue facing Royal Appliance is strategic. Do the Dirt Devil ads create the type of personal relevance or brand equity among the target group of consumers that will generate favorable brand attitudes and positive intentions to buy the Dirt Devil brand over its competitors? We believe the strategic approach to measuring advertising effectiveness discussed earlier can provide more useful information to Royal Appliance managers than the traditional copy testing methods commonly used to indicate ad effectiveness (Reynolds & Rochon, 1991).

To demonstrate the utility of the strategic approach over the traditional approach, we conducted two studies of ad effectiveness for Dirt Devil and competitive brands. One study examined the Dirt Devil advertising using more traditional copy testing procedures, whereas the other assessed the strategic effectiveness of Dirt Devil advertising based on a means–end approach. We describe each study and its results separately.

TRADITIONAL MEASURES
OF ADVERTISING EFFECTIVENESS

The purpose of the first study was to evaluate the effectiveness of Royal Appliance's advertising for their Dirt Devil brand using more traditional, copy testing approaches. We begin by describing the methods used, and then we discuss the results.

Advertisements

We examined two Dirt Devil television commercials from the 1993–1994 campaign. The first ad (called "Humor") was the mainstay of the campaign. This 15-second ad introduced two versions of the upright vacuum model using a somewhat humorous execution showing the company CEO with the golden retriever dog who ends up wearing sunglasses. The second commercial was a 30-second ad called "Montage" that contained small segments from previous Dirt Devil ads tied together with a musical voice-over of Bobby Goldsboro singing "The Little Things You Do." The ad showed the Dirt Devil upright vacuum being used to do lots of small chores around the house such as sweeping stairs, cleaning upholstery, and picking up animal hair. "Humor" accounted for about 80% of the media exposure, whereas "Montage" aired less than 20% of the time.

We compared the two Dirt Devil ads to three ads for competitor brands from Hoover, Eureka, and Regina. The Hoover and Eureka ads were straightforward visual presentations of the various attachments for the product and their ease of use in various household situations. The Regina ad had a "fantasy" theme, showing the vacuum picking up paper clips, marbles, quarters, and eventually sucking up ¾-inch nuts and bolts (apparently without damage or noise).

Methods Used in the Traditional Approach

We collected the traditional measures of advertising effectiveness in a field survey of 500 adult women conducted in five U.S. cities. Interviewers approached women in malls and invited them to participate in a "study of advertising." To be included, women had to be older than 25, have household incomes greater than $25,000 per year, and be somewhat likely to purchase a vacuum cleaner within the next year. After some introductory remarks, the interviewer asked subjects a series of questions designed to measure traditional indicators of ad effectiveness. These measures included brand name recall, unaided recall of brand advertising, and perceptions of the strength and weaknesses of brands. Then, about half of the women saw four ads (one Dirt Devil ad and the three competitor ads) and rated their affective reactions to each ad and brand.

Results of the Traditional Approach

In this section, we review the results produced by these traditional measures of advertising effectiveness.

Top-of-Mind Brand Awareness.   One goal of advertising is to build a strong connection between the brand and the product category. Top-of-mind awareness (or unaided brand recall) is a measure of the strength of this association. Consumers are more likely to purchase brands with strong top-of-mind recall, because easily recalled brands are included more often in the consideration sets of more consumers.

After responding to some initial warm-up and screening questions, we asked each woman, "What brand name comes to mind when I say vacuum cleaner?" If the Dirt Devil advertising is effective, top-of-mind recall should be roughly equivalent to its share of voice over the past several years, but this was not the case. Dirt Devil received few top-of-mind mentions (5%) compared to Hoover (46%) and Eureka (13%). Dirt Devil also received fewer second mentions (9% compared to 25% for Hoover and 17% for Eureka). Hoover brand vacuums appear to "own" the category (85% of subjects recalled the Hoover brand, whereas only 27% recalled Dirt Devil). This suggests that even though Royal Appliance's expensive advertising campaign ($210 million from 1989 to 1993) gained market access to the mass merchants, Royal's ads did not make a tight connection in consumers' minds between the Dirt Devil brand name and the product category.

Unaided Recall of Advertising. We can think of two possible reasons for a weak connection between the Dirt Devil brand and the category. Perhaps consumers did not see the ads because of low exposure to the target population due to poor media selection, or maybe the ads did not attract consumers' attention. To examine these possibilities, we asked the respondents, "What advertising for vacuum cleaners do you recall seeing within the last 60 days?" Unaided ad recall was considerably higher for Dirt Devil than for any of its competitors (24% of subjects mentioned Dirt Devil ads first, compared to 18% for Hoover and 9% for Eureka). This suggests that key consumer groups were exposed to the Dirt Devil ads, and the ads captured the attention of those consumers. Yet, given the huge Dirt Devil advantage in share of voice over several years, we might expect an even greater advantage in ad recall.

Thoughts or Feelings Associated With Brands. Consumers' top-of-mind thoughts or feelings about a brand reflect their most salient beliefs about its strengths and weaknesses. These beliefs about a brand are likely to be important components of brand equity. Positive meanings in consumers' minds are among the most valuable assets a brand can "own." We measured women's top-of-mind concepts for four competitive brands (Hoover, Dirt Devil, Eureka, Regina) by asking, "What comes to mind when I say [*brand name*] of vacuum cleaner?" We also asked, "Is that thought positive or negative?" If Royal Appliance's advertising created equity for the Dirt Devil brand, consumers' top-of-mind thoughts and feelings should reflect mostly positive, personally relevant meanings.

In fact, the Hoover brand name elicited more positive concepts than Dirt Devil. Nearly all consumers (92%) mentioned positive concepts associated with Hoover that reflected the perceived personal relevance of the brand—"dependable, superior quality, good reputation, and cleans well." Likewise, most consumers (85%) mentioned positive concepts associated with Dirt Devil, but these were beliefs about less central concepts such as "small unit for small jobs, convenient, and powerful." These top-of-mind thoughts and feelings suggest that the Dirt Devil brand derives much of its equity from its original handheld model. Apparently, Royal Appliance's massive advertising campaign has not leveraged this equity to their full-sized, upright vacuums.

Ad Affect. Next, we examined the women's reactions to the Dirt Devil ads. After completing the survey questions, we asked 250 of the women (randomly selected) to watch some ads for vacuum cleaners. The interviewer directed these consumers to a separate viewing room where they saw four recent ads—one of the Dirt Devil ads, and one ad each for Hoover, Eureka, and Regina. Half of the viewer group (125 women) saw the "humorous" Dirt Devil ad, whereas the other half viewed the "montage" ad. After seeing each ad, consumers indicated their affect toward it, using a 100-point scale to rate two items: (a) "The ad shows people I like" and (b) "The ad entertains me."

Most consumers had rather similar responses to the two Dirt Devil ads and the Hoover ad, although the montage ad scored slightly higher than the humor ad. Scores on the "shows people I like" scale were 50, 47, and 48, respectively, and 48, 42, and 42, respectively, on the "ad entertains me" scale. Consumers had less positive feelings about the ads for Regina and Eureka (both scored in the mid- to low 30s). In sum, consumers seemed to like both Dirt Devil ads, but not dramatically better than the main competitor's ad.

Product Affect.   After seeing each ad, the women used a 100-point scale to rate their feelings about each brand on two items: (a) "After seeing the ad, I have a more favorable view of the brand" and (b) "The brand is a superior product." Again, the Dirt Devil "montage" ad performed slightly better than the Dirt Devil "humor" ad (scores of 50 and 49 vs. 45 and 45, respectively). However, neither Dirt Devil ad created dramatically greater brand affect than did the other ads (48 and 48 for Hoover, 43 and 44 for Regina, and 41 and 42 for Eureka).

SUMMARY

The traditional measures suggest that the Dirt Devil advertisements may be slightly superior to the competition on some criteria, but not on others. Consumers positively evaluated the Dirt Devil ads and the brand. However, these ratings were not much different from other brands, so they may not have much behavioral significance. The Dirt Devil ads produced higher ad recall than competitive ads, which probably reflects the much higher media weight for Dirt Devil advertising. However, the weak measures of brand name recall suggest that the Dirt Devil ads were ineffective in creating top-of-mind awareness for the brand. In summary, the traditional measures do not indicate that Dirt Devil advertising was particularly effective (or ineffective). Instead, the results of the traditional approach indicate that all the ads were rather similar in measured effectiveness.

The traditional copy testing approach we used to evaluate ad effectiveness is similar to other ad testing systems such as McCollum–Spielman. Unfortunately, such measures of ad recall, ad affect, product affect, and changes in brand attitude provide little insight into why an ad generates affect or is remembered. The traditional approach may indicate that an ad is good or poor on some criteria of ad effectiveness, but it gives little guidance for how to make the ad more effective. Finally, the traditional approaches do not measure how well an ad communicates the marketing or positioning strategy.

To answer such questions, we need a deeper understanding of the meanings communicated by an advertisement. We need to understand how advertising builds (or erodes) the personally relevant meanings that constitute brand equity. We need a strategic assessment of advertising effectiveness.

THE STRATEGIC APPROACH
TO ADVERTISING EFFECTIVENESS

In this section, we examine the results of a second study in which we assess the strategic effectiveness of Dirt Devil advertising, using measurement methods based on the means–end view of personal relevance.

Methods Used in the Strategic Approach

Ads and Subjects. In the strategic assessment study, we identified the apparent advertising strategies portrayed in four vacuum cleaner ads by examining the meanings they communicated to consumers. We examined the two Dirt Devil ads, plus the ad for Hoover and the ad for Regina. Because each respondent evaluated only two ads, we needed two groups of women to assess the four ads. We recruited 25 women from the Dallas area for each group, using the same selection criteria as in the first study.

The Strategic Assessment Procedures. We assessed the strategic effectiveness of these ads using a system of interview and measurement methods called *Strata*. The Strata approach is based on means–end concepts and the MECCAS model. Strata provides measures of the strength with which the ad communicates the key concepts of the advertising strategy as well as the strengths of the linkages between those concepts.

We took the Strata measures during a 45- to 60-minute, one-on-one, computer-assisted interview in which the respondent evaluated two ads (Gutman & Reynolds, 1987). We always showed two ads together, and the respondent viewed each ad four times during the interview (four exposures to the pair of ads). Following each ad exposure, respondents assessed each ad using a series of computer-generated graphical devices and rating scales. To provide a deeper understanding of consumers' responses, the interviewer asked open-ended questions at key points, and recorded the answers verbatim for later analysis.

After the first viewing of the two ads, respondents gave their top-of-mind reactions regarding the main idea of each ad, described their key thoughts and feelings, and identified points of confusion. They also rated the extent to which each ad was consistent with how they think about the product and how well each ad reinforced their view of the product.

Following this, respondents viewed the two ads again and assessed the strength with which each ad communicated several message elements and consumer benefits (product attributes and functional consequences). We converted these judgments to a 0 (*not communicated at all*) to 100 (*perfectly communicated*) scale. Respondents also rated (on 100-point scales) their overall affective feelings for each ad and brand.

Then, after viewing both ads for a third time, respondents assessed how well each ad communicated various leverage point and driving force concepts (psychosocial consequences and values). Again, we converted these judgments to a 0 (*not communicated at all*) to 100 (*perfectly communicated*) scale. Next, respondents rated (using a 0–100 scale) the overall executional framework of each ad on three dimensions: (a) The ad shows how the product fits my lifestyle, (b) The ad shows an unrealistic view of vacuums, and (c) The ad shows the benefits of owning products made by this company.

Finally, the respondents saw the two ads for the fourth time. By adjusting a graphical display, respondents assessed how strongly each ad connected every possible pair of concepts communicated by that ad. We converted these judgments to a linkage score based on a 0 (*not linked or connected at all*) to 9 (*a perfect linkage*) scale.

By measuring how strongly the ad communicates each concept in the advertising strategy and how strongly the ad links the concepts, the Strata method assesses the strategic effectiveness of an ad in creating meaningful perceptions of personal relevance about the brand (Reynolds & Craddock, 1988). The Strata results also provide insight and guidance for improving an ad (cf. Reynolds & Gengler, 1991). We believe this strategic approach can give Royal Appliance more useful information about the effectiveness of the Dirt Devil advertising than the more traditional measures.

Results of the Strategic Approach

The Dirt Devil Ad—"Humor."   Figure 19.2 summarizes the results of the Strata assessment for the Dirt Devil "Humor" ad. The "diagonal step box" contains the key means–end concepts communicated by the ad. A thin line connects each concept with the mean strength of communication (ranging from 0 to 100). The mean strengths of association (ranging from 0 to 9) between each pair of concepts appear at the intersections of the lines connecting them.

We base our interpretations of these Strata partially on our experiences with other ads. We have found that better ads have linkage ratings in the 7 to 9 range. Also, better ads have average strength of communication ratings for the four components of advertising strategy—message element, consumer benefit, leverage point, and driving force—that range from 70 to 90, 60 to 80, 50 to 60, and 40 to 50, respectively. Relative to these guidelines, the assessment results shown in Fig. 19.2 indicate the humor ad did not deliver a meaningful strategy. The ad did not strongly communicate the concepts—most were below 40 and several were in the low 30s and 20s. Moreover, the ad formed only moderate

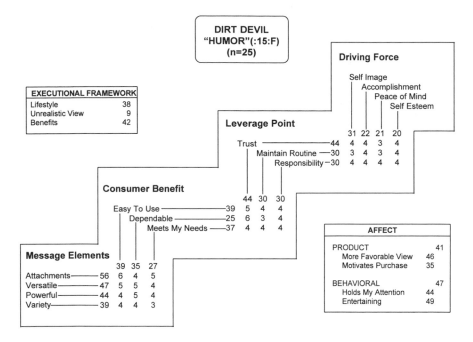

FIG. 19.2. Strata results for the Dirt Devil ad, "Humor."

connections between concepts (linkage ratings were in the 3 to 6 range; most connections were 4 or 5).

Two other sets of data in Fig. 19.2 are noteworthy. The box in the lower right of Fig. 19.2 displays the mean scores for product and ad affect (measured on a 100-point scale). Overall affect scores for the Dirt Devil brand and the ad were moderate (41 and 47, respectively). The box in the upper left of Fig. 19.2 displays the average ratings of the ad's executional framework.

In summary, the strategic assessment indicates that this Dirt Devil ad did not create much brand equity. The ad did not strongly communicate a chain of personally relevant concepts that connected key attributes of the brand to important consequences and personal values of the consumer. Finally, only two concepts—"meets my needs" (a consumer benefit) and "maintain routine" (a leverage point)—were significantly related to brand affect (they had the highest partial correlation with product affect). In our experience, better ads strongly communicate concepts at all four levels of ad strategy, and the concepts at each level tend to correlate with product affect. In sum, the Strata results indicate that "Humor" is a weak ad.

The Dirt Devil Ad—"Montage."   In contrast, the strategic assessment of the Dirt Devil "montage" ad indicates it is more effective than the "humor" ad. The Strata results shown in Fig. 19.3 reveal that this ad effectively communicates concepts at all four levels (many communication strengths are greater than 50, with several in the 70s and 80s). Moreover, the linkage scores are quite strong

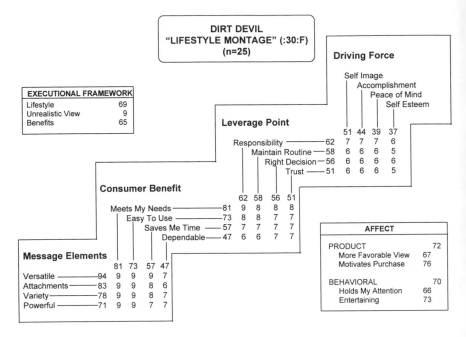

FIG. 19.3. Strata results for the Dirt Devil ad, "Montage."

(ranging from 6 to 9), indicating that the ad also communicated tight connections between the concepts. In addition, brand and ad affect scores were high (in the 70s), indicating very favorable consumer reactions to the ad.

Finally, elements at all four levels in the MECCAS model were related to brand affect. The ad communicated a means–end chain linking "powerful" to "meets my needs" to "responsibility," and on to "self-image." Because each concept correlated with brand affect, these meanings should increase consumers' motivation to purchase a Dirt Devil vacuum. Such a chain of personal relevance could be an effective advertising (and positioning) strategy for Dirt Devil vacuums. In sum, this ad was a winner in creating brand equity. The ad strongly communicated "strategic" concepts at all levels (nearly all scores were greater than 50), created strong linkages between concepts (many ratings from 8 to 9), and created positive brand evaluations.

The Hoover Ad—"Nobody Does It Better." The Hoover ad, "Nobody Does It Better," reflects a slightly different strategy than Dirt Devil's "montage" ad, yet it is nearly as effective in creating positive brand affect and motivating purchase. The Strata results presented in Fig. 19.4 show that this ad communicated many concepts rather well (most communication strength scores were 50 or greater; almost no 30s). Also, the linkage scores were moderately strong (range from 4 to 9). Overall brand and ad affect ratings in the low 60s are respectable. Several means–end concepts related to product affect formed a tightly connected means–end chain linking "attachments" to "easy to use" to "responsibility" and on to "self-image." In sum, the Hoover ad is fairly effective in communicating a meaningful strategy.

Note that the Dirt Devil and Hoover ads, "Montage" and "Nobody Does It Better," seem to be pursuing the same strategy at the leverage point and driving force levels. The key concepts for both ads were "meet my responsibility" and "self-esteem." However, these ads communicate different concepts at the message element and consumer benefit levels. These distinctions illustrate how two similar brands may be differentiated in consumers' minds.

The Regina Ad—"Nuts and Bolts." In contrast, the Regina ad is very weak. As shown in Fig. 19.5, the ad strongly communicated only one concept, "powerful." Unfortunately, "powerful" connected only weakly to other concepts and did not correlate with product affect. The ad communicated virtually no higher level concepts, and produced only modest affect scores for the brand and ad of about 50.

The qualitative results showed that this ad evoked as many counterarguments against purchase as it did positive arguments for purchase. Perhaps this was due to the executional framework that presented a "fantasy demonstration" of the Regina vacuum picking up nuts and bolts (and other items such as paper clips and marbles). Consumers rated the ad as presenting an unrealistic view of the brand and gave it low scores for "fits my lifestyle." Consumers suspect their vacuum will not pick up nuts and bolts without being damaged, and they are not sure why anyone would want to pick up nuts and bolts in the first place. In

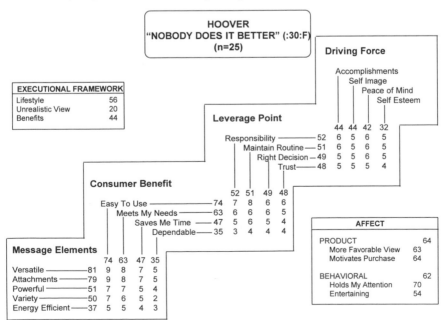

FIG. 19.4. Strata results for the Hoover ad, "Nobody Does It Better."

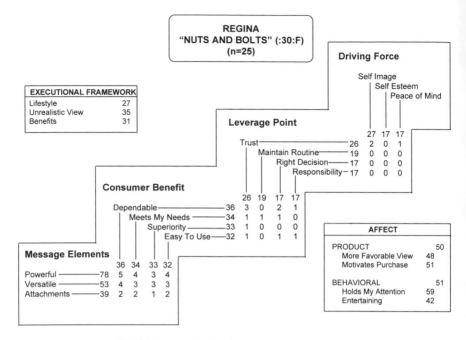

FIG 19.5. Strata results for the Regina ad, "Nuts and Bolts."

sum, the Regina ad did not communicate a means–end chain of personally relevant meanings that connected the brand to the consumer. This ad does not seem to have a communications strategy.

Comparing the Ads. Figure 19.6 summarizes the strategic assessment results for the four ads we tested. The strategic approach clearly shows that the "montage" ad from Dirt Devil is far superior to the "humor" ad and is slightly more effective than the Hoover ad. The "montage" Dirt Devil ad is effective because it strongly connects the product attributes of "strong and powerful" to "meets my needs" to "take care of my basic responsibilities" to a positive "self-image." In sum, the "montage" ad creates a means–end chain that represents how the brand is personally relevant to the consumer.

In contrast, the strategic analyses show the Dirt Devil (humor) ad and the Regina (nuts and bolts) ad to be ineffective. Because they did not communicate connections to upper level value concepts, these ads have no driving force.

Finally, Fig. 19.7 summarizes the mean affect scores for the ads and brands from both studies. Note that the traditional and strategic approaches to ad assessment were consistent in identifying the stronger and weaker ads, but the strategic approach revealed larger and clearer distinctions between the ads. Specifically, the Strata results showed that the "good" ads were much superior to the "bad" ads in communicating a strategy, not just slightly better as indicated by the traditional approach.

Components of Ad Strategy	Dirt Devil "Humor"	Dirt Devil "Montage"	Hoover "Nobody Better"	Regina "Nuts and Bolts"
Driving Force (0 to 100)	---- (0)	Self Image (51)	Self Image (44)	---- (0)
0 to 9	*0*	*7*	*5*	*0*
Leverage Point (0 to 100)	Maintain Daily Routine (30)	Take Care of Basic Responsibilities (62)	Take Care of Basic Responsibilities (52)	Trust Products Made by Company (26)
0 to 9	*4*	*9*	*7*	*3*
Consumer Benefit (0 to 100)	Vacuum Meets My Needs (27)	Vacuum Meets My Needs (81)	Vacuum is Easy to Use (74)	Vacuum is Dependable (36)
0 to 9	*0*	*9*	*9*	*2*
Message Element (0 to 100)	---- (0)	Strong and Powerful (71)	Multiple Attachments (79)	Multiple Attachments (39)
Motivates Purchase	35	76	64	51

FIG. 19.6. Comparisons of four ads on strategic assessment measures.

	Dirt Devil "Humor"		Dirt Devil "Montage"		Hoover "Nobody Better"		Regina "Nuts and Bolts"	
	Survey n=124	Strata n=25	Survey n=123	Strata n=25	Survey n=248	Strata n=25	Survey n=249	Strata n=25
Ad	44	47	49	70	45	62	37	51
Product	45	41	49	72	48	64	44	50

FIG. 19.7. Brand and ad affect scores from traditional and strategic assessment approaches.

Another advantage of the strategic approach is that it provides diagnostic information about why an ad is effective or not. Thus, the strategic approach gives guidance about how to "fix" or improve an ineffective ad (cf. Reynolds & Gengler, 1991). For instance, perhaps the humor ad could be reedited or reshot to better communicate the missing concepts and strengthen the connections between the concepts.

CONCLUSIONS

What can we conclude about the traditional and strategic approaches to measuring advertising effectiveness? Both approaches have utility. The traditional methods are useful for answering specific questions about advertising effects such as: Do consumers remember the ad? Do they recall the brand name? Did they change their belief about Z? However, many of the measures taken in traditional copy testing research do not have clear implications for marketing or advertising strategy. In contrast, the strategic approach places issues of ad effectiveness squarely within the broader perspective of marketing strategy. Effective ads contribute to marketing strategy by communicating the personal relevance of the brand to the consumer.

The strategic approach to measuring advertising effectiveness uses means–end concepts and the MECCAS model to specify an advertising strategy for a brand in terms of which attributes, consequences, and values are to be connected to create perceptions of personal relevance for the brand. Then we can use the Strata methods to assess the effectiveness of an ad in communicating that strategy to the consumer.

In our experience, the most effective ads strongly communicate the key concepts at each level of the ad strategy and also communicate how these concepts are linked together. These means–end perceptions of a brand's personal relevance usually create more positive brand and ad affect and enhance consumers' purchase motivations. Thus, these beliefs about a brand's personal relevance are the basis of brand equity.

REFERENCES

Gutman, J. (1982). A means-end chain model based on consumer categorization processes. *Journal of Marketing, 46*(1), 60–72.

Gutman, J. (1991). Exploring the nature of linkages between consequences and values. *Journal of Business Research, 22*(2), 143–148.

Gutman, J., & Reynolds, T. J. (1987). Coordinating assessment to strategy development: An advertising assessment paradigm based on the MECCAS model. In J. Olson & K. Sentis (Eds.), *Advertising and consumer psychology* (Vol. 3, pp. 242–258). New York: Praeger.

Olson, J. C., & Reynolds, T. J. (1983). Understanding consumers' cognitive structures: Implications for advertising strategy. In L. Percy & A. Woodside (Eds.), *Advertising and consumer psychology* (pp. 77–90). Lexington, MA: Lexington Books.

Perkins, W., & Reynolds, T. J. (1988). The explanatory power of values in preference judgments: Validation of the means-end perspective. In Michael J. Houston (Ed.), *Advances in consumer research* (Vol. 15, pp. 122–126). Provo, UT: Association for Consumer Research.

Reynolds, T. J., & Craddock, A. (1988). The application of the MECCAS model to the development and assessment of advertising strategy: A case study. *Journal of Advertising Research, 28*(2), 43–54.

Reynolds, T. J., & Gengler, C. (1991). A strategic framework for assessing advertising: The animatics vs. finished issue. *Journal of Advertising Research, 31,* 61–71.

Reynolds, T. J., & Gutman, J. (1984). Advertising is image management. *Journal of Advertising Research, 24,* 27–37.

Reynolds, T. J., & Rochon, J. P. (1991). Means-end based advertising research: Copy testing is not strategy assessment. *Journal of Business Research, 22*(2), 131–142.

Walker, B. A., & Olson, J. C. (1991). Means-end chains: Connecting products with self. *Journal of Business Research, 22*(2), 111–118.

Comments on Chapter 19

Christine Wright-Isak
Young & Rubicam, Advertising

PRACTICAL RELEVANCE OF THIS RESEARCH

In the "real world" we always find case examples especially instructive, and chapter 19 offers a fascinating one. Moreover, the discussion itself is based on taken-for-granted assumptions similar to those we hear voiced in agency–client debates over whether the advertising has delivered well.

The idea that copy testing measures effectiveness implies that delivery of the intended message is all there is to being effective. Later in the year when the budget renewal process is underway, we are reminded that sales of the product or service will be a major factor in gauging effectiveness. It is shortsighted to view copy testing as anything other than diagnostic information regarding only one portion of the criteria by which marketers evaluate the full contribution of advertising to their businesses. Chapter 19 does us a service by demonstrating that there is more to be considered.

In contrasting traditional copy testing approaches to judging effectiveness with what they call a strategic approach, Reynolds, Olson, and Rochon go beyond identifying shortcomings in current measurement. They contribute a useful alternative way of thinking for those managers who might read this volume, if only by reminding all of us that performance criteria should be related to intended strategy.

USEFULNESS OF THE FINDINGS

For agencies and clients the most profound limit to the usefulness of this research is its basic assumption that "the fundamental purpose of (brand oriented) advertising is to create, maintain or leverage brand equity" (p. 340). Although (brand-oriented) advertising is of course designed to build and manage equity, there are many situations in everyday agency life in which this is at best a secondary consideration. The introduction of new products and categories as well as price special advertising are two examples.

The importance of considering the purpose of advertising when we evaluate it is indisputable. However, we need to be careful about reducing this thought to just the criterion of personal relevance expressed as, "This brand is right for me. This brand will meet my needs." This perspective is too rational for many of the situations we address in the industry. Nevertheless relevance is a good

356

criterion for the situation in which the authors use it. Placing prime importance on personal relevance as the effectiveness criterion of a brand-building campaign works well for categories with utilitarian appeal to consumers of household products and services, many of which are the bread and butter of the industry.

However, the discussion in chapter 19 implies a system for universal copy evaluation that takes place at the level of strategy. Even in classic packaged goods marketing, there are categories in which *all* the leading brands are relevant. In such well-developed categories as bar soap, for example, the rational- utilitarian approach of linking product attributes to consumer end benefits has been accomplished for most of the leading brands. In this instance relevance gives way to building differentiation in order to gain competitive advantage. For long established major brands this becomes a task of rejuvenating the brand's unique qualities in consumer perceptions, and these are often not qualities physically inherent in the product.

The bar soap category continues to offer us an apt illustration. In the early 1980s, Dove differentiated itself from Caress on user imagery associations because most of the product attributes of these two skin care soaps were comparable. Establishing product differentiation (other than deodorant vs. skin care) was not a reasonable expectation of advertising. Consumer research suggested that establishing brand differentiation was feasible but not by using a rational appeal to product distinctiveness. Instead, Caress distinguished itself from Dove by user imagery, supplemented by references to the purpose of each brand (body bar vs. face soap). Indeed, the product differentiation that did occur in the category was by the new product development and market entry of the Lever 2000 brand, which accomplished both deodorancy and skin softening.

In the future advertising will have to justify its contribution in situations both intangible and abstract compared to those of traditional household products marketing. It will do so by addressing target constituents whose ways of ingesting messages are more complex than a personal relevance via the means–end calculation this model implies. For example, GE has had the "creation of goodwill" as a central objective of its advertising for more than 15 years. GE is certainly doing brand maintenance, management, and leveraging. However, they reach audiences that include the entire investment community, product and corporate division managers who make purchase decisions, and government regulators. The notion of personal relevance may be only indirect for these constituents and applying it to measuring BBDO's efforts to maintain GE's communications goals will be problematic using this model's definition of relevance.

FUTURE RESEARCH POSSIBILITIES

These marketing situations aside, the emphasis in this chapter on diagnosing an ad's effects against its strategic purpose has the clear merit of encouraging managers to think systematically about the role of the advertising they commission. This in turn can lead to making creative direction clearer and more focused. The result will benefit the client–agency partnership by encouraging agreement on reasonable objectives. In addition, the effort to gain insight into brand meanings that are relevant to the consumers who choose them is an important emphasis in the approach advocated in the chapter. Future research might take into account these alternative pathways to creating and managing equity by considering modifying the model to work in categories like perfume or cosmetics. It might also be expanded to include other promotional activities such as sales promotions or events marketing. In all cases it will be necessary to consider the nature of the strategies of persuasion that are required for success in these different motivational arenas.

20

Developing Copy Tests That Estimate Brand Usage

Brian Wansink
University of Illinois, Urbana–Champaign

Michael L. Ray
Stanford University

The growing interest in brand equity is resulting in new advertising objectives for some brands of consumer packaged goods. Some campaigns emphasize *using* the brand instead of simply *choosing* it over a competing brand. That is, many versatile, high-penetration packaged brands are well-suited for advertising campaigns that encourage loyal consumers to use the brand more frequently or in new ways (Wansink, 1994; Wansink & Ray, 1993, 1996). This chapter describes the copy testing measures that most accurately predict whether a campaign will generate increased usage. Such usage-related campaigns are most commonly employed by mature, dominant brands (such as Campbell's Soup), high-loyalty niche brands (such as Grey Poupon), and industry associations (such as the American Dairy Council).

Both industry professionals and academicians have criticized traditional copy testing methods for their inability to capture usage-related responses accurately (Marketing Science Institute, 1983). Measures of purchase intention and brand attitude, for instance, are no longer satisfactory when our interest is in usage. These measures are too insensitive when consumers are brand loyal. Brand attitude measures are often at a ceiling. Furthermore, estimates of purchase intentions become unreliable when the product is already in inventory and must be depleted before it can be repurchased. Indeed, recent studies have shown that the correlations between measures of brand attitude and subsequent usage range only from $-.10$ to $.23$ for heavy users (Wansink & Ray, 1992).

This chapter describes research that examines the validity of different types of usage-related measures that can be reasonably collected in a copy-testing environment. From a managerial standpoint, we suggest measures that would determine which of two campaigns (such as an "Mmm Mmm Good" campaign or a "Soup is Good Food" campaign for Campbell's Soup) would be more effective at increasing usage. In particular, this chapter makes three specific

359

contributions. First, it provides a basic framework for understanding the sequential effects of advertising on usage-related responses. Second, it suggests valid quantitative measures that estimate an ad's impact on usage. Last, it suggests cognitive response elicitation questions that are most sensitive to usage.

After outlining a basic framework for usage-related responses, the results of two copy testing studies are described. The first study shows the quantitative measures that correlated most highly with usage. The second study shows a method that maximizes the sensitivity of cognitive responses toward usage-related thoughts.

HOW ADVERTISING IMPACTS USAGE

An ad can be processed in either a peripheral way or a central way, depending on how much attention a consumer allocates to the ad (Petty, Cacioppo, & Schumann, 1983). Suppose a person spends little time thinking about an ad he or she has just seen. Even if exposure to this ad has no influence on consumer attitudes toward the brand (A_{brand}), the ad may still have an impact on consumption or usage if it simply raises his or her awareness of the brand (Ehrenberg, 1974), thereby increasing the chance that it might be considered for usage (Nedungadi, 1991). Consistent with this, a field study conducted by Seagrams suggested that changes in attitude need not precede changes in the usage frequency of a product. This study analyzed aggregated data from brand loyal consumers (Schiller, Schribner, & Belkin, 1982), showing that consumers who were frequently exposed to Seagrams ads also consumed more of their products. This increase in usage occurred "in the absence of any related increase in product beliefs or in attitude" (see Fig. 20.1). Although this study does not prove causality, its results are consistent with the notion that changes in usage may occur without accompanying changes in attitude.

The more frequently studied route to persuasion is the central route. It suggests that when a consumer views an ad and is highly involved with it, he or she silently generates thoughts about the brand, and these thoughts either alter or fortify beliefs and attitudes about the brand and its use. In turn, these beliefs and attitudes influence usage intentions that eventually influence usage. This perspective is consistent with learning theory and what we would expect when consumers process informational ads (Rossiter & Percy, 1987). Copy testing measures that examine centrally processed measures are the focus of this chapter. The low-involvement processing conditions that exist with peripherally processed messages are not further examined here.

Figure 20.1 shows the points at which we could sample the ad's impact. As researchers, our interest is in determining the measures that suggest future usage, thus eliminating the time and expense of having to collect actual usage measures. It is important to realize that two broad types of measures of ad

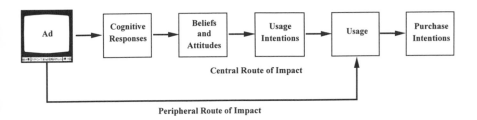

FIG. 20.1. How advertising impacts usage.

effectiveness can be taken in the laboratory without having to take actual usage measures in the field: (a) cognitive responses, and (b) quantitative measures of usage intentions. Both of these can be collected quickly and inexpensively, and can serve complementary purposes.

Determining the Quantitative Measures That Predict Usage

Measures of one's usage intentions (for a particular time period, such as "within the next 2 weeks") can be obtained either through likelihood measures, or through estimates of one's usage volume. Likelihood measures can be directly obtained by asking an individual how likely it will be that he or she uses the brand within an upcoming period. Answers are given on a 7-point scale ranging from 1 (*highly unlikely*) to 7 (*highly likely*). Usage intentions can also be measured by asking one to estimate the volume of a brand he or she might possibly consume within a similar time period.

These two different measures of usage intent have different relative strengths. With infrequent users of a brand, volume estimates will be skewed toward 0 units (especially over a relatively short period of time). This is partially a drawback of numerical estimates that provide no gradation between 0 and 1 unit. In such cases, volume estimates would provide less variance and less information than an estimate of usage likelihood. As a result, usage likelihood estimates would allow a greater gradation in response and would be more sensitive in detecting any potentially different effects these ads might have on usage.

In contrast, with frequent or heavy users of a brand, a volume estimate is likely to be more accurate than a likelihood estimate. This is because the distribution of these volume estimates is more likely to be normal (Pearl, 1981). As a result, a volume estimate of one's usage intent is likely to provide more variance and more information about the intended usage of heavy users than is a likelihood measure, which would undoubtedly be at or near 100% probable. Under these circumstances, volume estimates would be a more accurate estimate of a heavy user's usage volume of a brand.

Empirical Findings

The effectiveness of these different measures was examined by Wansink and Ray (1992) when they exposed 239 subjects from parent–teacher associations to a series of ads for one of three different brands (Campbell's Soup, Jell-O Brand Gelatin, and Ocean Spray Cranberry Sauce). The correspondence between intentions and usage was most impressive when the subjects were segmented into heavy users and light users based on their prior year's usage of the brand. Consumers who consumed more than the median amount for each brand were classified as relatively heavy users, and the rest as light users (Jacoby & Chestnut, 1978).

In general, both measures of usage intention (likelihood and volume estimates) were effective in predicting subsequent usage, depending on how frequently one has tended to consume the brand in the past. As shown in Table 20.1, heavy users of the brands were more accurate in estimating their usage volume than in estimating their likelihood of using these three products ($r =$ .62, .46, and .23, respectively). In contrast, light users of the brands were unable to accurately estimate their usage volume but were instead much more accurate in estimating the usage likelihood ($r =$ .42, .78, and .49, respectively). When contrasted with research that indicates that usage volume predictions are often very low (Cassidy, 1981; Pilgrim, 1957), the results from Table 20.1 show that volume predictions can be very accurate when frequent users are examined.

Implications for Increasing Predictive Validity

These results illustrate two key concepts. First, brand attitude measures will not always be sensitive enough to dectect usage-related responses from ads. Second, usage intentions can be measured through likelihood estimates or through volume estimates, and each measure is effective under different circumstances. As seen in Table 20.1, heavy users of a given brand are most accurate when predicting their future usage volume. Light users are most accurate when predicting their likelihood of consuming the brand.

These results can be extended to entire product categories. That is, if a researcher is trying to estimate the impact that an ad will have on the usage of a product category that is infrequently consumed (relative to other categories) likelihood measures may be more generally accurate than volume measures. However, if the product category is one that is frequently consumed (relative to other categories) volume measures may be more accurate. In this study, for example, the typical household ate 29.1 cans of soup per year, but only 2.7 cans of cranberry sauce. Given a larger sample of subjects, we would likely find that soup is a product category where usage intentions are best estimated through volume measures, whereas usage intentions for cranberry sauce would be best estimated through likelihood measures (see Fig. 20.2). This relationship should be even stronger when examining the heavy users of a frequently consumed

TABLE 20.1
Correlations Between Usage Intention Measures and Actual Usage

		Light Users			Heavy Users	
	$\bar{X}^a$	Likelihood of Usage[b]	Volume of Usage[c]	$\bar{X}$	Likelihood of Usage	Volume of Usage
Campbell's Soup	.9 cans	.42[*]	.15	4.2 cans	.19	.62[**]
Jell-O Brand Gelatin	.3 boxes	.78[**]	.58[*]	1.3 boxes	.23	.46*
Ocean Spray Cranberry Sauce	.1 cans	.49[*]	.22	.4 cans	.04	.21
All brands (aggregated)		.47[*]	.16		.20	.60[**]

[a]Number of units consumed each month. [b]1 = very unlikely; 9 = very likely. [c]Volume of usage in units.
[*]$p < .05$. [**]$p < .01$.

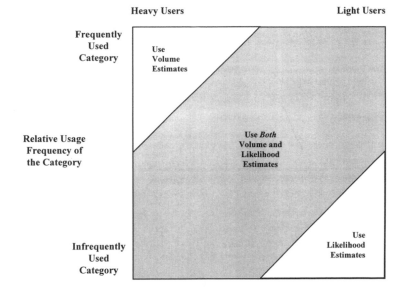

FIG. 20.2. Usage intention measures that correspond most closely to actual usage.

category, or when examining the light users of an infrequently consumed category. Indeed, as can be seen in Table 20.1, volume estimates provided relatively accurate estimates of usage for heavy users ($r = .62$) of soup, and likelihood estimates provided relatively accurate estimates of usage for light users ($r = .49$) of cranberry sauce.

The findings described here underscore the importance of usage-related measures over the simple measures of attitude that are typically collected during copy testing. Specifically, it is important to understand that volume estimates best approximate the actual usage of heavy users (or of frequently consumed brands) and that likelihood estimates are best used with light users (or with infrequently consumed brands). More specific diagnostic information, such as usage-related thoughts and feelings, can be obtained by examining the specific thoughts that consumers generate when viewing these ads.

ELICITING USAGE-RELATED COGNITIVE RESPONSES

Understanding the effectiveness of an ad is greatly aided by knowing a consumer's thoughts as he or she views that ad. These thoughts help us better estimate the impact these ads will have on attitudes and usage, and they also suggest ways in which the ads can be changed to be more effective. Unfortunately, the traditional procedure by which these thoughts are elicited may not yield valid or reliable findings (Russo, Johnson, & Stephens, 1989).

The initial research with cognitive responses (or verbal protocols) was pioneered by Greenwald (1968) and then introduced into advertising by Wright (1973). Their work indicated that cognitive responses can mirror the actual thoughts that occur to people as they evaluate a persuasive message. In these studies, cognitive responses are typically elicited with instructions such as, "Write down any thoughts that went through your mind while reading the ad." These written thoughts are typically coded as either counterarguments, support arguments, or source derogations (Smead, Wilcox, & Wilkes, 1981; Wright, 1973).

One problem with this coding scheme is that it does not specifically address thoughts that are usage related, nor does it necessarily encourage thoughts that could be of diagnostic value. Although a multitude of thoughts may be generated as one views an advertisement, only a small percentage of them will actually be communicated (Kidder, 1980; Wright & Rip, 1980). After subjects see an ad, they are typically asked to record their thoughts when viewing it. These instructions are general, and a portion of the random thoughts that result could be minimized if subjects had a better idea of what is expected of them (Ericsson & Simon, 1984). In short, when a researcher is focusing on usage-related thoughts, the conventional procedure of simply asking for general reactions may not be as useful as procedures or questions that are less ambiguous.

Two Options for Eliciting Usage-Related Responses

A person viewing an ad may generate many thoughts about cognitive responses, but not all of them will be communicated because of time constraints or cognitive capacity constraints (Ericsson & Simon, 1984). To uncover these thoughts about a particular target issue, researchers have used either preexposure elicitation exercises or directed postexposure instructions.

If a subject is given no instructions prior to their exposure to an ad, he or she is free to think of any issues that come to mind. Preexposure elicitation exercises (such as practice tests or examples) frame a subject's processing by suggesting a range of issues one might consider. One way this can be accomplished is by providing subjects with a hypothetical example or illustration of what another subject might have written when he or she viewed a related ad (Keller, 1987). A second way this is accomplished is by providing subjects with a practice trial that is followed with standardized feedback. The feedback, for instance, can be presented in the form of a prewritten checklist that instructs them to reread their responses to ensure that they are not simply writing down a replay of the ad (Batra, 1984). In short, providing subjects with preexposure elicitation exercises intensifies their processing of these target issues during exposure.

In contrast, giving directed postexposure instructions to subjects after they view an ad encourages them to cognitively edit their less relevant thoughts before writing them down. One way this can be accomplished is by instructing subjects to address specific issues of interest (Wright, 1980). For instance, a researcher can ask subjects how they feel about using the product, if they agree or disagree with the ad, or if it reminds them of any past experiences with the product (Wright & Rip, 1980).

Preexposure elicitation exercises and directed postexposure instructions both share risks of potential reactivity. The primary concern is that these procedures may "force" a subject to generate thoughts about a particular target issue that would have otherwise never occurred to them Nisbett & Wilson, 1977; Turner, 1986). As a result, such thoughts would be invalid, and would bias outcome measures such as beliefs, attitudes, or intentions. A direct way of testing for reactivity is by measuring the impact these different procedures have on critical outcome variables (Russo et al., 1989). Nonreactive procedures should have no influence on the ratings of outcome variable when compared to that of a control group. In other words, if these different procedures are nonreactive, there should be no difference in the ratings of A_{brand}, A_{ad}, and usage intentions among subjects who are given preexposure elicitation exercises, directed postexposure instructions, or neither.

Empirical Findings

The effectiveness of these two different elicitation methods was examined in a study that involved 74 adults who were recruited from parent–teacher associations, and who were given $6.00 for their effort (see Wansink, Ray, & Batra, 1994, for details). This study found that using either preexposure elicitation exercises or directed postexposure instructions increased the number of usage-related thoughts generated by subjects, but was not reactive. That is, there were no corresponding differences in the ratings of A_{brand}, A_{ad}, or usage intentions among subjects who were given preexposure elicitation exercises, directed postexposure instructions, or neither.

In a general sense, these results are consistent with what Batra (1984) found when examining different types of elicitation exercises for different dependent variables. Batra's results showed that general instructions can be as effective as directed instructions, but only when accompanied by some form of vivid preelicitation exercise or illustration, such as an example or a practice trial.

When should preexposure exercises be used in favor of directed postexposure instructions? It is important to realize that both options are not always available. Involving subjects in preexposure exercises is not always feasible, and it can be constrained by the experimental design or time limitations. Under such circumstances, directed postexposure instructions are the best alternative. When preexposure exercises can be used, Fig. 20.3 suggests that they might elicit more thoughts about a target issue. It is important to note that the combination of the two procedures, however, provides no greater sensitivity than does either by itself.

A General Method for Increasing Cognitive Response Sensitivity

Research dealing with cognitive responses is important because of the generalizations it makes regarding the cognitive response sensitivity (see also Wansink, Ray, & Baatra, 1994). In doing so, it suggests a general pretesting

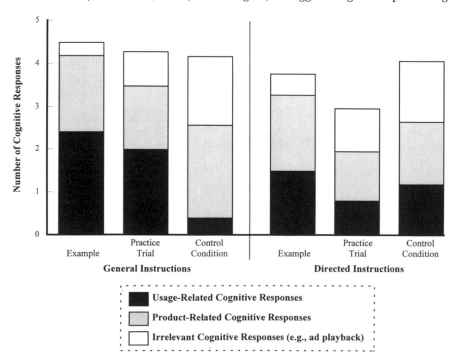

FIG. 20.3. Types of cognitive responses generated by various elicitation methodologies.

method that can help researchers determine what procedure will be most appropriate for eliciting usage-related cognitive responses. The general four-step method follows:

1. Select a number of preexposure elicitation exercises and directed postexposure instructions believed to provide the greatest level of sensitivity toward usage-related responses. Be certain to include a control condition.
2. Design the study by having the various procedures under examination represent between-subjects factors. Statistical power can be increased by having subjects respond to multiple ads. Care should be taken to ensure that subjects are from a comparable pool as those who will be involved in the future studies.
3. Include outcome variables of interest to confirm that the different procedures do not generate reactivity (such as A_{brand}, A_{ad}, and usage intentions).
4. Select the elicitation procedure that best achieves the objectives of the study without affecting outcome variables relative to the control condition. For instance, an objective may involve selecting the procedure that maximizes usage-related thoughts and minimizes unrelated thoughts such as ad playback.

This section emphasizes the importance of increasing the usage-related sensitivity of cognitive response elicitation procedures. Furthermore, it illustrates the steps a researcher must go through if he or she wishes to develop a stylized elicitation procedure for his or her own program of research. The study described here is taken from an ongoing program of research that suggests that either preexposure elicitation exercises (such as practice trials or prior exposure), or directed postexposure instructions can increase this sensitivity without appearing to be reactive.

SUMMARY

When the objective of an advertising campaign is to increase the usage frequency of a packaged good, copy testing measures must be sensitive to this objective. Because measuring actual usage can be prohibitive in terms of time and money, two more primary measures—cognitive responses and usage-intention measures—show promise because of their validity and diagnostic value.

These findings underscore the importance of taking usage-related measures in copy tests, instead of simply attitude measures of purchase intentions. Specifically, it is important to understand that volume estimates best approximate the actual usage of heavy users or frequently consumed brands, and that likelihood estimates are more accurate with light users or with infrequently consumed brands. Additional information about these ads can be obtained by examining the thoughts or cognitive responses that are generated by these ads.

These cognitive responses can best be examined using either preexposure elicitation exercises or directed postexposure instructions. Early evidence suggests that either procedure can effectively increase the number of thoughts a respondent communicates about a particular target issue, and that they may not be reactive.

ACKNOWLEDGMENTS

The first author is grateful to the Stanford Graduate School of Business Doctoral Program, and the University of Illinois for the generous financial support they have provided. He also gratefully acknowledges financial support received in conjunction with the Marketing Science Institute's Alden G. Clayton Doctoral Dissertation Proposal Competition award.

REFERENCES

Batra, R. (1984). *Low involvement message reception—Processes and advertising implications.* Unpublished doctoral dissertation, Graduate School of Business, Stanford University, Stanford, CA.

Cassidy, C. M. (1981). Collecting data on American food consumption patterns: An anthropological perspective. In Food and Nutrition Board National Research Council (Ed.), *Assessing changing food consumption patterns* (pp. 135-154). Washington, DC: National Academy Press.

Ehrenberg, A. S. C. (1974). Repetitive advertising and the consumer. *Journal of Advertising, 14*(2), 25-34.

Ericsson, K. A., & Simon, H. A. (1984). *Protocol analysis: Verbal reports ad data.* Cambridge, MA: MIT Press.

Greenwald, A. G. (1968). Cognitive learning, cognitive response to persuasion, and attitude change. In A. G. Greenwald, T. C. Brock, & T. C. Ostrom (Eds.), *Psychological foundations of attitudes* (pp. 63–102). New York: Academic Press.

Jacoby, J., & Chestnut, R. W. (1978). *Brand loyalty: Measurement and management.* New York: Wiley.

Keller, K. L. (1987, December). Memory factors in advertising: The effect of advertising retrieval cues on brand evaluations. *Journal of Consumer Research, 14,* 316–324.

Kidder, L. H. (1980). *Research methods in social relations.* New York: Holt, Rinehart & Winston.

Marketing Science Institute. (1983). *Beyond recall.* Cambridge, MA: Author.

Nedungadi, P. (1991, December). Recall and consumer consideration sets: Influencing choice without altering brand evaluations. *Journal of Consumer Research, 23–276.*

Nisbett, R. E., & Wilson, T. D. (1977). Telling more than we can know: Verbal reports on mental processes. *Psychological Review, 84,* 231–259.

Pearl, R. B. (1981). Possible alternative methods for data collection on food consumption and expenditures. In Food and Nutrition Board National Research Council (Ed.), *Assessing changing food consumption patterns* (pp. 198–203). Washington, DC: National Academy Press.

Petty, R. E., Cacioppo, J. T., & Schumann, D. W. (1983). Central and peripheral routes to advertising effectiveness: The moderating role of involvement. *Journal of Consumer Research, 10,* 134–148.

Pilgrim, F. J. (1957). The components of food acceptance and their measurement. In J. Brozek (Ed.), *Symposium on nutrition and behavior* (pp. 69–73). New York: National Academy Press.

Rossiter, J. R., & Percy, L. (1987). *Advertising and promotion management.* New York: McGraw-Hill.

Russo, J. E., Johnson, E. J., & Stephens, D. L. (1989). The validity of verbal protocols. *Memory and Cognition, 17*(6), 759–769.

Schiller, C., Schribner, R. J., & Belkin, M. (1982). *A study of the effectiveness of advertising frequency in magazines* (Report prepared by Time Incorporated in association with Joseph E. Seagram and Sons, Inc). New York: Time, Inc.

Smead, R. J., Wilcox, J. B., & Wilkes, R. E. (1981, June). How valid are product descriptions and protocols in choice experiments? *Journal of Consumer Research, 8,* 37–42.

Turner, C. K. (1986). Don't blame memory for people's faulty reports on what influences their judgments. *Personality and Social Psychology Bulletin, 14,* 622–629.

Wansink, B. (1994). Advertising's impact on category substitution. *Journal of Marketing Research, 21*(4), 95–105.

Wansink, B., & Ray, M. L. (1992, May–June). Estimating an advertisement's impact on one's consumption of a brand. *Journal of Advertising Research, 32,* 9–16.

Wansink, B., & Ray, M. L. (1993). Expansion advertising's impact on brand equity. In D. A. Aaker & A. L. Biel (Eds.), *Advertising and building strong brands* (pp. 177–194). Cambridge, MA: Lexington Books.

Wansink, B., & Ray, M. L. (1996). Advertising strategies to increase usage frequency. *Journal of Marketing, 60*(1), 31–46.

Wansink, B., Ray, M. L., & Batra, R. (1994). Increasing the sensitivity of cognitive responses. *Journal of Advertising, 23*(2), 62–74.

Wright, P. L. (1973, February). The cognitive processes mediating acceptance of advertising. *Journal of Marketing Research, 10,* 53–62.

Wright, P. L. (1980, September). Message-evoked thoughts: Persuasion research using thought verbalizations. *Journal of Consumer Research, 7,* 151–175.

Wright, P. L., & Rip, P. (1980). Retrospective reports on consumer decision processes. In J. C. Olson (Ed.), *Advances in consumer research* (Vol. 7, pp. 146–147). Ann Arbor, MI: Association for Consumer Research.

21

Evaluating the Effectiveness of Place-Based Media

James Lucas
Frankel & Company

David Prensky
Trenton State College

Place-based media have elicited a great deal of interest in recent years. This is evidenced by the emergence of new place-based vehicles such as instant coupon dispensers; video carts; in-store radio, TV, and video; package billboards; airport television; and electronic kiosks (Smith, 1993). The popularity of place-based media stems in part from manufacturers search for new marketing tactics to aid in the execution of strategies (Blattberg & Glazer, 1994). The popularity of in-store displays stems from their effectiveness, and growing competition for limited retail space has given rise to new techniques such as merchandising hardware, signage, and shelf tags.

At the same time, the physical layout of retail stores has been evolving. Mass merchandiser, department store, convenience store, gas station, and restaurant formats have changed dramatically not only in physical layout but in offerings as well. According to the Food Marketing Institute (1989), food stores have become larger, encompass a diverse range of formats, and have witnessed an emergence of nontraditional and nonfood departments. Additionally, studies by Nielsen Marketing Research (1990a, 1990b, 1990c) point to the blurring of traditional boundaries among grocery, drug, and mass merchandisers, and to changes in in-store merchandising activities. As a result, both retailers and manufacturers have been rethinking their approach to in-store communications with customers.

The focus of this chapter is place-based media. Place-based media encompass a wide range of away from home media, such as in-store displays, shelf-talkers, shopping carts, aisle signage, sampling, in-store television, and interactive kiosks. More specifically, the focus is on place-based media that are relatively proximate to the purchase. These include point-of-purchase and point-of-sale media that occur at the confluence of message, customers and product or service. The perspective developed in this chapter is based on a wide variety of product or service categories. The categories include, but are not limited to, packaged goods, restaurants, mass merchandisers, service retailers, entertainment, financial services, and the travel industry.

Our description of the perspective begins with a discussion of some of the main similarities and differences between place-based media and more traditional electronic and print media. We discuss and use a brand experience approach as a framework for looking at place-based media. This leads to a discussion of the multidimensional nature of the effectiveness of place-based media programs. Finally, we outline a multidimensional process for developing strategies and tactics that deal with multiple constituencies and for measuring program effectiveness through the development process.

DIFFERENCES BETWEEN PLACE-BASED
AND TRADITIONAL MEDIA

Place-based media and programs often have the same objectives as more traditional electronic and print media advertising. As is the case for many marketing communications, the communications objectives typically include generating awareness; conveying information and understanding; and stimulating trial, repeat, and trade-up purchases at the individual consumer level. To achieve these objectives, marketers must be aware of the intrusiveness and relevance of their communications. These individual-level objectives are intended to help the marketer achieve aggregate business objectives such as building brand equity and loyalty and increasing sales, profit, or market share.

Although place-based media have similar communication objectives as traditional advertising media, they differ in some important ways: proximity to purchase, short life span, and local variation in execution. Proximity to purchase is an important difference. Place-based media tend to be more proximate in place and time to purchases, and because of this proximity they are often targeted to more qualified prospects. This proximity also means that they are frequently called on to serve as environmental cues or reminders. The life span and the salience of place-based media also tend to be different. Because place-based media are often tied to promotions and trade deals, they tend to have short life spans, and they tend to be more subtle and generate less top-of-mind awareness. Place-based media tend to be more susceptible to local variations and inconsistent execution. It is difficult to make a "national buy" of place-based media, so they tend to be dependent on store configuration and proper execution by the sales force and retail trade personnel.

THE CHANGING MARKETING ENVIRONMENT

The marketing environment has evolved during the past decade. Some of this evolution has come at the hands of marketers themselves, some from a changing population, and some from other environmental pressures. Changes include the following:

- Fragmentation of the mass market.
- Rise of personalized buying strategies.
- Consumers who are more knowledgeable and critical of marketing efforts.
- More cluttered retail and marketing communications environments.
- Blurring of traditional boundaries among retail classes of trade and between retailers and manufacturers.
- Increased localization and micromarketing efforts.
- Rise of total quality management (TQM) and customer satisfaction programs.
- Increased accountability.
- Marketing information revolution.

The evolution of the marketing environment points to the need for a shift in how marketers approach communication planning.

THE BRAND EXPERIENCE™ APPROACH

Today's marketers can be thought of as managing a portfolio of marketing funds. This is an apt analogy in light of the general industry view that marketers must do more with less resources as companies downsize and seek to reduce costs. Increased accountability and increasingly detailed marketing information means more scrutiny of the way that managers achieve results as well as how they measure their achievements (Farquhar, Han, & Ijiri, 1991; Schultz & Wang, 1994; Srivastava & Shocker, 1991). Therefore, marketers must show that their communications programs effectively use the firms resources to achieve business objectives by demonstrating how they achieve communications objectives—affecting the knowledge, perceptions, and behaviors of consumers. For example, Schultz and Wang (1994) discussed the need for a fundamentally new approach for communications planning to replace the traditional emphasis on mass media.

The traditional role of mass media assumes the hierarchy of effects model that Lavidge and Steiner (1961) developed to describe the communications that influence consumers at each step in the purchase process. Lavidge and Steiner (1961) divided the purchase process into its component steps: awareness, knowledge, preference, and purchase. The hierarchy of effects model posits that consumers move from thinking to feeling to action as they become aware, gather information, form attitudes, and make purchase decisions. It emphasizes consumers orderly progression from cognition to affect to behavior, and assumes that marketers will develop communications programs that use appropriate content to influence consumers at each step as they proceed through the purchase process.

In our experience the hierarchical effects model is still valid in particular situations—for some new product introductions and new market expansions—but it is not equally applicable to all situations or all consumers. Some consumers might become aware of a new car model, gather information and develop attitudes toward it, and then buy. However, many advertising and consumer researchers criticize the model because of its strong assumption that consumers move from thinking to feeling to action. For example, some consumers might buy a new soda because they see a display for it in the store, and later form their attitudes toward it.

An approach that focuses on the dynamic complexity of the consumer purchase process and the changing marketing environment is needed. Such an approach must recognize the interrelationships among cognition, affect, and behavior but focus on changing behavior. It should recognize that consumers move back and forth among the component steps in the process and that their knowledge, preferences for a product, and behavior are affected simultaneously by many kinds of marketing communications. Because consumers must integrate the many messages that they receive through the multiple media now available, it is vital to devise some way to integrate the marketing communications efforts for a product (Schultz, Tannenbaum, & Lauterborn, 1993; Thorson & Moore, 1996). The stream of integrated marketing communications must be coherent and consistent because consumers will receive a flood of disarrayed information from many messages delivered through a variety of different media. Each component of the communications plan must be delivered in a way that provides a consistent image to consumers and that moves the consumer toward purchase, however and whenever it is received.

The Brand Experience™ approach is used as the starting point for our perspective. A consumer's brand experience is his or her overall experience or satisfaction with a brand and is shaped by many brand contacts. Brand contacts include advertising, public relations, packaging, promotions, product or service consumption, after-purchase experience, and so on (see Fig. 21.1). Thus, it is important to design brand contacts in a manner consistent with what is to be communicated about a brand to produce the desired perceptions and behavior. This is especially important for place-based programs that tend to be of shorter

Brand Contacts
Advertising
Public relations
Word-of-mouth
Promotions
In-store
After purchase experience
Product/service

Brand Experience

FIG. 21.1. Brand experience and brand contacts.

duration, be more proximate to purchase, and reach more qualified consumers. For example, a consumer who experiences an out-of-stock when he or she tries to buy a promoted item is likely to have a negative view of both retailer and manufacturer.

The Brand Experience™ perspective recognizes the interactive nature of contacts, perceptions, and behavior in creating the overall experience. The process that shapes consumer experiences of a brand is not the simple linear one that is described by the hierarchy of effects model. Brand experience is an integrative approach in that it views any brand contact as having a potential positive or negative effect on consumers. Moreover, because the goal is often to change the "brand landscape," an integrated approach is necessary if multiple brand contacts are to produce the desired experience for consumers and achieve business objectives.

Because Brand Experience™ focuses on the behaviors that result from brand contacts, it is consistent with the increasing need for accountability. This focus is also consistent with TQM and customer satisfaction approaches being adopted by many firms. Ongoing monitoring is a crucial component of this approach. Brand experience is monitored over time as a means for maintaining or improving "quality." It is based on the same logic as the process control charts used to monitor quality and continuous improvement in TQM programs (Deming, 1992; McClave & Benson, 1991).

Finally, a brand experience approach serves as a means to link the strategic with the tactical. It helps focus efforts against the brand contacts that produce desired changes in consumer knowledge, perceptions, and behavior. This requires: (a) an understanding of how contacts influence a customer's experience, and (b) monitoring the extent of influence on consumer behavior—for example, visits, trade-up purchases, sales, share, and so on.

THE MULTIDIMENSIONAL NATURE OF EFFECTIVENESS

At first glance, it appears that the effects of place-based media are easier to measure because they produce results quickly (Schultz, Robinson, & Petrison, 1993). In-store displays probably represent the best example of quick and measurable responses (Blattberg et al., 1994; Blattberg & Neslin, 1990; Lodish, 1986).[1] Although sales responses to in-store displays vary by category, it is not unusual to see significant increases in sales with the presence of in-store displays. This impact has captured the interest of manufacturers and retailers alike.

---

[1]The issue of short- and long-term effects as well as issues of profitability and the incremental contribution of displays, price reductions, coupons, and so on, are important issues not discussed here. For discussions of these issues see Jones (1990), Lodish, (1986), Blattberg and Neslin (1990), Schultz and Wang (1994), and Farquhar et al. (1991).

The difficulty of evaluating place-based programs becomes apparent in those situations where scanner data are not available. Such situations show that the difficulty is not simply the result of a lack of scanner data; rather, it stems from the multidimensional nature of effectiveness. Even with the advent of marketing mix models, it is difficult to evaluate the effect of individual place-based elements of a program because they typically coincide with other elements of the program or event. One of the drawbacks of such an approach is the limited ability of econometric models to separate simultaneous effects of several exogenous variables (Srivastava & Shocker, 1991).

First, in evaluating the effectiveness of place-based media, the different constituencies or audiences being addressed must be kept in mind, as well as numerous objectives against which effectiveness can be judged. This requires understanding of consumers, core and functional marketing groups, the sales force, and the trade and other channel members. A program typically has to deliver against goals for many, if not all, of these constituencies.

Second, measures of effectiveness vary through the course of the development process for a program. The measures by which one determines potential profitability versus post hoc profitability differ greatly.

Third, as is the case with traditional advertising programs, different vehicles or elements of a program are designed to play different roles. Therefore, they must be judged against different effectiveness criteria.

Constituencies

Although the brand experience of consumers represents an important focal point for this process, other participants or constituencies must be considered in the course of design and implementation of place-based media. Brand equity also resides with these nonconsumer audiences (e.g., service delivery, marketing support, and performance history of the manufacturer). Because place-based programs are heavily dependent on constituencies for their execution, their consideration is especially important. In essence, each new program represents an attempt not only to appeal to consumers, but to provide multiple constituencies with information relevant to execution of a program. The manufacturer must persuade all constituencies of the viability of the program (see Fig. 21.2).

Constituencies must understand how a place-based program works and perceive it to be worthwhile before they will invest time and effort. For example, proprietary research conducted among trade and retail constituencies across a number of different place-based programs, including a wide range of different types of program elements, has indicated a strong relationship between perceived effectiveness of a program element and proper execution and use ($r^2 = .54$; see Fig. 21.3). Such perceptions influence not only constituencies' willingness to use elements of place-based programs, but also their willingness to invest the time in executing them properly. Importantly, perceptions influence beliefs

FIG. 21.2. Measures of effectiveness of brand contacts for key constituencies.

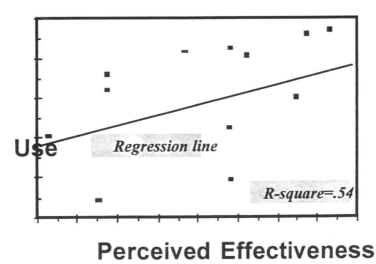

Perceived Effectiveness

FIG. 21.3. Relationship between perceived effectiveness and use of place-based elements.

about the types of programs and vehicles that should be used in the future, as well as future participation by trade customers (Blattberg & Glazer, 1994).

MEASURING EFFECTIVENESS THROUGH
THE DEVELOPMENT PROCESS

What constitutes an effective place-based program varies by constituency and stage in the developmental process. The development process has four stages: concept viability, strategic development, preproduction testing, and in-market monitoring (see Fig. 21.4).

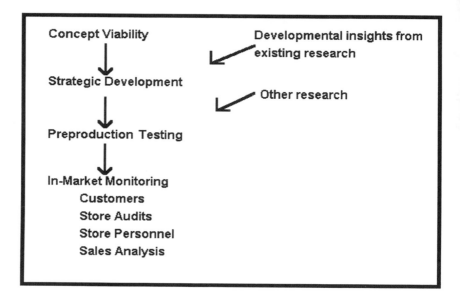

FIG. 21.4. An approach to measuring effectiveness throughout the development process.

Concept Viability Stage

We begin with what we refer to as the *concept viability stage*. Here proxy measures are used to gauge components of a potentially effective merchandising or promotional effort: (a) the property, which may encompass: celebrity spokespersons, current cultural artifacts (movies, electronic games, events, etc.), themes such as holidays, seasonal themes, and grand openings; and (b) offers that typically refer to the actual rules, terms, awards or rewards, and so on. Concept viability research helps determine consumer interest and appeal of properties and themes, as well as the relevancy and understandability of an offer. This stage includes consideration of:

- Properties
  - Celebrities.
  - Current cultural artifacts (movies, electronic games, or events).
  - Themes (holiday, seasonal, or grand openings).
- Offers
  - Structure, rules, awards, prizes, and so on.
- Measures
  - Appeal and interest.
  - Relevancy.
  - Understandability.
  - Image of brand.
  - Attitudes and behavior.

Strategic Development Stage

After determining the viability of a particular concept, it is important to develop and refine the strategic and tactical direction. This stage entails exploring which attributes and benefits are most leverageable, most consistent with the brand, and best able to help convey the communication objective. At this point in the process it is also important to obtain feedback from constituencies such as the sales force and retail and trade personnel regarding how easily the program can be executed.

The elements of the refined version of a concept must be tested among consumers to determine their appeal, and among other constituencies to judge their viability and interest. This stage includes consideration of:

Consumers:
   Appeal and interest
   Leverageable attributes and benefits
   Consistency with brand
   Communication objective
   Diagnostics

Other Constituencies:
   Operations/Sales
   Logistical viability

Retail Personnel
   Viability
   Helpfulness

Preproduction Testing

Preproduction testing provides invaluable diagnostic information about message playback and potential areas of confusion. At the same time, pretesting allows for an evaluation of how effectively each element of a place-based program is achieving its intended communication objectives. This step provides valuable direction for execution of the program.

Although environments are variable and norms are scarce, preproduction testing provides an excellent opportunity to learn before the program is executed. Often, this stage requires unique testing methods such as computer simulation, virtual reality, slide simulations, eye tracking, or time-lapsed video. It includes consideration of:

Consumers:
   Intrusiveness
   Message playback
   Confusion

Other Constituencies
(Sales and retail personnel):
   Diagnostic Feedback
   Versioning

In-Market Monitoring

In-market monitoring affords many opportunities to measure the various dimensions of effectiveness. It provides the best arena for understanding how brand contacts are affecting brand experience, as well as how effectively the program performed on measures important to other audiences. Has the effort attracted incremental customers, sales, and profits. Has the effort conveyed the communication objectives, and changed perceptions? Have the elements been used in the store, were they easy for store personnel to implement and use, and so on? Several methods of measurement are needed to answer these questions:

- Sales information.
- Store audits to measure use, placement, and other executional elements.
- Surveys of store personnel.
- Consumer surveys.

It is important to measure both attitudes and behavior, and it is important to study all major constituencies. This information serves not just to evaluate the effectiveness of the current program, but also to guide future efforts. In-market monitoring affords the most opportunity for measuring the major dimensions of effectiveness. It includes consideration of:

Consumers:	Other Constituencies:	Environmental Assessment:
Attitude, trial, and use	Surveys of store and sales personnel	Place conditions
Trade area analysis	Profitability	Execution
Exit surveys		Clutter
Sales/share analysis		

THE LOGIC FOR MEASURING EFFECTIVENESS

The logic behind measuring effectiveness, both at the individual and aggregate levels, stems from the desire to understand how brand contacts work and the type of impact they have on a brand.

Exploration and Understanding

Monitoring customers' brand experience can be viewed from both the individual consumer and aggregate business levels. Examination of the consumers brand experience at the individual level provides valuable diagnostic information about the influence of specific contacts on brand experience. Contacts will meet, exceed, and fall short of acceptable expectations, as shown in the top panel of Fig. 21.5. Exploration and understanding serve as the basis for the development and execution of effective marketing communications strategies. Qualitative research, communications testing, tracking studies, and other formal and informal measurements provide the information necessary for

Individual's Experience

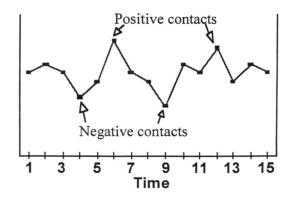

Aggregate Experience

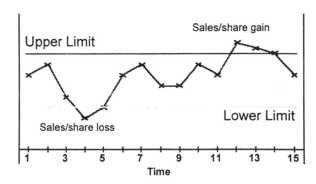

FIG. 21.5. Monitoring brand experience.

developing fact-based (i.e., empirically derived) communications strategies. Because this step requires understanding the consumers psychological and social purchase dynamics as well as environmental effects, it often requires more than a single study.

Evaluation

At the aggregate level, monitoring of brand experience provides a means of evaluating brand performance in a manner akin to the process control charts used in TQM. Aggregate-level monitoring provides a method for evaluating the impact of brand contacts and the effectiveness of strategy and tactics. This type of analysis should focus on the impact of program elements, environmental trends, and the relationship among the marketers own programs and those of competitors and other channel members. Aggregate-level monitoring is essential for completing the development process. It addresses the need for accountability and provides one of a marketing organization's most important tools for mapping future communication strategy and tactics.

DISCUSSION

The increased interest in and use of place-based media by both manufacturers and retailers make it an important topic of study. Although place-based media share many of the objectives of more traditional media, the ways in which they differ require a new way of looking at the development of communications strategy.

The Brand Experience™ approach represents a paradigm that provides a new way of looking at the development of communications strategy. Its focus on behavior helps it address many of the issues facing marketers today, such as multiple audiences and the proliferation of new media. The approach also takes into account the need for measurement at different points in the development process. Moreover, the brand experience approach is consistent with the manner in which many marketers make marketing decisions—for example, share and profit accountability, TQM, and customer satisfaction.

The brand experience approach serves two important functions. First, its objective is to develop brand contacts that produce a consistent brand experience. A behavioral focus, rather than a message content focus, helps ensure integration of communication efforts. Second, the logic underlying the brand experience approach provides a strong linkage between strategy and tactics—understanding how contacts affect consumer knowledge, perception, and behavior at the individual level as well as evaluating how well they meet business objectives at the aggregate level. When these two functions are well executed, the brand experience approach solves problems for marketers and for their retail clients.

REFERENCES

Blattberg, R., Glazer, R., & Little, J. (Eds.). (1994). *The marketing information revolution*. Boston: Harvard Business School Press.

Blattberg, R., & Glazer, R. (1994). Marketing in the information revolution. In R. Blattberg, R. Glazer, & J. Little (Eds.), *The marketing information revolution* (pp. 9–29). Boston: Harvard Business School Press.

Blattberg, R., & Neslin, S. (1990). *Sales promotion: Concepts, methods and strategies.* Englewood Cliffs, NJ: Prentice-Hall.

Deming, W. E. (1986). *Out of the crisis.* Boston: Center for Advanced Engineering Study.

Farquhar, P., Han, J., & Ijiri, Y. (1991). *Recognizing and measuring brand assets* (Working Paper, Rep. No. 91-119). Cambridge, MA: Marketing Science Institute.

Food Marketing Institute. (1989). *Facts about store development.* Washington, DC: Author.

Jones, J. P. (1990). The double jeopardy of sales promotions. *Harvard Business Review, 68,* 145–152.

Lavidge, R. J., & Steiner, G. A. (1961). A model for predictive measurements of advertising effectiveness. *Journal of Marketing, 25,* 59–62.

Lodish, L. (1986). *The advertising promotion challenge: Vaguely right or precisely wrong?* New York: Oxford University Press.

McClave, J., & Benson, P. G. (1991) *Statistics for business and economics* (5th ed.). San Francisco, CA: Dellen.

Nielsen Marketing Research. (1990a). *1990 annual review of retail grocery store trends.* Northbrook, IL: Author.

Nielsen Marketing Research. (1990b). *1990 annual review of drug store trends.* Northbrook, IL: Author.

Nielsen Marketing Research. (1990c). *1990 annual review of mass merchandiser trends.* Northbrook, IL: Author.

Schultz, D., Robinson, W., & Petrison, L. (1993). *Promotional essentials.* Lincolnwood, IL: NTC.

Schultz, D., Tannenbaum, S., & Lauterborn, R. (1993). *Integrated marketing communications.* Lincolnwood, IL: NTC.

Schultz, D., & Wang, P. (1994, April–May). Real world results. *Marketing Tools,* 40–47.

Smith, H. (1993, December). New media for a new age. *Promo,* 60–63.

Srivastava, R., & Shocker, A. (1991). *Brand equity: A perspective on its meaning and measurement* (Technical Working Paper, Rep. No. 91-124). Cambridge, MA: Marketing Science Institute.

Thorson, E., & Moore, G. (Eds.). (1996). *Integrated marketing communications: Synergy of persuasive voices.* Mahwah, NJ: Lawrence Erlbaum Associates.

VII

Afterword

22

An Interview With Mr. X

William D. Wells
University of Minnesota

Q. Please state your name and occupation.

A. My name is Mr. X. I'm a brand manager. I market a consumer product.

Q. You've read *Measuring Advertising Effectiveness*?

A. I have read *Measuring Adverting Effectiveness*, some of it with great interest.

Q. What did you find most interesting?

A. I was interested in Kuse's evidence in chapter 17 that attitude change predicts sales, and recall doesn't. Some research firms still push day-after recall scores. If Kuse is right, their numbers are not valid. Some academicians focus on recall. If Kuse is right, their work would be more useful if it looked at something more predictive.

Q. Anything else on chapter 17?

A. I was impressed by the idea that you can measure the persuasiveness of a sales proposition. If Kuse is right about that, I can test messages without the high cost of final production. That's important. And I was impressed by his wear-out model. If wear-out is as predictable as he says, I'll know when to change the copy.

Q. Anything else?

A. The chapter by Wansink and Ray reminded me that some advertisements are intended to persuade consumers to use products they have already purchased. In that case—and it's a common and important case—attitude toward the brand is not a good measurement of effectiveness. That point is easy to forget, and it's important to anyone who markets that kind of product. Most academic advertising researchers also overlook it.

Q. Anything else on making marketing decisions?

A. I was impressed by the experiment by Thorson and Zhao. If Thorson and Zhao are right, attention to TV commercials drops second by second, and attention to some commercials drops much faster than attention to others. That means I'm going to be skeptical of any copy test or lab experiment that requires, or even encourages, respondents to watch every second of every ad. If you eliminate ability to grab and hold attention, you eliminate an important ingredient.

Q. Anything else?

A. I make decisions every day. I base those decisions on my own view of what makes ads effective. Anything that improves that view is going to make me a better manager.

Q. Can you give me an example?

A. The Wyer–Srull theory that Gregan-Paxton and Logan describe in chapter 11 explains why consumers sometimes remember an advertisement better as time goes on, even when it has not been repeated. That never made sense before. The Wyer–Srull theory also told me that it's mental rehearsal that's important, not just the number of impressions.

Q. Why is that important?

A. I'd always thought of repetition as something that makes advertising more indelible. The Wyer–Srull theory says a lot more than that is going on. And the Wyer–Srull theory is not alone. The large-scale field experiment in chapter 14, the means–end chains in chapter 19, the processing models in chapters 6 and 7, and 16 and 18, all imply that some parts of some advertisements exit memory in seconds whereas other parts of other advertisements stay active long enough to change behavior. If Wyer and Srull and the others are right, our standard reach and frequency media models are not even halfway decent first approximations. The business schools teach those models and our media analysts use them.

Q. So the Wyer–Srull theory can be useful.

A. Anything that helps me understand consumers can be useful.

Q. Anything else?

A. I was interested in chapter 4 by Yi. It said an advertisement can make a claim by making a claim about a related attribute. I'd never thought of that before. I was also interested in priming. I was especially interested in the idea that competitors' messages can benefit my products. That was a new wrinkle.

Q. Anything else new?

A. The "truth effect" in chapter 5. If Law and Hawkins are right, repetition makes advertisements more believable. That was new. I'd always thought of repetition as making ads more memorable, not more believable. And preattentive processing in chapter 3. If Shapiro and his coauthors are right, unnoticed advertisements can change attitudes.

Q. How would you use something like that?

A. It's not the sort of thing I would apply tomorrow. But, as I said, I make decisions every day, based on my own ideas about how advertising works. Anything that improves that model makes me more effective.

Q. So relevance means more than immediate applications.

A. It includes any increase in my knowledge.

Q. Anything else?

A. I'm always on the lookout for new ways to get useful information.

Q. Examples?

A. Chapter 10, by Stephens and Russo, and chapter 9, by Nelson and her coauthors, devote a lot of space to improving thought listing. All of their suggestions make thought listing more sensitive and more reliable. The same would be true of buttressing in chapter 8. Thought listing is an important method, and anything that makes it more sensitive makes it more useful.

Q. Can you be more specific?

A. Stephens and Russo, Nelson and her coauthors, and Wansink and Ray show that if you give respondents clear instructions and some guided practice you get more detailed, intimate responses. That gives you a higher return on your research investment.

Q. Anything else?

A. In chapter 6, Haugtvedt and Priester said, "attitudes changed via central route processing are likely to be more persistent over time, more resistant to change in the face of attack, and more predictive of behavior than attitudes changed by peripheral route processing" (p. 79). If they are right about that, copy tests and academic experiments that ignore long-term effects are liable to produce wrong answers. If we're serious about measuring effectiveness, we need to check that out and deal with it one way or another. If Haugtvedt and Priester are right, immediate measurements are not even half the answer.

Q. Anything more on methods?

A. I've already mentioned Reynolds, Olson and Rochon's chapter on means–end analysis and Wansink and Ray's chapter on ads that are intended to persuade consumers to use products they have already purchased. Both chapters are also "how-to" methods manuals. Vuokko's chapter and Thorson and Zhao's chapter are "how-to" manuals of a different sort. They show how to conduct basic research with real advertisements and real consumers.

Q. Does research have to be realistic to be useful?

A. I'm never going to trust research that hasn't been confirmed with real advertisements and real consumers.

Q. What about the work you mentioned earlier? Some of it was typical academic research with MBA students and college sophomores.

A. That would be food for thought. I never read one theory or one experiment and say, "My God, I never thought of that before!" and rush out and apply it. I filter everything through my own experience and the experience of other managers.

Q. Would you say the more realistic the experiment the more you would trust it?

A. Definitely—and the more it has been confirmed by others. The experiment by Broach and his coauthors in chapter 12 would be a good example. As the discussants of that chapter pointed out, it was just one experiment and it used college students, so I'd be skeptical. But if others were to show that TV programs influence the first commercial in a pod, I'd be more inclined to try to use it. The same would be true of the experiment by Haugtvedt and Priester. I can see how Tonya Harding would provoke more central processing than

Nancy Kerrigan, but I'd want to check that out with real products, real advertisements, and real consumers. And I agree with Crimmins in chapter 7. I wouldn't stop with "self-conscious, deliberate, explicit processing" of product attributes. I'd find out whether Tonya Harding is congruent with the self-image of the customer. If she's not, she probably would be harmful.

Q. So relevance includes specifics you can use in making marketing decisions, improvements in your personal model of how advertising works, and new—or at least improved—research methods. Does it include anything else?

A. It's easy to forget things everybody knows. So reminders are highly relevant.

Q. For instance?

A. I know that consumers do not respond to advertisements for frequently purchased packaged goods the same way they respond to advertisements for durables or services. In the absence of the hard evidence in chapter 8, it's easy to assume almost unconsciously that advertisements are advertisements. I know that consumers do not respond to advertisements for "utilitarian" products the same way they respond to advertisements for "social identity" products. In the absence of the hard evidence in chapter 9, it's easy to assume, thoughtlessly, that that distinction doesn't matter. I should add that academic researchers are even more guilty of assuming that one advertisement represents all advertisements and that one product—even a fictional product—represents all products and all services.

Q. So relevance includes reinforcement of the obvious.

A. Yes. I know that the competitive situation influences how consumers interpret my copy. I know that the marketing environment, including what's in the news, influences reception of my advertisements. I know that place-based media are at least as important as mass media and should be analyzed just as carefully. I know that consumers do not respond to advertisements for unfamiliar brands in the same way they respond to advertisements for familiar brands. Reminders in these chapters keep those basics front and center.

Q. Some researchers forget those basics?

A. Some do, especially in academia.

Q. Does one thing that "everybody knows" stand out as more important than any other?

A. The Wyer–Srull theory, the ELM model, Lebenson and Blackston's survey findings, Vuokko's and Reynolds et al.'s field experiments, Nelson et al.'s laboratory experiments, and the experiments by Stephens and Russo, and Thorson and Zhao, all converge on the idea that personal involvement is the single most important individual difference in consumers' responses to marketing communications. Everybody knows that. Given all the evidence, it is quite surprising that so many research suppliers and so many academic experimenters make so little effort to make sure that their respondents are really prospects for the product featured in the advertisement. When researchers mix unknown proportions of prospects with unknown proportions of nonprospects, their measurements are less sensitive and less valid.

Q. Any other reservations about common practices?

A. In chapter 2, Cook and Kover mentioned the ARF validity study. That study said that "likability" is a good predictor of sales effectiveness. Ever since then, some research suppliers and some academic experimenters have concentrated on attitude toward the ad. In chapter 17, Kuse concluded that attitude toward the ad is not a good measure of sales effectiveness. If he's right, they're wrong. Or, following Lebenson and Blackston in chapter 8, he's right for some products and not for others.

Q. Any other reservations?

A. In chapter 15, Percy and Rossiter question the assumptions behind many favorite research methods. In chapter 17, Olshavsky and Kumar question the common assumption that most processing is entirely "stimulus based," as they call it. In chapter 9, Nelson and her coauthors question the common belief that consumers don't know and can't tell why they change attitudes or behavior. Contradiction of accepted dogma is still another form of relevance.

Q. So now we have five different forms of relevance: specifics that improve marketing decisions, additions to the knowledge base, new—or at least improved—methods, reinforcement of the obvious, and contradiction of the generally accepted. Is that about it?

A. There's one more, and in some ways it's the most important. Once in a while I run across a perspective that alters a wide range of evaluations.

Q. For example?

A. In chapter 8, Lebenson and Blackston demonstrated that an advertisement can have a "brand effect," a "call to action effect," a "feel good" effect, or some combination. That changes everything.

Q. Why does that change everything?

A. It says, along with Wright-Isak and her coauthors in chapter 1, Reynolds and his coauthors in chapter 19, and Percy and Rossiter in chapter 15, that the meaning of effectiveness depends on the nature of the product and the purpose of the advertising.

Q. Why is that so important?

A. Anyone who takes it seriously will pay close attention to what the communication is intended to accomplish. In copy research, that means less unthinking use of invalid but convenient measures. In academic advertising research it means more respect for the exact purpose of the communication. Sometimes the marketing environment requires a brand effect. Sometimes it requires a call to action effect or a feel good effect, or a combination. An ad that is positive on one of those dimensions is liable to be neutral or negative on the others. Academicians publish misleading findings when they ignore those critical situational differences. More attention to what the communication is intended to accomplish would make all advertising research more valid.

Q. Anything else that changes a wide range of evaluations?

A. I've already mentioned the idea, in the Gregan-Paxton and Loken chapter, that mental rehearsal is more important than number of impressions. That chapter, and all the chapters on the ELM model, show that the content of mental rehearsal alters the effects of all advertisements. That's why we need to find a way to add cognitive processing to media models. Anyone who figures out how to do that will make a fundamental contribution.

Q. Any other major implications?

A. Thorson and Zhao's observation in chapter 13 that an advertisement can be too original or too emotional, but can't be too relevant. If Thorson and Zhao are right about that, a lot of advertising people will have to reconsider what they mean by creativity.

Q. Why is that?

A. In some quarters, creativity means originality and emotionality, even at the expense of relevance. Thorson and Zhao's findings suggest that in advertising—as distinguished from entertainment—true creativity is the art of combining moderate originality and moderate emotionality with maximum relevance. That would change the way a lot of agency people and a lot of academic researchers think about persuasive communications.

Q. Anything else?

A. In chapter 7, Crimmins concluded that "self-conscious, deliberate, explicit processing"—such as that picked up by thought listing and other common research methods—applies to "only a small proportion of the attitudes we form and the decisions we make" (p. 102). In chapter 18, Mehta and Purvis agree with that conclusion. If they're right, methods that focus on explicit processing omit key aspects of reactions to advertisements. Remember Tonya Harding and Nancy Kerrigan. Crimmins' chapter also says that we need a better way to distinguish between "central" and "peripheral" content. As Crimmins noted, the present answer—whatever is processed centrally is central—is not very helpful.

Q. Most of these insights came from real-world applications.

A. They came from attempts to apply academic theories to real-world problems.

Q. In chapter 1, Wright-Isak and her coauthors—and in chapter 2, Cook and Kover—recounted differences between academicians and practitioners. In her discussion of chapters 1 and 2, Thorson said, "the purpose of academic advertising research is not to aid practitioners, but to develop a psychology and sociology of mediated persuasion" (p. 21). Do you agree that academicians and practitioners have separate objectives?

A. Yes and no. Although it seems obvious that academic researchers should focus on developing a "psychology and sociology of mediated persuasion," they will never know whether their models are valid until someone applies them to real products, real advertisements, and real consumers. Crimmins' chapter, Lebenson and Blackston's chapter, and Reynolds, Olson, and Rochon's chapter, among others, show how academic theories become more sophisticated when they are tested and amended in real-world environments. Academicians don't have the resources to do that on their own. At the same time, managers can't get along without theories of one sort or another. Without an intuitive grasp of what they're doing, they wouldn't know where to start. This is not to say that managers are going to wait around until academicians perfect their models. In the course of pursuing their own agendas, practitioners will learn more about how advertising works, invent better methods, confirm useful principles, and question generally accepted dogma. All that will make the theories better.

Q. So it's circular.

A. It's circular. Innovations arise in the real world and in academia, and the real world and academia correct each other. The chapters in this volume provide a long list of examples.

Q. Of the points we've covered, which is the most consequential?

A. Maybe the last. Academicians need more external validity. Practitioners need more internal validity. The way to make that happen is to increase contact between them. More contact will evoke more conflict. That's good. It makes the process self-correcting. We don't need duplication. We do need cooperative interaction that makes both parties more effective.

Q. How do we get that?

A. A broader worldview and less isolation. It's relatively easy to disparage the other side. It's much harder to employ the unfamiliar. But if we are to have more accurate real–world measurement, and if we are to have a valid "psychology and sociology of mediated persuasion" that's exactly what will be needed. Academicians and practitioners need each other because they have offsetting limitations. The way to improve measurement of advertising effectiveness is through exchange of models, methods, and conclusions. That was the purpose of this conference, and it is the key message of this volume.

Author Index

Subject Index